D0741856

DEMOCRACY'S
PRISONER

DEMOCRACY'S PRISONER

EUGENE V. DEBS,

THE GREAT WAR, AND

THE RIGHT TO DISSENT

Ernest Freeberg

HARVARD UNIVERSITY PRESS
Cambridge, Massachusetts
London, England
2008

*Publication of this book has been supported
through the generous provisions of the
S. M. Bessie Fund.*

Library of Congress Cataloging-in-Publication Data

Freeberg, Ernest.
Democracy's prisoner : Eugene V. Debs, the great war, and the right to dissent /
Ernest Freeberg.
p. cm.
Includes bibliographical references and index.
ISBN-13: 978-0-674-02792-3 (cloth : alk. paper)
1. Debs, Eugene V. (Eugene Victor), 1855–1926.   2. Socialists—United States—
Biography.   3. Freedom of speech—United States—History.   I. Title.
HX84.D3F74 2008
335'.3092—dc22
[B]   2007043807

To Charlie and Emma

Contents

Illustrations

DEMOCRACY'S PRISONER

Prologue:
Free Speech Campaign

O N THE EVENING of November 2, 1920, Warren G. Harding and his supporters gathered in his home to celebrate a resounding Republican victory. That day American voters made the Ohio senator their next president, part of a nationwide repudiation of the policies of Woodrow Wilson. Harding spent the evening smoking cigars in his library, while newspaper editors around the country struggled to explain his landslide victory.

Democratic candidate James Cox, who had run as the heir to Woodrow Wilson's legacy, was stunned into silence by the magnitude of his defeat. For several days after the election he made no public statement. Newspapers could only report that he planned to go squirrel hunting in order to forget his humiliating loss.

A smaller group of reporters gathered on election night at the gates of the Atlanta penitentiary, hoping to hear a concession speech from the Socialist candidate Eugene V. Debs. Serving a ten-year sentence for protesting America's role in World War I, Debs had been in jail for twenty months. In four previous campaigns for the White House he had spoken to adoring crowds across the country, but this time he spent his days tending to his fellow inmates in the prison hospital. As he put it, he was a "candidate in seclusion." Outside the penitentiary walls, Debs's allies proudly displayed photos of him wearing the shapeless denim coat

Our Candidate

"Our Candidate." *The Liberator,* April 1920.
Courtesy of Debs Collection, Indiana State University Library.

of a federal convict, and passed out campaign buttons for "Prisoner 9653." Though Wilson had asked Americans to treat the 1920 election as a "solemn referendum" on his plan for a league of nations, Socialists asked voters instead to consider it a test of the First Amendment. A vote for Debs, they argued, was the best way to protest against the federal government's attempt to silence thousands of men and women who had dared to speak against America's decision to join Europe's Great War. Close to one million Americans agreed, casting their ballots that day for a man whom the government had branded a dangerous felon and traitor to his country.

Prison rules barred Debs from speaking to reporters, but the warden allowed him to release an unusual concession statement. "I thank the capitalist masters for putting me here," he wrote with characteristic defiance. "They know where I belong under their criminal and corrupt system. It is the only compliment they could pay me." He called on his comrades to resume their work the next day, not to elect him president but to continue a revolutionary struggle that would end only "when capitalism is dead and labor is free."

At his trial Debs charged that the government was persecuting him, not for undermining the draft, but because he dared to challenge the "plutocrats" who ran the country and were reaping large profits from the war. Government prosecutors denied that they wanted to silence Debs for expressing his political views. They argued that he had always enjoyed the freedom to preach socialism but had crossed the line between legitimate dissent and criminal sedition when he gave a speech on June 16, 1918, to a Socialist gathering in Canton, Ohio. That month American soldiers were just entering the battle lines in France, joining their allies' struggle to repulse a desperate German advance. Though reports from the front were tightly censored, the American public got glimpses of the carnage. Papers ran casualty lists, along with reports about German bombs dropped on Paris and troop ships lost at sea. Millions of American men had already been drafted to fight, and that month the government announced plans to induct millions more.

In that charged atmosphere, Debs delivered one of the most famous protest speeches in American history. He suggested that the country was not fighting a noble war to save democracy, but was joining European imperialists in a greedy struggle over profits. He also denounced the government's domestic war on dissent, insisting that hundreds of his comrades had been jailed for telling the truth that rich men declare wars while working men die in them. Across the country newspaper editors clamored for Debs's arrest, and federal agents soon obliged them.

In court Debs did his best to put the law itself on trial. As he put it, "American institutions are on trial here before a court of American citizens." Playing to the wider jury of public opinion and the ultimate judgment of history, Debs apologized for nothing. Instead he insisted that the government was betraying the country by trying to stifle open and honest debate about the war. His followers saw Debs as a great democratic martyr, but the jury was less impressed. They agreed with federal prosecutors that, during his Canton speech, Debs had tried to convince young men to shirk their patriotic duty in a time of national crisis. The judge gave him a ten-year sentence. Since Debs was in his mid-sixties and in poor health, many of his friends believed he would likely die in jail.

For Debs's supporters, and many historians ever since, his imprisonment has served as a cautionary tale about the way the passions of war can undermine traditional democratic liberties. Of course, this was only the latest chapter in a story as old as the country itself. Fearing the prospect of being drawn into the French Revolutionary wars, President John Adams provoked the nation's first free speech fight when he used the Alien and Sedition Acts of 1798 to jail critics of his foreign policy. When the country invaded Mexico in 1846, Abraham Lincoln and Daniel Webster were among those who denounced their government for waging an immoral war of aggression. When Lincoln served as commander in chief, however, he used emergency war powers to shut down opposition newspapers and detain some of his critics.

But this familiar struggle between national security and individual liberty intensified in 1917 when Congress granted the Wilson administration unprecedented authority to control public opinion. Faced with the demand to draft, equip, and transport millions of men across the Atlantic, the federal government used these new powers aggressively, imposing a monopoly on the meaning of American patriotism that turned a dissenter like Debs into a felon.

Debs was only the most visible victim of these wartime speech laws. Federal authorities arrested more than two thousand war critics, and jailed twelve hundred of them; many more were silenced by a variety of state and local laws; much of the radicals' vibrant alternative press was driven into bankruptcy; and an untold number of socialists, religious pacifists, and German immigrants were threatened, brutalized, and even murdered by patriotic mobs whose anger had been fed by a powerful government program of war propaganda.

After the armistice, while Debs sat in jail, the public's fear of German militarism merged with fresh anxieties over the threat of Bolshevik revolution. Historians often remember the postwar decade as a time of conservative reaction when the nation seemed to be governed more by its fears than by its hopes. They point, for example, to the anticommunist panic remembered as the "Red Scare," the rise of the Ku Klux Klan in the early 1920s, the successful drive by many companies to break unions, the passage of new laws to restrict immigration, and the landslide victory of a conservative like Harding. Faced with the threats of war and revolution, many Americans chose national security over individual liberty, and retrenchment over reform.

Debs's tally of a million votes in the 1920 election reminds us, however, that the story is more complicated. Most Americans who cast their ballots for Debs did not share his enthusiasm for economic revolution. They were casting a protest vote, and the nature of that protest is best understood when we realize that his strange "jail house to the White House" campaign was just one part of a much broader campaign to win his release. For three years, while Debs sat in federal prison, he was the central symbol of a massive nationwide civil liberties movement that tried to pressure the federal government to repudiate its wartime arrests by granting an "amnesty" to America's wartime "political prisoners." In the war's aftermath, Americans heard eloquent arguments for free speech rights from a remarkable group of artists and intellectuals on both sides of the Atlantic, read jail-cell interviews and smuggled messages from Debs, and debated in their own communities the fate of their nation's most famous prisoner.

While many in the amnesty movement felt genuine sympathy for Debs and his jailed comrades, the stakes in this debate were even higher. For thousands of Americans, President Wilson's crusade to make the world "safe for democracy" had raised troubling questions about the nature and limits of democracy at home. The amnesty protest provided them with a way to think about how the right to free speech could survive in an age of total war, mass propaganda, and growing federal and corporate power. In this national debate over Debs's crime and punishment, many Americans applauded the government's actions and felt sure that Debs and his comrades were getting all that they deserved. The proponents of amnesty fought back, translating the public's growing sympathy for Debs into a wider call for tolerance and national reconciliation. As historians often note, the plight of conscientious objectors and war critics prompted a handful of liberals and libertarian radicals to form the American Civil Liberties Union, one of the enduring legacies of the amnesty campaign. Legal historians also note the even smaller number of judges and scholars who were disturbed by the Supreme Court's support for the wartime speech laws and responded by promoting a new and more expansive interpretation of the First Amendment.

While these played a crucial role in shaping the future of free speech in America, they were just one facet of a much broader amnesty movement. Many thousands of Americans attended amnesty rallies, marched in parades, signed petitions, walked picket lines, and wrote to their government to express their views on the Debs case. The White House and Justice Department were deluged with letters from citizens, of all political persuasions, who were anxious to protect what they considered to be a sacred but threatened American right of free speech. Their efforts remind us that the scope and meaning of the First Amendment are determined not only by Supreme Court justices, attorneys, and legal scholars, but by the much wider democratic process of citizens working together in social movements. In the end, the amnesty campaign not only liberated Debs and his comrades, but also forced the government to moderate its program of repression and surveillance. In the process, the activists who organized the amnesty movement pioneered a form of free speech politics that has played a crucial role in American society ever since.

Before we can appreciate this three-year campaign to free Debs and defend the First Amendment, we must first understand who Debs was, why so many Americans loved and hated him, and how the pressures of war turned this five-time presidential candidate into "Convict 9653."

Chapter 1

Dangerous Man

O N AN OCTOBER afternoon in 1908, reporters on the upper floors of the Times Building in New York heard a roaring mob moving along the street below. From their windows they watched as a "wildly enthusiastic" crowd of four thousand followed in the footsteps of Eugene V. Debs. The Socialist Party candidate had arrived that morning on his "Red Special" train, stumping for votes in his third campaign for the presidency.[1]

An apprehensive *New York Times* reporter noted that the crowd seemed to worship Debs, reaching out to "touch even so much as the hem" of his garment—as always, a modest suit. Tall, lean, and bespectacled, the candidate looked more like a small-town banker than a revolutionary messiah, but to his followers he seemed like the prophet of a new age. "There he is!" one woman shouted as he passed, "The living link between God and man!"[2]

Outside the Hippodrome where Debs would speak, scalpers sold tickets for triple their price, making a nice profit on a meeting devoted to ridding the world of such selfish impulses. Unlike their rivals in the mainstream parties, the Socialists charged admission to hear their candidate, funding their national campaign not with donations from wealthy industrialists but from the nickels and dimes of workers. And still, as reporters often noted with surprise, Debs spoke to overflowing crowds.

Not all of the seven thousand who filled the hall that night were committed radicals. Many came simply to see the man described by the *Brooklyn Eagle* as "the most picturesque figure in American public life today." But party rank and file did all they could to bring these newcomers into the movement. Women in white gowns and scarlet sashes sold campaign buttons, while others hawked subscriptions to the *Appeal to Reason,* the national newspaper dedicated to the proposition that "Socialism is not just a theory—it is a destiny." The curious and the converted snapped up copies of Debs's autograph, along with ten-cent translations of Marx and Engels, and tracts for workers with titles such as *Class Struggles in America, Socialism in the Home,* and *The Passing of Capitalism.*[3]

While the crowd bought this "constructive propaganda" by the boxful, the main attraction was Debs. When he arrived, the audience waved red flags in frenzied anticipation, but hushed when he took the stage, eager to hear his voice. As one recalled, it was a voice "that could do with a crowd what it willed, not because of the mind behind it but because of the great warm heart which the crowd felt speaking there."[4]

In 1908, America's political landscape was still dominated by men who could command a stage, welding jokes and anecdotes, arguments and indictments, into two- and three-hour speeches. That year Debs was running against another great orator, the Democrat William Jennings Bryan. But many who heard Debs speak claimed that he was unique. Others delivered rehearsed speeches, ornamented with elaborate flourishes and a grand peroration, but Debs seemed to speak straight from the heart. "He resorts to no tricks of rhetoric," an admirer observed, "no claptrap and stage effects, no empty pretense of deep emotion; but he stands frankly before his audiences and opens the doorways of his mind and heart that seem to be overflowing with terrible invective or the sweet waters of human kindness."[5]

Debs could be alternately angry and funny, sarcastic and sentimental, poetic and prophetic. But always he aimed his "terrible invective" at America's great capitalists and their retinue of bankers, judges, politicians, editors, and conservative union leaders. They were guilty, Debs charged, of a "crime against modern humanity." Like the abolitionists before him, he called workers to join a moral struggle against human bondage, the "wage-slavery" imposed by those who robbed millions of men, women, and children of the fruits of their labor. No less than the slave masters of the antebellum South, he told the New York crowd, America's new industrialists were making a mockery of the nation's democratic promise, using their control of the means of production to pervert the will of the majority. "Tell me whose tools you use," he explained, "and I will tell you whose slave you are." An ardent admirer of John Brown, Debs was doing his best to incite a slave insurrection in industrial America.[6]

Critics charged that Debs was a menace. As the nation buckled under the stresses of economic change, many political and religious leaders believed that he was making matters worse by fomenting envy and class hatred, pitting one group of Americans against another. As Theodore Roosevelt saw it, while Debs claimed to be the prophet of a new age of social cooperation, he was in fact one of America's most "undesirable citizens," an apostle of "bloodshed, anarchy and riot." If Debs and his allies ever succeeded in their misguided revolution, his critics held, they would only destroy a pillar of American freedom, the right of private property. In its place, they would establish a state tyranny over economic, social, and family life. In short, Debs did not represent one point of view on issues facing American society, but rather he threatened democratic liberty itself. As Roosevelt put it, socialism was "not merely false, but fatal."[7]

Though Debs was a fiery revolutionist on the stage, much of the party's platform aimed at more modest but immediate improvements in workers' lives. The Socialists wanted the same things advocated by progressive reformers at the time—free public kindergartens, improved school buildings, and a curriculum that taught American children both manual training and lessons in economics. Socialists supported women's suffrage and the right of voters to use initiative, referendum, and recall. They wanted free legal advice for the poor, a ban on the use of police as strikebreakers, democratic control of the banking system, and "adequate hospital service with no taint of charity." They called on the government to inspect food, fight diseases, and build parks and playgrounds. And they wanted pensions for public employees, homes for the "aged and invalid," and free cremation services for the deceased.[8]

The end of class struggles and class rule, of master and slave, of ignorance and vice, of poverty and shame, of cruelty and crime, the birth of freedom, the dawn of brotherhood, the beginning of MAN, that is the demand. This is Socialism.

Debs campaign literature.
Debs Collection, Indiana State University Library.

However, no list of platform planks can adequately convey the grand edifice that Socialists dreamed of building. Their ultimate goal was not to repair capitalism, but to abolish it. They hoped that social reforms not only would improve workers' lives, but would embolden them to demand much more. Coming from the radical wing of his party, Debs was sometimes impatient with those who advocated gradual reform and downplayed the call for revolution. He suspected that this "slow-shulism" might soothe the symptoms of exploitation without removing the root cause. In spite of this difference, all Socialists worked to establish a "cooperative commonwealth." Debs asked his audiences to envision a land where the plenty of America was shared harmoniously, where the system founded on individual greed was replaced by one based on mutual concern, through shared public ownership of the means of production.[9]

More an evangelist than an architect, Debs offered few specifics about how this new society might be run. "Socialism," as he sometimes put it, "is simply another word for brotherhood." He left it to other, more disciplined minds in the movement to work out the details. "You must not look to him for facts and figures," one reporter explained, "for he talks in picture signs and visions." In fact, even as Debs campaigned for the office, he conceded that he would make a terrible president. "When Socialism is on the verge of success," he once told journalist Lincoln Steffens, "the party will nominate an able executive and a clear-headed administrator . . . not Debs." In short, Debs thought of himself as a professional agitator, not a politician. He ran for president, time and again, because a national campaign gave him the best opportunity to educate his fellow citizens. Every whistle stop and every auditorium was another chance to cultivate class consciousness, preparing ground that a future generation of Socialists would harvest.[10]

In that work, Debs had an uncanny ability to make socialist rhetoric ring true, to help others see the possibility of a new world order. "We live in a system where we have to fight for mere existence," he told his audiences. "Only when our economic interest becomes mutual, when we socially own what we socially need and use, only then can we expand to our noblest proportion, only then can we develop and express the best that is in us, only then will we start the march of the divinest civilization that man has ever known." In his 1908 visit to downtown New York, the holy city of American capitalism, Debs's ability to conjure images of this new economic Eden converted some of the money-changers themselves. That evening, at a private gathering of the radicalized rich, he so inspired the crowd that ladies plucked off their jewels and tossed them into a hat, doing their part for a movement that aimed to yank them off the pedestals of privilege.[11]

In the early twentieth century, Debs found a growing audience for this vision of a cooperative commonwealth because so much in America was new, and so much was not working. Though relatively few embraced his radical solution, many shared his concerns about what was often called "the labor problem." In the decades following the Civil War, Americans had built the largest economy in the world. While this growth brought the nation unprecedented wealth, workers found themselves threatened by these powerful economic changes. New machines and forms of factory discipline made their skills less valuable, and bosses used immigrant labor to drive down wages and kill fledgling unions. In the vast new mills, factories, and railroad networks that served a national and global marketplace, workers toiled as much as twelve hours per day, often in dangerous or unhealthy conditions, and with no safety net of insurance. The instability of unregulated markets made matters worse, as cyclical economic busts left thousands out of work altogether.[12]

Workers responded with strikes, some of them bloody and desperate. They won scattered victories, but they lost more often, as capitalists fought back with mercenary squads of detectives, private militia, and strikebreakers. Judges usually sided with the factory owners, issuing injunctions against strikes, blocking legislation to protect women and children in the workplace, and sometimes jailing union leaders. As the mighty powers of property clashed with a growing force of industrial workers, many feared that the country was being drawn into a new civil war.

Since 1894, Debs had often been at the center of this conflict. That year he led one of the most disruptive labor protests in American history, a strike by the American Railway Union (ARU) against the Pullman Palace Sleeping Car Company. Owner George Pullman required all of his workers to live in his Illinois factory town, where he charged a premium for rent and all other services. In the midst of a national depression in the early 1890s, Pullman's workers were squeezed by rising rents and severe wage cuts. When a committee of workers petitioned for relief, Pullman fired several who were members of the ARU. His employees went on strike, and Pullman retaliated by locking them out of their jobs and their homes, while refusing appeals for arbitration.[13]

As head of the large but fragile new union, Debs advised his members to avoid a confrontation with the united forces of the railroad owners. But when the union voted to strike in support of the Pullman workers, Debs prepared for a showdown between "the producing classes and the money power." On his orders, 150,000 ARU workers refused to handle Pullman's sleeping cars. The railroad owners, in turn, stood by Pullman, refusing to allow their trains to move *without* his cars. This standoff paralyzed two dozen of the country's key rail lines for several days, strangling interstate commerce west of Chicago.[14]

Though Debs called on his men to be nonviolent, clashes broke out when the railroads sent in thousands of special deputies against the strikers. As violence escalated, President Grover Cleveland ordered federal troops into Chicago to end the strike by force, citing the federal government's obligation to keep mail trains running. For ignoring a judge's injunction to send his men back to work, Debs was sentenced to six months in Illinois' Woodstock jail, his first encounter with what he came to call "capitalist justice."

Throughout the strike, the nation's business-friendly newspapers portrayed "Dictator Debs" as a power-crazed tyrant who "leans too decidedly to the side of revolution." National papers ran lurid and exaggerated headlines about the reign of anarchy in Chicago, and as one historian put it, Debs was "vilified and abused as few men have been." The *New York Times* called him an "enemy of the human race" and, after Pullman, many Americans could think of "King Debs" only as the embodiment of reckless class warfare.[15]

For Debs, the government's willingness to use court injunctions, guns, and prisons against the railroad workers proved that an unholy alliance between government and capitalism was subverting American democracy. Up to that point he had considered himself a Democrat, even serving a term as a representative in the Indiana legislature in 1885. After the Pullman strike, he lost faith that either of the country's main political parties would protect the interests of working people. He had also seen the power of the mainstream press to turn public opinion against workers, and concluded that the legal system itself was a servant of big business. In the words of one biographer, Debs decided that "the machinery of state was owned and operated like any other business concern by the capitalist interests." Casting about for some understanding of the forces that had brought the nation to open class warfare, and him to a jail cell, Debs found some answers in a volume of Karl Marx's *Das Kapital* sent to him by a socialist. He later claimed that he converted to socialism while doing time in the Woodstock prison.[16]

After his release, Debs continued to agitate on behalf of the underdog, first supporting the Populist third-party movement in 1896, then planning a socialist colony in the American West, and finally helping to found the Socialist Party of America in 1901. After that he made his living as a professional revolutionary, running as the Socialist candidate for president every four years, making the lecture circuit between campaigns, and writing for socialist papers such as the *National Rip-Saw* and the *Texas Rebel*. Crisscrossing the country by train, he spoke at union halls, strike rallies, Socialist conventions, and public lyceums, doing all in his power to fan the embers of class consciousness.[17]

As he traveled, Debs found that workers were often divided against themselves. Natives resented immigrants; whites shunned blacks, who in turn often served as strikebreakers. The labor movement also feuded bitterly over tactics and goals. Although Socialists had an important minority voice in many unions, and controlled "revolutionary" unions in some trades, most organized workers favored the more conservative approach of the American Federation of Labor (AFL). Led by Samuel Gompers, the AFL wanted no part of a working-class revolution and avoided direct participation in the political process. Accepting the capitalist wage system, Gompers fought only for the right to organize skilled craftsmen, according to their trades, and to use the collective power of this "craft unionism" to win "bread and butter" concessions for these elite workers. The Socialists charged that this approach divided workers and distracted them from the real source of economic injustice. Debs regularly denounced Gompers as a lackey of the master class and urged workers to create more militant industrial unions that would unite the skilled and unskilled in each industry. These new unions would give workers true clout on the economic front, he believed, while the Socialist Party would serve as the political voice of the working class. In every speech, Debs urged American workers to recognize their common interests and their common enemy. "Do you not know," he implored them, "that the very hour you are united your fetters fall from your limbs, your slavery ends?"[18]

When Debs began preaching socialism in 1900, the movement was just one of dozens proposed by reformers and revolutionaries to deal with the social crisis caused by rapid industrialization. By 1912, when Socialists chose Debs to be their candidate for a fourth consecutive time, their movement had emerged as the most successful vehicle for radical dissent. In cities across the East and Midwest, a small army of speakers distributed campaign literature and preached the cause, sometimes supported by "stereopticon slides" that helped workers visualize key tenets of the class struggle. The party had 150,000 members, who worked to elect hundreds of their comrades to posts as mayors, aldermen, city commissioners, and state representatives.[19]

Socialists also developed a vigorous press. Thirteen daily newspapers—eight in the foreign languages of immigrant workers—dozens of weekly papers, and a handful of monthly journals provided radical readers with an alternative to what they called the "capitalist press." The party owned and ran some of these papers; others belonged to other organizations and individuals. Most impressive of all was the *Appeal to Reason,* a weekly paper run out of Girard, Kansas, that was owned by Francis Wayland, a millionaire who brought his entrepreneurial talents into the Socialist movement. For several years Debs was a regular contributor to the *Appeal.* During election years, when excitement about his candidacy peaked, so did the paper's subscription list, reaching a nationwide circulation of over seven hundred thousand.[20]

The party also created an alternative educational system. Funded by an heiress with a socialist conscience, New York's Rand School of Social Science trained party fieldworkers and provided safe haven for radical intellectuals like John Spargo, a former English miner who helped found the school, and Scott Nearing, a charismatic young economist who had been fired from the University of Pennsylvania for his outspoken critique of capitalism. Socialists also educated workers through meetings and discussion groups, held almost every night in many American cities, and a small army of soapbox orators whose harangues against capitalism became a familiar sound on America's busiest commercial thoroughfares.

The centerpiece of the Socialists' propaganda campaign was Eugene Debs, who toured the country in a Red Special railcar that was crammed with posters, pamphlets, and a moving host of reporters and local party dignitaries. At times Debs was joined on these trips by his younger brother Theodore. Like Eugene, Theodore was tall, angular, bald, and in a less public way a ferocious fighter for the cause. He ran their office, conducted much of the correspondence, and advised his more famous brother on a daily basis. In return they split the income Debs made from his writings and speaking tours. Some whispered that Theodore also made sure that his brother did not spend too much time in the nation's barrooms.

At the height of these campaign tours, Debs would often give several hundred speeches a month, never failing to mesmerize an audience. "He moves quickly from side to side," one reporter observed. "He bends over the front of the platform and reaches out with his long arms, as if seeking to draw his hearers to him. . . . He appeals personally to the men and women before him. He talks to each man and each woman individually." When Debs kicked off his 1912 campaign before a sold-out crowd in Madison Square Garden, he received a twenty-nine-minute standing ovation—a sight that a *Times* reporter found "startling." In New Kensington, Pennsylvania, enthusiastic crowds overwhelmed a stand of bleachers, sending Socialists careening down in a "maddening crash." Through the streets of Baltimore, thousands marched behind four brass bands playing revolutionary songs like the "Internationale." "No saviour from on high delivers," they sang, "No faith have we in prince or peer/ Our own right hand the chains must shiver/ Chains of hatred, greed and fear." In Boston, Debs roused an audience that included many Harvard students when he denounced "the almost universal poverty" that capitalism had imposed on "the useful workers of this nation." He painted a vivid picture of "the slaughter of workers in the mines and mills" and predicted an impending battle between "the multi-millionaire and the pauper."[21]

As a description of the nation's class structure, this stark vision of a death struggle between elite power-mongers and abused workers obscured as much as it explained. But such rhetoric touched an emotional core in many Americans who resented the way new concentrations of wealth mocked the nation's cherished principle of equality of opportunity. Even for some who were skeptical about socialism, Debs gave voice to those fears, translating their anxiety into a clear and thrilling lingo of moral outrage.

Moderates in the party fretted that Debs was too extreme, a champion of what they called "impossiblism." To them, his predictions of an imminent revolution were fantasies that ignored the stolid conservatism of most American workers. Still, Debs was nominated, time and again, because even his rivals had to admit that he was the man most likely to win votes, the one who could gather crowds and stir hearts. The Jewish garment cutters on the Lower East Side, the railroad men of the Midwest, the tenant farmers of Texas and Oklahoma, and the bohemian artists and poets of Greenwich Village and San Francisco—all were moved by the man who could make the clichés of Marxian dogma glow with flesh-and-blood possibility. For the party's rank-and-file delegates, Debs was the fist-shaking embodiment of their movement, a beloved prophet of the pending clash between the haves and the have-nots.[22]

Part of Debs's appeal came from his claim to be not just a champion but also a member of the working class. Largely self-educated, he had dropped out of public school at the age of fourteen to take a job on the railroads, where he worked his way up in the ranks of union leadership. As he enjoyed pointing out on the campaign trail, he was the only union man on the ballot. His opponents in the mainstream parties were invariably the sons of privilege who had never done manual labor, nor even been forced to look for a job. "Not one has ever been slugged by a capitalist policeman," he scoffed, proudly claiming the distinction of being the only candidate who knew the inside of a jail cell. To his supporters, the fact that he was one of the "most hated men in America" only proved that he was a threat to the economic elite.[23]

Although Debs claimed that the Socialist Party was run by and for the "horny handed sons of toil," his message appealed to many middle-class men and women. A reporter covering a Debs speech in Los Angeles, for example, was surprised to find only a "sprinkling" of working-class people in the audience. Most wore white collars, and yet "they cheered and applauded every sentiment." These bourgeois Socialists were not just the lunatic fringe of radical bohemians, those whom scoffers liked to call "the longhaired men and shorthaired women." Instead Debs attracted "ladies by hundreds" and liberal Christians searching for a political platform that matched their social gospel. College students and professors turned out when he toured university towns, and socialism appealed to the romantic and rebellious impulses of an entire generation of young painters, writers, and poets. Many responded because Debs cast his radicalism in an American grain. Critics often portrayed socialism as an alien ideology, imported by disgruntled immigrants who failed to appreciate the American promise. But Debs was born and raised in the Midwest, and his fight against capitalism was inspired as much by Tom Paine, Walt Whitman, and Wendell Phillips as it was by Karl Marx.[24]

Debs called on workers and their middle-class allies to form a "conquering army," one powerful enough to demand "the unconditional surrender of the capitalist class." The leaders of capitalist America, however, had no intention of surrendering and fought back energetically. As early as 1900, Mark Hannah, the Ohio businessman who had engineered President William McKinley's electoral victory, warned that the nation was moving toward an apocalyptic struggle between capitalism and socialism. As Debs's movement grew, others in the business community heeded Hannah's warning. In 1912, John Kirby, the president of the National Association of Manufacturers, urged his fellow businessmen to unite against the socialist menace. Particularly alarmed by the economic heresies popular on college campuses, Kirby urged businessmen to "throw down the gauntlet," challenging the Socialists' "remarkable band of proselytizing missionaries promulgating hare-brained theories."[25]

While Kirby encouraged reasoned debate over economic principles, many others tried slander instead. Though he was one of America's most notorious radicals, Debs lived a conventional middle-class lifestyle with his wife, Kate, a prim and dignified woman who was loyal to her husband though not passionate about his cause. The childless couple lived in a modest Victorian house a few blocks from the main street in Terre Haute, Indiana, a small industrial city on the banks of the Wabash River. His critics charged, however, that Debs had stashed away huge profits in his career as a professional troublemaker. He traveled in a "Magnificent Palace Car," the *Detroit Free Press* charged, while his "flunkies" guarded their leader "from the common herd." The Catholic Church led this defamation campaign, describing his house as a luxurious mansion built by "scab labor." A Chicago bishop denounced socialism as "an insult to the workingman." If Debs ever won an election, he warned, the state would become "the only owner and the laboring man must feed at his master's crib." In a favorite line of attack, Catholic leaders often described Debs and his allies as sexual libertines, eager to nationalize women, smash the family, and turn America's children into wards of the state. In the heat of the 1912 campaign, a New York priest told his flock that men like Debs were "the mad-dog of society, and should be silenced, if need be, by the bullet."[26]

Though often threatened, Debs was never physically assaulted. Some of his comrades were not so lucky. Socialist organizer Kate Richards O'Hare was doused with a fire hose when she spoke against the use of child labor in a Georgia mill. At a 1912 campaign parade in New York, the police attacked the Socialist standard-bearers, seizing their red flags and trampling them in the street. Across the country, radical speeches were broken up by police, often on orders from city officials. Socialists found little relief in the courts, as judges often considered their gatherings to be, almost by definition, a breach of the peace. A Socialist mayor in Schenectady was hauled to jail for speaking without permit to a group of striking mill workers. "Lincoln says . . ." was all he could say before the police grabbed him. The radical press was likewise harried. While Debs worked for the *Appeal to Reason,* the paper faced government surveillance, mail tampering, and spurious libel suits, harassment that ultimately may have been what drove editor Francis Wayland to commit suicide.[27]

In the 1912 election, Woodrow Wilson and Theodore Roosevelt tried a different approach to silencing Debs and the Socialists. Hoping to quell working-class unrest, they co-opted many of the radicals' reform proposals. Leading the Progressive "Bull Moose" Party, Roosevelt called for reforms that Socialists had been championing for years—women's suffrage, the right of referendum and initiative, the direct election of senators, stricter regulation of the economy through food and drug laws, a minimum wage, and a ban on child labor. Old-guard Republicans denounced this "manifesto of revolution," calling it "frankly Socialistic." The Socialists agreed, protesting that "Ruse-evelt" was stealing their platform. Bull Moose supporters freely admitted that they hoped

to defeat radicalism by taking over "the reasonable part" of its program. On the stump in 1912, Roosevelt warned voters that if they failed
to adopt these reforms, they would play into the hands of Eugene
Debs, an agitator who had no conception of the fragile balance of
compromise that made democracy function. "Mr. Debs wishes to pull
down in a spirit of hate," he charged. "I wish to build up in a spirit of
brotherly love."[28]

Democratic nominee Woodrow Wilson was more temperate in his attacks. While serving as president of Princeton, and then governor of
New Jersey, he had known many Socialists who were "honest and serious men," most of them intellectuals from the moderate wing of the
party. But he also warned voters about the rising threat of socialism, describing it as an angry and irrational "protest." He predicted that unless
government acted quickly, workers would lose their faith in the common good and become prey to radical schemes that would destroy
American enterprise. He vowed to ease social unrest by breaking up the
trusts, restoring hope to the man "who is knocking and fighting at the
closed doors of opportunity."[29]

Debs believed that Roosevelt, Wilson, and their liberal supporters
were ignoring the stark fact that workers and owners were enemies,
their interests irreconcilable. In his view, the mainstream politicians
hoped to ease the symptoms of economic injustice while ignoring their
cause, the private property rights that protected America's industrial
masters. Roosevelt and Wilson promised to regulate corporations, while
Debs insisted that the people should "take them," harnessing their pro-
ductive power to serve the public good, and not the greed of a few.[30]

Both his admirers and his enemies often described Debs as a dreamer.
Witness to some of the nation's bitterest labor battles, he knew the
harsh realities of class conflict in America. He interpreted these clashes,
however, as the terrible pangs of a hopeful birth, signs that confirmed
his faith in the imminent arrival of the great worker's revolution. He saw
this transformation coming, just around the corner, for more than two
decades. He demanded it, predicted it, scanned the horizon for it. With
the advantage of hindsight, Debs can seem to be a man deeply deluded,
one who saw portents of a future that never arrived, who saw the death

of capitalism, and the birth of a classless utopia, far more clearly than he saw the political and social reality in front of his face. Many Americans at the time thought just that about Debs. "He is too good for this world," they concluded. "His visions and dreams are the fanciful out-pourings of a generous but impractical soul."[31]

Debs was clearly swimming against the strong current of public opinion. Most of America's editors, preachers, and politicians united in their praise of the free enterprise system. They sanctioned the culture's deep and abiding faith that capitalism offered the surest path to individual success and social progress. Everywhere, Americans felt what William James called the "circumpressure" of this consensus, reinforcing the belief that private property was not betraying the country's democratic ideals, as Debs contended, but was a pillar of the American "way of life."

Still, by 1912 many thousands of Americans considered socialism to be what James called a "live hypothesis." The nation's choice between capitalism and socialism was as yet unresolved. The vision Debs conjured of a cooperative commonwealth stirred imaginations, and cast a corrosive doubt on the profit motive as an engine of freedom and progress. As James understood, Americans would never resolve the struggle between capitalism and socialism by calm and rational inquiry into economic laws. The decision facing them at the start of the twentieth century was moral rather than scientific, a question about the best way to live, a matter more of faith than of reason. And on such social questions, James pointed out, "faith in a fact can help create the fact." People on all sides of this struggle understood that the question hung in the balance, that socialism was neither destined to prevail nor doomed to fail. The Socialist plan to reorder society might be realized—if men like Debs could convince enough people to believe in it, to desire it, and to devote their lives to it.

If, as James suggested, emotional commitment is an essential component of turning such dreams into realities, then Debs was powerfully equipped to change American minds. Socialist intellectuals often regretted that their candidate was not better grounded in the scientific principles of socialism, better able to grapple with the intricacies of Marxian theory and with the problems of applied economics. But they had to concede, as they sent him time after time into the fray of a national campaign, that Debs had the electrifying power of a true believer and the ability to touch the hearts of Americans from every walk of life. After hearing Debs speak, one agnostic reporter put it this way—"If Socialism is a dangerous and pernicious thing, then Eugene V. Debs is a dangerous man."[32]

As results came in from the 1912 election, that danger seemed greater than ever. Just as Republicans had feared, Roosevelt's third-party campaign split the party, handing a rare presidential victory to the Democrats. Even more surprising to many commentators, Debs received almost a million votes, nearly doubling his 1908 tally. "Socialism mounts like a tide," a party member crowed. "The Socialist Party has come to stay." Editors of mainstream papers confessed that they found the growth of public support for Eugene Debs to be "astonishing."[33]

The Socialists had momentum, and reason to hope for even better results in 1916. Debs felt sure that the "ladylike" Woodrow Wilson would have no success in reforming the nation's system of "entrenched privilege." In the years ahead, the rift between the rich and poor would only widen, fueling the fires of revolutionary indignation among America's working class. Debs felt sure that history was on the side of socialism.[34]

While Americans prepared for a pending civil war between capitalism and the rising power of socialism, a quite different war broke out in Europe in August 1914. Over the next three years the United States would be drawn into that conflict, an experience that would have a profound impact, not only on its place in the world, but also on its domestic politics. When Congress declared war on Germany in 1917, public officials and many private citizens also launched an undeclared war on the Socialists for their stand against the war.

Before the war, Debs and his comrades had often been forced to defend their right to speak, fighting skirmishes against court injunctions, police threats, and press harassment. In spite of these challenges, the Socialists did enjoy a remarkable freedom to promote their revolution. Some observers considered this a sign that the nation's respect for free speech was alive and well, while others urged the authorities to do more to silence those radicals who seemed so determined to foment class envy and violence. But until America entered the war, Debs spoke freely, attacking the nation's "plutocracy" in the radical press and on hundreds of platforms across America. Though he denounced the legal system as the handmaiden of capitalism, it granted him enough freedom to make a fair living as a professional revolutionist.

The war would soon change all this. Though Americans professed a respect for the First Amendment, most also believed that, in times of national peril, the individual's right to free speech was less important than the community's right to defend itself. When Debs and his allies disagreed, and vowed to rally working-class opposition to the war, they added force to the old criticism that they were disloyal, an untrustworthy "enemy within." In the charged emotional atmosphere of war, many more Americans would soon come to see Eugene Debs as a "dangerous man."

Chapter 2

Never Be a Soldier

I N 1914 JOHN REED had earned an international reputation as a war correspondent for his exciting depictions of the Mexican Revolution. Traveling with Pancho Villa's ragged revolutionary army, the Harvard-educated bohemian thrilled his readers with tales of a romantic, sun-soaked people's insurgency. On a new assignment covering the outbreak of war in Europe, Reed found something quite different. In the trenches of France, war was incomprehensibly vast, mechanical, and destructive. Writing for the radical journal *The Masses,* he described "holes torn in bodies with jagged pieces of melanite shells . . . sounds that make deaf . . . gases that destroy eye-sight . . . wounded men dying day by day and hour by hour within forty yards of twenty thousand human beings, who won't stop killing each other long enough to gather them up." The experience left Reed profoundly unsettled.[1]

For American radicals, the war also shattered illusions about the power of the international socialist movement. On both sides of the Atlantic, socialists had long argued that war was a symptom of the disease of capitalism and that socialism would be its cure. As Reed put it, the conflict was "a falling out among commercial rivals" who were greedy for global markets. European socialists had seen the war coming and had vowed to work together to prevent it. Enjoying more political clout than their American comrades, they planned to thwart their own governments' war declarations by blocking military funding in their parliaments, and by leading workers in a general strike that would cripple their nations' war machines before they reached the battlefield.[2]

Instead, as New York's Socialist congressman Meyer London put it, "the nightmare had full sway." When the "hour of danger" arrived in the summer of 1914, a majority of German socialists had chosen to support national "self-defense" over the international solidarity of the working class. Many of their counterparts in France and England soon followed suit. Jean Juares in France, one of the few who stood by his prewar principles, was silenced by an assassin's bullet. The socialist strategy to conquer war proved to be only a pathetic "hallucination," London moaned, and the workers of Europe had been "at each other's throats ever since."[3]

American radicals were deeply disappointed by this failure of nerve. As one of them put it, "When the great day of our opportunity came, we who ought to have witnessed for our faith by a united and supreme heroism proved ourselves to be the cowards of history." Thousands quit the party in disillusionment, while Socialist leaders tried in vain to organize an international peace conference. As the bloodbath in Europe grew worse, they groped to formulate a "constructive" response. Some thought that any effort by Socialists to stop the killing was futile and would only expose the party's impotence; others formulated blueprints for a peace treaty that would impose socialist reforms on the postwar world. Yet another faction urged the party to seize this moment to intensify its revolutionary propaganda. After the capitalist nations of Europe were done destroying one another, those workers lucky enough to survive would likely be eager to hear the socialist solution to war.[4]

In 1914 Debs spoke to his party most often through editorials in the *National Rip-Saw,* a socialist paper that vowed to be "Blind as a Bat to All but the Right." The *Rip-Saw* also sponsored his speaking tours, sharing the proceeds he gathered from ticket sales. In the months after war broke out, Debs traveled the nation's rural heartland, speaking to college students in Ann Arbor, miners in Idaho, and sharecroppers in Texas and Oklahoma. As he grappled with the meaning of the war, Debs drew freely from all sides of his party's debate, sometimes arguing that nothing could be done to halt the conflict, other times endorsing the plan to mediate peace, and never missing a chance to denounce the conflict as the perfect expression of capitalism. "Capitalist nations not only exploit their workers," he explained, "but ruthlessly invade, plunder and ravage one another. The profit system is responsible for it all."[5]

While Socialists debated their options in 1914, they agreed on one thing—that they should do everything possible to keep America out of the conflict. John Reed summed up the radicals' consensus when he warned his comrades, "This is not Our War."[6]

On this point at least, the Socialists swam in the mainstream of American opinion in the first year of the war. While many in the nation of immigrants were tugged by native sympathies for one side or another, most believed that the United States should not get involved in this Old World madness. Speaker of the House Champ Clark spoke for most when he said that one day a "dry as dust historian" might be able to explain why Europeans were slaughtering one another, but that Americans in 1914 were dumbfounded. "Whoever got it up," Clark pleaded, "we want it to stop." Although President Wilson privately believed that a German victory would be "a disaster to the world," he called on Americans to remain "impartial in thought as well as in action." He declared a national day of prayer for world peace, asked moviegoers to refrain from showing "approval or disapproval" when they watched war newsreels, and offered his services to Europe as a mediator.[7]

Locked in a death grip, the belligerents rebuffed Wilson's public and private offers to negotiate a truce. At home, his efforts were better appreciated, particularly by the nation's various peace organizations. For several decades progressive reformers, social gospel ministers, and humanitarian philanthropists had been developing ideas to end all war, and the outbreak in Europe only stimulated their efforts. They hoped that, finally, their plans for international mediation, collective security, and economic embargoes would earn a respectful hearing from a desperate world. In early 1915, famed social worker Jane Addams helped found the Women's Peace Party, which soon had forty thousand members, and presided over an international women's peace conference that advanced new strategies for conflict mediation. Henry Ford launched his much-ridiculed Peace Ship, carrying a delegation of American pacifists on a quixotic voyage to Stockholm. Another coalition of liberals, settlement workers, and socialists formed the American Union Against Militarism, which proposed, among other things, the public ownership of all armaments factories in order to remove the profit motive from mass destruction.[8]

Though Wilson remained noncommittal about these various suggestions, he gave them a sympathetic hearing, and none doubted that he wanted to help restore the peace in Europe. He was a longtime member of the American Peace Society and had appointed several pacifists to his cabinet. The most notable of these, Secretary of State William Jennings Bryan, devoted great energy in the first years of the administration to drafting dozens of arbitration treaties, designed to ensure the peaceful resolution of international grievances. When war broke out, Bryan felt sure that it was America's destiny, "as the leading exponent of Christianity," to make peace by standing above the fray and serving as a neutral arbiter. Wilson's own desire for American neutrality was motivated by a compound of hope and fear—hope that the nation could serve the world as a "great and lasting influence for peace," and fear that America's ethnically diverse population might be drawn by the war into "divided camps of hostile opinion, hot against each other."[9]

However, as the war ground on, the president found it increasingly difficult to preserve the nation's neutrality. With massive armies bogged down across Europe, both the Allies and the Central Powers desperately needed the loans and supplies that American bankers and businessmen were eager to provide. At first, acting on Bryan's suggestion, Wilson prohibited any financial support to the warring parties, until it became clear that he could not starve Europe's war machines without doing the same to the American economy and unintentionally helping the more self-sufficient Germans. In October he made a fateful decision to reopen the flow of capital to Europe. American ships were soon entangled in Britain's naval blockade. The British seized American cargo bound for Germany, blacklisted businesses that traded with their enemies, opened American mail, and even blocked humanitarian missions to the Central Powers. In vain Wilson demanded the "freedom of the seas" guaranteed by international law for the citizens of neutral nations.[10]

While many criticized Wilson for failing to take a tougher stand against England for violating American rights, public opinion veered sharply against the Germans when they countered the British blockade with the even more controversial use of submarine warfare in the Atlantic. The greatest shock to American neutrality came in May 1915 when a German U-boat torpedoed the British passenger liner *Lusitania*, killing more than a thousand passengers, including 128 Americans. While the Germans argued that the ship was a legitimate target because it carried war material along with its passengers, Wilson insisted that the attack was a barbaric violation of American rights. Under the threat of war, the Germans pledged to halt submarine attacks on unarmed merchant vessels and to negotiate an indemnity for American losses.

As the prospect of imminent conflict receded, Wilson claimed that Americans had proven themselves to be "too proud to fight." Still, the incident made clear that the country's neutrality was a fragile barrier that could be swept away at any time. Bryan resigned to protest the belligerent tone of Wilson's ultimatum to Germany, but Debs joined many other peace advocates in praising the president's "moral self-restraint." The sinking of the *Lusitania* was a "fiendish crime," Debs conceded, and proof that German autocrats were the "deadliest menace that confronts the modern world." Still, Americans should not meet this danger by preparing for war, he insisted, but should set a higher example by calling for peace, and backing this up with unilateral disarmament. The death of hundreds of innocent civilians on the *Lusitania,* the Socialist Party declared, should remind Americans of the "fiendish savagery of warfare," and "should inspire us with stronger determination than ever to maintain peace and civilization at any cost."[11]

Such talk infuriated Theodore Roosevelt, who toured the country warning that the president had fallen under the sway of "the professional pacifists, the peace-at-any-price, non-resistance, universal arbitration people." In an increasingly dangerous world, he charged, Wilson was leaving the country "helpless and naked." Calling for "action" instead of "elocution," he urged a crash program of arms buildup, fresh efforts to "Americanize" immigrants, and universal military training. He insisted that war training would instill a sense of national purpose in young men and keep them from becoming "soft and flabby physically and morally." For Roosevelt and his allies, this "preparedness" program was not just a temporary expedient in the face of an immediate threat, but a massive reform program that would modernize the army and unify a fractious and polyglot American society.[12]

Roosevelt was the headline-grabbing front man for the National Security League (NSL), one of several organizations that promoted this preparedness agenda. Dominated by conservative nationalists in the Republican Party and underwritten by wealthy industrialists, the NSL organized preparedness parades, produced films depicting a foreign invasion of America, and ran a camp in Plattsburg, New York, that gave American businessmen and college students a chance to experience the rigors and pleasures of army life, turning them into "missionaries in the cause of patriotic service."[13]

At the start of the war, Wilson had resisted pressure to expand the nation's quite modest military forces, believing that the creation of a large peacetime army would be both unconstitutional and, under the circumstances, dangerously provocative. "We shall not alter our attitude," he announced, "because some among us are nervous or excited." The president's lofty detachment from the threat of war was harder to maintain in the face of growing public anger against Germany, fueled by submarine attacks, British propaganda about the German "rape of Belgium," and the steady drumbeat of the National Security League. While most Americans still wanted to avoid war, many now decided that the nation's neutrality, and its honor, should be backed by more military muscle. Facing reelection in 1916, Wilson literally rushed to get ahead of the parade, appearing as the guest of honor in several "preparedness day" marches. Insisting that he was still a "partisan of peace," he warned Americans that they were "daily treading amidst intricate dangers" and should prepare for the worst. He signed defense bills to expand the navy and to create the National Council of Defense, an advisory body that would plan for the mobilization of the American economy in case of war. Though he rejected Roosevelt's call for universal military service, Wilson started a more limited program of military recruitment and training.[14]

By supporting a moderate version of preparedness, Wilson effectively blunted criticism from the National Security League and robbed conservative Republicans of an issue in the pending election campaign of

1916. But the president's war preparations met intense criticism from some in his own party, as well as the feminists, social reform progressives, and moderate Socialists who had become crucial supporters. "You are sowing the seeds of militarism," the liberal pacifist Oswald Garrison Villard told Wilson. Villard was the grandson of abolitionist William Lloyd Garrison and the owner of the influential *New York Post* and the liberal journal *The Nation*. He had supported Wilson in 1912, and when the war broke out he still enjoyed enviable access to the president, an honor he mistook for influence. Predicting that the president would soon enjoy "the wonderful privilege" of negotiating peace in Europe, Villard had asked the president for a "share, however small," in this glorious task. Two years later, Villard grew disillusioned, as the president seemed to be falling into the clutches of Washington's "military clique."[15]

Many congressmen from the South and Midwest shared this concern, charging that "preparedness" was just a government program to create more millionaires. William Jennings Bryan toured the country, attacking the administration's "scaredness" program as both dangerous and un-Christian. In Georgia, populist editor Tom Watson called Wilson's plan "the insane notion that belligerence of mind, belligerence of preparation, and belligerence of attitude and conduct *lead to peace*." The American Union Against Militarism sent speakers on a national tour to challenge the president's arms buildup, accompanied by a giant papier-mâché dinosaur named "Jingo," a caricature of an American militarist who was "ALL ARMOR PLATE — NO BRAINS." In a congressional hearing, Jane Addams claimed to speak for many of the Chicago immigrants she worked with, whom she described as "utterly bewildered by all this sudden talk of the citizens arming and training for war. It upsets their notion of what America is and what they thought, before they came to this country, America was going to be."[16]

The Socialists emphasized the economic causes of war and the workers' stake in keeping the peace. A bigger military, they charged, would benefit only those conservative businessmen who longed for the permanent "militarization" of society. This "so-called citizen army," one predicted, "will be used to destroy collective action on the part of the workers and to shoot them when they strike." If the only way to save civilization is to join a "race of armed murderers," Debs wrote, then humankind is not worth saving. Making a point that would soon land him in prison, he added that "as far as Socialists are concerned, the aristocracies, bureaucracies, and plutocracies who are responsible for war may also fight the battles." In a series of editorials, Debs urged his readers to "Never Be a Soldier." The army turned a man into a "vile and abject thing," he wrote, "the hired assassin of his capitalist master." Debs did not repudiate all violence. Over the years he had often claimed that, when the social revolution finally arrived, he would gladly man the barricades. But until then, he declared, he would let himself "be shot" before he would help to defend American capitalism. Rising to a pinnacle of purple rhetoric, he told the master class to "rip out their own loins and livers, riot in their own blood and entrails and offer up their own mangled and putrescent carcasses on the blood-drenched altar of Mars and Mammon."[17]

An official in the War Department was incensed by this kind of talk, especially when he learned that Socialists were plastering these angry pacifist rants on walls and billboards in American cities. He forwarded a copy of Debs's comments to attorneys in the Justice Department, and asked them to take legal action to silence him. Federal prosecutors agreed that the language was extreme, but they could find no law on the books that would allow them to arrest Debs. This was an oversight that Attorney General Thomas Gregory was already trying to remedy, drafting a bill that would give the government the power to punish disloyal speech. Still divided over the war, Congress failed to act on Gregory's request.[18]

Debs fought the preparedness battle with bold and broad epigrams that captured the mood of the more militant rank-and-file Socialists. "I have no country to fight for," he wrote, "my Country is the Earth and I am a citizen of the world." He was an internationalist, but one whose position on the war appealed to the isolationist sentiment of his midwestern audiences. "We have no fear of invasion," he told them. "The enemy we need to prepare against is a domestic and not a foreign one." And so, while Debs often spoke against the war in these years, he devoted as much time to fighting on quite different fronts. He drummed up sup-

port for a new socialist correspondence college and defended Margaret
Sanger, who was being prosecuted for giving workers information about
birth control. He spoke for the miners crushed in bitter strikes in Calu-
met, Michigan, and Ludlow, Colorado, and attacked the Wilson administration's military ventures in Mexico. He defended Tom Mooney, the
labor organizer who faced a death sentence for throwing a bomb at
a San Francisco preparedness parade—a charge that Debs and many
others considered a blatant capitalist "frame-up." And he denounced
the racism of D. W. Griffith's *Birth of a Nation,* the epic film that drew
large white crowds and strong black protests in 1915. Ida Wells-Barnett
joined many other black leaders in thanking Debs. "Of all the millions
of white men in this country," she told him, "you are the only one I
know that has had the courage to speak out against this diabolical production as it deserves."[19]

By May 1915, Socialist leaders finally agreed on a "constructive" response to the war, issuing a manifesto that called for an immediate
peace without "indemnities and annexations," a program of universal
disarmament, and the creation of an "international parliament" to preserve the peace, which they called a "United States of the World." They
asked Debs to join a delegation to present this plan to Wilson, but he
declined. "I see no possible good in us as socialists calling on a capitalist
president," he told them, "and asking him to do a thing he is committed
not to do." And so Debs missed a chance to meet the man who would
soon become his nemesis.[20]

When the Socialist delegation called on Wilson, they were delighted
to hear that he was already working on a "similar plan" to end the war
and build a new international order founded on a league of nations. The
president offered the same assurances to other pacifist groups. When a
committee of liberals and socialists from the American Union Against
Militarism visited the White House, Wilson disarmed them by taking
them into his "intellectual bosom" and sympathizing with their fears. "I
am just as opposed to militarism as any man living," he told them, but
he argued that the arms buildup was a tool that would allow America to
lead the postwar world in the creation of an international peacekeeping
body. The petitioners warned him that the "reactionary" forces of big
business would use America's new military force to pursue the "aggressive grabbing for the trade of the world." Wilson professed to share

their concern, but insisted that a strong American army would have just the opposite effect, empowering the country to lead a "world federation" for the "international enforcement of peace." Guns, bombs, and battleships were the unsavory means to a beautiful end, one long cherished by conservative peace advocates, liberal Christians, and Socialists alike.[21]

"We all liked him," the socialist editor Max Eastman reported, "and we all sincerely believed that he sincerely believes he is antimilitarist."[22]

A party referendum in 1915 showed that more than 90 percent of American Socialists remained unconvinced and opposed the president's military preparations. Some influential moderates in the party, however, were having second thoughts. Although novelist Upton Sinclair had once been an enthusiastic advocate of the radicals' scheme to end all war through a general strike, he now concluded that German militarism posed a grave threat that Americans could not afford to ignore. The Kaiser's men were "barbarians," he believed, and their victory in Europe would be "the worst calamity to civilization in the whole of human history." Sinclair not only supported military preparations, but decided that Americans had a moral obligation to join the Allies in their struggle. As Wilson began to articulate his vision of a postwar peace, founded on some of the radicals' own ideas, Sinclair concluded that Socialists should cast their lot with the president.[23]

Sinclair wrote to Debs, asking him to sign a petition supporting "democratic defense." He urged Debs and other Socialists not only to accept Wilson's preparedness plan, but to use their influence to turn this new army into a democratizing force. Instead of fighting against preparedness, he argued, Socialists should insist on government ownership of munitions factories and embrace the reform possibilities of universal military service. This new model army would not have to impose the tyranny of mindless drill and regimentation, but could be used to encourage young men and women to improve their "physical culture" through a healthful program of outdoor activities and public service. In the future, when Socialists controlled the government and further wars were unthinkable, they could put this democratized army to work "building the cooperative commonwealth."

Debs refused to sign Sinclair's petition. "I appreciate fully the spirit and intent of your undertaking," he wrote to his friend, "but I know of no reason why the workers should fight for what the capitalists own or slaughter one another for countries that belong to their masters." Once the snarling dogs of war were unleashed, Debs did not think they could be harnessed to pull the sled of socialism.[24]

A small but influential group of Socialist intellectuals did agree with Sinclair. As one put it, the party's claim that this was just a capitalist war over markets was "trite and sectarian." Charles Edward Russell, a leading Socialist writer and intellectual, warned that pacifism at this moment could be suicidal for social revolutionaries. "If Germany wins," he insisted, "good night to Socialism—and every progressive cause. The world will be turned into an armed camp." Until he came out in support of the Allies, Russell had been a popular and influential figure in the party, one of Debs's closest rivals for the presidential nomination and a likely choice to succeed him in that post. Now Russell's stand for preparedness destroyed his standing in the party. As with Sinclair's petition, Debs firmly rejected Russell's argument but defended his right to express his opinion in the face of strong opposition from his comrades.[25]

In spite of Debs's conciliatory words, the debate over preparedness revealed fractures that would split the party once the war began. Many attacked Sinclair, Russell, and others for falling prey to the war party's "hysterical preparedness campaign." In 1915 party members voted to expel any Socialist who held elected office and voted for the arms buildup. Some who supported preparedness fought back, accusing German immigrants in the party's leadership of being "Kaiser-worshippers" who were motivated not by radical ideals but by a secret loyalty to their fatherland. A bitter fight within the party was brewing, and as the Socialists looked forward to 1916, many pinned their hopes on Debs, hoping that he might once again accept the presidential nomination and unify the party at this crucial moment.[26]

Debs refused to consider a fifth run for the White House, declaring, "There are thousands of comrades who are at least as well qualified as I am for the nomination." He was, in fact, deeply tired and in poor health. Decades of being on the road, campaigning and lecturing, had taken its toll. Though he relished the chance to mingle with comrades, he had grown weary of the months spent "in exile" from his home.

Making matters worse, his itineraries were exhausting. Night after night Debs emerged from a meeting physically drained, drenched with sweat from his exertions on the platform. Plunged into the cold air of an open automobile, or the stuffy confines of a railroad car, he would spend much of the night heading to his next engagement. One bitter winter night in Idaho, he bounced along seventeen miles of muddy roads in an open buggy, in a vain attempt to catch a train that never arrived. "I am willing to be killed for the cause," he complained to his booking agent, "but I don't want to die a fool's death." Each time he returned from one of these tours, he collapsed, often spending weeks in bed trying to recuperate from what his brother described as "nervous and physical exhaustion." Debs was sure that another run for president would kill him.[27]

The Socialists turned instead to Allan Benson. A journalist with no leadership experience in the party, Benson captured the attention of his comrades through a series of anti-war articles for the *Appeal to Reason*. With single-minded devotion, he championed a plan he felt sure not only would keep America out of the war, but would prevent all future wars. He proposed that, unless threatened by immediate invasion, the country should declare war only through a national referendum. This would give the war power to the working-class majority, a group that Benson assumed had little desire to fight.

Many party leaders ridiculed Benson's plan to destroy war by democratizing it. Morris Hillquit, leader of the party's New York wing, fretted that his "perfectly wild" scheme would make a "laughing stock" of the party, particularly the provision that those men who voted for war should be the first ones drafted. Debs, however, called the referendum idea "unassailable," and it was popular enough with the party's rank and file to earn Benson the nomination. In a year when millions of young men were dying in the mud at Verdun and the Somme, Benson believed that the quest for peace was the only issue worth talking about, and he hoped to win the votes of all those Americans who were ready to take a radical stand against war.[28]

In spite of strong anti-war sentiment in the country, Benson's campaign failed to ignite much interest. He was a journalist, not a platform speaker, and he headed out on the campaign trail with a sense of dread.

Even worse, many radicals had already decided to vote for Wilson, believing that the incumbent offered the best way to promote social justice and world peace. The president had delivered a remarkable slate of domestic reforms in his first term, supporting the eight-hour day for rail workers, a ban on child labor, some protection for unions, tariff reduction, and the creation of the Federal Reserve and the Federal Trade Commission. Under Wilson's leadership, the usually fractious Democratic Party had become an effective vehicle for change, advancing causes held dear by progressives and moderate Socialists.[29]

Many Socialists also believed that Wilson offered the best chance of staying out of the war. The Democrats emphasized this point in their campaign. "You are Working—Not Fighting!" they reminded voters. "Alive and Happy;—Not Cannon Fodder!" A number of radicals were ready to concede that the president had indeed "kept us out of war," just as his campaign slogan proclaimed. John Spargo noted that, at a time when much of the world had become a slaughterhouse, the president had managed to keep the United States a "great sanitary center of health and healing." These Socialists were also impressed by Wilson's plan for a new international order after the war. "Wilson aggressively believes not only in keeping out of war," as Max Eastman put it, "but in organizing the nations to prevent war." The president spoke in hazy but noble terms about disarmament, open diplomacy, and a world league that would create peace through collective security. Benson's referendum plan was more radical, but simple-minded by comparison, and many in the anti-war movement concluded that a vote for Benson would be nothing more than a feeble symbolic gesture at a time when more decisive action was needed. In addition to wining Eastman's and Spargo's votes, Wilson was also supported by John Reed, Jack London, Helen Keller, Upton Sinclair, and a number of other middle-class radicals and peace progressives.[30]

During the 1916 campaign Wilson revealed a less tolerant side to his personality that might have given these left-wing admirers reason to pause. While rallying public support for preparedness, the president often questioned the loyalty of those "hyphenate" Americans who opposed his plan, many of whom were working against his reelection. Marching under a banner that demanded "Absolute and Unqualified

Loyalty to Our Country," Wilson warned that there was "a disloyalty active in the United States," one that must be "absolutely crushed." He disclaimed any interest in using violence against this "subtle minority." Rather, he urged Americans to unleash their "spiritual force" to teach these dissenters that "loyalty to this flag is the first test of tolerance." The president believed that he was artfully leading the American people toward a "single way of thinking" about the war. Those who disagreed with him, he implied many times in 1916, were not just wrong, but were not true Americans.[31]

Wilson's threats against the "disloyal" were dangerous in part because they were so vague, failing to distinguish between the German agents who were, in fact, spreading anti-war propaganda in the country, and those Americans who had their own objections to the nation's foreign policy and every right to express them. As war fears mounted, others made Wilson's point more clearly, stigmatizing those who opposed preparedness as cowards, traitors, and even "milk-faced grubs." The much beloved Jane Addams found herself ostracized, while William Jennings Bryan faced death threats for questioning America's arms program. As the country moved toward war in 1916, the change in the public mood was already evident. "There is in America today," Walter Lippmann observed, "the beginning of that very military arrogance which we are told this war is being fought to abolish. It shows itself in contempt for all efforts toward peace, in programs of armament that are the vistas of a nightmare, in denunciation of the virtues that make a free and tolerant people, in a hatred of other points of view, in the attempt to haze and ostracize those who have different opinions, and in the assertion of a brittle, touchy impatience at the thought that anything human can be adjusted without slamming the table and rattling the windows."[32]

Thanks in part to support from liberals, progressive reformers, and moderate Socialists, Wilson won a narrow victory over Republican Charles Evans Hughes, a former New York governor and Supreme Court justice. Benson ended with a disappointing tally of less than six hundred thousand votes, two-thirds of the support that Debs had received in the happier days of 1912. Unable to stay out of the race entirely, Debs made a lively run for Congress in Indiana's fifth district.

He came in second, a respectable showing in a campaign that attracted much attention in the radical press, and gave Debs another platform for opposing the country's drift toward war. "If I were in congress," he told his neighbors, "I would be shot before I would vote a dollar for such a war."[33]

Those "fighting pacifists" who voted for Wilson felt vindicated when the president appeared before Congress on January 22, 1917, and once again called on the Europeans to accept his lead in forging a "peace without victory." Wilson vowed that, when the killing stopped, America would join with other nations to create a new kind of peace, founded on moral right rather than military might. "It is taken for granted," he insisted, "that the peace must be followed by some definite concert of power which will make it virtually impossible that any such catastrophe should ever overwhelm us again." "There will be no war," he assured his advisor Colonel Edward House. "This country does not intend to become involved in this war."[34]

Even as the president spoke, the Kaiser's generals were formulating plans to deliver a knockout punch on the Western front in the summer of 1917. A week after Wilson's plea for peace, the German ambassador informed the administration that his country would resume submarine attacks on all ships entering French and British waters. Calling on Americans to view the situation from "the lofty heights of impartiality," the Germans justified this as an unavoidable response to the British blockade that was inflicting starvation on the German people. The Kaiser's military planners realized that renewed attacks on American merchant ships would force Wilson to act against them, but they gambled that his administration would be unable to organize a significant military force in time to make a difference on the battlefield.

Faced with this blow to the nation's "dignity and honour," Wilson broke diplomatic ties and asked Congress for permission to arm America's merchant ships, an escalation that was blocked by a filibuster from Wisconsin senator Robert La Follette, sparking bitter attacks on his patriotism. Clinging to a slender hope that war could yet be avoided, Wilson warned Germany not to act on its "sudden and deplorable renunciation of its assurances." A month later, on March 1, American newspapers published excerpts of an intercepted telegram from German foreign secretary Arthur Zimmermann, revealing Germany's attempt to forge a military alliance with Mexico against the United States. In mid-March, three American freighters were sunk by German torpedoes in the Mediterranean. The nation's long and tumultuous quest for neutrality was coming to an end, and Wilson's call for a declaration of war was expected at any time.[35]

In this charged environment, Debs toured the Northeast that March, speaking to packed halls of workers and radicals who were hungry for leadership and inspiration in this moment of crisis. All Socialists knew that their movement stood at a crucial juncture. When war came, would they stand firm in their opposition, or cave under the pressure to conform as their comrades in Europe had done? The more pragmatic warned that protesting the nation's war effort would be tantamount to suicide, confirming the old slander that Socialists were disloyal and bringing the wrath of war-crazed patriots down upon them. These moderates argued that by supporting Wilson and his war, the party could expect to play a role in shaping the government's war policy and might be able to use this influence to advance the socialist agenda.

Rejecting this line of reasoning, Debs urged his fellow radicals to stand firm by their pacifist principles. He knew this would invite persecution, but thought of this as a refining fire that would drive the impure, the mere "vote-getters," out of their movement, leaving behind a core of true revolutionists. In America and in Europe, Debs argued, reactionary forces were ascendant, but the war would soon sweep them away. Cracks in the foundation of ruling-class power were already obvious; that very month, Russian revolutionaries had toppled the czar. Debs greeted the news with euphoria. "Out of Russia, the land of despotism and dungeons, of exile and death to political agitators flashed the red flame of revolution in the night of Capitalism's wars." Though Russia's future remained uncertain, Debs joined radicals around the globe in welcoming this ray of hope in the dark hour of world war.[36]

The large and enthusiastic crowds that greeted Debs in those weeks convinced him that many American workers were ready to face this revolutionary test. Five thousand heard Debs in Buffalo's Music Hall, where his speech left them "wild with enthusiasm." In Boston, crowds braved a spring blizzard to attend his meeting. There Debs asked them, "Must we send the workers of one country against those of another because a citizen has been torpedoed on the high seas, while we do nothing about the 600,000 workingmen that are crushed each year needlessly under our industrial machinery?" In New York, two thousand had to be turned away from his address at Cooper Union. The *Times* reported that Debs pushed his audience "almost to a state of frenzy" when he vowed "I will never go to war for a capitalist Government." If Wilson tried to force war on the country, Debs told them, workers should respond by forming a "revolutionary union" that would "paralyze" the country in a general strike.[37]

In the years since his great presidential campaign in 1912, Debs had at times felt nagging doubts about the value of his work. Traveling the same circuit covered by other lyceum speakers who peddled a wide range of intellectual wares, he worried that he was losing the revolutionary spark, becoming just another public entertainer stumping the backwoods in search of a buck. Speaking for money, he complained, left his "lips polluted and the inspiration smothered." In his early sixties, and often in frail health, Debs sensed that his long career was almost over, the social revolution he yearned for as elusive as ever.

Now, as the crisis of war approached, he preached revolution to crowds who hung on his words and seemed ready to defy their government. He felt rejuvenated by the experience, back on the front lines of world revolution at a time when the old order seemed ready to topple. He crowed to his brother back in Terre Haute that he was giving some of the best speeches of his life and felt "fine as a bear." Moderates in the Socialist movement thought, instead, that Debs had lost his grip on reality. As one put it, the idea that American workers were about to throw down their tools in a mass protest, forsaking their own government in a time of war, was "one of the most absurd and preposterous things ever known among men."[38]

On the evening of April 2, Wilson asked Congress to declare war on Germany. To meet the formidable challenges ahead, he warned lawmakers, he would soon ask for unprecedented powers to mobilize the country's men and resources. He would need to impose heavy new taxes, extend "liberal financial credits" to the Allies, and conscript at least a half million men—a figure that vastly underestimated the number that would eventually be drafted.

Ignoring a rising tide of anti-German feeling in the country, Wilson insisted that Americans were heading into this war "without rancor." The enemy, he argued, was the Kaiser's military autocracy, which had taken the German people to war without their "previous knowledge and approval." The German imperial government was an anachronism in the age of democracy, a throwback to "the old, unhappy days when peoples were nowhere consulted by their rulers and wars were provoked and waged in the interests of dynasties or of little groups of ambitious men who were accustomed to use their fellow men as pawns or tools."

By contrast, the American people would fight "without selfish object," inspired by the need to defend their traditional rights and the chance to build a new world order "planted upon the foundations of political liberty." Many who heard the president's words were stirred by his call to "dedicate everything that we are and everything that we have" to this crusade that would spread the nation's highest ideals across the globe. "The world," as the president said that night, "must be made safe for democracy."

It was a noble and inspiring phrase, and one that American dissenters would soon be mocking from their jail cells.

Chapter 3

War Declarations

I N APRIL 1917 the Wilson administration faced the daunting task of creating a military force capable of making good on America's declaration of war. The "reasonable" preparedness program that had sparked such controversy in 1916 now proved to be only a small down payment on the actual debt. The government needed to recruit, train, and equip an army of several million, build the ships to transport many of them to France, and create an air force where there was none. To do the job, and quickly, Americans would have to conduct a national draft, raise vast sums through taxation and bond sales, and convert much of their economy to wartime production.[1]

In addition to orchestrating train schedules, fixing the price of pork, and drilling young men on the parade grounds, the administration also asked Congress for unprecedented powers to control public opinion. Europeans had already learned that the vast machines of modern warfare ran on the fuel of national morale. As the philosopher John Dewey put it with some discomfort, the government needed to "conscript thought."[2]

Government leaders felt an urgent need to instill a sense of national purpose because Americans remained bitterly divided about the war. For many, the conflict was still distant and incomprehensible. Christian pacifists, agrarian populists, and many progressive reformers believed that Wilson's decision to intervene in Europe betrayed the nation's highest principles, while the Socialists still insisted that the country would be fighting "for the interest of financial freebooters only." Most of the liberal peace organizations either disbanded or supported Wilson's war to end all wars, but many individuals from those groups dreaded the prospect of having to choose between their country and their conscience.

Public demonstrations on April 2 illustrate the country's divided mind. As news spread that the president was about to deliver his war address, thousands gathered on the capitol grounds to protest, many wearing white arm bands declaring "We Want Peace," while thousand more came to the city to join counterdemonstrations. Capitol police managed to preserve order, but in other cities war protestors were attacked by patriotic mobs, often led by men in uniform. In Philadelphia the mayor banned all public demonstrations in order to keep the peace. In Baltimore, four thousand pro-war demonstrators, led by professors from Johns Hopkins University, "smashed a big pacifist meeting to bits," driving the peace activist and former Stanford president David Starr Jordan from the stage. The police managed to restore order only after clubbing a flag-waving banker into a stupor and arresting many. Across Manhattan, stage performances were interrupted that night as audiences demanded to hear "The Star-Spangled Banner," while vendors did a booming business selling flags to crowds who sang patriotic songs in the streets. At a Socialist rally in Carnegie Hall, however, the audience hissed Wilson's war plans and threatened revolution.[3]

This battle in the streets was echoed in the halls of Congress, where Senator Robert La Follette led a beleaguered coalition who continued to resist the call for war. Echoing an argument dear to the radicals, George Norris, the progressive Republican senator from Nebraska, insisted that America was "going into war upon the command of gold" and that his fellow countrymen were "about to put the dollar sign on the American flag." The majority in Congress believed that the nation had been driven to war by Germany's flagrant abuse of the country's rights and its honor. Most also shared Wilson's belief that America would fight selflessly, fulfilling its unique mission to bring democracy and a higher moral order to world affairs. In their view, this cause was as righteous as it was unavoidable. Continued opposition then, at a time when the nation demanded unity of purpose, seemed to be a despicable betrayal. At the end of several days of bitter debate, six senators and fifty congressmen rejected Wilson's call for war. As the most visible anti-war leader in Congress, La Follette was derided as a servant of the Kaiser.[4]

The American entry into the war also left many in the nation's largest ethnic groups torn by divided loyalties. Through the uneasy years of neutrality, leaders of the German- and Irish-American communities criticized Wilson's approach to neutrality, which they claimed favored the Allies. Firing back, Wilson made "Americanism" a key theme of his 1916 election campaign and threatened those who were trying to pour "the poison of disloyalty into the very artery of our national life." In his war address to Congress on April 2, Wilson again vowed that those who hoped to undermine America's will to fight would face "stern repression."[5]

In some respects the Socialists posed the greatest threat to the government's drive to create a national consensus. The day after Congress declared war, two hundred party leaders gathered in St. Louis for an emergency convention. Debs was not there, once again laid low by illness, but most of the delegates shared his view that the time had come to make "revolutionary history" by standing firm against American intervention. After a week of intense deliberations, the convention issued a proclamation declaring the party's "unalterable opposition" to the war. Mocking Wilson's claim that his call to war expressed the public will, they called it "a crime against the people of the United States." The world would not be made safer or more democratic, they charged, by adding one more nation's army to the "mad orgy of death and destruction." This "St. Louis Proclamation" called on Socialists across the country to join in "continuous, active, and public opposition to the war," including the draft and the sale of war bonds. The party planned demonstrations, petitions, and a propaganda campaign that would teach American workers "the true relation between capitalism and war." From his bedside Debs applauded his comrades' defiant stand, telling them that "there must be no fear, no evasion, and no compromise."[6]

A fraction of the St. Louis delegates supported John Spargo's "minority report." A leading voice of the party's moderates, Spargo urged his comrades to accept the war as an unavoidable "fact," and to work *with* rather than *against* the government. Socialists needed a "constructive" policy, he insisted, one that would allow them to press for economic reforms during the war, including a high tax on war profits, public ownership of key industries, and strong protection for free speech rights. This, Spargo pleaded, was the only way that the party could help to "minimize the suffering and misery" that were sure to come once Americans plunged into the fighting.[7]

In a national referendum, the party's rank and file endorsed the more militant majority report by an overwhelming margin, prompting Spargo, Upton Sinclair, and a number of other "pro-war" Socialists to leave the party. In their place, many more flocked to join the party, drawn by its stand against the war. Though fractious and decentralized, the party had enormous potential as a vehicle for encouraging and organizing the nation's anti-war forces. It had many regional and national newspapers and magazines, a number of popular stump speakers led by Eugene Debs, and an active network of local chapters experienced in the democratic arts of soapbox oratory and printed propaganda. The Socialists looked forward to the 1917 election campaign, when they could offer voters a chance to voice their anger over the "capitalist" plan to send millions of young men off to fight in the bloody trenches of France.

In the face of this opposition, the Wilson administration developed a two-pronged strategy to impose unity where there was none. A week after declaring war, the government created the Committee on Public Information (CPI), headed by the energetic progressive journalist George Creel. Mobilizing powerful tools of mass persuasion, Creel hired thousands of writers, scholars, artists, and filmmakers to make the government's case for war. As Creel later put it, the CPI embarked on a grand experiment in "advertising America," at home and around the world. This publicity bureau churned out pamphlets, press releases, films, and talking points for a volunteer army of "Four Minute Men," cataloging the atrocities of the German army and extolling Wilson's war crusade. Though Creel insisted that his agency fought foreign propaganda with the power of truth, many of his employees conceded that much of the CPI's work was badly biased, and in some cases entirely fabricated.

Whatever the committee's value as a source of information about the causes and prosecution of the war, Creel turned the CPI into a megaphone that for the next eighteen months gave the government the loudest voice in the marketplace of ideas.

The administration complemented the seductions of this public relations campaign with an aggressive program of legal repression. As early as 1916, in the midst of the preparedness debate, Attorney General Thomas Gregory asked Congress for more power to punish the disloyal. Except for a new law criminalizing threats against the president, Congress ignored Gregory's request—a reflection, perhaps, of its own divided feelings about the war. Just hours after Wilson called the country to war, the Justice Department once again called for greater powers to control information and punish subversive speech, many contained in a subsection of a larger bill known as the Espionage Act.[8]

As the name implies, much of the Espionage Act dealt with the real threat of German spies, sabotage, and clandestine propaganda. Through the troubled years of neutrality, government investigators had uncovered numerous German conspiracies, often clumsy attempts to undermine American support for the Allies and to slow the production of war material that was bound for their enemies. German agents funded American newspapers and speakers, supported labor agitation in war-related industries, and were implicated in a series of explosions and fires at munitions factories. Provisions of the new "spy bill" that targeted these activities were uncontroversial, though in the end they proved futile. During the war, the Justice Department did not convict a single German spy or saboteur under the Espionage Act.[9]

However, the bill also gave the administration unprecedented powers to regulate public discussion of the war. The target was not German spies but American citizens and their newspapers. Soon after the bill was introduced, the *New York Times* warned that the public was not sufficiently alarmed by the attorney general's proposal, one that "strikes at one of the fundamental principles of the American Government— liberty of speech and the press." The *Times* and other papers were particularly concerned about the government's plan to censor newspapers. A new censorship board, led by George Creel and the secretaries of the army and navy, would monitor the nation's press and punish those who published, or even attempted to collect, any information that the president had previously determined could be "useful to an enemy."

Editors across the country attacked this "monstrous abuse of legislative authority," an executive power grab that struck more than one as positively "Prussian," under the circumstances the darkest of adjectives. According to Gregory's plan, the president would have the power to declare specific aspects of the war effort off-limits to journalists. Thundering editorials warned that this would do nothing to stop German spies, but would allow the president's underlings to stifle legitimate criticism of their conduct. "The bureaucrat entrenched behind this law," one paper warned, "might conceal his errors until he had blundered away an army or a fleet." Censorship, then, was not only a violation of traditional American rights, but bad military policy.

Editors pointed out that, when it came to sensitive military information, they already followed a voluntary system of self-censorship. "Does anybody believe," one asked, "that there is in the United States a single newspaper that would willingly convey to the enemy that which should be concealed from him?" As radicals like Debs often pointed out, the mainstream papers had been avid supporters of military preparedness, and most had welcomed the war declaration. In fact, editors were far more enthusiastic about the war than many of their readers were. Eager to do their part, they resented Wilson's lack of faith in their judgment and claimed that he was impugning their patriotism.[10]

The mainstream press enjoyed strong and articulate allies in Congress, including some who owned newspapers themselves. Congressman Medill McCormick, part owner of the *Chicago Tribune,* argued that "the American people are used to the utmost candor in matters dealing with the administration of the country's affairs. Why should there be a dark secrecy imposed in wartime?" In the Senate opposition was led by William Borah, a progressive Republican from Idaho. "Some Senators seem to think that the Constitution is suspended in time of war," he told his colleagues, "but that is absurd." Borah and his allies vowed to deny the president this unprecedented new power, "drastic and nebulous in its terms and uncertain in its import." "War is the natural enemy of freedom," added Hiram Johnson, another progressive Republican who opposed the bill. In the name of war, Congress already had granted the president "practically autocratic powers financially," and he warned that, in the months ahead, executive power would only grow. "But we must stop short," he told the Senate, "of successful assault upon democracy's basic principles."[11]

Perhaps caught off guard by this barrage of criticism, proponents of the bill implored their fellow lawmakers to trust the president's good intentions. "If we cannot give our Executive power," Senator Overman complained, "then God help this country." The best reply to that line of argument came from New York's freshman congressman Fiorello La Guardia. "The law admittedly makes the president a despot," he scoffed, "but with the comforting assurance that the despot about to be created has the present expectation to be a very lenient, benevolent despot." Supporters of the bill pressed on, insisting that in times of war every person and every institution must be willing to yield a measure of peacetime freedom for the good of the cause. One senator wondered aloud why so many thought "that there is something about a newspaper man that makes him above the law, and a sort of sacred personage," a faith that he clearly did not share.[12]

In the face of what the *Times* called a "storm of criticism," the bill's supporters backpedaled, considering a range of amendments. A bipartisan coalition of free press forces, in turn, vowed to kill the censorship clause entirely. Just as the idea seemed doomed to defeat, Wilson intervened, insisting that this power was "absolutely necessary to the public safety." He assured the country that he welcomed "patriotic and intelligent criticism," and reminded Congress that the proposed law included a clause denying any intention to restrict "discussion, comments, or criticism" of the government. The law would be used, the president explained, not to silence the vast majority of journalists who were already practicing "patriotic reticence," but to punish the small but unspecified number who "cannot be relied upon."[13]

Wilson's unusual personal plea revived a debate that had grown increasingly bitter. Not long after, the *Times* reported that "Senators and Representatives talked censorship wherever they met today. Their opinions were expressed in no uncertain language." Many lawmakers were reluctant to deny such an urgent request from the commander in chief who was about to take the country into battle, but the bill's opponents remained adamant. After almost two months of debate and a search for compromise, Congress dropped the censorship provision from the bill.[14]

Coming at a time of intense war pressure, this decision to deny the president censorship power was a remarkable victory for the First Amendment. Spilling from the halls of Congress into the newspapers and other public forums, the debate inspired wide affirmation of the value of a free press, the first of many national discussions about the issue that would be provoked by the war.

While the fight over the censorship clause absorbed public attention in the summer of 1917, a smaller group of free speech advocates pressed for further changes in the Espionage Act. When the House Judiciary Committee opened hearings on the bill, two dozen professors, peace activists, labor leaders, and free speech attorneys testified, rehearsing arguments against the law that would eventually find their way to the Supreme Court. Many of them were concerned about a provision that would give the postmaster general the power to deny mailing privileges to any publication "advocating or urging treason, insurrection, or forcible resistance to any law of the United States." The censorship clause defeated by Congress would have punished the publication of specific war-related information on topics determined beforehand by the president. But the "mailability" clause gave an indirect, but potentially much broader, censorship power to Wilson's postmaster, a conservative and crotchety Texan named Albert Burleson. The bill would allow him to punish a paper, not for revealing sensitive military secrets, but for using a tone that struck him as "treasonous." With little debate and perhaps unintentionally, Congress was granting the Post Office what one historian has called "virtual dictatorial control" over the nation's journals and newspapers.[15]

Those testifying against the Espionage Act also objected to the provision that banned the "willful" distribution of "false reports or false statements with intent to interfere" with the war effort, and a related measure making it illegal to "willfully cause or attempt to cause disaffection in the military." None at the hearing challenged the government's right to punish an army mutineer or an enemy agent caught trying to undermine the soldiers' morale. They feared, however, that anyone who spoke against the war might be accused by a zealous prosecutor of trying to promote "disaffection" among the troops. A peace activist from New York told the lawmakers that she found the "disaffection" clause to be a "pretty vague phrase," one that would give the government a powerful tool to stifle open and honest dissent. Arkansas congressman Thaddeus Caraway reassured her that the law was not designed to stop citizens like her from engaging in political organizing, "trying to persuade the public that it is time to cease hostilities." Congress only wanted to punish those who intended to "cause disaffection among the soldiers themselves; that is, to stir up rebellion, stir up insurrections, and things of that kind."

Others remained skeptical, and for good reason. As the hearing continued, several lawmakers made it clear that they took a much broader view of this "disaffection" clause. Harriet Thomas, a leader of the Women's Peace Party, startled the committee when she told them, "It seems to me that under this act I would be liable to imprisonment for life, or a more drastic penalty, perhaps, if I should say that I would rather my sons be shot for refusing to go out and kill and bear arms against a supposed enemy of this country." A congressman interrupted her to ask, "Then you do not honor your citizenship in this country?" Thomas stood her ground. "I feel I have a right to interpret my loyalty to my own country in my own terms of citizenship, and according to my own conscience, and I do not need any bill to tell me what my love of country shall represent."[16]

At that point, several on the committee told her that, once the Espionage Act passed, she would no longer have a right to make those kinds of provocative statements. "If your speech goes to the point of being treasonous," one scolded her, "you are denied that right, and you ought to be." Another exasperated congressman summed up the government's position this way: "People should go ahead and obey the law, keep their mouths shut, and let the Government run the war." Thomas tartly congratulated the committee for at last making clear the true intentions of the Espionage Act.[17]

The congressmen continued to insist that the speech clauses of the Espionage Act did not threaten any person's legitimate First Amendment rights. In the midst of the hearing, however, distinctions between acceptable and treasonous speech that once seemed clear to them began to break down. After several hours of discussion, one citizen pointed out that there was a "distinct vagueness among the members of the committee as to how far this abridgment of speech is going." The lawmakers then countered by pointing out that the Espionage Act targeted only those who *intended* to cause disaffection among the troops. And yet, as Wellesley civics professor Emily Balch suggested, "the question of intent is a very delicate one." Balch insisted that, even as the nation girded for battle, pacifists had the right to share their views on the war with their fellow citizens, and to petition their government to repeal conscription. A zealous prosecutor, on the other hand, might well decide that a speaker who objected to the war or to conscription was motivated by an unspoken desire to discourage young men from doing their duty. Under the proposed bill, this person could be accused of spreading "disaffection," and face the prospect of life in prison.[18]

In any case of this kind, the speaker's intention would ultimately be determined by a jury, and several lawmakers assured the bill's critics that this would protect speakers from overzealous government prosecution. New York attorney Gilbert Roe told the committee that, in cases of this kind, a jury usually was slim protection indeed. For years Roe had donated his services to the Free Speech League of New York, defending the First Amendment rights of radicals convicted for espousing a variety of unpopular causes. In Roe's experience, the members of a jury saw the prosecuting attorney as "the embodiment of the authority of the United States," an aura of power and virtue that would only be amplified by the emotions of war. He warned that, if that prosecutor charged a defendant with trying to aid the enemy, the jury would rush in a guilty verdict in the time it took to "go out of their room and return."

Rehearsing arguments he would one day bring before the Supreme Court in the Debs case, Roe insisted that, without careful safeguards, Congress was about to pass a law that was "so indefinite that it simply becomes a vehicle for oppression." "If you will pardon the statement," he concluded, "I hardly see how it would be safe to say the Lord's Prayer if this bill becomes a law. When we pray that our trespasses might be forgiven us as we forgive those who trespass against us, I think it might be construed that we were praying for the forgiveness of our enemies, the Germans."[19]

The criticisms raised by Roe and others at the hearing were not without effect on the lawmakers, who insisted that they had no desire to stifle free speech but only wanted to "protect our national defense secrets." The final version of the bill that came before Congress was a bit less vague, and a bit less harsh. The term *disaffection* was dropped; instead, the bill stated that no one "shall willfully cause or attempt to cause insubordination, disloyalty, mutiny or refusal of duty in the military, . . . or shall willfully obstruct the recruitment or enlistment services of the United States." The threat of a life sentence was eliminated, making the maximum sentence a still-formidable twenty years in prison. The clause granting "mailability" powers to the Post Office remained. When Congress passed the final version of the Espionage Act on June 15, civil libertarians warned that the government had just set a "trap to catch and jail true Americans" who disagreed with the war.[20]

In 1917, as Americans debated the limits of free speech in times of war, all sides expressed a reverence for the First Amendment. As they spoke, however, a wave of legal and vigilante persecution broke out across the country against those who dared to speak against the nation's decision to go to war. As one witness put it, a "feeling of something akin to terrorism" was spreading, with mob attacks on war dissenters often condoned by local police and led by soldiers in uniform. A coalition of liberals and socialists, including Jane Addams, Max Eastman, and Oswald Garrison Villard, sent the president an urgent petition, warning that "halls have been refused for public discussion, meetings have been broken up, speakers have been arrested, censorship has been exercised not to prevent the transmission of information to enemy countries, but to prevent a free discussion by American citizens of our own problems and policies." They asked the president to speak out against these attacks on what they called the nation's "immemorial rights and privileges."[21]

Given the president's demand for censorship powers and his repeated threats against the "disloyal," the notion that he might intervene to protect the rights of war dissenters may seem misguided and naive. At the start of the war, however, Wilson's allies on the left put much trust in his liberal inclinations, encouraged by the president's private assurances that he "chimed in" with their concerns about free speech. "You may be sure I have the matter in mind," he told them, "and will act, I hope, at the right time in the spirit of suggestion."

In the opening months of the war the president made no public statements against these attacks, however, and even seemed to condone them. In a widely publicized Flag Day speech, he denounced those who were spreading "thinly disguised disloyalties." Some Americans still clung to the nation's "ancient tradition of isolation," he warned, while others denied that America was fighting to defend democracy. Wilson charged these people with trying to "undermine the Government with false professions of loyalty to its principles." These dissenters cared nothing about American ideals, he suggested, but were motivated by a secret desire to aid the Kaiser. Sounding more like a biblical patriarch than an American liberal, Wilson concluded with a stern warning: "Woe be to the man or group of men that seeks to stand in our way in this day of high resolution when every principle we hold dearest is to be vindicated and made secure for the salvation of the nations." Sure that he was leading America into a noble "People's War," Wilson equated dissent with treason, blurring the distinction between German spies and American dissenters.[22]

America's mainstream newspaper editors also showed little concern about these attacks on the war protestors, even as they fought to defend their own First Amendment rights. While opposing the government's censorship plan, the papers emphasized time and again their support for the war effort, offering this as proof that they were "responsible" patriots. As a result, editors had little trouble distinguishing their rights from those claimed by the men and women who opposed the war. As one put it, "When it comes to dealing with spies and traitors, we care not how drastic legislation may be." In Debs's hometown, the local paper wished aloud that all the anti-war socialists could be either swept into a Prussian prison camp or boiled in oil. Ignoring mounting evidence to the contrary, the *New York Times* claimed that "the whole nation has cheerfully volunteered to serve in the war." Such a comment defied reality, unless one equated the dissenters with foreign agents.

"The conspirators, pacifists of the malignant type who are associated with anarchistic societies, are not of the nation," the *Times* explained. "They have no right to be accounted citizens of the Republic."[23]

In the halls of Congress and on the nation's editorial pages, those who wanted to silence war critics made a distinction between *liberty* and *license*. Patriotic citizens, they argued, used their liberty responsibly, and therefore enjoyed the right to speak freely. Radicals who spoke against government policy, and openly worked for social revolution, were not entitled to First Amendment rights; theirs was not responsible speech but "license," an antisocial activity that the Bill of Rights was never designed to protect. An editor for the *Philadelphia Inquirer* summed up the prevailing view this way: "It should not be necessary to indulge in endless debates upon the question of how far a man is permitted to go in insulting the flag and the Nation which affords him protection. If that is free speech, then the less of that kind we have the better it will be for the country."[24]

When the Wilson administration announced its plan for "national selective service," his supporters looked anxiously toward June 5. On that day all American men between the ages of 21 and 30 were required to register for the military draft, a crucial first test of the public's true feelings about the war. Many congressmen who had voted for war only later realized that the president intended to send a large army overseas, and some were reluctant to abandon the nation's tradition of voluntary military service. Acknowledging the war's unpopularity in his home state of Missouri, Speaker of the House Champ Clark compared conscription to slavery, an analogy that radicals would soon be making at their peril. Others, recalling the draft riots of 1863, predicted bloody resistance when the federal government tried to coerce young Americans into taking up arms. Proponents of the draft insisted that it was more fair, democratic, and efficient; besides, in the first month after the war declaration, only thirty-five hundred men were enthusiastic enough about fighting to enlist.[25]

While Debs stopped short of recommending violent resistance, he counseled working men not to join the army. "Don't you take a fit and rush to the front until you see [the bankers] there," he advised his readers. "They own the country and if they don't set the example of fighting for it, why should you?" If volunteering was foolhardy, then conscription was "nothing short of criminal," he insisted. He portrayed the draft as a diabolical capitalist machine designed to turn working men into unthinking enemies of their own class. Such talk, Debs understood, would likely be "construed as treason by the authorities." To that he replied, "So be it."[26]

As Registration Day approached, Congress was still wrangling over the Espionage Act's censorship clause. As a result, local prosecutors had to find other ways to silence those who were trying to rally public opposition to the draft. In Pittsburgh, for example, a minister was charged with "disorderly conduct" for making an anti-war speech. In Ohio, the Socialist politician Charles Ruthenberg and others were jailed on similar charges for holding an anti-conscription meeting. And the anarchists Emma Goldman and Alexander Berkman were arrested in New York for creating a No Conscription League, and "conspiring" to convince young men not to comply with the law.[27]

On June 5 government officials were delighted to find that Registration Day passed with comparatively little violence. Inspired by lavish patriotic festivities, or pressured by neighbors and the local draft board, almost ten million men registered, signing their names to what the president called "these lists of honor." By the end of summer thousands of them would be "selected" by their local draft boards to begin military training, the first wave of a new national army that would be four million strong by the end of the war. With evident relief, federal officials and newspaper editors cheered the orderly turnout as a noble expression of the nation's war spirit. Ignoring the coercive nature of the enterprise, Wilson praised the response as evidence that the nation's young men had "volunteered in mass."[28]

That enthusiasm soon turned to anxiety, as draft boards realized that more than 10 percent had failed to register, and in some regions over half chose not to cooperate. Others signed up using fictitious addresses or fled the country entirely. In addition, more than 60 percent of these supposedly eager volunteers requested personal exemptions, while chapels did a booming business creating husbands who hoped that, as married men, they could escape service.[29]

Tens of thousands declared themselves to be conscientious objectors. While the conscription law exempted members of the established "peace churches," such as the Quakers and Mennonites, draft boards were less willing to accommodate the pacifist scruples of men from smaller evangelical sects in the South and the Jehovah's Witnesses, as well as those political radicals who declared a moral rather than religious foundation for their pacifism. None were entirely excused from service on those grounds, as the law required them to be drafted but provided with noncombatant jobs. Guided by Secretary of War Newton Baker, until that spring a declared pacifist himself, the army handled these men with a mix of tolerance and vicious persecution. Some were allowed to perform "alternative service," many more were convinced or coerced into joining the fight, while hundreds of the most uncompromising pacifists were sent to military stockades, where they often faced brutal treatment, including solitary confinement and torture.[30]

Concerted opposition to the draft was particularly strong in the South and Midwest. In the pages of his *Jeffersonian,* Georgia's populist editor Tom Watson savaged Wilson for taking the country to war. "Where Morgan's money went," he told his followers, "your boy's blood must go, ELSE MORGAN WILL LOSE HIS MONEY!" Watson raised more than a hundred thousand dollars from readers eager to support his legal challenge to the draft law. When a federal judge ruled against him, Watson vowed to continue his fight. "The masses," he insisted, "especially the rural masses—are with me." Many farmers' organizations passed resolutions condemning conscription, and in Oklahoma hundreds of tenant farmers joined an ill-fated protest movement known as the "Green Corn Rebellion." Expecting reinforcements from outraged radicals across the country, they began a march on Washington to force a halt to the war. This rebellion was quickly smashed by a local posse, but across the rural South many conscripts continued to resist the authorities, sometimes violently, and arrests were reported from New England to Texas.[31]

As the first wave of drafted men arrived at hastily constructed military camps in the summer of 1917, the Socialist Party organized mass demonstrations against the war and the draft, which often were broken up by police or soldiers. The most visible protests came from the People's Council, a loose-knit coalition of various branches of the battered peace movement. Led by the radical economist Scott Nearing, the group demanded "immediate peace" and an end to war profiteering, an agenda that led the *New York Times* to denounce them as "the Kaiser's Council." When they called a national convention in September 1917, several midwestern states denied them a meeting place, while vigilantes sent death threats. The mayor of Chicago did grant them permission to meet in his city, but the governor of Illinois countered by sending in state militia to break up what he called a "treasonable conspiracy which must not find refuge under the guarantee of freedom of speech."[32]

The People's Council also faced a challenge from Samuel Gompers, head of the American Federation of Labor, the nation's most powerful union organization. Gompers was eager to discredit the radicals' claim that most workers opposed the war and were being dragged to the slaughter by their industrial masters. "That is a lie," he charged, "and we are going to make the whole country see that it is a lie." Gompers challenged the People's Council by forming the rival American Alliance for Labor and Democracy, an organization that worked to "stamp out sedition and to confuse and confound the traitors who talk peace and anti-Americanism." The AFL leader was probably correct that, once Wilson declared war, a majority of American workers felt it their patriotic duty to support the cause—though it is hard to gauge their enthusiasm. While Gompers's Alliance enjoyed support from some pro-war Socialists like John Spargo, critics charged that this was not a spontaneous, grassroots expression of working-class patriotism. In fact, the Alliance was paid for by the National Security League, George Creel's Committee on Public Information, and the president's "secret" war fund.[33]

Through the summer of 1917, Debs continued to write editorials for the *National Rip-Saw* that denounced the draft as immoral and unconstitutional, a program of "murder by coercion" that repudiated "every principle of democracy." Few read those remarks, however, because a postal inspector decided that the paper contained "objectionable" material that made it "unmailable."[34]

Just as opponents of the Espionage Act had feared, Postmaster Burleson took a broad view of his new power to deny mailing privileges to publications that undermined the war effort. He ordered his agents to stifle any publication that might interfere with the success of Liberty Loan drives, discourage army recruitment, or otherwise "embarrass or hamper the Government in conducting the war." In the summer of 1917 his inspectors found more than a dozen radical publications that matched that description, as well as many religious and German-American papers. The Socialists tried to appeal, sending a committee to Washington that included labor lawyer Clarence Darrow. The postmaster was unyielding, refusing even to offer clear guidelines that might help editors stay within bounds of the law in the future. The delegation could only report that he was prepared to "go right on choking the Socialist press if it does not please him."[35]

Many of Wilson's allies on the left urged him to rein in his postmaster. Upton Sinclair, Oswald Garrison Villard, the *New Republic*'s Herbert Croly, and Max Eastman of the *Masses* each warned that Burleson was an unreasoning autocrat who was driving many small papers into bankruptcy. "How can we advocate democracy for foreign peoples," Sinclair asked, "when we suppress it among our own?" Once again, the president expressed his sympathy. He overturned Burleson's decision in a couple of cases, but when his postmaster threatened to resign, the president backed off. "A line must be drawn," he told Eastman after an issue of the *Masses* was withheld. "We are trying, it may be clumsily but genuinely, to draw it without fear or favor or prejudice."[36]

In the Department of Justice, federal attorneys were also struggling to establish the "line" between legitimate criticism of the government and felonious subversion. While some in the attorney general's office urged restraint, across the country federal prosecutors took a broad view of their mandate under the Espionage Act. Just as Gilbert Roe had predicted, they arrested thousands of Americans for speaking against the war or the draft law, on the grounds that such talk might discourage young men from doing their duty. An Iowa man received twenty years for predicting that American boys would leave for Europe as heroes but return to fill the insane asylums. Others went to jail for distributing a pamphlet that a federal prosecutor thought "overstated the horrors of war." A Rhode Island socialist was arrested for saying that "war is organized murder and that soldiers are uniformed murderers." A Montana man was prosecuted when he called the president "a Wall Street tool" during a "hot and furious saloon argument." In South Dakota, twenty-seven socialist farmers were convicted for sending a petition to local officials and their governor, opposing conscription and complaining about their county's draft quota. Others were jailed for calling the food conservation program "bosh," demanding Wilson's impeachment, suggesting that draftees were "dying like flies" in the army camps, or describing the government's war budget as "an orgy of prodigal waste."

Pacifist ministers also felt the government's wrath, including a Vermont preacher who got fifteen years for distributing a pamphlet that declared, "Christ has no kingdom here. His servants must not fight." Because they resisted war and equated patriotism with idolatry, the Jehovah's Witnesses were particular targets for prosecution. Seven of their directors went to jail, with a twenty-year term meted out to their leader, Joseph Rutherford.[37]

State and local prosecutors found their own ways to silence war dissenters. A New York City policeman, for example, used a flag desecration ordinance to jail a man who was wearing a flag pin that declared "Our Rights: But No War." Minnesota passed its own Espionage Act and used it to arrest a man who discouraged women from knitting socks for the Red Cross. Dozens of states passed conspiracy and sedition laws and used them to jail members of the Industrial Workers of the World (IWW), while others tried to drive politically suspect teachers out of the classroom. In Los Angeles, police accused a group of Christian pacifists of disturbing the peace. They faced fines and jail terms for holding a "quiet afternoon meeting" in a private room, where one man declared it hard to imagine "the Prince of Peace" buying a Liberty bond, or "thrusting a bayonet into the breast of a brother."[38]

Patriots in many communities decided that government prosecutors were not working fast enough to sweep pacifists, pro-German subversives, and radicals off the streets, and created their own "vigilance" or "public safety" committees. Some Justice Department attorneys worried about the "spy mania" that was sweeping the country, but their boss encouraged these activities. Attorney General Gregory invited the public to provide his office with tips about suspicious activity, eliciting an avalanche of mostly specious accusations. He also granted a quasi-official status to the largest of these vigilante organizations, the American

Protective League. Acting with his blessing, these citizen-spies tampered with mail, searched homes without warrants, and swamped authorities with hundreds of thousands of reports on alleged disloyal activities in their neighborhoods.[39]

Members of another organization, the American Defense Society, patrolled the streets of New York attacking soapbox orators. The Society lobbied Congress to ban the teaching of the German language in public schools, urged the immediate detention of all "enemy aliens and sympathizers," and encouraged its members to keep records on every voter in their districts, marking them loyal, disloyal, or "doubtful." One leader explained the group's approach with the maxim, "Those who are not for us, must be against us."[40]

The radicals charged that these attacks were motivated more by class warfare than by any concern for winning the war in Europe. The leaders of most of these patriotic organizations were businessmen, civic leaders in their communities, while their victims most often were working-class radicals, immigrants, or religious sectarians. By the end of the war, Socialists would estimate that fifteen hundred of their five thousand local chapters had been destroyed by violence or intimidation. As one historian put it, "almost immediately after the beginning of World War I the people of the political right used the war as an excuse to attack people of the left."[41]

Privately, Wilson worried about the excesses of these vigilante organizations, but his attorney general ignored him and boasted that the country had never been so "thoroughly policed." "I have today several hundred thousand private citizens," Gregory said, who were helping the government keep an eye on "disloyal individuals and making reports of disloyal utterances." Increasingly, the vigilantes did much more, expressing their patriotism through violence or coercion. In small towns and city neighborhoods, they humiliated suspect citizens, forcing them to kiss the flag or empty their savings accounts to buy war bonds. They drove teachers and other public employees from their jobs, dragged German immigrants through the streets, and tarred and feathered some who showed "lukewarmness" toward the war. The radical unionists in the IWW bore the brunt of many attacks. They were falsely accused of advocating draft evasion, and their halls were raided and vandalized, in many cases by soldiers. A mob in Butte, Montana, dragged one of their organizers behind an automobile, then lynched him. Attorney General Gregory denounced such violence, but at other times he only seemed to encourage it. When asked about war dissenters in November 1917, he said, "May God have mercy on them, for they need expect none from an outraged people and an avenging government." The National Civil Liberties Bureau cataloged several hundred vigilante attacks during the war, and found that only two mob leaders were ever prosecuted. Said one historian, "During World War I, physical violence and murder seemed to become legal, as long as the victim was allegedly disloyal or pro-German."[42]

The threat of violence silenced many. Booking agents for the Chautauqua and Lyceum circuits announced that, for the duration of the war, the public wanted to hear only from pro-war patriots. Struggling with ill health, Debs had arranged only one platform appearance for the summer of 1917, at a Fourth of July gathering in St. Peter, Minnesota. Even this talk was canceled, however, when some local citizens, backed by that state's Safety Commission, decided "it would be dangerous" for Debs to speak there. Max Eastman understood that danger firsthand. He had to abandon a Midwest speaking tour after soldiers broke up his meeting in Fargo, North Dakota, and he narrowly escaped being lynched. Tom Watson canceled his plan to organize a national convention of war dissenters when he received threats against his life.[43]

As the first wave of persecution broke against the radicals, Debs urged his comrades to stand firm. Invoking Tom Paine's call to persevere in the "time that tries men's souls," he called on "every warrior of the revolution to stand by the Socialist Party." And yet, as his comrades read this editorial, Debs was fishing in a Minnesota lake, beginning a long vacation prescribed by his doctors to treat his "nervous and physical exhaustion." When the Socialists had gathered in St. Louis to debate their response to the war, Debs had been confined to bed, "utterly exhausted." He suffered from a variety of ailments, including back pain, digestive problems, and the symptoms of a weakened heart. His doctor told him that unless he took an extended rest, he would not live long. While his beloved Socialist Party faced a struggle for its life, Debs had to confront his own mortality. Under doctor's orders, he retreated to a friend's summer cottage. Only weeks into his therapy he was catching bass, breathing the pine-scented air, and sleeping more soundly. "We're outdoors all day long," he wrote Theodore, "& when I get back I'll be strong as a lion . . . & then we'll make up for lost time."[44]

In August, Debs moved on to Boulder, Colorado, to continue his recovery at a sanitarium run by the Seventh-Day Adventists. At first the spa's managers balked at the prospect of providing safe haven to one of America's most notorious infidels, and when Debs arrived he was told there were no vacancies. After an emergency meeting, the sanitarium directors relented. Oblivious to the uproar he had caused, Debs was soon surrounded by a new batch of admirers, some encouraging the kindly old radical to tell them all about socialism. Finding that Debs had a "dilated heart," the doctor warned that he would not live long without proper treatment and put the patient on a strict vegetarian diet. Debs swore off alcohol, an old weakness but strictly forbidden at the sanitarium, and embraced his new routine of cool night air, cold water, daily massages, and regular exercise. After only a week he felt that "the tide has turned & that life is coming instead of going."

So many old friends came looking for the celebrity patient that his doctor soon forbade visitors and screened his phone calls. Debs dwelled for some months in semi-isolation, linked only by mail to the wider world. Each day brought news about what John Reed described as the nation's descent into "judicial tyranny, bureaucratic suppression and industrial barbarism." In the September issue of the *Masses*, Reed summarized what he called "the blackest month for free men our generation has known." The anarchists Emma Goldman and Alexander Berkman had received two-year sentences for opposing the draft. Passing sentence, the judge had insisted that their First Amendment rights had not been violated because "free speech does not mean license." Postmaster Burleson's crusade to silence the radical press continued, as his agents blocked eighteen publications from the mail, including Reed's own journal. When the *Masses* editors asked the postal inspector to point out which passages had offended, he refused, saying, "If I told you what we objected to, you'd manage to get around the law some way." Reed concluded bitterly that Americans no longer had any free speech rights "worth the powder to blow them to hell."

With federal and state prosecutors pressing the attack, nothing restrained mobs from venting their patriotic fury against radicals and other suspect minorities. That summer soldiers attacked a Socialist parade in Boston, beating the marchers, trampling their banners, and ransacking the party's headquarters. In Oakland soldiers set fire to the offices of the Industrial Workers of the World. In East St. Louis a white mob burned a black neighborhood and killed more than thirty men and women. In the nation's capitol, rampaging soldiers and "government clerks" attacked suffragists who were picketing the White House, pelting them with eggs and destroying their signs. And in Bisbee, Arizona, gun-wielding vigilantes rounded up miners who were striking peacefully but were suspected of ties to the radical IWW. They detained more than a thousand miners without charges, corralled them into boxcars, and "deported" them from town, dumping them without food and water in the desert.

After decades on the front lines of social struggle, Debs was now strangely removed from these conflicts, insulated by the structured daily routine of his mountain idyll. In between long walks and "electric baths," he continued to file editorials for the *Rip-Saw*, which teetered on the edge of bankruptcy thanks to Burleson's attacks. The paper suffered another blow in July when Kate Richards O'Hare, who shared ownership of the paper with her husband, Frank, was arrested in North Dakota for giving an anti-war speech. Prosecutors accused her of saying that American women were "nothing more or less than brood sows to raise children to get into the Army and be made into fertilizer"—a charge that O'Hare insisted was a malicious distortion of a speech she had given many times before without incident. "She is guilty of having publicly expressed her honest convictions," Debs wrote in her defense. "If she is convicted she will go to prison without a flicker. There is not a recreant drop in her veins."[45]

In addition to his monthly contribution to the *Rip Saw*, Debs also passed leisurely hours in the mountains of Colorado writing playful and cryptic love letters to a Terre Haute neighbor, Mabel Dunlap Curry. Married to a professor, Curry had grown to feel confined by the genteel social circle of university life. Increasingly radicalized, she first worked for women's suffrage, and then cast her lot with the class struggle by joining the Terre Haute chapter of the Socialist Party. There she met Debs while volunteering for his 1916 congressional campaign, and by August 1917 Debs confided, "You have been and are more to me than can ever be expressed in words." Debs and Curry still respected and admired their own spouses, but in each other they had found soul mates. In his letters Debs shared advice and gossip about local and national politics, praised Curry's writings and her "considerable mental, moral and spiritual endowment," and gave free reign to a giddy playfulness that appears nowhere else in his letters. In her replies Curry confided that she was "about to fall in love."[46]

Strolling in mountain canyons, picking flowers, and dreaming up silly lyrics and puns to please Mabel Curry, Debs was far removed from one of his party's most important political battles, the 1917 election campaign. While their press was battered and many of their meetings were disrupted, Socialists hoped that the electoral process would provide them with a chance to "re-establish the democracy that is being wrested from them." The party was exhilarated to find that their stand against the war had won them thousands of new converts, people eager to cast a protest vote. That summer Socialist candidates made strong showings in primary elections for state and local offices across the Northeast and Midwest, and one Socialist editor ecstatically predicted that 1917 would mark the beginning of "*the* political revolution."[47]

All eyes turned that fall to Morris Hillquit's campaign to be the next mayor of New York. In spite of government warnings that his speeches were being carefully monitored, he told massive and excited crowds that "we have a right, with intelligence and love of country, to criticize the officers of our Government when they are wrong or stupid, or both." Drawing financial and moral support from radicals around the country, Hillquit described his campaign as "a loud and emphatic rising of the multitude in protest." His opponents interpreted his support quite differently, charging that the Socialists were agents of the Kaiser. "German sympathizers are now working along lines that tend to cover the chances of detection," the *Times* explained. "Many of them have joined the Socialist Party, and are preaching sedition under the guise of Socialist doctrine."[48]

Following the contest in the newspaper, Debs wrote to Hillquit, "I can smell the battle from afar, and it distresses me not a little not to be on the firing line where I belong." In the end, Hillquit won 20 percent of the vote, a marked increase in the party's support, and a moral victory of sorts. In New York and in other races across the country, Socialist candidates only managed to win minor offices, but party leaders made much of their showing, one piece of good news in a time of relentless defeat and humiliation. The sanctity of an electoral campaign had thrown a brief wall of protection around the Socialist candidates, allowing them to explain the party's views on the war with a minimum of state interference. Once the campaign ended, however, the persecution resumed.[49]

Debs returned to Terre Haute in the late fall and remained there through the winter, still under doctor's orders to "keep free from excitement." On many days he could not drag himself from bed, still too weak to stand. Theodore handled much of his correspondence and kept busy turning down the calls for help that arrived each day from his comrades across the country. "No one regrets this more than [Debs]," he explained, who yearned to be "at the front with the comrades who are bearing the banner through these trying days." From his sickbed, Debs did what he could to support those who were suffering for their anti-war principles. He wrote to encourage Robert La Follette, who faced the threat of a Senate censure for his stand against the war. He protested the postmaster's continued suppression of the radical press, calling Burleson "a survival of the stone age." He joined a chorus of protests against one of the worst outrages of mob violence, the kidnapping of pacifist preacher Herbert Bigelow. Masked men in Klan robes seized Bigelow as he prepared to give an anti-war speech in Kentucky. They tied him to a tree, stripped him, cut his hair and poured crude oil on his head, and then whipped him brutally, all in the name of "the women and children of Belgium and France."[50]

This outrage prompted wide protests among liberal and radical groups, who once again pleaded with Wilson to provide more protection for democratic debate about the war. In response, the president offered a vague but "earnest protest against any manifestation of the spirit of lawlessness anywhere or in any cause." Debs found this entirely unsatisfactory. The president had "flayed pacifists," he wrote, but "dealt in the most polite and lady-like manner with the broadcloth, lynch fiends, mob leaders and man-whippers who incarnate the prevailing system in all its satanic, sodden beastliness to the disgrace of humanity to the last generation."[51]

Much that Debs wrote that spring never made it to print, or was watered down by editors eager to avoid the postmaster's wrath. As one explained the situation to Debs, "the editor in chief of the Socialist Press is Burleson. Whenever a Socialist editor prints anything that is distasteful to the fancy of the Texas landlord, the paper is put out of commission." And so the editorials Debs wrote in these months were angry but vague, a call to arms with no clear battle plan.[52]

Otherwise, all Debs could do was watch helplessly as his friends and political allies went to jail, radical papers were driven into bankruptcy, and his party was splintered and humiliated by government harassment. In early March the government indicted five of the Socialists' most prominent leaders. Kate O'Hare lost her case and faced five years at Leavenworth. Another friend, Rose Pastor Stokes, had been arrested in Kansas City for saying, "I am for the people and the government is for the profiteers." Such comments, the prosecutors charged, had a tendency to "chill enthusiasm" for the war. Debs's mail was filled with news of these setbacks, and pleas for help, but there was little he could do but urge his comrades to support the party's legal defense funds. "We who are out of jail today," he told them, "may be in jail tomorrow."[53]

Chapter 4

Canton Picnic

I N MAY 1918 the *Rip-Saw* announced that Debs had at last recovered enough strength to return to a limited program of speaking engagements. He would start close to home in Indiana. If his strength held up and the police did not interfere, then in mid-June he would travel to Canton, Ohio, where he would be the main attraction at the state party's annual picnic. The doctor feared that even this modest schedule might trigger a relapse and warned Debs not to overtax himself. However, many of his beleaguered comrades expected much from the return of the "lion-hearted old agitator." As the editor of his own paper put it, "Amidst all the turmoil of war and its resultant social turbulence, the giant form of Gene Debs towers, like a lighthouse above a seething sea." With that final tribute the paper folded, driven out of business by the postmaster.[1]

While Debs rarely talked about such mundane matters as money, his financial situation may well have played a role in his decision to return to the platform. Kate Debs was supported in part by a modest inheritance, but much of the family income came from Debs's speaking engagements, and he had not been on the circuit in more than a year. The little money he made from journalism had likewise dried up as most of his outlets had gone the way of the *Rip-Saw*.

Balancing the conflicting demands of his physical and financial health was difficult, but Debs faced an even more challenging dilemma as he prepared to return to public life. If he defended the Socialist position on the war, he would invite arrest and a long prison term; under the circumstances, saying anything about the government's war policy was bound to provoke the authorities. On the other hand, remaining silent, capitulating to the threat of prosecution, would bring a sorry end to his long career as a professional rebel. Staying safe while others went to prison, he believed, would betray both his principles and his friends. "I cannot be free," he told a party organizer, "while my comrades and fellow workers are jailed for warning people about this war."[2]

Many of Debs's friends believed that he knew from the start that he would be arrested. When one comrade from Terre Haute warned him to be careful because federal authorities were sure to be monitoring his speeches, Debs replied, "Of course, I'll take about two jumps and they'll nail me, but that's all right." He seemed to face the prospect stoically, accepting that the trajectory of his life's work left him little choice but to stand with his comrades and take the consequences, however grim. "Gene was ready to make his last gift to the working class," one comrade felt sure. In this Debs seemed to be motivated less by political strategy, or a need to vindicate his constitutional rights, than by a desire to preserve his own integrity. "I would rather a thousand times be a free soul in jail," as he put it, "than be a sycophant and coward in the streets."[3]

Debs's biographers have also concluded that he returned to the platform in May 1918 expecting and even hoping to be arrested. Ray Ginger, for example, suggests that Debs spent the first year of the war in a malaise, paralyzed not only by his physical ailments but also by a sense of despair. According to Ginger, Debs finally summoned untapped reserves of moral courage and returned to public life determined to speak his mind regardless of the personal costs. This "beautiful plan" was almost stymied, he tells us, when Debs began speaking in Indiana and found it more difficult than he had expected to get himself arrested.[4]

Some evidence suggests a more ambiguous story. As Debs took to the platform, one relatively impartial observer saw no sign that he was actively courting his own arrest. Claude Bowers, an Indiana Democrat who had once been Debs's political rival, heard him give a speech in

Fort Wayne. He did not notice "a single word to which the most super-sensitive patriot could take exception," Bowers said. "It seemed to me that he had prepared his speech with the realization that every word would be microscopically examined by secret agents." Following the newspaper reports of Debs's other meetings across Indiana, Bowers concluded that Debs continued to steer a course well inside the limits of the law.[5]

Debs showed a similar caution on June 16, the very day he was arrested for his speech to the Socialist picnic in Canton, Ohio. In a hotel lobby he was approached by Clyde Miller, a young reporter covering the speech for the *Cleveland Plain Dealer*. When Miller asked for his views on the war, Debs told him, "In a world that is fighting to make the world safe for democracy, one must be very careful of what one says if one wants to keep out of prison." While these are hardly the words of a man frustrated because he could not get himself arrested, Debs then threw caution to the winds, telling Miller that he continued to support the "main ideas" of the Socialists' anti-war St. Louis platform.

Given his contempt for the "capitalist press," Debs surely suspected that Miller was an unsympathetic witness. In fact, the thirty-year-old journalist was an ardent patriot who had tried more than once to enlist, only to be rejected because of poor eyesight. Denied this chance to serve his country with a gun, Miller had decided instead to enlist his pen. At the *Plain Dealer* he made the domestic war on radicals his beat, and liked to think that his work was helping to fill the city's prison with traitors and slackers. He came to Canton expecting to find a dangerous radical, and Debs did not disappoint. Though Miller was confused by the old man's "gentleness of manner," in their brief interview Debs said enough to convince him that he was an "evil man."[6]

As far as Miller was concerned, Debs's qualified support for the St. Louis Proclamation was a shocking admission, proof that he was "a traitor to his country." That summer, as American doughboys were dying in the trenches of France, Debs still embraced his party's plan to undermine the nation's will to fight. Either too shocked or too rushed, Miller failed to ask Debs the right follow-up questions about this stand on the war. Debs had given his party's anti-war policy only a qualified endorsement. "In light of recent events," he told Miller, he "favored a restatement" of the party's views on the war. While Debs continued to insist that he opposed every fight except the one against capitalism, his ideas about America's role in the European war were in flux.

A month earlier Debs had urged those Socialist leaders not already in jail to gather for a reconsideration of the St. Louis Proclamation. He published a lengthy article that reminded his fellow radicals of the obvious—that defending the party's war policy had become a "criminal offense." However noble in principle, their stand had been disastrous in effect, and a new federal law would soon make matters even worse. In the spring of 1918, Attorney General Gregory complained that too many disloyal citizens were slipping through the net of the Espionage Act, and Congress responded with amendments known as the Sedition Act. Under these revisions, prosecutors no longer needed to prove that defendants were trying to convince young men to violate the draft law. Instead, the act punished the use of any "disloyal, profane, scurrilous, or abusive language" that might encourage feelings of "contempt, scorn, contumely or disrepute" toward the nation's constitution, political system, flag, or military uniform. As one historian puts it, this sweeping new government power "appealed to those superpatriots who yearned for a return to Star Chamber," a group that included a large majority of congressmen.[7]

Of course, stirring up "scorn and contempt" toward the capitalist government was the cornerstone of the Socialist program, and was likely to be judged so by many federal prosecutors. Under these circumstances, Debs insisted, if Socialists stood by their St. Louis pledge to actively oppose the war and the draft, they would only provide the government with a "bludgeon . . . with which to strike us down."[8]

Debs's new thinking about the war was inspired as much by revolutionary optimism as it was by fear of government repression. While conservative forces seemed triumphant across America and most of Europe, "the most extraordinary and unexpected developments" had occurred in Russia, where the Bolsheviks had won a surprise victory for international socialism. Debs thrilled to see Lenin and his party building a "triumphant democracy," one that beckoned all of humanity "toward a higher civilization and the federation of the world." In what seemed like socialism's darkest hour, Russia suddenly showed a way forward.[9]

The Soviet experiment was inspiring but still quite fragile, and in the spring of 1918 its very survival was threatened by the Kaiser's army. When the Bolsheviks came to power in the late 1917, Lenin made good on his vow to take Russia out of the war. Ignoring threats and entreaties from Russia's former allies, the Bolsheviks signed a separate treaty with Germany at Brest-Litovsk. Even though the agreement imposed harsh terms on Russia, the Germans soon tossed it aside and invaded. Debs feared that unless the world intervened, and soon, the Bolsheviks would be overthrown "and the nascent democracy may lie weltering in its own blood and ruins."

Under those circumstances, many American radicals who had once opposed the war now reversed themselves. The war that had once looked like a pointless capitalist scramble for colonies and war contracts had now become a fight to save world socialism. Wilson made this change of course easier for American radicals by making overtures to the new Soviet government. Hoping to lure the Bolsheviks back into the war, he sent them a sympathetic greeting and castigated the Germans for interfering with Russia's "struggle for freedom." Debs praised the president's "splendid and inspiring message." In the struggle to save Russia's working-class republic, President Wilson now appeared to be an unlikely ally.[10]

Under these new circumstances, some radicals decided to spare themselves further government persecution by endorsing Wilson's plan for a new international order outlined in his Fourteen Points. Debs watched his comrades abandon the party's stand against war with mixed emotions, sometimes criticizing them for betraying their jailed comrades, while other times acknowledging that the St. Louis Proclamation had become outdated, even "flagrantly wrong." Publicly, Debs denied that he was changing his mind, particularly when capitalist editors spread the rumor that he was being "whipped into line by threatening public sentiment, and at this late hour is humbly clambering aboard the bandwagon." "I have never yielded to threats or to intimidation in any form," he shot back, "and I am not cowardly enough to seek refuge, as so many do, in the popular side of a public question." Privately, however, Debs told party leaders that continuing to stand by their anti-war platform looked like a "colossal blunder."[11]

Ironically, the Socialists decided not to act on Debs's call for a meeting because the threat of government prosecution made it impossible to have an open and fair discussion about the war. Those who continued to oppose it could never say so in public without risking a jail term. Thus silenced, party leaders decided that they had no choice but to stand by their anti-war principles, even though some now considered them outdated and counterproductive. They agreed, however, to hold a private meeting in August to explore their options.[12]

And so, when Debs arrived in Canton to deliver what became known as his greatest speech against war, his own thoughts about that war were ambivalent. Privately, he was mulling the idea that it might be worthwhile to fight a war against Germany if it saved the Russian revolution. On the other hand, he recognized that a change of course in the summer of 1918 would divide the party, give comfort to America's superpatriots, and betray those noble comrades who had suffered in the defense of the party's anti-war principles. In the end, Debs chose to stand by his friends, regardless of the consequences for himself and his party.

When Debs arrived at Canton's Nimisilla Park on the afternoon of June 16, he was greeted by the affectionate cheers of more than a thousand of the party faithful. Volunteers from the local vigilance committees worked through the crowd, checking the draft registration cards of the young men, hoping to ferret out "slackers." The proceedings were also watched by federal agents, including one stenographer taking notes on the speech. Several of these hostile witnesses noticed that the speaker's platform featured no American flag or patriotic bunting, a glaring omission at a time when every public gathering was draped in red, white, and blue. The meeting did open with a solemn reading of the Declaration of Independence, offered "without comment."

Debs was introduced by Marguerite Prevey. After making a small fortune in Akron real estate, Prevey had turned her home into a haven for Ohio radicals. She coordinated Debs's tours through the state, and he often stayed with her. She was a wealthy matron, but no "parlor pink"; during a strike in one of Akron's rubber factories, she gave safe harbor to some IWW organizers and fended off a vigilante mob by waving pistols on her front porch. Prevey introduced Debs that afternoon by ridiculing the rumors that he was changing his mind about the war. He laughed along with the crowd at the absurdity of the suggestion.[13]

Debs opened his speech by acknowledging three Socialist comrades who were imprisoned in the Canton workhouse, just on the edge of the park. That morning he had stopped by to visit them in their cells. "They may put those boys in jail," Debs told the cheering crowd, "and some of the rest of us in jail, but they can not put the Socialist movement in jail." The men were serving one-year sentences for opposing the draft, and Debs praised them for being willing to suffer for their principles. "If it had not been for the men and women who, in the past, have had the moral courage to go to jail, we would still be in the jungles."

Still, it is not clear that Debs intended that afternoon to join them on that civilizing mission behind bars. He began his speech with a disclaimer, reminding the crowd that he would have to be "exceedingly careful, prudent, as to what I say, and even more careful and more prudent as to how I say it." The audience understood his meaning perfectly, and cheered when he added, "I may not be able to say all that I think; but I am not going to say anything that I do not think."

In the years ahead, Socialists would look back on the speech Debs gave that afternoon as a grand gesture of defiance, a willing embrace of martyrdom. But only a small portion of his talk involved the war. As the Supreme Court would later observe, much of what he said was standard socialist fare. After decades on the platform, Debs could snap the old ideas and phrases together like the well-worn pieces of a favorite puzzle. He urged American workers to join the Socialist Party and form industrial unions, breaking free of the tyranny of Samuel Gompers's conservative AFL. He made a plea for Tom Mooney, and received the loudest applause of the day when he praised the Russian Bolsheviks. "Those Russian comrades of ours have made greater sacrifices, have shed more heroic blood, than any like number of men and women anywhere on earth; they have laid the foundation of the first real Democracy that ever drew the breath of life in this world."

Debs speaking in Canton, Ohio.
National Archives and Record Administration, Great Lakes Region (Chicago).

Inevitably, Debs turned to the war, the issue that hung over this and every other gathering of men and women in the summer of 1918. While he did not directly criticize America's decision to go to war, he did mount a sustained attack on the government's prosecution of anti-war dissenters. "They tell us that we live in a great Republic; our institutions are Democratic; we are a free people." As the audience laughed at Debs's sarcasm, he added, "This is too much, even as a joke. It is not a subject of levity; it is an exceedingly serious matter."

Debs then reviewed what he believed was a long train of injustices, abuses of the law that made a mockery of America's democratic ideals. Kate O'Hare, a woman he loved "like a younger sister," had just been sentenced to five years in prison. "Just think of sending a woman to the penitentiary for talking," Debs said, playing for a laugh before turning somber. "The United States, under the rule of the plutocracy, is the only country that would send a woman to the penitentiary for five years for exercising her constitutional right of free speech." He reminded his audience that Scott Nearing, "the greatest teacher in the United

Debs addresses the crowd at Nimisilla Park, Canton, Ohio.
National Archives and Record Administration, Great Lakes Region (Chicago).

States," had been fired and blacklisted by the University of Pennsylvania for daring to teach "true economics." Max Eastman was under indictment and the *Masses* was shut down, "just as papers with which I have been connected are all suppressed." "They are afraid that we might contaminate you," he told the crowd. "You are their wards; they are your guardians."

Debs also defended the IWW, whose leaders faced a mass trial that summer in Chicago. And he remembered his friend Rose Pastor Stokes, who had been convicted for saying that "a Government could not serve both the profiteers and the victims of the profiteers."

"What had she said?" Debs asked. "Not any more than I have said here this afternoon. I want to admit—I want to admit, without argument, that if Rose Pastor Stokes is guilty, so am I. If she is guilty, I wouldn't be cowardly enough to plead my innocence. And if she ought to be sent to the penitentiary for ten years, so ought I." Prosecutors would later wrench this comment out of its context, claiming that Debs had declared his own guilt and was daring the authorities to arrest him.

But Debs insisted that these men and women were not guilty, and had been denied their "legal, constitutional right" to speak their minds. He was not protesting the government's war on Germany, but its home-front campaign to silence war critics.

In each case, Debs added, these comrades were not really being punished for betraying their country; the Socialists, he pointed out, had been enemies of the Kaiser and German militarism long before the war. No, the radicals were being persecuted for daring to challenge the despotism of their own nation's "Wall Street gentry." Those masters of "corporate capital" were manipulating public opinion, buying up the press, the pulpits, and the judges. When war broke out, Debs explained, they "wrapped themselves up in the American flag" and seized the opportunity to silence anyone who exposed the profit motive lurking behind their false patriotism.

"They would have you believe that the Socialist party consists in the main of disloyalists and traitors," he told the crowd. "It is true in a sense not at all to their discredit. We frankly admit that we *are* disloyalists and traitors to the real traitors to this nation." At a time when all citizens were being urged to sacrifice for the war, to eat less wheat, pay more for coal, and send their loved ones into battle, a handful of Americans were reaping enormous profits. These people, he charged, were America's true "arch-enemy."

As Debs rehearsed the socialist arguments against war that day, he made no references to the draft law, or the war then raging in Europe. Instead he couched the argument in broad historical terms, spending more time on the plight of serfs in medieval Europe than on proletarians in modern-day Ohio. Still, Debs moved onto dangerous ground when he told his comrades:

> They have always taught you that it is your patriotic duty to go to war and to have yourselves slaughtered at command. But in all of the history of the world you, the people, never had a voice in declaring war. . . . And here let me state a fact—and it cannot be repeated too often: the working class who fight the battles, the working class who make the sacrifices, the working class who shed the blood, the working class who furnish the corpses, the working class have never yet had a

voice in declaring war. . . . If war is right, let it be declared by the people—you, who have your lives to lose; you certainly ought to declare war, if you consider a war necessary.

Ohio was in the throes of a scorching heat wave, but Debs did not remove his vest and coat. He leaned forward across the railing of the park gazebo, basking in the smiles beaming from under a sea of straw summer hats. "This assemblage is exceedingly good to look upon," he told the high-spirited crowd. Once again, he drew new life from his audience, and gave it back in return, convincing them that they were the advance guard of a new and better humanity.

"The party has been killed recently," he joked, "which no doubt accounts for its extraordinary activity. There is nothing that helps the Socialist Party so much as receiving an occasional death blow." Debs assured his comrades that their victory was inevitable, and was coming soon. "We are going to destroy all enslaving and degrading capitalist institutions and re-create them as free and humanizing institutions. The world is daily changing before our eyes. The sun of capitalism is setting; the sun of Socialism is rising. It is our duty to build the new nation and the free republic."

In the meantime, Debs urged his friends to stand firm, to do their part, and not to falter in the face of persecution. "Do not worry over the charge of treason to your masters," he told them, "but be concerned about the treason that involves yourselves. Be true to yourself and you cannot be a traitor to any good cause on earth."

As Clyde Miller listened to Debs that afternoon, he could not decide whether the man was "extremely vicious or extremely misguided." After phoning in his story to the *Plain Dealer*, he called his friend Edwin Wertz, the federal prosecutor for the district of Northern Ohio. All through the war the two worked as a team against the radicals, the prosecutor providing the reporter with thrilling stories, and enjoying flattering media coverage in return. Wertz needed little convincing that Debs was a dangerous man; he was the one who sent a stenographer to make a record of the speech. If Wertz had not already planned to arrest Debs for violating the Espionage Act, then Miller effectively maneuvered him into taking action. Along with his story on the Canton speech, he included a sidebar that quoted Wertz's reaction to Debs's remarks. "No man," Wertz declared, "even though four times the candidate of his party for the highest office in the land, can violate the basic law of the land." Though he knew nothing more about the speech than what Miller had told him over the phone, Wertz added, "I shall ask for his indictment."[14]

Miller's story, with Wertz's comment, was reprinted by papers across the country, run under the headline "Debs Invites Arrest." While this enhanced the prosecutor's national profile, it also put pressure on him to make good on his threat. Across the country editors thundered against the speech, one calling Debs a "treasonably-inclined blatherskite." "He voices the sentiment of a very few," a Terre Haute paper declared, "some of whom are already in prison and all of whom should be there and probably soon will be." The *Plain Dealer* kept the heat on Edwin Wertz, running an editorial the following day demanding to know why Debs remained a free man. "Debs is still at large," Miller's paper complained, "preaching the same kind of doctrine that shocked loyal Ohioans when uttered at Canton. . . . What are the federal authorities doing to call Eugene V. Debs to account?"[15]

Though Wertz had publicly committed himself to arresting Debs, before taking on America's most famous radical he decided to get a second opinion. He sent a transcript of the speech to John Lord O'Brian, the special assistant in Washington in charge of federal prosecutions under the Espionage Act. O'Brian replied that many of the offending passages singled out by Wertz were, in his view, protected speech. "For instance," he explained, "criticism of the courts for their administration of the war laws can hardly be called an attack on the 'form of government of the United States' . . . and Debs's references to the St Louis platform are not sufficiently clear and definite." As O'Brian understood the statute, Debs was entirely free to "abuse the actions of the plutocrats of this country, real or imaginary."

O'Brian conceded that some of Debs's remarks might have "crossed the line between lawful and unlawful utterances." When Debs mocked the idea that Americans were fighting a war "to make the world safe for democracy," when he accused the Allies of pursuing plunder, when he told his audience that they were "fit for something better than slavery and cannon fodder," he might well have gone "close to, if not over, the line." But still O'Brian hesitated and told Wertz that the case was "by no means a clear one."[16]

While the lawyers deliberated and newspaper editors demanded action, Debs denied that he had broken the law in his Canton speech. Speaking from a "flag-bedecked" platform at an Indianapolis ball field, he "repudiated the statements attributed to him" in the newspapers, and protested that he had been "grossly misrepresented." He was the victim of newspaper lies, he claimed, because he had dared to speak against war profiteering. "I never once mentioned the United States in that speech when I referred to the avarice of nations," he protested, "and very clearly referred to treaties of nations made before the present war began." Remarkably, Debs added that he was "with the government in the prosecution of the war" and supported the president's plan for peace.[17]

If Debs was correctly quoted, such comments undermine the idea that he was eagerly courting his own arrest. His ideas on the war were changing, at least open to reconsideration, and he saw the value of striking a compromise that would save the party from continued persecution. Personally, he felt conflicting pulls, bound by friendship and honor to support his friends in jail but understandably reluctant to join them. Debs seemed to be searching for a middle ground that did not exist, refusing to run away from the threat of prosecution, but not embracing it either. His dilemma was captured in the advice he gave to a young friend at the time. "Don't go to jail," he advised, "until you are forced."[18]

His ambivalence was resolved on July 1, when federal agents placed him under arrest. Though Justice Department attorneys told Wertz that they did not consider it "advisable," he went ahead with the indictment. Debs was in Cleveland, on his way to another speaking engagement, when he was approached by U.S. marshals. "I am glad to meet you, Mr. Debs," one said. "I have a warrant for your arrest." Before any of his comrades knew what had happened, Debs was on his way to the federal building, and then to the county jail for the night. Prosecutor Wertz told the press, "No man is too big to be held responsible for his actions under the Espionage Act or any other law of the United States."

When the Cleveland crowd realized what had happened to their guest of honor, they passed the hat, raising almost a thousand dollars for Debs's defense. Party leaders condemned the government's decision. "It was a stupid thing for the authorities to do," one moderate leader told the press. "Debs was in favor of a revision of the St. Louis platform opposing the war. He was attempting to convert other Socialists to his way of thinking. His arrest at this time will only serve to alienate from the Administration the sympathy of many who would have come around to its support." Perhaps the arrest helped to alienate Debs himself. After entering a plea of "not guilty," he told reporters he would "rather die than repudiate the platform of the St. Louis Convention." Canceling the rest of his speaking engagements, he boarded a train for home.[19]

On July 4, 1918, the citizens of Terre Haute observed that holiday with wartime intensity. The downtown streets were ablaze with bunting and flags, and families poured into the fairgrounds for an afternoon of patriotic oratory, capped by an aerial display by two army planes.

Eugene Debs spent the afternoon sitting on the porch of his trim Victorian home on Eighth Street, sipping lemonade with two visitors from bohemian New York—journalist John Reed and the cartoonist Art Young. The pair had traveled down from Chicago, where they were reporting on the mass trial of more than a hundred leaders of the IWW. Debs was in bed when they arrived, suffering another bout of lumbago, but he got up to join his comrades.[20]

Like Debs, his two visitors would soon face their own day in court for publishing anti-war statements in the *Masses*. Among other offenses, Young had drawn cartoons lampooning the war as a satanic bloodbath, embraced only by big-bellied profiteers. Reed had reprinted a wire story about shell shock under the provocative headline, "Knit a Straight-Jacket for Your Soldier Boy."[21]

As they sat in the shade of Debs's front porch, the strains of patriotic music drifted from downtown. While Art Young sketched Debs, Reed watched the neighbors walking down Eighth Street on their way to the festivities. They cast "furtive glances" as they scurried past the "House of the Traitor," wearing expressions that Reed described as "a compound half of eager malice, and half of a sort of fear." Though many in the town had opposed America's entry into the war, a year later Debs now seemed like an "enemy in their midst."

Reed's observation might be attributed to the journalist's conspiratorial imagination; he was, after all, an abused radical himself, and one with an unusual relish for a fight. After their own arrests, Reed and Young had both experienced the chill of ostracism back in New York, where some of their former friends and employers kept their distance. On that afternoon, however, Debs confirmed that he had become a pariah in his own town. When Reed asked him if he feared a vigilante attack, Debs shot back, "I know that so long as I keep my eye on them they won't do anything. As a rule they're cowardly curs anyway."[22]

Debs had never been threatened by his neighbors, but the concern was not idle. Like many places in the country, Terre Haute had its share of patriotic violence against those suspected of disloyalty. Schoolteachers and college professors had been fired for their views, German books were burned in the streets, vigilantes attacked stores owned by German-Americans, beat the editor of the local Socialist paper "almost to death," and lynched an immigrant coal miner who was unwilling to buy war bonds. At a Memorial Day service a Methodist minister in town told the assembled that every American should be required to kiss the flag. Those unwilling to demonstrate "absolute allegiance," he continued, should be "lined up before a stone wall and shot."[23]

Throughout his long career as America's best-known radical, Debs had always remained a valued citizen of Terre Haute. Few in town shared his political ideals, the city's mayor had observed in calmer days, but no one in town enjoyed more of the "affection, love, and profound respect of the entire community." In turn, Debs made his living attacking capitalists as a class, but befriended the captains of industry in his own hometown. When the war broke out, his friend Herman Hulman, the wealthy owner of a grocery business, pleaded with Debs not to go "on record for Treason." "It is now or never for all of us," he insisted as he vainly urged Debs to buy a liberty bond or make some other gesture of solidarity with his fellow citizens. "If we waver until the guns are roaring around Terre Haute," Hulman warned, *"We lose."*[24]

In such a state of heightened anxiety, tolerance became more difficult, and after Debs was arrested, his neighbors lost their patience. On that Fourth of July, the local papers gave voice to the town's new attitude toward its most famous citizen. "Flying at organized government," the paper chided, had always been Debs's "pet hobby," nothing more than a business trick that "swells receipts on the Chautauqua circuit." Now he had pushed the "socialist meal ticket" too far. "Mr. Debs will have to hit on some other sort of entertainment for his Chautauqua circuit," another editor scoffed. "He might learn to yodel, inflate a saxophone or perform on the Swiss bells. His jazz patriotism and economic theories grate on Uncle Sam's nerves."[25]

The government was about to silence Debs, perhaps for many years, and many of his neighbors considered it long overdue.

Chapter 5

Cleveland

O N SUNDAY, SEPTEMBER 9, the day before his trial, Debs arrived in Cleveland for a brief meeting with his attorneys. Clarence Darrow, who had defended Debs after the Pullman strike, once again offered his services. Instead, Debs chose to work with his party's lawyers, a four-person team headed by Seymour Stedman. Back in June, when charges against him were pending, he had denied making any seditious remarks and blamed the press for twisting his words. Now he decided to deny nothing, resting his defense on the claim that the Espionage Act was an unconstitutional violation of his First Amendment rights.[1]

Convinced that his conviction in the lower court was inevitable, Debs wasted little time talking legal strategy that day and left for Detroit to preside over a fiery protest meeting. "I may be sent to prison by the powers of militarism," he told three thousand cheering radicals, "but they have not the power to conquer the power you now possess. My message from behind bars will be all the more powerful. I would much rather be a man in jail than a coward outside of it." Debs predicted that, far from silencing him, his pending legal defeat would become a moral victory for the movement.[2]

Socialists from across the nation traveled to Cleveland that week, eager to witness a trial that some predicted would go down in history as a turning point in the triumphant march of the social revolution. Here, as their movement's Christ faced his Pilate, they were determined to bear witness. Entering the courthouse, they were frisked for weapons by vigilante guards from the local chapter of the American Protective League. Federal agents mingled in the crowd and took a few suspicious-looking socialists, and at least one journalist, to an adjoining room for interrogation. The authorities had reason to be on edge; a week earlier, four people had been killed and dozens wounded by a suitcase bomb that exploded in the crowded hall of Chicago's federal building, the scene of the IWW's mass trial.[3]

Among the radical faithful who gathered in Cleveland was Max Eastman, covering the trial for his new journal, the *Liberator.* Eastman was not just an observer of the wartime prosecutions but a celebrated survivor, one of the few radicals who had successfully talked his way out of a jail sentence, winning a hung jury for the *Masses* editors. Although federal prosecutors planned a retrial, Eastman and his partners refused to be silenced. In February 1918 they launched the *Liberator,* a journal that aimed to be "more diplomatic than militant," walking the fine line between free-thinking radicalism and the wrath of Postmaster Burleson. For Eastman this task was made easier by the fact that he had changed his mind and now supported Wilson's war.[4]

Surveying the courtroom on the first morning of the trial, Eastman noted its "flamboyant solemnity." Morning sunlight streamed through windows that vaulted to a gilded ceiling where cherubim guarded the tablets of God's ancient law. Judge David Westenhaver sat high on a platform of marble and oak. "I always want to like the judge when I go into a courtroom," Eastman mused. "It is such an opportunity for human nature to be beautiful." In Westenhaver, he found that opportunity squandered. The handsome and cosmopolitan journalist cast a condescending look at the bald, jowly, and bespectacled judge and decided that he had the "soul of a small-town lawyer."[5]

In quieter times, a fair-minded radical might have found things to admire about Judge Westenhaver. He had begun his career providing legal advice to Cleveland's controversial mayor Tom Johnson, a progressive reformer celebrated for taking on business interests in his city. And Westenhaver was a close friend and former law partner of Secretary of

War Newton Baker—another progressive and lapsed pacifist who played a moderating role in the administration's campaign against dissenters. Westenhaver was a Democrat who had only recently been elevated to his position, thanks to this connection with the Wilson White House.[6]

But for the radicals who packed the courtroom to watch their leader stand trial, the man was a stooge, his robes not a symbol of disinterested justice but the uniform of a capitalist lackey. The courts, no less than the newspapers, the schools, and the Congress, were run by and for the master class. Debs had made the point in the Canton speech, as he had many times before. Federal judges were not chosen by the working-class majority, he charged, but "the corporations and the trusts dictate their appointment."

The jury selection process only seemed to confirm this suspicion that the courts were tools of capitalist power. Under federal law, the pool of potential jurors was drawn from names recommended by county judges, black-cloaked guardians of the respectable class, and then further winnowed by two commissioners, one a Democrat, the other a Republican. As one journalist summed up this arrangement, even though Ohio was a hotbed of radicalism at the time, "if the name of any Socialist ever got into the jury-box, it would be an accident."[7]

Hands folded, Debs leaned forward, watching with wry interest as his defense team tried to keep out of the jury box any man who was likely to condemn him simply for being a Socialist. The judge rejected their attempt to disqualify all military veterans and government employees. They had little more success in challenging men who expressed a poor opinion of socialism. Almost all potential jurors admitted some bias against the party and its principles.

"Have you ever expressed any opinion with regard to Mr. Debs?" one juror after another was asked.[8]

"Well," one replied, "my opinion is not altogether favorable to Mr. Debs."

Another admitted he was "rather opposed" to socialism.

"Your lack of sympathy for the Socialists would include Mr. Debs, would it not?" a prospective juror was asked. "I take them as a party," he replied.

Stedman argued that this political bias would lead jurors to prejudge Debs, but Westenhaver overruled. Given the national mood and the local pool of potential jurors, he reasoned that no jury could be convened if those opposed to socialism were excluded. "The Socialist Party will not be tried here," he promised. Debs would get a fair trial based on the specific charge that he had intended to disrupt the government's war effort. After four hours the defense exhausted all of its opportunities to challenge, but only managed to eliminate two jurors who seemed especially eager to punish anyone who dared to interfere with the war.[9]

Socialists complained that the resulting jury epitomized the interests of the capitalist class. Cleveland, the fifth largest city in America, had a growing, assertive, and ethnically diverse working class. Socialists had won a third of the votes in the city's 1917 mayoral race, before most of their candidates had gone to prison. But the jury was drawn exclusively from the city's established Yankee middle class. They were merchants and farmers, most around seventy years old, all but one comfortably retired. Debs thought they had "dressed-up faces" and "smug bodies," while another radical described them as old men "with eyes blinded by securities, and ears stuffed by stocks and bonds." And, in a touch of poetic serendipity worthy of Dickens, the jury foreman's name was Cyrus Stoner.[10]

While Stoner and his fellow jurymen claimed not to know much about socialism, their daily newspapers told them plenty about the war. That week in Cleveland, headlines announced that American troops were making their first major offensive on the Western front. Editorials denounced the Kaiser's soldiers for using crucified kittens to booby-trap America's animal-loving doughboys, and for bombing Allied hospitals and then plundering their victims. The Bolsheviks, meanwhile, had murdered the czar's family, and Petrograd was in flames. Closer to home, defense plant workers in Bridgeport, Connecticut, were on strike, threatening to paralyze the Allied war effort. Wilson warned them to return to work or face conscription into the army. And in Cleveland, jurors and their neighbors had lived for months in a war-saturated environment of coal shortages, "meatless and wheatless" meals, American Protective League raids on suspected spies and subversives, and daily headlines mourning the "sons of Cleveland" who had fallen in France or drowned in the Atlantic. In this "present high state of patriotic tension," Eastman realized that Debs was doomed. "Nothing matters much in these cases but the indictment."[11]

Against all odds, Debs's lawyers struggled on, unwilling to concede defeat. Victories for Espionage Act defendants were rare, but not unknown. A small handful of federal judges insisted on a narrow interpretation of the wartime speech laws, standing against what they considered to be an abuse of the federal police power. When they did, they found themselves ostracized, denounced as traitors by the press, and threatened with impeachment.[12]

The legal victories won in their courts were no doubt inspirational for Stedman, but not typical. Closer to Cleveland, the recently concluded trial of the IWW leadership offered a more ominous precedent. After a five-month trial, the Chicago jury needed only one hour to review thousands of specific charges, and bring in a guilty verdict against 101 defendants. Judge Kennesaw Mountain Landis then handed down severe sentences, in some cases twenty years at Leavenworth. At the trial, Landis offered an understanding of the First Amendment that reflected the legal consensus at the time and was applauded on the editorial pages of mainstream newspapers. As Americans debated the pros and cons of going to war, all had been free to express their views, he explained. But once war was declared, "that right ceases." In effect, Landis argued that free speech rights were different in times of peace than in times of war, that the need for public unity in a time of crisis trumped the individual's right to disagree.[13]

Debs's lawyer Seymour Stedman assumed that Westenhaver and the Cleveland jury would take the same view. Even as the trial began, he looked ahead to the appeal, believing that the Supreme Court offered Debs his best chance of keeping out of prison.

In the government's opening statement, assistant prosecutor F. B. Kavanaugh told the jury that they were about to decide the fate of a dangerous man who had "opposed the ideals for which the American flag stands." He proceeded to outline the charges. While the grand jury had approved ten of them, all for the same speech, the prosecution had withdrawn five before the trial and the judge dropped a sixth one—

those that claimed that Debs used "false reports and false statements" to undermine the war effort. Whether Debs had spoken damning truths, insidious falsehoods, or personal opinions would be irrelevant to the case, and he would be given no opportunity to defend himself by trying to prove that he was right about the war. According to the four remaining charges, Debs had made remarks "calculated to promote insubordination" and "propagate obstruction to the draft." Kavanaugh concluded by suggesting that Debs was no ordinary traitor, but the "palpitating pulse of the sedition crusade." As the young prosecutor finished his speech and headed to his seat, Debs congratulated him on a job well done.[14]

Although Debs had initially urged his lawyers not to make any opening argument, Stedman won a concession on this point and proceeded with a half-hour speech to the jury. Millions of Americans, he told them, were awaiting their decision. "Their question is not what this jury thinks about the war, or about socialism, or about anything other than this one thing: 'What does this jury think about the right of Free Speech?' What is this jury going to do about the right of Gene Debs to express to all men the promptings of his soul?"[15]

Those Americans who were following the Debs trial in the press had very little idea about what Debs's soul had actually prompted him to say on that day in Canton. Editors knew that publishing the offending comments might court government prosecution, so the only public accounts of Debs's alleged crime were the brief but unflattering summaries in the press. But Stedman told the jurors that Americans would not want Debs to be judged for a handful of controversial comments he made on one day in June, but for his life of service to humanity. He reminded them of the prosecutor's words, that Debs would be judged not for his ideas but for his "works." "The defense accepts the challenge," Stedman countered. "You shall know him by his works, by the works of his whole life."

Stirred by this tribute to their hero, some in the gallery burst into applause. Stunned, the judge allowed this lapse in legal decorum to go on for a full minute. Then he lashed out against those who were turning his courtroom into a Debs rally. He was "exceedingly wroth," the *Times* reported, and ordered the bailiff to round up any who were clapping.

Seven were brought before the bar. Some quavered, protesting their innocence, while others proudly confessed their contempt of court.

Eastman thought that the judge's attempt to defend the dignity of the court had the opposite effect. "It was a terrible moment," he reported, "and everybody felt a little foolishly sick, the way you feel in school when some dreadful sinner is hauled up before the teacher." One of Debs's lawyers, William Cunnea, further deflated Westenhaver's dignity by openly chiding him, "I don't like to see you sit up there and play God to your fellow men." Remarkably, the judge conceded the point. Confessing that he may have been "unduly vexed," he ordered the clappers to be charged but released without bail, and then adjourned court for the day.[16]

Among the radicals caught in the bailiff's net was Rose Pastor Stokes, a fact that dominated the next day's headlines across the country. One of America's best-known radicals, Stokes had been a poor Jewish immigrant, toiling in a cigar factory, when she met the handsome socialist millionaire Graham Phelps Stokes. They fell in love, and even the most partisan capitalist paper could not resist the romance of their marriage, a Cinderella story with a revolutionary twist. Stokes used her influential position to fight for a variety of high-profile radical causes. She organized defense committees to support jailed strike leaders and anarchists, campaigned unsuccessfully to force the University of Pennsylvania to reinstate Scott Nearing, and pleaded in vain with President Wilson to spare the life of Joe Hill, the IWW songwriter and union organizer who was framed for murder and executed by a Utah firing squad in 1915.[17]

When the United States entered the war, both Rose and her husband sided with the "pro-war" Socialists who believed that German militarism had to be stopped at any cost. They quit the party after the St. Louis convention and worked briefly with other pro-war socialists and labor progressives on an ill-fated plan to create a new socialist party that would put "America first." By January 1918 Stokes had second thoughts, regretting that she had come "blindly to stand for war." Resentful of the way her radical friends were being treated, she decided that Wilson's crusade was more likely to spread America's imperialism than its democracy. "I believed in this war because it was inevitable,"

Debs with Rose Stokes and Max Eastman on the eve of Debs's trial.
From Max Eastman, *The Trial of Eugene Debs: With Debs' Address to the
Court on Receiving Sentence.* Liberator Pamphlets No. 3. New York: Liberator
Pub. Co., 1918. Courtesy of Debs Collection, Indiana State University Library.

she later explained, "but those great things the war stood for—freedom
of speech and freedom of thought—have been removed, and hence the
war is no longer worth fighting." Against her husband's wishes, she returned to the Socialists and their stand against war, a first break that
would eventually lead to a bitter divorce.[18]

After giving a speech to a Kansas City woman's club, Stokes felt she
had been misquoted by the local paper. Trying to clarify her views in
a letter to the editor, she wrote, "No government which is for the
profiteers can be also for the people, and I am for the people, while the
government is for the profiteers." That letter proved to be a final provocation to the government agents who were following her, tipped off by
her husband's wealthy uncle. After a widely publicized three-day trial,
she had been convicted and sentenced to ten years in prison, one of
the verdicts that Debs had protested in his Canton speech. Out on

bail, Rose was still appealing her case when she traveled to Cleveland to support Eugene Debs. There, smiling like an "unrepentant sinner," she had again provoked the authorities by clapping in Judge Westenhaver's courtroom.[19]

In the evenings and during lunch breaks, Stokes, Eastman, and other comrades gathered around Debs at the Hollenden, a grand seven-story hotel near the courthouse. Bills for this festive reunion and bittersweet farewell party were paid by William Bross Lloyd, a wealthy radical who would soon face his own trial for being a communist. As Debs embraced old friends, he talked as if he was just another foot soldier, doing his fair share of suffering for the movement. But the young Socialists who traveled to Cleveland to bear witness to the trial understood the distinctive place Debs held in their movement. Though sensitive about his age, at sixty-two Debs was the grand old man of American radicalism. And now, in frail health, their hero faced the prospect of a lengthy jail sentence, an exile from his family and his work that might well end only with his death. Scott Nearing, who awaited his own day in court, was deeply moved by his visit with Debs in Cleveland. "He was an old man," Nearing marveled, "broken in health, facing, without flinching, without budging an eyelid, a possibility of twenty years in jail . . . I never in my life came in contact with so radiant a spirit as I did that afternoon when Debs was getting ready to take his place in the Federal Court and receive a penitentiary sentence."[20]

Another young idealist who made the pilgrimage to Cleveland was David Karsner, a journalist from the *New York Call,* one of the most influential socialist newspapers in the country, and one of the few that had not yet been silenced by the postmaster. For Karsner's daily dispatches on the trial, Debs served up a series of pithy but noble statements. "We shall not tarry here very long," he predicted in cadences honed over years on the platform. "This is but another milestone along the pathway of progress." Sure that he was both serving the cause of social justice and recording one of American history's greatest moments, Karsner scribbled Debs's remarks down eagerly, then telegraphed them back to New York for mass distribution to the party faithful.

The following morning Judge Westenhaver began the proceedings by imposing a modest fine on the seven clapping radicals. Defiant as ever,

Stokes planned to refuse to pay, which would force the judge to imprison her. She yielded only after friends talked her out of a confrontation that would have compounded her legal troubles. After the trial Stokes would exact a small measure of revenge, touring the country and denouncing Westenhaver as "a man who rocked back and forth in his chair and only needed some knitting in his hand to complete the picture."[21]

As the jury settled in for the first day of testimony, the prosecution outlined their case against Debs. First they would establish just what he had said that day, producing two witnesses who had made a stenographic record of the speech. They would then move on to show what he had *intended*. Witnesses would show that, while Debs had been "careful" in his remarks in Canton, he had been motivated by an unspoken desire to subvert the draft and interfere with the war effort—a goal that was clearly laid out in the St. Louis Proclamation that Debs had endorsed. Next, the prosecution would show that, when Debs defended Stokes, O'Hare, and others who were already convicted of violating the Espionage Act, he revealed his own intention to break the law. Finally, the prosecution would prove that draft-age men listened to Debs that day and might have been talked into refusing to do their duty.

The prosecutors stumbled when they put their first witness on the stand. Virgil Steiner was working as a car salesman when Wertz enlisted him to attend the Canton speech and make a transcription. As the defense brought out in cross-examination, Steiner had a couple years of experience as a stenographer but was not skilled enough to make an accurate record of Debs's two-hour torrent of words. Not long after Debs began, Steiner had lost his way. Exhausted in his attempt to keep pace, he had given up for long stretches of time, only "jumping in" when he thought he heard a particularly treasonous sentiment. "There were some few sentences which I was unable to get," he admitted on the stand. But after he read his mangled version of the speech into the court record, Debs's attorneys pointed out that this key piece of government evidence only reflected about forty minutes of the two-hour speech. "My practice has been taking letters," Steiner protested weakly. "I have not had experience in taking speeches."

The young man was close to tears after he stepped down from cross-examination. And again Debs comforted the instrument of his own imprisonment, urging the lad "not to feel humiliated in the least." Patting Steiner's face with motherly solicitude, Debs told him that "his abilities in that line had been unfairly taxed."[22]

Ironically, a fuller record of the Canton speech was provided by the Socialists themselves. The local branch had hired a more competent stenographer to record the day's proceedings. Edward Sterling had a dozen years of experience at the job, and as he read his own transcript out loud in court, he even added dramatic flourishes. Eastman thought Sterling was trying to underscore those passages he found particularly odious, but others in the room felt he was only paying tribute to the power of Debs's words. Either way, some in the gallery were moved to tears by Sterling's impersonation of their beloved leader, while the prosecutors affected a pose of "infinite weariness." The two versions of the speech introduced by the government as evidence were different in many respects, though no one disputed that they were roughly the same in those places where they "collided."[23]

Debs spent that evening in his hotel room, drinking a fair amount of whiskey. That was not an unusual event, but one biographer has suggested that he may have been driven to the bottle that night less by worries about his impending imprisonment than by the experience of hearing his own words so badly mangled.[24]

Once the jury heard what Debs had said that day in Canton, the prosecution turned next to proving what he had *intended.* Wertz needed to show that, behind Debs's cryptic and general comments against war, lurked an unspoken desire to obstruct military recruitment. Acting on advice from the Justice Department, the prosecution attempted to place Debs's speech into the wider context of his previous statements about the war, particularly his views on the St. Louis Proclamation.

Toward that end, Clyde Miller took the stand, the key witness in a trial he had done so much to instigate. Guided by his friend Wertz, he told the jury about his brief interview with Debs in the hotel lobby on the day of the speech, where Debs had affirmed his support for the basic principles of the party's anti-war platform. Miller also told the jury about a second meeting with Debs on the day he was arrested. In the federal marshal's office in Cleveland, Miller had again asked Debs for his thoughts on the St. Louis platform. Feeling more defiant under those circumstances, and unaware that this reporter was an enthusiastic agent for the prosecution, Debs told him that he repudiated nothing and was willing "to die for those principles." Miller's testimony helped the prosecution to establish a link between the general anti-war statements Debs made in the Canton speech and the much clearer and more confrontational language that his party had adopted in St. Louis.[25]

While Miller had been shocked both times by Debs's unpatriotic remarks, something about the old radical moved him, and this came out in the testimony. During the second interview, Miller had told Debs that it was a shame that his ideas "were so different from the views of the rest of us."

"Well, you may be right and I may be wrong," Debs had freely conceded. "I may be quite wrong in this, but I don't see it now. I don't claim to be infallible." This humility had touched Miller. Though Debs preached dangerous doctrines, the young patriot had to admit that he had a kind heart, and was even remarkably "Christ-like." Perhaps because his personal admiration for Debs conflicted with his political convictions, Miller appeared to some observers to be a reluctant witness. He was "in some discomfiture," Karsner thought, "in having to testify against the old agitator."[26]

After Miller delivered his testimony, Debs left his chair and put his arm around the young journalist's shoulders. "Mr. Miller," he whispered, "all that you say about me is true. You quoted me straight and accurate. I don't want you ever to feel that you have done me an injury by testifying against me. You had to do it, and you did it like a gentleman." Looking down with his "kindly blue eyes," Debs predicted that, within twenty years, one of them would change his mind about the war. Miller, as it turned out, would come to regret his testimony against Debs much sooner.[27]

Next the prosecution put on the stand Charles Ruthenberg, one of the three Ohio Socialists whom Debs had visited in the Canton jail that day. Wertz dragged Ruthenberg from his prison cell to confirm something that had already been established, that Debs was a Socialist who stood by his party's anti-war St. Louis Proclamation. Watching from the gallery, Max Eastman suspected that the prosecutors used Ruthenberg only in order to associate Debs with one of Cleveland's most notorious radicals, a man already convicted for making unpatriotic remarks. The implied message, Eastman mused, was that "all Socialists ought to be in jail."

In cross-examination, Stedman used Ruthenberg's testimony to put distance between Debs and the St. Louis platform. The witness confirmed that Debs had not written the document and had not even attended the convention. Stedman also reminded the jury that, as Miller had also testified, Debs gave only a halfhearted endorsement of his party's anti-war platform before his Canton speech, suggesting that it needed to be revised.

Any advantage Stedman may have gained from this point was undermined when the prosecution called Joseph Triner to the stand. Working as a special agent for Naval Intelligence, Triner had spied on the meeting of Socialist Party secretaries held in Chicago in August, two months after the Canton speech. Once again, Socialist leaders decided that it was too dangerous to even discuss their views on the war. Debs, however, was no longer in a cautious mood. Triner dropped in for ten minutes, just long enough to hear Debs say, "They may call me a disloyalist and brand me a traitor, but I shall stick to my principles. The master class pretend to wage this war for democracy, but by persecuting us they have branded this pretension a lie." In words more direct than any he delivered in Canton, Debs declared, "There is only one war in which I have any interest, and that is for the workers of the world against the capitalists." No longer interested in compromise, he urged his comrades to stand by the St. Louis platform and those who had gone to jail in its defense.[28]

After linking the evasive remarks in Debs's Canton speech with his support for the party's anti-war platform, the prosecution concluded by proving that draft-age men heard Debs speak in Canton and might have been convinced to shirk their duty. Wertz produced several of them, not radicals but journalists who were covering the speech. One was a twenty-six-year-old who testified that he had heard Debs make some anti-war remarks, and added that he had seen no American flags on the bandstand.

In defense, Stedman pointed out that Debs had not been in charge of decorating the park that afternoon. Further, he pointed out that none of the young men produced by the prosecution had actually failed to do their duty. All admitted under cross-examination that they had registered, and one was already in uniform. If Debs had tried to talk them out of doing their duty, clearly he had failed.

Although the prosecution had produced no evidence that Debs had convinced anyone to become a slacker, the threat of such disloyalty was quite real. In 1918 the government sounded the alarm that "thousands upon thousands" of eligible men either had not registered or had deserted. As everyone in the Cleveland courtroom was aware, all through that summer the Justice Department staged massive dragnets through many American cities, often using deputized soldiers, sailors, and patriotic volunteers from the American Protective League. The largest and most controversial of these "slacker raids" was conducted in New York just a week before the Debs trial began. Tens of thousands of young men were forced to produce their draft cards, sometimes at the point of a bayonet. Close to twelve thousand were detained, though in the end only a fraction of them proved guilty of evading the draft.[29]

When the *Nation* denounced the raids by declaring "Civil Liberty Dead," the Post Office banned that issue of the magazine from the mail. Editor Oswald Garrison Villard had to use some of his dwindling influence with President Wilson to get the order overturned. But New York papers boiled with indignation over what one called the government's "shameful abuse of power." Under mounting criticism from liberals in the Senate, Attorney General Gregory conceded that the use of vigilantes and soldiers had been "ill-judged," but he blamed their violent and illegal acts on "an excess of zeal for the public good" and vowed to continue the practice. Under these circumstances, the Cleveland jury would have no trouble concluding that, if Debs was sowing seeds of resentment against the draft, they were likely to fall on fertile ground.[30]

As the prosecution introduced its case over the first two days of the trial, Seymour Stedman had interrupted dozens of times, establishing objections that would become the basis of a Supreme Court appeal. Through these, the contours of a conventional legal defense emerged. He attacked the centerpiece of the government's case, the speech transcript, as incomplete and faulty. He challenged the government's attempt to prove Debs's malicious intentions by linking his Canton speech to the St. Louis Proclamation. The St. Louis platform was not in itself illegal, Stedman pointed out, because it had been written months before the Espionage Act had passed. Further, Debs had not written it and had not even attended the convention, and he had told Miller that he favored "revisions." And finally, the government had produced draft-age men who had heard the speech, but none who showed any inclination to avoid the draft. In sum, the prosecution's case left Debs's lawyers with some legal grounds on which to make an appeal.[31]

But Debs was convinced that none of these legal strategies would work. Even worse, making such arguments seemed to acknowledge the government's right to prosecute him for expressing his views on the war. In Canton Debs had been indirect, taunting but not directly challenging the law. Now he was determined to concede nothing, to offer no apologies or prevarications, and to try no legal evasions. He wanted, instead, to put the law itself on trial. "I have nothing to take back," he insisted. "All I have said I believe to be true."[32]

And so, when the prosecution concluded its case just before noon on Wednesday, September 11, Stedman rose and told the surprised prosecutors, "Let's see—you rest? *We rest.*" Rather than call witnesses, the defense would only offer Debs, who would speak on his own behalf.

During a brief recess no one in the packed gallery moved for fear of losing their seats. All week in court, Debs had remained polite, attentive, and mostly silent. Now the great orator would have his say. The courtroom was packed—the dozen aisles of stiff wooden benches were full, the window ledges served as makeshift seats, and hundreds more waited outside. Judge Westenhaver began the afternoon session with a warning to the audience against another partisan outburst. Then Debs rose, gazed at the judge a full minute, and began what would become the most famous speech of his long career on the public stage.[33]

"For the first time in my life," Debs started, "I appear before a jury in a court of law to answer to an indictment for crime." This was an odd claim to make for one of America's most famous prisoners, the working-class hero and newspaper villain of the Pullman strike. But his rhetorical point was clear. "I am not a lawyer. I know little about court procedure, about rules of evidence or legal practice." Ignorant of legal conventions, Debs intended to follow a higher moral authority, a standard of justice that dwarfed the dignity of Westenhaver and his jury.[34]

Debs told the jurors that he fully realized their power over his physical being. They could brand him a felon, and send him, perhaps, to end his life in a prison cell. "Gentlemen," he added, "I do not fear to face you in this hour of accusation, nor do I shrink from the consequences of my utterances or my acts. Standing before you, charged as I am with crime, I can yet look the Court in the face, I can look you in the face, I can look the world in the face, for in my conscience, in my soul, there is festering no accusation of guilt." Debs freely admitted "the truth of all that has been testified to in this proceeding. . . . I would not retract a word that I have uttered that I believe to be true to save myself from going to the penitentiary for the rest of my days." In fact, Debs joked that the prosecutors should have saved themselves the trouble of proving things he not only would not deny but had taken "very considerable pride in."[35]

As Debs paced under the gloomy light of high chandeliers, the violent shade of a late summer thunderstorm darkened the room. Nature itself, his friends concluded, was empathizing with the clash of elemental forces taking place in that courtroom. "His utterance became more clear and piercing against that impending shadow," Eastman wrote, "and it made the simplicity of his faith seem almost like a portent in this time of terrible and dark events."[36]

Debs moved immediately to what he considered to be the real issue in the trial, and the ultimate meaning of his life's work—the conflict between the reactionary forces of wealth and the progressive demands for industrial democracy. Insisting he had been put on trial for his faith in socialism, he was determined to defend it, regardless of the consequences. "There is not a single falsehood in that speech," he told the jury. "If there is a single statement in it that will not bear the light of truth, I will retract it. I will make all of the reparation in my power. But if what I said is true, and I believe it is, then whatever fate or fortune may have in store for me I shall preserve inviolate the integrity of my soul and stand by it to the end."[37]

"I have been accused of having obstructed the war," Debs proceeded. "I admit it. Gentlemen, I abhor war. I would oppose the war if I stood alone." But he did not consider himself to be alone; rather, his stand at Canton was just another chapter in a long history of men and women who stood against the violent and "tragic history of the race." Jesus, he preached to the jury, had also been convicted for his "dangerous doctrine" of human love and the threat he posed to the "profiteers, high priests, the lawyers, the judges, the merchants, the bankers." Socrates was likewise martyred for his defense of "new ideals." Debs then praised the Bolsheviks, comparing them to America's own immortal revolutionaries.

At that point prosecutor Wertz had heard enough. Jumping to his feet, he called on the judge to force Debs to "confine his remarks to the evidence." Though Westenhaver had begun the trial determined to prevent his courtroom from becoming a socialist soapbox, now that things were winding down he decided to loosen his grip. He was comforted, no doubt, by the fact that Debs had just offered what sounded like a full and open confession. "I think we will let him talk in his own way," Westenhaver decided.[38]

With no hope that he could sway the jury in front of him, Debs spoke as if he was only concerned about the ultimate judgment of history. Socialists, he explained, were only the latest expression of the power of a moral minority in American life. The founding fathers had been despised radicals in their day. Before the Civil War, most Americans regarded the abolitionists as "monsters of depravity." But now parents taught children to "revere their memories, while all of their detractors are in oblivion." Just as the abolitionists once fought chattel slavery, the Socialists worked to abolish wage slavery. "It is because I happen to be in this minority that I stand in your presence today, charged with crime. It is because I believe as the revolutionary fathers believed in their day, that a change was due in the interests of the people, that the time had come for a better form of government, for an improved system, a higher social order, a nobler humanity and a grander civilization."[39]

As Debs spoke, he worked the entire room, turning from the jury to the judge, and spending as much time turned around, speaking to his friends in the gallery, the socialists with "stars in their eyes." He waved his right hand to underscore his points, as he gave the jury his views on internationalism. "I believe in patriotism," he explained. "I have never uttered a word against the flag. I love the flag as a symbol of freedom." But during the war, patriotism had been used for "base purposes," the love of country twisted into an irrational hatred of others. The much-condemned St. Louis platform, he insisted, was not an attack on America, but an expression of the party's faith in universal brotherhood. The Socialist Party never aimed to destroy the American war effort, Debs contended, but to rally working people everywhere to end all wars.

As Debs spoke on, Westenhaver wagged his head from time to time, wearing what Eastman described as an "amused, attentive, patronizing smile." All of Debs's "humane and patriotic remarks," the judge was thinking, were only a smokescreen designed to obscure the agenda of a dangerous "revolutionary internationalist." The longer Debs spoke, the clearer it became to the judge that this man had nothing but contempt for a citizen's "patriotic obligations" to obey the law. While Debs claimed to believe in peaceful democratic change, Westenhaver concluded that he had devoted himself to a worker's revolution that could only be achieved through violence.[40]

Max Eastman, on the other hand, believed that his hero had transported the entire proceeding to a loftier realm of thought. "With a very genial—and privately almost uproarious—scorn for the whole legal apparatus in which they were trying to tie up his clear-motived intelligence," Eastman marveled, "he simply remained high up in the region of truth and noble feeling, where he lives, and compelled the court to come up there and listen to him or not listen at all."[41]

Midway through his two-hour speech, Debs arrived at his sole line of legal defense. "I believe in free speech, in war as well as in peace," he explained. "I would not, under any circumstances, gag the lips of my bitterest enemy. I would under no circumstances suppress free speech. It is far more dangerous to attempt to gag the people than to allow them to speak freely of what is in their hearts." The real attack on America, he continued, was not his Canton speech but the government's systematic attempt to "gag a free people. . . . If the Espionage Law stands, then the Constitution of the United States is dead."[42]

While his lawyers would develop this line of argument in their appeal to the Supreme Court, Debs moved quickly back to his defense of socialism. Through the long dark afternoon, he wove together ideas, images, and allusions that he had polished in hundreds of platform speeches, some decades old and others of more recent vintage. Once again he defended American radicals from the charge that they were friends of the Kaiser. Socialists had long opposed German militarism, but the greater enemy, he told the jury, was the profit system run by imperialist warmongers in every country. Debs then produced a copy of Woodrow Wilson's *New Freedom,* his 1912 campaign manifesto, and read passages in which the future president warned voters that their government had fallen under the control of an "unholy alliance of bosses and Big Business." That, Debs argued, was just what Socialists were saying when they denounced war profiteers. "The President of the United States tells us that our government has passed into the control of special interests," he charged, but "when we Socialists make the same contention, we are branded as disloyalists, and we are indicted as criminals."[43]

Moving to his finale, Debs said, "I am the smallest part of this trial. I have lived long enough to appreciate my own personal insignificance in relation to a great issue that involves the welfare of the whole people. What you may choose to do to me will be of small consequence after all. I am not on trial here. There is an infinitely greater issue that is being tried today in this court, though you may not be conscious of it. American institutions are on trial before a court of American citizens. Time will tell."

After thanking the judge and jury for their patient attention, Debs concluded, "My fate is in your hands. I am prepared for your verdict." He bowed deeply, and returned to his seat. The room was hushed. Some in the jury box even shed tears. Socialists in the gallery believed that they had just witnessed a milestone in mankind's march toward the cooperative commonwealth. Debs had once again worked his magic.

As far as Edwin Wertz was concerned, the defendant's remarkable powers of persuasion were just what made him so "dangerous." Conceding that Debs was "a man of much personal charm and impressive personality," the prosecutor felt that these were the very qualities that enabled him to "mislead the unthinking and afford them an excuse for violating the law." When Wertz rose to take his turn before the jury, that was his line of attack.

After the soaring oratory of the previous two hours, Wertz tried a folksier approach. "Here is the situation in a nutshell," he announced, then drew an analogy between Debs and a barnyard disaster. He told the jury that while driving in the country one day, he had seen a barn on fire. The farmer, eager to save his flock of sheep, was herding them out the door. But as soon as he did, "an old ewe at the head of the flock started around the barn as fast as she could go, and every sheep took after her into the barn on the other side where the flames were the worst."

Wertz moved to the moral of the story. "If this old ewe," he pointed to Debs, "wants to violate this law that Congress has passed, he has a right to go to the penitentiary, but I object to him taking the rest of the flock to the penitentiary, and making traitors out of the rest of the people that he assumes to represent, because of his smattering of what the law is, and his smattering of what the constitution is, and of what he assumes to be his rights in this country."

Debs was a dangerous amateur when it came to understanding the Constitution, Wertz continued. "He knows just enough . . . to get him in trouble." Debs told the jury that the First Amendment bars Congress from making any law limiting the right of free speech. Wertz countered by pointing out that the law had always recognized a number of limits on free speech, in cases of slander, libel, obscenity, and threats to public safety. Using an example that would soon be enshrined in a Supreme Court decision, the prosecutor argued that according to Debs's theory, "a man could go into a crowded theatre . . . and yell 'fire' when there was no fire, and people trampled to death, and he would not be punished for it because the Constitution says he has the right of free speech."[44]

In his own plea, Debs had ranged far beyond the legal issues at stake in the trial, and Wertz energetically followed right after him. After setting the jury straight on the First Amendment, he moved on to rescue the New Testament. "These men who get an idea that all the righteousness, and all the high character, and all the principles in the world, is embodied in themselves, and that no one else has any, they are the fellows that when they get into trouble they always lean to the bible and hold up the picture of the crucified Christ and would have you believe that they are in the same class." Wertz then reminded the jury that Debs had conveniently ignored the "Master's" instruction to "render unto Caesar the things that are Caesar's." Once Congress declared war, he continued, "the body of Eugene Debs," no less than the products of America's mills, mines, and farms, belonged to his government, to be used as it saw fit.[45]

Wertz took on Debs's plea for internationalism with similar earthy dispatch. "In other words, pitch them all together—all of the nations in one pot. Then you will have internationalism, with the Socialists on top." Wertz handled the radical critique of war profiteering with another folksy analogy. Complaining about war profits was like putting a mustard plaster on a mosquito bite. "That is the attitude that these people take; if somebody makes a little money building ships or producing war material, they want to overturn the government."

"Is there any doubt what he was trying to do when he took this 'holy thou' attitude," Wertz asked the jury, "assuming to be the Jesus Christ of these other fellows that did something in this country? . . . If it was any other country in the world he would be facing a firing squad, after a trial on the head of a drum, and not after days and days of pain and effort to give him a fair, just and equitable trial"[46]

Even the judge seemed embarrassed by Wertz's performance. Looking on from the gallery, Max Eastman was disgusted. "As clearly as Debs symbolized in his presence the hope of evolution," he fumed, "this man was the mud from which it moves." Angered by some remarks Wertz made about his friend Kate Richards O'Hare, Debs did not congratulate the prosecutor for a job well done. As he left the courtroom that afternoon, Debs was thronged by admirers, including a young girl who pressed through the crowd, presented him with a bouquet of roses, and then fainted into his arms.[47]

In his instructions to the jury the following morning, Westenhaver began by reminding them that Debs was not on trial for his political views, a claim obscured by the closing arguments from both the prosecution and the defense. Socialism, the judge repeated, was not on trial. Further, he warned the jury not to be blinded by the patriotic feelings of "righteous indignation" that were inevitable in wartime. The defendant was entitled to be tried by a careful review of evidence, related to a specific charge, the same due process applied in times of war as in times of peace.

Under the First Amendment, Westenhaver explained, Debs was entitled to criticize the government's prosecution of the war. "Disapproval of war is, of course, not a crime, nor is the advocacy of peace." What the jury had to determine, then, was what Debs *intended* when he spoke in Canton. Was he simply sharing his political views with his fellow citizens, or did he mean to encourage men to avoid the draft? Was he simply providing useful information on an important public issue, or was he inciting his followers to break the law?

According to prevailing legal standards of the time, the government did not have to prove that Debs had actually been successful in these efforts, only that he had tried. The judge reminded the jury that the prosecution had introduced "scraps" of evidence about things Debs had said before and after the Canton speech, interviews and private conversations that showed his support for his party's anti-war platform. But Debs was not on trial for those statements, Westenhaver reminded the jury. The prosecution had offered them only as a way to help establish "the state of mind of the defendant" when he gave the speech for which he was arrested.

Finally, Westenhaver instructed the jury to disregard the key legal argument made by Debs and his attorneys that the Espionage Act was a violation of basic constitutional rights to free speech. "The law was on the statute book, and it was the part of no man to question its authenticity," the judge declared. In his view, the law did not contradict the First Amendment; Congress had always retained the power to limit speech in times of war in order to fulfill its obligation to protect "the public peace and the public safety." Westenhaver explained that, if he was wrong about that, the nine members of the Supreme Court, not the nine men of the Cleveland jury, were the only ones entitled to correct him and to overturn the law.

After the judge concluded his charge, the jury filed out at eleven in the morning. In many other cases across the country, federal judges had turned their charge into an opportunity to vent their righteous fury against the defendants, but Debs and Stedman agreed that Westenhaver had been remarkably fair. Still, everyone expected a quick verdict, and few left the courtroom. As rain fell outside, Debs passed the time replying to some of the hundreds of telegrams he had received from supporters around the country, and regaling his friends with his favorite anecdotes about Lincoln. Among his visitors was newspaper poet Edmund Vance Cook, who shared a poem he had just written, the first of dozens inspired by the old man's calm defiance of the American legal system. "Standing like a shaft of light/ Cloud by day and fire by night/ For the thing you think is right/ Dominating all your scene/ None may daunt you, brave Eugene!"[48]

The jury did not return until five that evening. Eastman joked that the crude antics of prosecutor Wertz must have accounted for at least half of their six hours of indecision. As the judge called for the verdict, Rose Pastor Stokes crossed the railing and sat by Debs, their hands entwined. Foreman Stoner pronounced Debs guilty on three counts. On that June afternoon at Canton, the jury ruled, he had "attempted to incite insubordination, disloyalty, mutiny and refusal of duty in the military and naval forces." In the same speech, he had obstructed or attempted to obstruct the recruiting and enlistment service. And he had used "language intended to incite, provoke, and encourage resistance to the United States and to promote the cause of the enemy." The jury cleared Debs of the last remaining charge, "opposition to the cause of the United States." But that was little consolation; each of the three guilty verdicts carried with it a maximum penalty of twenty years in jail, quite likely a life sentence for a man of Debs's age and condition. As he had throughout the trial, Debs took the news with a calmness that impressed even his detractors.

The following morning Debs appeared before Westenhaver to receive his sentence. He was asked if he had any last words. As Scott Nearing observed, Debs never missed a chance to "tell someone about socialism." With the jury gone, he lectured the judge, offering a more compressed and poetic coda to his speech of the day before.

"Your honor," he began, "years ago I recognized my kinship with all living beings, and I made up my mind that I was not one bit better than the meanest of earth. I said then, I say now, that while there is a lower class, I am in it; while there is a criminal element, I am of it; while there is a soul in prison, I am not free."

For decades Debs had gathered scrapbooks of newspaper clippings, most tracing his career and important controversies of the day. He also saved any story he found about his heroes from American history. Scattered throughout these books were items on the life and martyrdom of the militant abolitionist John Brown. Debs greatly admired Brown's willingness to live and die for the slave, and as he prepared his own defense, he returned to this story of a man who turned a military blunder at the Harper's Ferry arsenal into a moral victory in a Virginia courthouse.

Just as Brown had denounced the hypocrisies of Christian slaveholders, Debs argued that the justice administered by the court served only the master class. The Espionage Act was "a despotic enactment in flagrant conflict with the democratic principles and with the spirit of free institutions." Though he considered the law unjust, he thought it was only one small expression of a much greater injustice at the foundation of the entire "social system in which we live." He told the judge that 5 percent of Americans owned two-thirds of the nation's wealth, while the 65 percent who made up the working class owned only 5 percent. Debs was on trial, he insisted, for siding with these men, women, and children who suffered under "the remorseless grasp of mammon." "I can see them dwarfed, diseased, stunted, their little lives broken, and their hopes blasted, because in the high noon of our twentieth century civilization, money is still so much more important than human life."[49]

"I could have been in Congress long ago," Debs concluded. "I have preferred to go to prison. The choice has been deliberately made." He predicted that his path would be vindicated in time. "This order of things cannot always endure," he reasoned, "finally the right must prevail. I never more clearly comprehended than now the great struggle between the powers of greed on the one hand and upon the other the rising hosts of freedom." Again Debs thanked the court for its courtesy and stood ready to hear Westenhaver's sentence.[50]

After his initial outburst on the first morning of the trial, Westenhaver had retained an evenhanded control of the proceedings. He had allowed Debs to produce his own brand of political theater, and his charge to the jury, the defendant freely admitted, had been "masterly and scrupulously fair." But as the judge delivered his sentence, he could not to forego this chance to have the final word. Dropping the mask of impartiality, he initiated what the *New York Times* called a "spontaneous debate . . . on socialism vs. patriotism."[51]

As Westenhaver had listened to Debs hold court during the trial, he had concluded that, however sincere the defendant might be, he was preaching "anarchy, pure and simple." The old radical's much vaunted idealism, the judge now charged, was no "higher, purer, nobler than the idealisms of thousands of young men I have seen marching down the streets of Cleveland to defend our country." With many of those young men even then dying in France, Westenhaver did not see Debs as a champion of the underdog, but as a man devoted to tearing down all that made America strong, undermining the country in its hour of need.

> I cannot accept the attitude of mind of any one who claims any right to dispense anybody from observing the laws of our land for the protection of peace and safety while thousands of young men are defending the country against the common enemy. Any one who strikes the sword from the hand of those young men or causes another young man to refuse to do his duty when called to serve by their side, or any one who obstructs the recruiting service does just as much injury and wrong to our country as if he were a soldier in the ranks of the German army.[52]

Westenhaver then sentenced Debs to three concurrent ten-year sentences. Because the federal penitentiaries were overcrowded, the judge ordered him sent to West Virginia's state penitentiary in Moundsville.

Across the country, newspaper editors praised the jury's decision and Westenhaver's rejoinder to Debs at the trial. Debs "will receive little sympathy and deserves none," pronounced the *Cleveland Plain Dealer.* "America is a better place for free men to dwell in now that Debs is sent on the trail of so many of his followers—the trail that leads from the freedom they desecrate to the cell door that opens inward." The "law of consequences" had caught up with Debs at last, the *Los Angeles Times* crowed, pointing out that it had been calling him a traitor for decades. "At last the prison doors open for one of the most dangerous disloyalists that ever attempted to undermine the authority of a sovereign people." Dismissing Debs's First Amendment defense, the *New York Herald* countered that the four-time presidential candidate only revealed his ignorance of American law. "Perfect freedom of speech is not denied in this country even in war except in one direction," the paper explained. "Those who misuse that privilege in order to thwart the national will and to assist the enemy are bound to suffer the consequences, and they are victims only of their own baseness and folly." The American majority had always granted Debs and his followers a generous tolerance, the *Christian Science Monitor* reasoned; rather than gratefully acknowledging the privilege of free speech and using his formidable talents to build harmony between the classes, Debs had abused his rights at a time when the nation faced a great peril, and now deserved to be punished.[53]

Radicals, of course, saw the matter differently. To them, the trial had been a travesty of justice, the final insult that would finally stir workers to open revolt. On the day that news of the conviction spread across the country, John Reed led a rally for Debs in the Bronx, featuring what the *Herald* called "the usual outbursts against government" At another New York meeting a week later, Rose Stokes urged her comrades to unite in their outrage. The jury had "gone to sleep before the civil war," she told the crowd. "The only slaves they knew of were the colored slaves of the civil war, and having freed those slaves, they had no appreciation of the fact that industrial development in this country had produced another slave—the wage slave, for whose freedom Debs was fighting as ardently as Lincoln ever fought for the freedom of the colored slave." Stokes predicted that if the government dared to go ahead with their plan to put Debs in jail, they would provoke these wage slaves into a furious revolt against their oppressors.[54]

The entire trial had been cathartic for Debs. At the start the judge, jury, and even his neighbors seemed like enemies. By the end his optimism had returned, along with his taste for the revolutionary fight. He had done his duty to the movement, had proven himself willing to make the greatest of sacrifices, had stood on the side of the angels in the cosmic clash of economic forces. And in their attempt to silence Debs, the government had provided him with a powerful platform, thrusting him back to the center of national attention. Just then the war no longer seemed to be the death knell of his long career, but its great culmination. "I have no complaint to make," he told David Karsner as they left Cleveland. "It will come out all right in God's good time."[55]

Chapter 6

Appeal

WHILE THE WAR divided Socialists in the spring of 1917, eighteen months of mob violence and government persecution had the opposite effect, temporarily uniting them in the face of a common enemy. Though it came late in the war, the Debs trial intensified this feeling. Here was final proof, many radicals contended, that the plutocrats were waging "open warfare" on their class enemies. "Nothing that has happened in the United States this year has stirred so many people just this way," John Reed contended. The long jail terms handed out to conscientious objectors and Socialist leaders, and the almost complete destruction of the radical press had not "deeply moved" most Americans. "But the arrest and indictment of Gene Debs—of Gene Debs as a traitor to his country! That was like a slap in the face to thousands of simple people—many of them not Socialists at all—who had heard him speak and therefore loved him."[1]

The arrest shocked many radicals, but Debs's performance at the trial had inspired them. Other dissenters had ably defended themselves in court, as one editor saw it, but none had so defiantly challenged the government's assault on free speech. Translated into many languages, and widely reprinted in the socialist press, Debs's courtroom speeches served as a "clarion call" to America's battered radicals. "We were ready for unvarnished speech," they agreed, "and Debs's declaration before the court brought the whole Party, from Canada to Mexico, from the Atlantic to the Pacific, to its feet, in one burst of enthusiastic acclaim."[2]

Younger comrades sent Debs poems, glorifying his suffering. "Go take your place with Socrates and Christ," one urged, while the muse inspired dozens of other radical poets in the same direction. Horace Traubel, the disciple of Walt Whitman, echoed his mentor when he called his old friend Debs "a ray of light in a dark place . . . a ripe harvest field that no mortal eye can see the end of . . . something big without a name."[3]

Upton Sinclair paid homage to Debs by working him into his latest novel, *Jimmie Higgins.* The story traced the experiences of a humble mechanic who began the war loyal to the Socialists' anti-war convictions, but was drawn by bitter experience into fighting the Huns, all the while preserving his passion for class warfare. As he had with *The Jungle,* Sinclair dashed off the tale at a feverish pace, publishing it in serial form, eager to create not timeless art but timely propaganda. Appearing the month of the Cleveland trial, the first chapter featured a sentimental portrait of Debs, thinly fictionalized as "The Candidate," a loving tribute to America's best-known defendant. Sinclair sent a copy of *Jimmie Higgins* to Wilson, urging him to print and distribute the book at government expense as a testament to the wisdom of the president's policies. Several New York editors took a different view, advising federal prosecutors to inspect the novel for traces of treason.[4]

Debs read Sinclair's tribute just days after the trial. Most pro- and anti-war Socialists feuded bitterly, but these two had remained friends. Debs thanked the novelist for his testimonial, as well as his "comradely, humane" attempts to defend the free speech rights of radicals. He was similarly moved by all of the "lavish praise" that poured into his Terre Haute office after the trial. But he told his admirers that his contribution to the cause was "almost contemptible" when compared with the "heroic services" of Lenin and Trotsky, and all those American dissenters who had suffered beyond the protective glare of publicity.[5]

Eager to capitalize on their leader's fresh notoriety, the party organized a national speaking tour, including an entire "Debs week" of mass rallies in New York. Judge Westenhaver had no interest in allowing Debs to convert his conviction into a recruiting tool for the Socialist

Party. He ordered him to remain at home in Terre Haute, or in the judicial district of Northern Ohio where he had been tried. If Debs made any more speeches that violated the Espionage Act, the judge threatened, he would revoke Debs's bail, sending him to a Cleveland jail to wait for the Supreme Court's decision on his appeal.

Geographically constrained but politically unbowed, Debs set out to turn northern Ohio into a "burned-over district" for the workers' revolution. All through the war, the industrial centers of Cleveland, Akron, and Toledo had been the site of passionate clashes between radicals and patriots. A week after his conviction, Debs was the main attraction at "packed and overflowing" meetings in these cities. Some of them, he crowed to Max Eastman, "fairly bristled with the spirit of revolution."[6]

At a December meeting in Toledo, for example, Debs admitted with evident pleasure that he was "on dangerous ground" as he repeated his claim that "in all of history the working class has never declared war." While government agents took notes and a ring of uniformed policemen watched the crowd for unpatriotic outbursts, Debs rehearsed his favorite swipes at "the system." "When men under command go out and slaughter thousands of other men whom they do not know and who have never injured them, this is not murder—it is patriotism." A reporter described the audience as a mix of undercover agents, workers with "tousled hair and swarthy faces," and "well groomed men and women" who were just curious to see America's most notorious traitor.[7]

In a change of course that outraged many American radicals, Wilson sent thousands of troops to Russia that summer, waging a halfhearted and undeclared war against the Soviets. At the same time, Debs proclaimed that "every drop of blood in my veins is Bolshevik," a remark that always won a roar of applause from his audiences. "Every worker who is against the Bolsheviki," he said, "stands in his own light, spits in his own face." Critics, including the conservative labor leader Samuel Gompers, were telling American workers that the Bolsheviks were not the vanguard of the working man's liberation, but dangerous despots. They had disbanded the country's Constituent Assembly, Gompers pointed out, and ruled with bloody terror. Debs countered that the Bolsheviki could not be expected to "give a perfect democracy within twenty-four hours time." Jesus and Jefferson, he liked to say, had been the Bolsheviks of their day.[8]

Lenin returned the compliment. As Debs prepared for his trial in the summer of 1918, the Russian leader sent an open letter to American workers, smuggled into the country by the poet-reporter Carl Sandburg. Widely published in what remained of the country's left-wing press, the letter praised Debs as "one of the best loved leaders of the American proletariat." "I am not surprised that this fearless man was thrown into prison by the American bourgeoisie," Lenin stated prematurely. "Let them brutalize true internationalists," he taunted from afar. "The greater the bitterness and brutality they sow, the nearer is the day of the victorious proletarian revolution."[9]

The Bolsheviks had arrested several Americans, including a diplomat, and they threatened at least one with execution. The Wilson administration denounced these violations of international law, and worked through the Norwegian government to negotiate their release. The Russians proposed a swap, exchanging the American hostages for Debs. And the *New York Times* reported that, at a secret convention in Moscow, the "soviet dictators" had appointed him the president of the future Soviet Republic of America. Picking up the story, Debs's hometown newspaper announced, "[Lenin] Gives Debs This Country."[10]

These fantasies enraged newspaper editors across Ohio, who pleaded with federal prosecutors to silence this "clever exponent of false doctrine." One urged the government to exile Debs to Russia. "There he may learn the lesson of law and order and come, if he escapes the dagger of his friends the bolsheviki, to realize that he has been treated immeasurably better than he deserved." These papers assured their readers that federal agents were on the case, sending copies of Debs's recent speeches to the Justice Department for further review. "Let 'em do their damndest and dirtiest," Theodore Debs scoffed. "It will not influence Gene in the least."[11]

Publicly, Debs played the role of a defiant revolutionary martyr with his usual vigor. Privately, he was suffering physically, emotionally, and financially. The Debs brothers struggled to keep their Terre Haute office afloat, all the while sinking deeper in debt. Without income for much of the war, they lived on edge, expecting a police raid on their offices at any time. Though Debs enjoyed some rousing meetings in northern Ohio, at times he was deeply discouraged. "The secret service agents follow me everywhere," he complained, "and the people are so largely intimidated, that my work is made the more difficult and the returns more meager and fruitless on that account." In some places city officials denied the use of meeting spaces, while the police in Lima broke up a rally by threatening to drench the audience with a fire hose. "Radicals Fear Bath," mocked the *Cleveland Plain Dealer.* A number of dates were canceled not by government repression but by public anxiety about the dreaded Spanish influenza that was killing millions across the globe that fall.[12]

Under this strain, Debs suffered what Theodore called "a nervous and physical breakdown" in November. As he enjoyed what might well be his last few months of freedom, he also faced an emotional torment, the pending separation from his lover Mabel Curry. Their relationship remained a guarded secret, known to Theodore and few others. Both remained dutifully married, respectful and even loving toward their spouses. Curry confided to Rose Pastor Stokes her fears about the toll prison would take on Debs. "No one knows as I know what just a year would do! The separation would kill him. *This I know.*" Always forced to live apart, the couple now faced the prospect of total, even final, separation, a bitter end to the unfulfilled dream that they might, somehow, live together one day.[13]

Though the war was over, the trials of anti-war radicals ground forward. Stokes remained free while her case was appealed. The editors of the *Masses* faced a retrial, with Max Eastman serving once again as star witness for his own defense. Emboldened by Debs's example, he concluded with an eloquent three-hour speech extolling the value of dissent in a democracy. Even one of the prosecuting attorneys was moved, telling Eastman that "as an address of a man accused of a crime, it would probably live as one of the greatest addresses in modern times." Two holdout jurors were similarly affected, and the five editors won another hung jury and their freedom.[14]

The radical economist Scott Nearing also managed to face down his accusers in a New York courtroom. In February 1919 the leader of the anti-war People's Council went on trial for writing *The Great Madness,* a pamphlet distributed by the socialist Rand School that described the American war effort as "the greatest victory that the American plutocracy has won over the American democracy since the declaration of war with Spain in 1898." The prosecutor condemned Nearing for dulling Americans' enthusiasm for the war, while he countered that if the government had the power to silence any discouraging word, free and fair discussion was at an end in America.[15]

Inspired by Debs's "radiant" example, Nearing chose to "deny nothing," and used his trial as a forum to promote socialism. Defended by the tireless Seymour Stedman, Nearing testified for days, piling the witness stand high with textbooks and charts, lecturing on socialist theory and defending his right to speak, educate, and agitate on this or any other vital public question. The handsome young rebel professor impressed even his prosecutors with his calm, rational, and sober demeanor. After a thirty-hour deliberation, ten jurors were unable to convince two holdouts, both Russian immigrants. The jury acquitted Nearing for writing the pamphlet, while paradoxically convicting the Rand School for distributing it. The judge ordered the school to pay a three thousand dollar fine. This partial victory led the *New York Call* to predict in the spring of 1919, quite prematurely, that the government's campaign against radicals was almost over.

For his part, Debs did not expect that his Supreme Court appeal would provide either liberty or justice. The real fight for free speech, he believed, would not be won in lawyers' briefs, but on street corners, public squares, and factory floors. This was ultimately a battle, not for individual liberties as defined by the courts, but for control of the entire democratic process, at the ballot box and in the workplace. An example from his hometown underscored the nature of this contest. When Debs had declined his party's invitation to run for Congress that fall, his comrades nominated Shubert Sebree, an enthusiastic young radical who worked in a Terre Haute glass factory. When Sebree began to campaign, his boss had him fired, blacklisted, and "hounded out of town." Debs took such incidents as proof that the ruling class had dropped any pretense of democratic practice and fair play, revealing the naked power struggle that lay beneath. No doubt comforting himself as much as his young friend, he could only tell Sebree, "Your day will come as sure as the truth prevails."[16]

And when that day finally came, Debs thought, it would be delivered not by nine robed judges in Washington but by the working people themselves, rising to claim their rights. Debs had long anticipated that moment, and now events at home and abroad encouraged his wildest hopes. Surviving Allied pressure and a brutal civil war, the Bolsheviks held on to power in Russia, and communist-inspired revolts were erupting across war-ravaged Europe. In America, he saw signs that workers were ready to bring on a social revolution through more peaceful democratic means. As he toured Ohio, he campaigned for Charles Ruthenberg, the Socialist candidate for Congress who had testified at his trial and remained behind bars in Canton. Buoyed by an "extraordinary" turnout at meetings that fall, Debs felt sure that "all things are coming our way." As Election Day neared, he reminded workers that they outnumbered their masters twenty to one, and that the ballot box could become the instrument of their liberation. As he had every November for many years, he asked them if they would be "blind and stupid and spineless enough in light of the frightful happenings of the last few years to vote the same corrupt old ruling-class ticket?"[17]

And again American workers let Debs down. In Ohio, Ruthenberg was unable to repeat his impressive showing of the year before. In New York City the party suffered similar setbacks in a series of ferocious contests marred by ballot fraud, intimidation of immigrant voters, and brutal attacks on Socialist poll watchers. In key races, Republicans and Democrats joined to support "fusion" candidates against the Socialists. Many ballots disappeared, while hundreds of others were torn up or otherwise disqualified under suspicious circumstances. In the heat of the campaign, a Socialist speaker was almost killed, knifed by a Tammany Hall "gangster" as he spoke from the bed of a truck. In the end, Socialist congressman Meyer London, one of the party's few voices in Washington, lost his seat. In another New York congressional race, Scott Nearing was defeated by Fiorella LaGuardia, just back from the war and campaigning in his uniform. Although the party made a strong showing in the upper Midwest, only Victor Berger in Milwaukee, still awaiting his own sedition trial, won a seat in Congress. "Wartime attacks" on the party "had taken their toll," historian James Weinstein concluded. "Even where the locals had not been entirely disrupted, their energies were often dissipated in defending their right to exist."

Making matters worse, when Berger arrived in Washington that spring, his fellow congressmen refused, by a vote of 309 to 1, to allow him to take his seat.[18]

Socialists were familiar with defeat, but voters also repudiated the Wilson administration, ignoring the president's appeal for a Democratic majority in Congress. In a controversial move, Wilson had asked Americans to treat the 1918 election as a referendum on his leadership, and they had rejected him. Republicans promised to resist the "tyranny" of Wilson's White House, particularly the government's interference in the economy, while simultaneously stepping up the war on "socialism, Bolshevism and the destructive elements of society." Voters gave them control of both houses, a humiliating defeat for the president.[19]

While Debs toured Ohio hoping to stir revolution, and Seymour Stedman prepared briefs for the Supreme Court, a small but influential group of liberals and pro-war socialists urged Wilson to use the armistice as an opportunity to begin the process of national reconciliation. At the *Nation*, Oswald Garrison Villard argued that the fate of the president's democratic crusade now hung in the balance, that his plan to build world peace was being undermined by his war on radicals at home. As the Republicans' recent victory made clear, the president desperately needed the support of America's "liberal forces" if he hoped to salvage his plans for a progressive peace based on mutual disarmament, limited indemnities, national self-determination, and collective security. But all through the war the very people who were his most likely allies had been "by his own act scattered, silenced, disorganized, some in prison." As the war drew to a close, the *Nation* argued that the president never should have allowed the "dull and narrow" postmaster general, and the "even narrower" attorney general, to suppress public debate. Only conservative hyperpatriots had been free to speak, and they were the enemies of Wilson's foreign policy and his progressive reforms at home. "If he loses his great fight for humanity," Villard predicted, "it will be because he was deliberately silent when freedom of speech and the right of conscience were struck down in America." Although Villard blamed Wilson, at this early stage he put the burden of reconciliation on the victims, advising liberals and Socialists to overlook the president's "errors of judgment" and to "pull together" behind him during the crucial period of postwar reconstruction.[20]

Upton Sinclair also urged the president to use the armistice as a chance to rebuild his tattered coalition of supporters on the left. Throughout the war, Sinclair had worked to minimize the damage that the conflict was doing to the Socialist Party. When he quit the party in 1917, he was shut out of the radical journals that had always afforded him a modest income and a sure outlet for his propaganda. Instead, he founded his own magazine, *Upton Sinclair's,* a monthly that embodied his talent for self-promotion and his good-natured tolerance for opposing viewpoints. In these pages, Sinclair threw his prodigious moral fervor behind Wilson's war on German militarism, while urging all Socialists to think of their split as temporary, rooted in honest differences of opinion among people who still shared a common political goal.

The embitterment caused by the government persecution of dissenters, however, made reconciliation unlikely. Many Socialists denounced Sinclair as a "Judas Iscariot," while one crazed radical threatened assassination. Until the man was arrested, Sinclair was forced to carry guns and keep his shades drawn. He parried these attacks with good humor, only complaining that the pistols he carried wore holes in his pockets. He was much more concerned about the Wilson administration's heavy-handed use of its censorship powers against the radical press. Many of Postmaster Burleson's victims were the muckraking novelist's old friends and occasional employers. Frank Harris, editor of *Pearson's,* spent the war years hovering on the edge of bankruptcy, his left-wing literary magazine repeatedly barred from the mail for allegedly subversive content. Harris was deeply disturbed by the Debs trial, but muted his criticism in the vain hope of saving his magazine. Sinclair was also friends with Max Eastman and most of his fellow editors at the *Masses.* He praised the Greenwich Village radicals as the "brainiest" journalists in America and regretted that they chose to bang those brains against the thick wall of the Espionage Act.[21]

Sinclair sent Wilson polite letters, hoping to use his influence to keep their journals out of Burleson's control. He conceded that in times of war the government had the right to silence those who would hurt the war effort. And he sympathized with Wilson's claim that the line dividing acceptable dissent from dangerous sedition was hard to draw. Sinclair insisted, however, that the postmaster general was too blunt an instrument for this delicate job. It is also hard to draw a line, he told the president, "as to the amount of ignorance permitted to a government official. But Mr. Burleson is assuredly on the wrong side of any line that could be drawn by any one."[22]

During the war, Wilson usually disarmed such criticisms with a show of sympathy. He promised Sinclair, Eastman, and other allies on the left that he would investigate their concerns. On several occasions he did intervene, urging Burleson to use "the utmost caution and liberality in all our censorship." Though he conceded that many of the radical publications "intended to have sinister results," he advised Burleson not to do "any more suppressing." Unmoved, Burleson replied that he was simply fulfilling his legal obligations, and he continued to ignore his boss's call for moderation. For a man determined to impose his ideals on a war-torn world, Wilson showed remarkable deference to his postmaster.[23]

Years later, H. L. Mencken chided his friend Upton Sinclair. "You have done more or less hollering for free speech," he wrote, "but how much of it did you do during the war, when free speech was most in danger?" As Sinclair's letters to Wilson suggest, the charge was not entirely fair. Sinclair did defend free speech, but as he struggled to reconcile freedom of thought with national security, he proposed compromises that pleased no one. To curb Burleson's censorship powers, for example, he suggested that the government should give war critics a free hand to print their views, as long as they granted the government equal space on their pages for an official rebuttal. Wilson was intrigued by the idea, and Max Eastman, Frank Harris, and Abraham Cahan at the *Jewish Daily Forward* were surprisingly willing to compromise this much editorial control in order to escape the threat of bankruptcy. Only the *New York Call* denounced this "cowardly compromise" as an egregious violation of the First Amendment. But Sinclair's idea went no further, and Burleson continued to bar disloyal publications from the mail.

In the final months of the war Sinclair also lobbied the administration to adopt a more lenient approach to the punishment of anti-war speakers. He told Wilson that Debs, Stokes, Nearing, and other indicted radicals "have given a life-time's devotion to the highest ideals of humanity, and [their] only fault is that they have not been able to adjust their minds to the sudden and desperate emergency." Again, Sinclair did not challenge the administration's right to "restrain them" while soldiers fought. In fact, he even accepted the attorney general's view that federal prosecution was comparatively humane. If the government did not take these obstructionists off the streets, Gregory reasoned, violent patriotic mobs would, with far uglier results. However, Sinclair urged Wilson not to treat these "political prisoners" like common criminals, but to put them in a separate prison farm where they would be lightly guarded and humanely treated as long as they promised not to engage in any further pacifist propaganda. Sinclair added that the farm work would be bracing and healthful for the imprisoned radicals, public-spirited citizens who might even welcome the chance to grow vegetables for the common good. Again, Wilson showed a glimmer of respectful interest in Sinclair's odd plan for a pastoral gulag, but then dropped the idea.[24]

Although he considered the administration's overzealous prosecution of dissenters to be Wilson's "one serious blunder" during the war, Sinclair muted his criticism until the armistice. Believing that the fate of civilization hung in the balance, and trusting that the president's liberal instincts would eventually prevail, he stood behind the administration until the Kaiser was defeated. "When the war is over," he assured his readers, "we expect that there will again be free speech and free press in America; if it is denied, we shall help to try to win it, and perhaps we shall then gratify those correspondents who want to see us in jail."[25]

Two weeks after the armistice, Sinclair heard from Louise Bryant, the radical writer who was John Reed's companion. The couple had recently returned from Russia, and Reed was busy completing his master work on the revolution, Ten Days That Shook the World. Bryant confessed to Sinclair that she felt "deeply discouraged" about the political mood in America, and especially about the prospect of Debs going to jail. "In a few days our President is sailing for France and nothing at all has been done about our political prisoners—and, of course, nothing will be done while he is away." Like Sinclair, Bryant had supported the war but had deep misgivings about the toll it had taken on American liberty. "I love America enough to go to jail to keep it free," she told Sinclair. "I know you do too and since there is no longer a German menace, it seems to me that we have to take a stand." Sinclair agreed that, now that the war for democracy in Europe was over, it was time to renew the struggle at home. He told another friend, with evident glee, "My little venture in respectability is ended and for good."[26]

Sinclair launched an energetic campaign to convince the Wilson administration to pardon the political prisoners, hoping to add public pressure to the private persuasion he had tried throughout the war. Few radicals better understood the art of thrusting a cause into public view. He started with a press release announcing his new "clean slate campaign," a petition drive calling on Wilson to grant amnesty to Debs and others convicted under the wartime laws. The armistice, Sinclair announced, had removed "the last reason that could by any possibility justify the holding of pacifists and anti-militarists in jail." Debs and the others were perhaps mistaken, he said, but they were undeniably sincere. Thinking he might yet flatter Wilson onto the high road of reconciliation, Sinclair concluded that those who still wanted Debs punished "are not the friends of your policies of enlightenment and justice, but on the contrary their bitter enemies." In this group Sinclair no doubt included Postmaster Burleson, a man he now openly denounced as an "ignoramus."[27]

During the war, Wilson had cultivated his relationship with Sinclair, valuing the writer's mostly futile attempt to bring Socialists into the war camp. But as the conflict drew to a close, he grew silent. Any message Sinclair received from the president came only through his secretary, Joseph Tumulty, and these were cordial but evasive.

In the absence of a clear statement from the president, those trying to discern how the administration would handle civil liberties after the armistice had reasons for optimism, and cause for concern. All through the war, Wilson had taken an ambiguous approach to the problem, issuing ominous threats against dissenters, and then belated protests against the mob violence that his own comments seemed to encourage. While claiming to welcome legitimate criticism, he mostly stood by as federal prosecutors and the postmaster crushed those radicals who dared to speak against the war. And now, as he sailed for France in early December, he was clearly preoccupied with the peace negotiations. More than ever this vital public question was left in the hands of his subordinates.

As one historian put it, the president "seemed to hope that the [civil liberties] issue would disappear in peacetime."

Without clear direction from the president, his advisors took an inconsistent approach to the controversy in the first months after the armistice. Secretary of War Newton Baker heartened American liberals by pardoning many conscientious objectors held in military prisons and reducing sentences on soldiers convicted for minor offenses. Attorney General Thomas Gregory moved in a similar direction, though more slowly. As the war ended, he continued to defend the wartime prosecutions, and warned the public that groups like the new Civil Liberties Union were only using talk about free speech as a smokescreen to hide their pro-German or Bolshevik agendas. Still, Gregory told his prosecutors to be cautious with new indictments, and he ordered a review of all convictions under the Espionage Act. Postmaster Burleson, however, still hunted for subversive publications. Long after the armistice, journalists continued to work under the chilling effect of his censorship threat.

These contradictory policies mirrored public opinion as the war drew to a close. Many Americans had no desire to forgive those who had betrayed their country in the moment of national crisis. Others agreed with Sinclair that it was time for a national reconciliation. Now that the war was over, sending Debs to jail for opposing the war seemed vindictive, an act that would accomplish no military purpose but would add more fuel to the fires of radical indignation. The Supreme Court, they hoped, would end the matter by ruling that the Espionage Act convictions had been an unconstitutional violation of the First Amendment.[28]

In 1919 the Supreme Court was not a promising venue for radicals to defend their civil liberties. With the exception of Louis Brandeis, a liberal Jew who was a recent and controversial addition to the court, the nation's top justices were staunch conservatives. Associate Justice Oliver Wendell Holmes Jr. was less predictable, a brilliant iconoclast who enjoyed the company of young liberals. Nothing in Holmes's record, however, suggested that he would sympathize with an idealist like Debs. He was a steely-eyed pragmatist who thought of the law as an expression of the majority's will to power. Truth, as he famously put it, was determined by "the majority vote of that nation that can lick all others." A Civil War veteran who had been wounded in battle, Holmes believed that the majority had a primordial right to defend itself by drafting men and sending them to the front. "No society had ever admitted that it could not sacrifice individual welfare to its own existence," he wrote. "If conscripts are necessary for its army, it seizes them, and marches them, with bayonets in their rear, to death." He once confided to a friend that sentimental reformers and pacifists made him want to "vomit," and he considered those radicals trapped by the Espionage Act to be "poor devils," deluded not only by a false political ideology but also by the fantasy that they enjoyed some natural right to stand in the way of their country's march to war.[29]

During the Cleveland trial, Debs's lawyers had allowed him to offer his own defense, a passionate but unlawyerly plea for his First Amendment rights. In the Supreme Court appeal, Seymour Stedman filed a brief that fleshed out a more detailed legal argument. He charged that prosecutors had unfairly introduced and emphasized the St. Louis anti-war manifesto, leading jurors to judge Debs for words he had never spoken. He also objected that the prosecution had never specified which parts of the Canton speech broke the law. Their "insufficient indictment" allowed jurors to judge Debs for his many harsh statements against capitalism, words that were clearly legal but bound to prejudice the jury. The heart of their appeal, however, was the claim that the Espionage Act, as applied during the war, violated the free speech rights guaranteed by the First Amendment.[30]

When the Supreme Court agreed to review the Debs case and several other Espionage Act convictions, civil libertarians believed the stakes were enormously high. In their view, if the court upheld the wartime prosecutions, this would grant the federal government the power to limit speech whenever it interfered with some other public good. As Gilbert Roe put it, "If the free speech clause of the Constitution only means that one may advocate what Congress has not by statute forbidden one to advocate, then it does not mean anything."

None felt the urgency of this controversy more keenly than Roe, a progressive New York attorney who was a veteran of many free speech battles. For two decades he had volunteered his services to the Free

Speech League, a small group that provided legal aid to radicals of all kinds. Roe had protected Upton Sinclair from libel charges, defended Emma Goldman and the Wobblies in various courts, and helped Max Eastman and the *Masses* win a rare, but temporary, victory over the postmaster. At the start of the war he had testified against the Espionage Act, warning senators that the law was vague and liable to abuse. Now he believed that events had confirmed his fears; an act supposed to target mutineers and spies had been used, instead, to punish citizens for speaking their minds on a vital matter of government policy.[31]

The Supreme Court could put a stop to this, and Roe was eager to persuade them to do so. "I have spent a good deal of time in the last few years in the historical study of the free speech clause," he wrote to Stedman. "The ordinary interpretation of that clause makes it simply waste paper." Believing that the Debs case offered good grounds for a strong and high-profile constitutional challenge, he asked Stedman for permission to file an amicus brief. Though sympathetic toward Debs, Roe cared less about keeping him out of prison than he did about saving the First Amendment.[32]

As well as anyone, Roe realized that he faced an uphill battle. Over the decades, federal judges tended to ignore First Amendment arguments, and only a handful of lawyers even bothered to make them. In many cases before the war, when a radical tried to claim protection under the First Amendment, the state countered that such rights did not belong to people whose words disturbed the public peace or shocked the community's sense of decency. This argument usually won the day with judges and juries, who embraced the axiom that *liberty* did not mean *license*. In his brief, Roe argued that this conventional view of free speech was all wrong, that it betrayed the founder's strong commitment to open and unfettered public debate. According to Roe, judges all too often ignored the First Amendment's revolutionary origins, and instead got their ideas about free speech from the eighteenth-century English jurist William Blackstone. In his influential 1769 summary of English common law, Blackstone had defined free speech as the absence of censorship and licensing laws. The government could impose no "previous restraint," as he put it, but was free to punish a speaker after the fact if it judged that the words threatened the public good.[33]

In their brief against Debs, government attorneys claimed that this "Blackstone doctrine" remained the "prevailing view" in 1919. Many jurists and legal scholars agreed that when the founders drafted the First Amendment, they only intended to safeguard this traditional English liberty. Some important legal scholars disagreed with this view, but federal prosecutors reminded the Supreme Court that their own most distinguished jurist had embraced Blackstone's definition of free speech in an important 1907 case. The Constitution prevents "previous restraints," Holmes had written, but does not interfere with "the subsequent punishment of such as may be deemed contrary to the public welfare."[34]

For free speech advocates, nothing made the limitations of the Blackstone doctrine more obvious than Burleson's heavy-handed use of the Espionage Act. The postmaster's defenders often pointed out that those radical publications he had driven into bankruptcy were not victims of "prior restraint." Just as Blackstone required, editors had been free to print their subversive newspapers and magazines—they were just not free to mail them.

In his brief, Roe set out to slay Blackstone, whose views on free speech cast such a long shadow over American thinking about the First Amendment. He reminded the court that Blackstone was an English Tory, a "conservative of conservatives." Dead well before the Bill of Rights had been written, he had only intended to summarize the English common law of his day and never dreamed of offering Americans a blueprint for democratic liberty. Roe reminded the court that Blackstone also believed in witches, adding that the dead Englishman's ideas about free speech, like his thoughts on sorcery, deserved nothing more than "historical interest." Until American judges exorcized Blackstone, Roe contended, the First Amendment would remain "utterly useless as a guarantee of liberty of any sort whatsoever."[35]

Roe offered the court an alternative ancestry for the First Amendment, finding precedent not in English law books but in America's democratic revolution. He reminded the judges that Jefferson and Madison considered freedom of speech and conscience to be cornerstones of individual liberty and democratic self-government. In their fight to establish religious freedom in Virginia, the two had defined free speech in

a way that would have shocked Blackstone. The government should interfere with a speaker, they argued, only "when principles break out
into overt acts against peace and good order." Roe insisted that, when
the revolutionary generation ratified the First Amendment, and later
elected Jefferson president, they were endorsing this more expansive
view of the meaning and value of free speech.[36]

Even if one accepted Roe's alternate history of the First Amendment's origins, difficult questions remained. Legal precedent and common sense both suggested that the even the most libertarian of founders never intended to banish all limits on free speech. No judge or
commentator, then or since, had ever argued that the Bill of Rights
should be taken literally, that Congress could make "no laws" curbing
speech and the press. According to one influential jurist, such an idea
was "too wild to be indulged in by any rational man." At the Cleveland
trial, prosecutor Wertz reminded jurors of the legal truism that the right
to free speech had to be balanced against other competing goods. No
one was free to libel another, for example, or to spread obscene material, or to use language to commit fraud. And so, federal attorneys insisted that the Espionage Act was not a new intrusion on Americans'
right to speak their minds, but expressed another traditional exception
to the First Amendment, a ban on speech that incites others to commit
crimes. "The defendant was not prosecuted for hostile criticism of the
war," they insisted. "He was prosecuted for a willful and deliberate attempt to obstruct the execution of a Government policy."[37]

In his brief, Roe conceded that speech rights were not absolute and
that incitement to crime was an exception supported by long precedent.
He also granted that the government had an important obligation to
raise an army and was entitled to take steps to make that possible. If
prosecutors had used the Espionage Act only to punish those who
clearly attempted to interfere with recruitment, he agreed, the government would have been within its rights and no constitutional objection
to the law could be raised. The problem was not in the letter of the Espionage Act, he contended, but in the way it had been applied, in the
heat of war, by zealous judges, prosecutors, and juries. They had ranged
far beyond the law's original purpose, Roe argued, thanks to the court's
use of what was known as the "bad tendency" test.

Under this test, prosecutors did not have to prove that a defendant had actually caused harm or directly urged anyone to commit a crime. Instead, juries were instructed to convict a speaker if they concluded that the "natural consequences" of his speech would be harmful. As in most of the wartime speech cases, the government could not show that Debs had directly advised anyone to break the draft law, and could produce no man who had failed to register after hearing the Canton speech. Instead, Westenhaver told jurors to find Debs guilty if they thought that the "natural tendency" of his words would be to discourage young men from doing their duty. Under this test, prosecutors also needed to show that the speaker had *intended* to cause this harm. As Roe pointed out, this rarely offered the defendant meaningful protection. If a patriotic jury decided that a speaker's words were dangerous, it was bound to assume that they revealed the defendant's bad intentions. Roe protested that, in the heat of war, such loose guidelines allowed jurors to pass judgment based on conjecture rather than solid evidence, giving free rein to their political biases. As a result of a vague law badly applied, "the constitutional guarantee of free speech and free press is wiped out."[38]

In place of "bad tendency," Roe and Stedman urged the Supreme Court to embrace a more protective free speech test proposed by Judge Learned Hand. A hero to civil libertarians, Hand was one of the few federal judges who resisted the government's campaign against dissent. When New York's postmaster banned the *Masses* from the mail in 1917, Roe had gone to Judge Hand's court to ask for an injunction to keep the magazine in circulation. After reviewing the anti-war cartoons and essays in the *Masses*, Hand agreed with federal prosecutors that they might well "enervate public feeling at home" and give comfort to America's enemies. Under the "bad tendency" test, such conclusions would have been enough to justify government interference, but Hand decided that the authors were expressing a political opinion, just what the First Amendment had been designed to protect. He argued that, when Congress passed the Espionage Act, it had not intended to punish all "hostile criticism." Like Roe, the judge believed that prosecutors had twisted the law's meaning, equating all dissent with incitement to crime, erasing a distinction that he called "a hard-bought acquisition in the fight for freedom."

Hand granted the injunction to stop the postmaster, and proposed a new free speech test designed to limit the reach of the Espionage Act. He argued that speakers should be punished only if they openly and *directly* urged others to resist the law. Even the harshest criticism of the government should be tolerated, Hand concluded, as long as the speaker was not explicitly advocating a crime. In their briefs, both Stedman and Roe commended Judge Hand's "direct advocacy" test. Stedman told the Supreme Court that if this standard had been applied in Cleveland, the jury could not possibly have convicted Debs. "Search this speech through from first to last," he asked the judges, "and what is there in it that may be read as an incitement or encouragement toward dereliction of military or civic duty in relation to the war?"[39]

Federal prosecutors thought much less of Hand's innovation and reminded the justices that his ruling in the *Masses* case had been overturned by a higher court. Dismissing Hand's arguments, the appeals court found no grounds for abandoning the "bad tendency" test, which was supported by precedents "too plain for controversy." Justice Department attorneys agreed. They warned that if Hand's test prevailed, they would be powerless to stop men like Debs who "fight from cover," hiding their subversive intentions in "veiled, indirect, or rhetorical language." Debs had praised other jailed offenders and told his followers not to worry about "treason to their masters." Minutes before his speech, he had endorsed the St. Louis Proclamation, which vowed opposition to the draft. As he began his speech, he even announced that he would be careful about his words to avoid arrest. Prosecutors insisted that the jury should be allowed to put the pieces together, drawing the obvious conclusion that Debs was trying to subvert the war effort on that day in Canton.[40]

No less than Roe and Stedman, the Justice Department's attorneys believed that the First Amendment was a crucial pillar of American democracy. They argued, however, that the same Constitution that enshrined free speech also gave Congress the power to declare and conduct war, and thus to ensure "national self-preservation." Free speech rights were not absolute, but were constrained by the conflicting values of public safety and the efficient prosecution of the war. They reasoned that if Congress could draft a man and send him to the front, it also had the right to silence those who tried to interfere with that solemn purpose.

In their briefs for Debs, Stedman and Roe rejected the government's claim that its "war purposes" trumped the individual's right to object. After all, they pointed out, the Bill of Rights had been passed at a time when the country faced the perils of another European conflict, by men who knew firsthand the pressures of war, and yet they made no exception for war in the First Amendment. Americans had gone to battle many times since then, and in each case some had protested that decision. Even in the great national crisis of civil war, Roe contended, Lincoln had never taken such harsh measures to stifle his critics. If the Supreme Court failed to stop the Wilson administration's attempt to crush war protesters, Debs's lawyers concluded, they would be complicit in a "careless sweeping aside of the most vital principle of American freedom."[41]

On March 10 the Supreme Court unanimously confirmed the guilty verdict. Writing the decision, Justice Oliver Wendell Holmes Jr. affirmed the traditional "bad tendency" test. He conceded that most of the Canton speech was standard socialist fare, and perfectly legal. "With that we have nothing to do," he wrote, but added that "if a part of the manifest intent of the more general utterances was to encourage those present to obstruct the recruiting service and if in such passages such encouragement was directly given, the immunity of the general theme may not be enough to protect the speech." While Holmes's use of the phrases "manifest intent" and "encouragement directly given" might imply that he was endorsing Hand's idea that only "direct advocacy" of crime should be punished, the justice did not have this in mind. Instead, he proceeded to review, and tacitly approve, the evidence that Debs had *indirectly* encouraged his audience to disobey the draft law—by praising his convicted comrades, defending the St. Louis Proclamation, and condemning war as a tool of capitalist oppression. Siding with government prosecutors, Holmes agreed that such evidence established Debs's true but unspoken intention to "obstruct the recruiting service." The government's method for uncovering the defendant's hidden motivations was supported by precedent that Holmes called "too well established and too manifestly good sense to need citation of the books."[42]

Holmes concluded by praising Judge Westenhaver's instructions to the jury, in which he told them not to convict Debs for his opinions, but only if they believed that "the words used had as their natural tendency and reasonably probable effect to obstruct the recruiting service, &c., and unless the defendant had the specific intent to do so in his mind." Endorsing the lower court's use of the traditional "bad tendency" test to convict Debs, Holmes ignored Roe's argument that such an approach made a mockery of the First Amendment.[43]

Holmes acknowledged Debs's elaborate free speech defense only when he claimed that the court had already "disposed of" that issue a week earlier, in its first ruling on an Espionage Act case. In a decision also written by Holmes, a unanimous court endorsed the conviction of Charles Schenck, the secretary of a New York branch of the Socialist Party who had been arrested for printing and spreading a leaflet protesting the draft. "A conscript is little better than a convict," Schenck had claimed. "He is deprived of all freedom of conscience in being forced to kill against his will." Calling the draft unconstitutional, the pamphlet urged Americans to "assert and support your rights" by joining the Socialist Party, writing to congressmen, and petitioning for the "repeal of the act." Even though Schenck had urged readers to change the law, not to break it, the judge advised the jury to convict him if they decided that his words had a "bad tendency." They did, and Holmes agreed with their decision. "Of course the document would not have been sent unless it had been intended to have some effect," he wrote, "and we do not see what effect it could be expected to have upon persons subject to the draft except to influence them to obstruct the carrying of it out."

Dismissing Schenck's free speech defense, Holmes argued that an individual's right to speak had to be balanced against the majority's right to protect itself, a calculation that changed with the context. In times of national peril, Holmes reasoned, the court should favor the majority, which enjoyed a right to self-preservation that was more fundamental than the individual's right of dissent. "It is a question of proximity and degree," he explained. "When a nation is at war many things that might be said in time of peace are such a hindrance to its effort that their utterance will not be endured so long as men fight and no Court could regard them as protected by any constitutional right." In short, Holmes argued that free speech meant one thing in times of peace, and another in times of war. "The question in every case is whether the words used are used in such circumstances and are of such a nature as to create a clear and present danger that they will bring about the substantive evils that Congress has a right to prevent."

Civil libertarians would soon turn Holmes's own words against him, insisting that Schenck, Debs, and most of the other Espionage Act prisoners had posed no such "clear and present danger" to the public. Legal scholars also noted that, contrary to Holmes's assertion, the facts of the two cases were quite different; Schenck had passed out anti-draft leaflets to young men, while Debs had only offered vague criticisms of the war, and to a general audience. In the spring of 1919 both points were lost on Holmes. Applying the traditional "bad tendency" test, he spoke for a unanimous court and conventional legal wisdom when he ordered both men to prison. Privately he told friends that he hoped that Wilson would offer Debs and most of the others a pardon. Holmes was sure that Debs had violated a valid law, but he thought that the government had been unwise to press the point. As he put it, "fools, knaves and ignorant persons were bound to say he was convicted because he was a dangerous agitator and that obstructing the draft was a pretence."[44]

While Holmes and other government officials insisted that Debs, Schenck, and others were not being punished for expressing their political views, many editorial observers claimed that Debs was quite properly being sent away for an entire career of preaching what the *Washington Post* called "Debsism." When the country enjoyed peace, Americans could afford to tolerate his revolutionary talk and his contempt for the government. In a time of national peril, however, the majority had every right to defend itself. "No country can afford to permit the constant preaching among its people of ideas which in their logical development mean the destruction of governmental forms and the paralysis of law and order." The *New York Times* agreed. While admiring Debs for showing "the courage of his convictions," the paper dismissed his "theory" that "the government had no power to defend itself against unbridled speech, even though that speech might lead to the Government's own destruction." Again moving far beyond Debs's alleged crime, the *Times* reasoned that he was being justly punished for an entire career devoted to "fighting to overturn or revolutionize the Constitution. He is its enemy. How, therefore, could he reasonably expect that it would fail to defend itself against him?"[45]

Free speech advocates were understandably disappointed by the Supreme Court's decision. In a raucous public meeting in New York, Roe charged that the justices had set back the First Amendment by two hundred years. In the calmer forum of the *New Republic*, University of Chicago law professor Ernest Freund claimed that Holmes had ignored the fundamental speech questions raised by the Debs case, taking "the very essentials of the entire problem for granted." Freund did not doubt that Congress had a right to pass laws to protect the recruiting service, but he argued that Debs's prosecutors had offered no evidence of "actual obstruction or an attempt to interfere with any of the processes of recruiting." Freund scolded Holmes for ignoring the challenge this raised to the First Amendment. "How can it be denied that the upholding of such a finding upon such evidence involves the question of the limits of permissible speech?"

Like Roe, Freund believed that the Debs case proved that the court's approach to free speech was inadequate, unable to meet the challenges posed by modern warfare. Traditionally, the jury system served as a check on government power, but the Espionage Act convictions showed that "its checking function fails where government policies are supported by majority opinion." The court's "bad tendency" doctrine also proved to offer scant protection for open public debate. If speaking against government policy could so easily be interpreted as incitement to crime, then all who dared to think differently would be left "adrift on a sea of doubt and conjecture." Reverence for the ideal of free speech was not enough, Freund contended, because "the real securities of rights will always have to be found in the painstaking care given to working out of legal principles. To know what you may do and what you may not do, and how far you may go in criticism, is the first condition of political liberty; to be permitted to agitate at your own peril, subject to a jury's guessing at motive, tendency and possible effect, makes the right of free speech a precarious gift."

Freund's criticism was seconded by Harvard law professor Zechariah

Chafee. In explaining his view that free speech rights vary according to context, Holmes had written in the Schenck decision that "the most stringent protection of free speech would not protect a man from falsely shouting fire in a theatre and causing a panic," a now famous legal metaphor that Holmes may well have borrowed from the crude rant of Debs's Cleveland prosecutor, Edwin Wertz. Chafee agreed with Freund that this crowded-theater analogy was "manifestly inappropriate." "How about the man," Chafee asked, "who gets up in a theatre between the acts and informs the audience honestly but perhaps mistakenly that the fire exits are too few or locked? He is a much closer parallel to Schenck or Debs."[46]

Freund conceded that a majority of Americans were "gratified" to learn that Debs would soon be heading to prison, but he believed they were making a grave mistake. "Stamp a man like Debs or a woman like Kate O'Hare as felons," he wrote, "and you dignify the term felony instead of degrading them, and every thief and robber will be justified in feeling that some of the stigma has been taken from his crime and punishment."[47]

Chapter 7

Long Trolley to Prison

"I DEFY THE SUPREME COURT to do its worst," Debs declared when he heard Holmes's decision. Of course, the court already had; within the month, federal authorities would summon him to prison. Debs "celebrated" the news by taking his wife to the picture show. "I am not concerned," he told reporters, "with what those be-powdered, be-wigged corporation attorneys at Washington do."[1]

While Debs growled defiance, some of his friends tried a more conciliatory approach, hoping to convince Wilson to grant a pardon. More than a dozen pro-war socialists, including Upton Sinclair, John Spargo, and Charlotte Perkins Gilman, sent a clemency petition to the White House. Conceding that Debs had broken the law, they "respectfully" urged the president to consider the man's age and his years of "devoted service to the cause of human freedom." Debs had never intended to defy the law, they insisted. His only crime was his "honest expression of opinion."[2]

The president's secretary Joseph Tumulty forwarded the request to Wilson, who was still in Paris occupied with peace negotiations. In his private reply, Wilson continued his ambivalent response to the wartime prosecutions. "If the Attorney General consents I am willing to grant the respite in the cases of Eugene Debs and others," the president cabled back to Tumulty. Then Wilson closed the door as quickly as he had opened it. "I doubt the wisdom and public effect of such an action," he continued, "and hope that you will discuss it in the most serious way with [Attorney General] Palmer and let me know the result of the conference before I act." In short, Wilson made clear that he opposed clemency, while passing responsibility to his attorney general.[3]

That spring, the attorney general's office was continuing to review the speech-law convictions, including the Debs case. After Thomas Gregory retired, the process had continued under his successor, A. Mitchell Palmer, a reform-minded Pennsylvania Quaker who served during the war as custodian of property seized from enemy aliens. Taking over the Justice Department in early March, Palmer took a tolerant approach, pardoning hundreds of conscientious objectors and Espionage Act offenders, and vacating the charges in many pending trials. In some cases, his attorneys concluded that the prosecution's evidence had been dubious, and in others that judges had allowed their patriotic anger to bias the jury. The Justice Department also freed prisoners who had, in its view, already served enough time, concluding that the ten- and twenty-year sentences so freely handed out during the war had been excessive.

But the Debs case was different, the stakes higher on all sides, and Palmer received strong advice not to grant a pardon. From Ohio, Judge Westenhaver repeated his view that Debs was a reckless "revolutionary internationalist." Commuting his sentence, the judge warned, would only invite "his followers to indulge in crime." Ohio's senator Atlee Pomerene, an ally of the administration, reminded Palmer that even after his conviction Debs had missed no opportunity to "abuse and vilify" the courts, and to praise Lenin and Trotsky as "the greatest statesmen of the age." This was not just another "crack-brained individual who had gone wrong," the senator insisted, and he pressured the new attorney general not to flinch at the prospect of sending this four-time presidential candidate to prison. "This is no time to trifle with outlaws whether they are in Russia or in America. If law and order are to prevail an example must be made of some of these men, such as Debs."[4]

Alfred Bettman, a Justice Department attorney supervising the wartime cases, was the lone voice in the administration who favored a pardon. He agreed that Debs had been justly convicted, but he doubted that the man had done any harm to the war effort. Most at the Canton picnic, Bettman scoffed, surely recognized that Debs was "playing with a lot of ideas which he himself did not understand." He warned Palmer to consider the political consequences of sending the Socialist icon to prison. Before the war Debs had been "on the decline," an old man with diminishing power even within his own party. The trial had revived his standing among radicals, and imprisonment would grant him the status of a martyr. Let him go, Bettman argued, and he would sink into obscurity.[5]

From across the country, individual citizens, union locals, and patriotic clubs volunteered their own advice to the attorney general. Some pleaded for clemency, others threatened that if Debs went to prison, Washington would be swamped in a revolutionary deluge. But many more demanded that Debs not be allowed to escape "unwhipped of the justice he has so long defied."

In the end, Palmer advised against a pardon for Debs. In a private telegram to Wilson, he explained that the trial had been fair, and the verdict upheld by a unanimous Supreme Court. Since his arrest, Debs had "violently criticized" that court and, according to some press reports, even threatened a general strike. Palmer concluded that it was "imperative" that the forces of law and order should stand firm against these insults. The attorney general's personal ambitions may have reinforced his legal judgment in this case. With his eye on the 1920 presidential race, Palmer understood that taking a tough stand against Debs would improve his reputation as a guardian of law and order, while helping to deflect Republican criticism that the Democrats had been too complacent about the radical threat. With the president's tacit support, Palmer denied the clemency request on April 3, announcing that letting Debs go free would be a "grievous wrong to the country."[6]

Across the nation, editors praised Palmer for sending a message "that there is to be no pandering to the anarchists and bolshevists." "Debs is a public menace," said the *Washington Post*, "and the country will be better off with him behind bars." A judge from Austin, Texas, joined hundreds of others in congratulating the attorney general. "From what I know of the Debs case," Judge D. J. Pickle added, "I believe he should have been shot."[7]

Those working to save Debs saw a glimmer of hope in the attorney general's comments. Palmer had pointed out that Debs had never personally asked for a pardon, and so the government had no reason to act on his behalf. This seemed to imply that the administration might feel differently if Debs showed more remorse for his crimes. But Debs scorned the idea of asking for a pardon. Pleading for his freedom would accomplish nothing, he recognized, while diminishing the symbolic power of his stand against the Espionage Act. Upping the ante in this confrontation, he announced that not only would he not ask for a pardon, he would not even accept one if offered, unless the other speech-law prisoners were liberated at the same time. "During my incarceration my comrades will be true and my enemies will be satisfied, and therefore, as far as I am concerned all is well with the world." He would go to jail and trust that the workers of America would one day force the government to regret its hubris.[8]

Clyde Miller, the reporter who had testified against Debs in Cleveland, was already feeling a very personal sense of regret. As he had hoped, right after the trial he had finally gone to France, serving in the Army Educational Corps. Seeing the carnage of the Western Front, Miller gained a new appreciation for Debs's position on the war. When he returned, he contacted his friend Newton Baker, the secretary of war, and tried to enlist his help in convincing the president to pardon Debs. Baker did not share Miller's new appreciation for Debs. "You have done your duty," he told him. "Do not undo it." Most likely, Wilson never heard this plea from the man who had done as much as anyone to have Debs arrested.[9]

"My heart cries out," Helen Keller wrote to Debs when she heard the news that his appeal had been denied. "I should be proud if the Supreme Court convicted me of abhorring war, and doing all in my power to oppose it. . . . The wise fools who sit in the high places of justice fail to see that in revolutionary times like the present vital issues are settled, not by statutes, decrees and authorities, but in spite of them."[10]

Keller was not the only radical who looked for the matter to be resolved outside the master class's hall of justice. For decades Debs had tirelessly championed the cause of the working class. His friends considered it inconceivable that these workers would now sit by and do nothing. "Has capitalism gone completely mad?" David Karsner asked. "Does it believe that the workers of America will allow the prison doors to shut upon the frail figure of Gene Debs?" Debs had intimated more than once that his imprisonment would be the last outrage that would spur the workers to revolutionary action. "The miners in my own state . . . will start the strike," Debs reportedly threatened. A delegation had assured him that if he went to prison, "no more coal would be mined in Indiana" until he was released. The coal strike, he suggested, would soon be followed by a paralyzing "general strike" on May 1, when American workers would take to the streets to demand freedom for all the jailed radicals.[11]

Debs later denied that he had ever threatened a general strike, but some of his more radical supporters embraced an even more unlikely scheme. Just back from Russia, where he had seen firsthand the power of revolutionary discipline, John Reed shared Debs's dream that his imprisonment might serve as the tipping point for proletarian revolt. At a packed meeting in Cleveland, he asked the crowd to raise their hands, swearing an oath that "either Gene Debs would get out of jail or we would all get in." Envisioning the Moundsville penitentiary as America's own Bastille, Reed eagerly blew on the spark of outrage, hoping for a revolutionary flame.[12]

In New York other radical groups made their own plans to storm the prison walls. A government spy attended a massive socialist rally in Brooklyn on April 11. "This is the heart of the enemy (Bolshevik) country," the informer reported. "So far as I could see or hear I was the only Gentile in the audience." The first order of business was greeting Ludwig Martens, the controversial Soviet ambassador whom the administration refused to recognize and later deported as an enemy subversive. But the loudest applause of the evening came when the Irish radical Jim Larkin spoke of Debs. "When he goes in either we are men or we are creatures that once were men," he shouted as the audience roared back. "I spoke to him a few days ago, and I told him in our name that the heart of the Socialist movement is beating true and will be found true unto death." Larkin urged the men to quietly form themselves into a "disciplined army," and to stand by for the signal to go "over the top."[13]

Perhaps the loudest yawp of outrage against Debs's pending imprisonment came from Georgia's populist firebrand Tom Watson. "It is a burning shame that Debs was ever prosecuted," Watson raged. "It will be *lasting infamy* if he is ever garbed as a felon." Watson rejected socialism and considered Debs a "political foe," while Debs considered Watson's racist populism to be "sincere, but stupid." Still, the two shared long careers built on contempt for America's "money-bag aristocracy," and they agreed that Wilson had taken the nation to war to protect Wall Street loans. As editor of the *Jeffersonian,* Watson attacked the war, mounted a vain legal challenge to the draft law, and heaped vivid scorn on government restrictions on free speech. "No king that ever lived," he charged, "ever wielded more autocratic control than President Wilson has demanded." Such talk roused the ire of the postmaster, who shut down Watson's paper in the summer of 1917. Federal prosecutors threatened to bring Espionage Act charges, until Watson agreed to hold his tongue for the rest of the war. Not long after, a hapless Iowa supporter got ten years for reprinting some of his editorials.[14]

Watson returned to the newspaper business after the armistice and renewed his attacks on Wilson, demanding the repeal of wartime restrictions on freedom of speech and the press, and clemency for victims of the Espionage Act. He praised Debs as a patriot who was about to be imprisoned for exercising his democratic right to free speech. Making a comparison that was no doubt unwelcome by Debs, Watson classed him with two other "illustrious" American prisoners of conscience, the Confederate leaders Alexander Stephens and Jefferson Davis. "If such as he are to be buried alive," Watson fumed, while the "turbid reptiles" of the Wilson administration "ride the Universe, it is time to ask God how he can stand such enormities."[15]

Unlike Watson, Debs felt surprisingly little malice toward the president. Even as he faced prison, Debs thought that "Wilson has a vision. . . . There is some light on his social horizon, however much it may be obscured by the clouds that hover over and around him." Still in Paris, Wilson had answered every appeal for a pardon with silence, but Debs did not blame him for his administration's "repressive measures." As he put it, "There are tremendous forces behind the President, or before him, I don't know which, that won't let him be free."[16]

While Wilson said nothing, the vast majority of America's opinion leaders stood firm against Debs. Public opinion on such matters is hard to gauge, particularly before the days of scientific polling, but the unflagging support for citizen patriotic leagues, the spread of new state laws against sedition, continued mob attacks on radicals, and the bulk of letters sent to Washington on the matter all suggest that most Americans in the spring of 1919 thought of Debs not as the victim of capitalist persecution but as a traitor who was finally getting his due. Debs expected nothing different from those he called "the hirelings of the master class, such as politicians, pulpiteers and editorial scribblers." What stung him, and shocked many of his radical friends, was the indifference, even the antagonism, of the great majority of American workers. "I did not think that [Debs] would go to prison," Mabel Curry confessed to Rose Pastor Stokes as she prepared to see her lover depart. "Are the workers going to let their greatest leader rot in jail? Damn Gompers and his whole cowardly crew!"[17]

While Debs dreamed that the stresses of the war might radicalize the working class in America, as indeed it had in some circles, the conflict arguably had the opposite effect on the mass of American workers. Most were patriotic, willing to fight their bosses over hours and wages but uninterested in toppling the social order. In the heat of a rally, some of the more radical might applaud John Reed's call to storm the penitentiary, but most had no intention of actually "going over the top" for Debs or throwing themselves on a Brooklyn barricade. When radicals vowed a general strike if Debs went to jail, the *Washington Post* could safely dismiss such threats as "the veriest rot," the delusion of an "acute attack of megalomania."[18]

The only glimmer of physical confrontation came in Toledo, where radicals organized a protest rally on March 30, urging workers to hear Debs's last speech before he was sent to "an American Hell-hole for ten years." Posters called workers to prepare for a general strike, in order to "break down the iron bars that will enclose our 'Gene.'" Six thousand people showed up that afternoon to hear Debs, only to be told that the mayor had ordered the city's Memorial Hall closed. Chanting "To hell with the mayor!" the crowd smashed windows and doors, while one man climbed a monument and goaded them to take the hall, even if they had "to wade through blood" to do it. For several hours three hundred policemen chased, clubbed, and arrested the demonstrators, while the mayor proclaimed his city permanently closed to speakers with "radical tendencies." Through it all, Debs was not even in town. Again feeling ill, he had gone home to Terre Haute to await the government's order to turn himself in.[19]

On the morning of April 12, prosecutor Wertz phoned Debs, ordering him to report to Cleveland as soon as possible. Debs spent much of this last day of freedom with his wife Kate, his brother Theodore, and the rest of the family, interrupted by a stream of neighbors stopping in to wish an awkward farewell. Throughout the day, messengers brought telegrams from comrades around the country, and bouquets that Kate Debs piled in their back room. David Karsner arrived that afternoon to cover the story for the *New York Call.* As he sat taking notes in what he thought of as "sacred premises," he felt sure that this day would be re-membered as "the greatest single incident in the history of the Ameri-can labor movement."[20]

Karsner strained to capture every detail for his readers, and for posterity. The leaves, he noted, were just budding that afternoon. A gardener turned the soil in the backyard, preparing the ground for Mrs. Debs's roses. She occupied herself with various small preparations, while Debs praised her courage. Never very enthusiastic about her hus-band's radicalism, Kate did not share his views on the war, but she never made these doubts public. "She has stood shoulder to shoulder with me through every storm," Debs told Karsner, "and she is standing firm now." Kate's mother was less stoic, weeping softly until she was com-forted by her son-in-law. "It's all right, mother," Debs assured her as he patted her cheek. "It will come out all right in the end."[21]

Karsner was enthralled, but to avoid intruding on the family's last hours together he excused himself and took a stroll around town. Ten months earlier, John Reed thought Debs's neighbors were hostile to the traitor in their midst, but Karsner found that the working-class prophet was not without honor in his hometown. "Everybody in Terre Haute loves Debs," a local editor told him, though he estimated that no more than five in a hundred had any use for socialism. As a man in a nearby saloon put it, Debs had "some cranky notions in his head." After a slow gulp of beer, the man added that he wanted Debs to be sent to jail, but just for a single day, long enough to prove that "the law is bigger than he is." "Do you know," Karsner predicted to another old man chomping a cigar on Wabash Avenue, "some day Terre Haute will honor itself by erecting a huge monument to the memory of Debs?" The man was skeptical. Though he had nothing to say against Debs, he told the young visitor from New York that the town "ain't much on monuments."[22]

That afternoon the Debs brothers stopped by their office, where Eugene rendezvoused with Mabel Curry. As Theodore left them alone, the two embraced, perhaps for the last time. "We faced our fate," Curry confided to Rose Stokes. "There never was a more marvelous drama on the stage of life." Their parting hurt Curry terribly—much more, she felt, than the prim and stoic Kate Debs was suffering. "Yes, Rose, my heart is breaking. . . . It is all within and its power and passion almost rends my soul."

Curry longed to declare her love for Debs openly, to break the bonds of social convention just as he dreamed of liberating workers from the chains of capitalism. But Debs and Theodore both urged her not to "smash anything." "His wife and my husband cannot be hurt and humiliated for the sake of our happiness," Curry explained to Stokes. The world was maddened by war and on the brink of red revolution; her lover and confidant was on his way to jail and she might never see him again. And still Curry was forced to suffer in silence and observe Victorian proprieties. "Can't you see how desperate I am?" she exclaimed. "I've gotten to hating the 'respectable' people with whom I associate."

A couple hundred friends met Debs that evening as he walked to the station to catch the train to Cleveland. They gave him "three cheers" and pressed around him for a last hug or handshake. As the train pulled out Debs continued to wave and tossed a kiss to his wife. Mabel Curry was unable to face the scene. In the past, whenever Debs left town, the two shared a secret signal, waving farewells as his train passed the crossing by her house. On this night she could not bear that sight. Instead she roamed aimlessly in a remote part of town, as far as possible from the train that carried Debs away.[23]

✿　　✿　　✿

On the overnight trip to Cleveland, Debs traveled with his brother-in-law Arthur Bauer, and with Karsner, whom Debs affectionately called "Davy." They sat in the club car till midnight, as Debs smoked cigars and told tales of his decades on the road. Karsner asked him what he thought about a proposal Scott Nearing had recently made at a meeting in New York, that the party should nominate Debs for his fifth run for the presidency in 1920. "There is better timber in the woods than I," Debs demurred, though Karsner clearly remained keen on the idea. More than once Debs called on the reporter to take dictation, so that he might relay through the *New York Call* a parting message to the comrades. "I shall be in prison in the days to come," he said as his young disciple scribbled, "but my revolutionary spirit will be abroad and I shall not be inactive. Let us all in this supreme hour measure up to our full stature and work as one for the great cause that means emancipation for us all." As the train rolled through the dark toward Cleveland, both men had their eye on a loftier destination.

When Debs got off the train the following morning, the streets were plastered with posters, printed in revolutionary red, calling workers to a rally for Debs that afternoon. Eager to get their prisoner out of town before thousands of angry radicals gathered in the city's "Free Speech Park," the federal marshal took some procedural shortcuts to hurry things along, ignoring Karsner's bellowed protest that they were "kidnapping" their prisoner. They put Debs in their automobile to drive him to the train station, while Karsner and three other comrades followed in a separate car. Along the way, the marshals did their best to shake them. As Debs bounced in the back, they careened wildly down city streets, ignoring even the frantic gestures of traffic cops. Desperate not to lose him, his friends followed close behind, though it meant "sometimes scratching the paint off moving trolleys and brushing other speeding automobiles." The guards in the lead car slowed only once, along Euclid Avenue, to point out Rockefeller's mansion and the house of reform governor Tom Johnson. This strange "mad race" ended an hour later, at a small rail station on the edge of town, where, to the marshal's evident disappointment, Karsner and Bauer insisted that they would ride with Debs all the way to the gates of Moundsville Prison.

As the train rolled across northern Ohio toward Youngstown, the

Eugene V. Debs, taken into custody in Cleveland.
Debs Collection, Indiana State University Library.

guards explained that they were taking the long road to West Virginia that day. Skirting major cities, they would use a series of regional trolleys, changing cars eight times in backwater towns like Leetonia, East Liverpool, and Steubenville. Though Debs joked that he did not mind the longer trip since he had nothing but time, Karsner seethed. Expecting to travel the central corridor through Ohio's industrial towns, he had planned to telegraph ahead so that Socialists could "organize speedy demonstrations at every city and town on the road." Now, instead of blazing a triumphant martyr's trail to prison, Debs would spend long hours hopping from one trolley to another, unknown to the picnickers and other Sunday travelers they met along the route.[24]

The 150-mile trip was grueling. Though Debs began the day in high spirits, hours of rocking across Ohio took their toll. By the afternoon he grew grim, his shoulders drooping, and finally he began to nod off. Karsner was deeply moved by the sight of "the sad and sleeping figure . . . with head bent on his bosom, his great frame cramped in a straw trolley seat." The unflinching revolutionist was also a tired old man, denied not only his freedom but also some of his dignity. "Life's grayest shadows hold no sadder picture than this," Karsner thought as he photographed the sight for his paper.[25]

After a stop in Wheeling, where Debs bolted a quick dinner of pork chops and coffee, the group made the last leg of the journey, arriving in Moundsville at ten o'clock that night. Debs insisted on carrying his own suitcase as they walked toward the massive dark turrets of the old state prison. Drawing near, they heard the muffled voices of prisoners within and saw the strange patterns of light streaming through iron bars. With little further ceremony, Debs entered the turnstile and began to serve his ten-year sentence. Karsner and Bauer would return the following morning to take their final leave. Meanwhile, Karsner went to find a telegraph so he could call in one final statement that Debs wanted to send to his comrades around the country, jotted on the back of an envelope that afternoon as they rumbled across Ohio: "I enter the prison doors a flaming revolutionist—my head erect, my spirit untamed and my soul unconquerable."[26]

Many of Debs's friends across the country felt impotent rage when they learned from Karsner's reports that the government had actually gone through with its threat to put their beloved leader behind bars. This was, in their minds, an unthinkable act of state tyranny. While Socialists had long argued that the power structure of American society was tilted in favor of the master class, most still retained a deep respect for America's democratic institutions, and they felt betrayed.

They also noted with bitter irony that America's workers had done

DEBS GOES TO PRISON

BY DAVID KARSNER

Published by
IRVING KAYE DAVIS & CO.
42 WEST 28TH STREET, NEW YORK

David Karsner, *Debs Goes to Prison.*
Courtesy of Debs Collection, Indiana State University Library.

nothing to come to his aid. Those for whom he had worked all his life, the million who had voted for him and the many more who admired him, had all been cowed into what one union organizer called a "terrible silence." "But will that silence continue?" he challenged his fellow laborers. "If they remain silent and do nothing for the liberation of Debs it will be the greatest triumph of reaction and a death blow to everything that is progressive." This writer predicted that the country would soon "ring with protests."[27]

There is little evidence, however, that in the spring of 1919 the majority of Americans were troubled by the news that Debs had gone to jail. Radicals often claimed that workers had been cowed into silence, that they opposed the government's decision but were afraid to speak out for fear that they might also be arrested. More likely, most who gave the matter any thought believed that Debs was being justly punished for betraying his country at a perilous moment. Since no paper had dared to publish the Canton speech, few could have known what Debs had actually said that day. But most no doubt accepted the government's argument that in times of national emergency, the demands of national security were more important than the individual's right to free speech.

However, as Debs entered the penitentiary in April 1919, the signs of an emerging national debate over Wilson's wartime policies on free speech were already evident. Civil libertarians were gathering information on wartime prosecutions, writing legal briefs and organizing the first of many public demonstrations. The Supreme Court upheld the Espionage Act, but other legal scholars had begun to publish challenges to Oliver Wendell Holmes's reading of the First Amendment. While most mainstream newspapers bade Debs good riddance, some of Wilson's most influential liberal and socialist allies pressed for clemency and were losing patience with their president. And a small but growing number of citizens, radical labor unions, and liberal civic groups looked for new ways to register their concern about the war's legacy of repression. Despite the differences in their ideas about the nature and limits of free speech, they would eventually unite behind the goal of winning freedom for Debs and the other imprisoned war dissenters. With growing momentum, this "amnesty" movement would soon engage millions of Americans in a broad national debate about the government's wartime speech policies.

As Debs put it, "great issues are not decided by the courts, but by the people." Rolling across Ohio on his way to prison, he assured Karsner that "the final resort is the people, and that court will be heard from in due time."[28]

Chapter 8

Moundsville

Though Debs entered the prison gates proclaiming himself a "flaming revolutionist," once inside he faced a warden who was determined not to let his institution become a "showcase" for socialism. "The Soviets might be all right in Russia," Joseph Terrell warned Debs, "but in Moundsville I am the supreme dictator."[1]

Terrell, a genial southerner in his mid-forties, felt little sympathy for Debs's radical politics. Back in 1894 he had been working as an apprentice telegraph operator when Debs gained notoriety as the leader of the Pullman strike. While most of his fellow workers praised Debs, Terrell told them that "the best and quickest way to end that strike" would be to hang its leader. Through a twist of fate, twenty-five years later Debs had become the warden's "most famous boarder." "If you want to get along here and be treated like a man," Terrell told him, "do exactly what I tell you to do and you will have no trouble." He made Debs promise not to preach socialism to his fellow prisoners. "Warden, your every order and wish will be obeyed by me to the letter," Debs assured him.[2]

Terrell was charmed by the old radical's warm personality, so different from the angry agitator he had read about in the nation's editorial pages. Escorting Debs to his cell that night, he thought about another famous political prisoner, the Confederacy's Jefferson Davis. Growing up in Virginia, Terrell heard stories about the way the South's once-proud president had been humiliated by Union troops, manacled in irons in a federal "dungeon." Thinking of Debs as another fallen icon of a "failed revolution," Terrell resolved not to repeat that mistake.[3]

The warden had strategic as well as sentimental motives for treating Debs with kindness. As David Karsner's hovering presence at the prison gate made clear, America's radicals would be watching for any sign that their leader was being mistreated. Federal authorities had given Terrell no special guidance about how to handle Debs, but the warden decided on his own not to do anything that might further antagonize his supporters. The next morning, after Debs had been fitted for an especially long suit of prison gray, he was called to the warden's office. There Terrell assured him, "As far as I can conscientiously go I will see that you are treated like a man and not as a criminal because I know you are not in the latter class."[4]

Though a prison physical revealed that Debs had a bad heart, he told Terrell that he wanted no special favors and would do any job assigned to him, "even to scrubbing floors." The warden gave him light duties in the prison hospital, where he could "lend a hand when he felt like it." He also arranged for Debs to have his own small private room there. Its unbarred windows overlooked the prison's landscaped courtyard, where he could stroll and smoke his pipe, enjoying the fountain and flowers.

Debs was grateful, and wrote to assure his anxious brother that the facilities were more comfortable than many hotels. Warden Terrell was a "gentleman in the true sense of that term," Debs thought. "I was never treated more considerately in my life." When Kate Debs visited a few weeks later, she too was relieved to find that the warden treated her "like a lady." Back home in Terre Haute some of her neighbors now regarded her as "the consort of a criminal," a slight that stung the prim wife of America's celebrity prisoner. Terrell granted her extra visiting privileges and invited her to stay with his family while she was in town.[5]

Kate was pleased to find her husband looking rested and healthy. In fact, Debs found the first months in prison to be invigorating, and even inspiring. After years of stressful work and months of anxiety during the war and his own trial, enforced isolation now gave him a rare chance to rest and reflect. He assured his friends that "prison is just now my part, and I'm taking it just as calmly and serenely as if it were staged in some delightful retreat for my special delectation." He even enjoyed the food, which Terrell let him take in his own room instead of the common mess hall, and he soon gained over ten pounds.[6]

Just as Terrell had intended, this kind treatment robbed Karsner's dispatches of some of their sting. Still, the young reporter did his best to keep Socialist indignation at a boil. The great Debs had fallen into the hands of a bourgeois do-gooder, Karsner suggested, a clean-cut and "typical" politician who treated the prisoner kindly because he feared the smoldering wrath of American radicals. When Debs read Karsner's stories, he asked his friend to go easier on the warden. Debs had been at Moundsville long enough to appreciate not only his own treatment but also the various reforms that Terrell had introduced to improve the lives of the other prisoners. "He occupies a very trying and difficult position," he told Karsner, "and my being here under the circumstances does not make things any easier for him."[7]

Soon Karsner was also disarmed by the warden's geniality. Determined not to "put Debs on exhibition or permit him to be paraded through the newspapers every day," the warden denied access to most journalists. He made an exception, though, for Karsner, on the grounds that, in addition to being a reporter, he served as a liaison between Debs and his family and friends. While Terrell thought that Karsner was a bit excitable and his reports on Debs more "imaginative" than accurate, he decided that the chain-smoking journalist was otherwise a "square shooter." He complained only when Karsner published a story that misspelled his daughter's name. "While I am always in a forgiving mood," he kidded the earnest young reporter, "I doubt if I can ever forget it. . . . If I thought I could get any justice in these plutocratic courts you write so much about, I would sue you for damages."[8]

Karsner did all he could to make sure Debs was not forgotten behind bars. The *Call* published regular excerpts from Debs's published writings. The headlines proclaimed, "Though Behind Bars Debs Speaks," sending federal authorities scrambling to make sure Debs was not leaking new statements to the press. Karsner also produced a stream of profiles and news items about "Our Gene" and a hastily assembled pamphlet telling the story of Debs's trolley ride to prison. As these reports spread across the country, Moundsville became a mecca for radi-

cals in the early summer of 1919. One afternoon a troop of fifty socialists from a nearby town marched on the prison to pay tribute to their
leader, while Rose Pastor Stokes told Debs that a young woman she
knew was painstakingly saving her pennies for train fare to West Virginia. Terrell at first suspended the usual prison regulations regarding
visitors but soon found he had to limit Debs's company to family and
close friends.[9]

Mabel Curry came to see the man she described to Stokes as her
"*great great* lover." Perhaps sensing that she was not just another emissary from the Socialist Party, the warden urged her to stay an extra day,
and broke another prison rule by giving the couple almost an hour
alone. As they embraced in the warden's office, Debs told her that God
must have put the idea in the warden's mind, "for he knew he would
have gone mad if he had not seen me alone." While Curry also found
Debs looking fit and rested, the sight of him in prison was a shock. She
went back to her hotel room and "vomited as if I had been poisoned."[10]

One evening the warden allowed another, quite different visitor to
see Debs, a prominent local businessman eager to match wits with
Debs over "property ownership and the rights of labor." After several
hours in Debs's room, the man left that evening exhilarated but discon-
certed. "You know," he told the warden as they walked out, "I would be
afraid to talk with Debs very much for fear he might convert me."
Terrel agreed that Debs had an uncanny ability to wrap his strange
ideas in "the most wonderful flow of language to which I had ever listened."[11]

Prison offered certain mind-expanding experiences for Debs as well.
For decades he had been preaching about the problem of crime. Criminals were not evil, he had argued, but were the victims of social conditions created by capitalism. Always a champion of the underdog, Debs
now lived among some of society's most disenfranchised men. "I belong
in prison," he told Karsner. "I belong where men are made to suffer for
the wrongs committed against them by a brutalizing system." Though
Debs had promised the warden he would not talk socialism to other
inmates, he spoke through the power of practical example. From across
the country hundreds of well-wishers sent him presents—flowers,
cakes, books, and boxes of fruit. Keeping little for himself, he spread

these gifts among the other inmates, white and black, who were delighted to be "smoking high grade cigars and eating choice candy, the
like of which they had never before tasted." Debs also forced fine cigars
on the warden and sent special boxes of candy to his daughter. Some of
the most hardened convicts still suspected that Debs was some kind of
"schemer and palaverer," but most were won over by his kindness. Sitting on the hospital porch in the evenings, he was surrounded by men
who wanted his advice and sympathy, or his help writing letters home.
With growing admiration, the warden conceded that Debs was one of
the few men he had ever known who "practiced absolutely what he
preached."[12]

On Easter Sunday 1919, Debs joined his fellow prisoners for a worship service in the chapel. Over the years he had often professed his admiration for Jesus. The "tramp of Galilee," as he called him, was the
first and greatest social revolutionary and friend of the poor. He balanced his respect for Jesus, however, with contempt for most forms of
Christianity and had not set foot in a church in years. Debs felt profoundly moved by that Easter service in Moundsville, however. "In the
very midst of all their sorrows and their miseries," he found, "there was
a wonderful spirit that shone in the faces of all the prisoners. I would
not have missed this experience for anything in the world." In his small
monastic room, Debs hung a portrait of Jesus cut from a magazine.

In Moundsville, Debs also felt close to one of his patron saints, the
militant abolitionist John Brown. Over the years Debs had collected
newspaper articles about Brown, and he once made a pilgrimage to
Harper's Ferry, the site of Brown's bungled slave insurrection. Unlike
most white Americans, who shared Woodrow Wilson's view that Brown
had been "fanatical almost to the point of madness," Debs saw the old
abolitionist as a kindred spirit in the long fight for human liberation.
Now fate had delivered Debs to a West Virginia cell not far from the
one where Brown spent his last days and finally gave his life for the
cause of emancipation. Debs and Karsner swapped stories about Brown,
and Debs showed his friend two prized possessions he had brought with
him to prison—a candle and button that had once belonged to Brown,
holy relics of American radicalism.[13]

Debs's friends and admirers joined him in searching for solace in the lessons of history. In the countless letters, telegrams, and poems that poured in for Debs each day, they drew analogies between his imprisonment and the noble sacrifices of history's great revolutionaries. Many compared Debs's suffering to the martyrdom of Christ, no doubt reinforcing his own attempt to find some comfort in that quarter. Another admirer offered a "dream picture" in which the ghost of Lincoln passed on the title "Emancipator" to Debs. Others fanned out across the pages of history for appropriate comparisons; he was, they said, just like William Lloyd Garrison, or Galileo, or Savanarola. In the face of a stunning setback, Debs and his friends hungered for evidence that personal defeat was only a prelude to historical triumph for those who stood by their principles.[14]

Almost as soon as Debs had arrived, prison censors struggled to keep up with the sheer volume of his mail, often more than a hundred letters and packages a day. Warden Terrell solved the problem with characteristic generosity. The censors opened all letters, but only a small fraction were reviewed, and by the warden himself. Most passed to Debs without the usual supervision. In return, Debs agreed to burn most of his mail after reading it.

According to prison rules, Debs was allowed to send only one personal letter a week, with no mention of politics. But Terrell let him forward bundles of his mail to Theodore, with the brief outlines of a reply jotted in the margins of each letter. Back in the Terre Haute office, Theodore and Mabel Curry labored long hours typing these scribbled comments into full letters. By this cumbersome indirect route, Debs maintained a connection with his many friends and admirers in the outside world. He thanked Helen Keller for her public tribute to him, praising her as "the incarnation of the revolutionary spirit." He urged Upton Sinclair to continue his push for an amnesty for wartime prisoners. He also sent short cryptic love letters to Curry. While they could not write openly to each other because of the censor, they worked out code names that gave them a bit more freedom from prying eyes. In a strange twist, Debs adopted the identity of "Mrs. Wilson."[15]

When Terrell dipped into some of the letters Debs was receiving, he found them to be fascinating reading, and with permission kept some for souvenirs. The warden was both amused and alarmed by the various

"cranks" who wrote to assure Debs that an army of radical workers
would soon arrive to liberate him. In the first few days after Debs arrived, he considered withholding the most "inflammatory" letters, but
soon concluded that Debs was a peaceful man who wanted no part of
such schemes. Still, as a precaution he hired more guards and mounted
new floodlights on the prison walls, dispelling the shadows where quixotic revolutionaries might gather in the night.[16]

A raid on Moundsville never materialized, but violence broke out elsewhere in the country, much of it sparked by more than three thousand
labor strikes that rocked the country in 1919. Tensions between labor
and capital had been muted during the war, thanks to rising wages and
government mediation designed to prevent disruptions in military production. All of that changed in the months after the armistice. Dropping its brief flirtation with "wartime socialism," the Wilson administration withdrew its support for organized labor just as the country faced
the postwar problems of economic recession, rising prices, and the return of millions of soldiers into the labor force. At the same time, many
industrialists were determined to roll back the advances won by unions
during the war. In thousands of shops and factories across the country,
workers fought wage cuts while employers demanded a return to the
"open shop." In Seattle, sixty thousand workers crippled the city in
a five-day general strike that Mayor Ole Hanson put down only by calling in federal troops. Bostonians feared criminal anarchy when their
police force went on strike in September. That same month 350,000
steelworkers also struck, prompting violence that brought federal
troops into Gary, Indiana. And that fall coal miners threatened to paralyze the national economy by walking off their jobs, a strike that was
smashed when Attorney General Palmer invoked the government's wartime powers and won a sweeping federal injunction against the United
Mine Workers.[17]

In each of these conflicts, politicians, capitalists, and newspaper editors claimed that workers had been provoked, not by rising prices and
unfair labor conditions, but by the seductions of Bolshevist agitators.
Faced with the worst year of labor violence in the nation's history, many
Americans feared that the threat of German militarism had been re-

placed by something even worse, the "red menace" of a worldwide communist revolution. That spring Lenin and his followers had promised just that. As Allied troops withdrew from Russia and the Bolsheviks consolidated power, they called thirty-nine revolutionary parties to meet in Moscow for an international summit, in order to prepare for the "final battle" against "the imperial conspiracy of Capital." The manifesto issued by this Third International called on radical workers around the world to arm themselves immediately and begin the "annihilation of the enemy's apparatus of government." A communist uprising across Europe not only was inevitable, the group proclaimed, but would arrive in a matter of weeks. Communist victories in Hungary and Germany that year seemed to confirm this prediction.[18]

Lenin conceded, however, that Americans lagged behind on the path toward proletarian revolution. On this point historians agree, concluding that radicals played a minimal role in organizing the labor unrest that gripped the country in 1919. The beleaguered Socialist Party had limited influence in most of the labor movement. The IWW fared better in this regard, but wartime persecutions had shattered their movement and sent most of their leaders to jail. Pockets of radicalism survived; however, as one socialist put it, the vast majority of unions remained "conservative to the bone." Following the lead of Gompers and his allies in the AFL, most American workers were as eager to fight communism as they were to battle their bosses for higher wages and shorter hours.[19]

While American radicals could take little credit for the labor militancy that spread across the country in 1919, they welcomed these conflicts as a rare opportunity to encourage the spirit of revolt in the American working class. At this volatile moment, when workers clashed with soldiers and police, and the government showed its true colors by smashing strikes with troops and injunctions, radicals believed that workers were on the verge of demanding revolutionary change. Surveying events from the Socialist Party headquarters, Adolph Germer assured Debs that "enough hell will break loose in the next year or so to tear the prison bars open and liberate those who have fallen victim of the war insanity." Encouraged by the working-class unrest at home and abroad, many Socialists believed that the campaign to free Debs had the potential to become "the rallying spirit of the social-revolution." Toward that end, Socialists announced plans for massive demonstrations across the country on May Day 1919, protests that would make clear that the struggle to free Debs was part of a wider war against capitalism.[20]

As May Day approached, tensions mounted when the government intercepted thirty-six bombs that had been mailed to industrialists and key figures in the federal government, each one packed with enough dynamite to "blow a man to pieces." Only one went off, in the hands of a Georgia senator's maid. The intended victims of these "infernal machines" included Postmaster Burleson, Attorney General Palmer, and Justice Oliver Wendell Holmes; the last, some papers pointed out, had recently sent Debs to prison, a connection that seemed to implicate Debs in a shocking conspiracy to "spread terror throughout the country." While police never found the culprit, the *Washington Post* blamed the plot on "criminal talk, indulged in the guise of free speech."[21]

In this charged atmosphere, radicals gathered in cities across the country on May Day, demanding the release of Debs, Tom Mooney, and the rest of the "class war prisoners." At many of these meetings, organizers read from the speeches of their jailed comrades, reserving the grand finale for Debs. Though Debs was shut behind prison walls, in city squares and meeting halls across the country he was cheered by crowds who roared their approval as they heard once again his bitter denunciations of the Supreme Court and his lavish praise for the Bolsheviks.

Many town and city governments banned these meetings. In others, vigilante mobs did their best to stifle them. A "furious street battle" erupted in Boston when police and soldiers tried to stop radicals from marching behind a red flag. Several policemen were shot or stabbed, scores of marchers were "badly beaten," and more than a hundred were arrested. In New York, seventeen hundred policemen battled soldiers who were trying to smash a May Day concert at Madison Square Garden. Four hundred soldiers and sailors had better luck finding a defenseless target across town. They stormed the offices of the *New York Call* and scattered the families who had gathered there not to demand the release of Debs but to celebrate the grand opening of the paper's new facilities. "The men were beaten in a manner beyond description," a bystander reported. "Blood flowed freely, and the crying and shrieking was horrible." In the Bronx, police broke up an amnesty parade and arrested its leader, a man who wore a scarlet hat band that read "Free Political Prisoners." Soapboxers in Brooklyn railed against Judge Westenhaver and paraded behind a banner demanding "Freedom for Our Comrade, Eugene Debs."

The worst violence of the day broke out in Cleveland, when marchers resisted attempts by soldiers to wrench red flags from their hands. Dozens of shots were fired as police, vigilantes, and radicals waged a ragged nine-hour street fight. Two were killed and hundreds were injured, including many policemen. The crowd finally scattered when charged by army tanks. The party's Cleveland headquarters was "totally wrecked," one paper reported, "by angry civilians bent on putting an end to the demonstration."

Around the country, observers drew different morals from the day that the *Liberator* described as the Socialist Party's "baptism of blood." Ignoring the fact that radicals had not instigated most of the violence, many editors interpreted the riots as further evidence that the Soviet menace had arrived on American shores. The *Christian Science Monitor* charged that the protestors were "working frankly for . . . the overthrow of present forms of government." The *Washington Post* agreed and called on the government to deport "undesirable aliens" and to draw a more cautious line "between free speech and treason." "Otherwise," the paper concluded, "we may as well invite [Lenin and Trotsky] to come here and set up business at once." A senate committee that had been investigating German propaganda now turned its attention to exposing the agents of Bolshevism in America; in addition to Eugene Debs and other quite predictable suspects, the committee pointed a finger at Jane Addams, Oswald Garrison Villard, Roger Baldwin, Gilbert Roe, and others who worked for peace and civil liberties organizations. Congressmen criticized the Wilson administration for not being tougher on radicals, and announced plans to pass new legislation that would give the government more power to deport alien radicals and punish seditious talk.[22]

As the country plunged into what historians now call the "Red Scare," extremists on the left and the right provoked each other, stirring passions that undermined any hope for restoring civil discourse after the armistice. Embittered by their wartime experience, some on the left believed that they were in a death struggle against reactionaries who had dropped all pretense of respect for democratic rights. Fighting back with militant threats and street protests, the radicals only confirmed the patriots' suspicion that the country faced the danger of a violent insurrection. Occupying a shrinking middle ground, a number of liberals and pro-war socialists tried to break this cycle of fear and recrimination. The country faced no serious threat from left-wing revolutionaries, they insisted. The public's growing anxiety about Bolshevism was being fueled by false charges, spread by business interests who hoped to use this red-baiting to discredit all progressive movements, treating all forms of protest and demands for reform as symptoms of a mythical Bolshevist conspiracy. Further, the liberals argued that if America did face mounting revolutionary pressure in 1919, the surest way to deflate it would be to respect the speech rights of radicals and release those convicted under the wartime laws. Leaving them in jail, they warned, was only making a volatile situation worse, giving radicals a good reason to take to the streets. In this way, the national debate over Debs and his fellow prisoners became entwined with the new struggle over the threat of communist revolution.[23]

During the war, many of the president's friends on the left had misgivings about the erosion of First Amendment freedoms. A few protested to the president, but most remained silent, accepting this as a necessary evil in a time of national emergency. John Dewey explained this with an odd analogy that made sense to many at the time: if the government had a right to ask citizens to ration their use of staples like meat, sugar, and gasoline, then it only made sense that Americans should be prepared to give up a portion of their free speech rights as well. If the government seemed overzealous in its attempts to jail speakers and silence newspapers, the president's progressive supporters blamed these abuses on his less high-minded subordinates. Wilson, they assumed, regretted these as necessary evils in wartime and would move quickly to correct the problem once the war ended.[24]

After the armistice, however, the president spent most of the next six months in Europe, preoccupied with peace negotiations and out of touch with domestic developments. When he returned to America in the "red" summer of 1919, many liberals and pro-war Socialists believed that the time had come for him to assert leadership on this issue, acting decisively to restore civil liberties.

Clarence Darrow was among those trying to sway Wilson. The nation's most famous lawyer not only had supported the war but had defended the government's decision to jail dissenters. In 1917 he told audiences across the country that a nation fighting for its survival cannot afford to tolerate those who give comfort to the enemy, no matter how pure their motives. As he put it, "times of war are not times of sanity and cannot be." Once peace returned, Darrow felt sure that the friends of free speech would insist that "all the old protections and safeguards remain secure." In this, the famous cynic showed a remarkable innocence.

By the summer of 1919 Darrow began to worry that Wilson was not moving quickly enough to restore those freedoms. He wrote to the president, explaining that he had a "deep affection" for Debs ever since he had defended him during the Pullman strike. Darrow conceded that while the nation was at war the government had a "stern duty" to silence anyone who stood in the way of the government's prosecution of the war. The "law of self-preservation," as he put it, always trumped the Constitution. But Darrow tried to convince Wilson that once peace returned, so should the First Amendment. "I am most anxious that this Government, which has always tolerated differences and upheld the freedom of thought and speech, should show that stern measures were only used for self-protection and that it has acted without malice or hatred and is willing and anxious not only to be just, but forgiving."[25]

Such a grand gesture of national reconciliation appealed to the president. On the day he left France to return home, Wilson cabled to his secretary Tumulty, announcing, "It is my desire to grant complete amnesty and pardon to all American citizens in prison or under arrest on account of anything they have said in speech or in print concerning their personal opinions with regard to the activities of the Government of the United States during the period of the war. It seems to me that this would be not only a generous act but a just act to accompany the signing of the peace." As he prepared to sell the controversial Versailles Treaty to the American people, Wilson seemed to think that this pardon would be not only "generous" but politically prudent.[26]

Attorney General Palmer immediately sent a return telegram to Wilson, urging him to say nothing more about a pardon until the two had a chance to consult. Wilson agreed and, once he had returned to Washington, Palmer laid out the case against issuing a general amnesty for wartime dissenters. In spite of the fact that his own assistants now admitted that many convictions under the Espionage Act were unjustified, Palmer insisted that no American had been sent to jail for "mere expression of opinion." Rather, they were being punished for "obstructing the war." A unanimous Supreme Court, he reminded the president, rejected the First Amendment claims of Debs and the other Espionage Act defendants.[27]

Palmer also argued that a general amnesty would plunge the Justice Department into a thicket of legal complexities. How would prison wardens know just who the president intended to pardon? If he declared amnesty for all those who had been punished merely for expressing "opinions," as the president had suggested, none would agree about who qualified. If the pardon extended to all those convicted under the Espionage Act, actual bombers and the merely bombastic would go free together. Better, Palmer believed, to decide each case on its own merits, something that the Justice Department had been doing for months. Hundreds of sentences had already been commuted, he reminded the president, and more recommendations for pardon were on the way.[28]

For Palmer, the Debs case posed a unique challenge. He had no doubt that Debs deserved to be in prison. The man had proudly confessed, after all, and though his voice was now muffled behind prison walls, the world still heard enough to know that he remained as defiant as ever. Palmer conceded that his ten-year sentence was excessive and should be commuted at an appropriate time. But in the summer of 1919 he believed that freeing Debs would be a terrible political mistake, one that would only give comfort to Wilson's enemies on both sides of the political spectrum. Radicals would be emboldened; conservatives would denounce the administration for not being tough enough against the Bolshevists.

In the months after the May Day riots, the public fear of revolution-ary radicalism had only grown. On the evening of June 2, unknown conspirators set off eight explosions across the country, including one that smashed the front of the attorney general's house, spreading grisly scraps of the bomber over an entire block. Palmer's office warned the country that more bomb attacks were imminent as part of a conspiracy to "destroy the government at one fell swoop." While he had taken a comparatively liberal approach to the radical threat up to that point, Palmer now yielded to mounting public pressure to crack down. Sup-ported by a large appropriation from Congress, he appointed J. Edgar Hoover to head a new bureau to spy on radicals.[29]

In the midst of a sweeping national panic over the dangers of radical-ism, Palmer reasoned that the public would see a Debs pardon not as a grand gesture of presidential generosity but as a capitulation to the threat of terrorism. America's bomb throwers and street fighters would gloat, thinking that their violent tactics had succeeded. Conservatives, on the other hand, would regard the decision as further proof of their charge that the Wilson administration had been too soft on radicals. Al-ready looking ahead to the race for the Democratic nomination in 1920, Palmer decided that an amnesty proclamation might please a small co-alition of liberals but would outrage a much larger number of Ameri-cans who believed that Debs deserved everything he got, and more.[30]

It is not clear which of these arguments Wilson found most compel-ling, but he agreed to set aside the amnesty question until after the pressing matter of the peace treaty was resolved. The president was also distracted by serious health problems that summer, symptoms of an im-pending stroke that had plagued him for months. Ignoring the amnesty question in his public statements, the president focused all the energy he could muster on a futile attempt to rally Senate support for his treaty and some halfhearted measures to resolve the postwar economic prob-lems of rising prices, labor strikes, and food profiteering.[31]

The amnesty question would not die, however, as many of Wilson's old allies on the left grew impatient with his delay. In the pages of the *Nation,* Villard now scolded the man he had once embraced as a politi-cal soul mate. "What is wrong with Mr. Wilson that he appears so de-void of the magnanimity which should be inseparable from the just and the truly great man?" Villard fumed. "It is, or ought to be, a humiliation

to every American that there should be such a thing as a political prisoner in America." Because Villard had opposed the war and attacked
the treaty as unjust, Wilson now felt nothing but contempt for the liberal editor. In turn, Villard told his audiences that the president had apparently never drunk enough of "the milk of human kindness."[32]

The National Civil Liberties Bureau (NCLB) tried a more tactful approach. Speaking through John Nevin Sayre, a trusted relative of the
president, the group sent Wilson a detailed brief in favor of a general
amnesty. Like Darrow, these civil libertarians argued that the Espionage Act had been an emergency wartime measure and that further
punishment served no useful purpose. Contradicting Palmer, they insisted that most of those convicted *had* been punished for "expressions
of opinion, rather than overt acts." Because the law had been vaguely
written and inconsistently applied, they insisted, convictions had been
determined by "the temper of popular opinion" and the "preconcep-
tions and personality of each judge." While they did not challenge the
government's right to jail those who actively worked to undermine the
war effort, they provided Wilson with many specific cases that supported their view that wartime prosecutions had strayed beyond these
bounds and violated the free speech rights of American citizens.[33]

The NCLB added a more pragmatic political reason for amnesty,
suggesting that a pardon would be the best way to defuse the growing
threat of revolutionary violence. Leaving these prisoners in jail, they
warned, would "only widen . . . dangerous breeches which divide modern society." "It seems to be coming true," Sayre concluded, "that the
blood of martyrs (even if they are only supposed ones) is the seed of
radical organization."[34]

These arguments impressed the president, who forwarded the petition to Palmer, asking him to give it a careful review. The amnesty question is a "perplexing matter," he told the attorney general, "in which . . .
I am anxious to act at an early date." Once again Palmer convinced him
to wait, insisting that "the time is not yet ripe."[35]

Each day since the president had returned from Europe, the pro-war
socialist John Spargo had eagerly scanned the morning papers, expecting news that Wilson had declared amnesty for the wartime prisoners.
Now, at summer's end, he told Wilson, "You have disappointed every
liberal that I know, just as you have disappointed me." Spargo urged the

president to act, not only to correct an injustice, but to protect his political program. As Wilson prepared to fight a major battle with Congress over the ratification of his treaty, a generous amnesty would help him win back the support of the "many thousands of liberals and radicals" who had supported the war but who now felt deeply alienated by the administration's "excessive and brutal treatment" of dissenters.[36]

Like the NCLB, Spargo warned Wilson that leaving Debs in prison not only alienated liberals, but encouraged the most dangerous and irresponsible elements of the American radical movement. During the war, Spargo had watched with growing alarm as many of his former comrades in the party moved further to the left, entranced by a Bolshevik movement that he considered to be a travesty of socialist ideals and "the biggest mistake in history." He warned the president that these deluded radicals were planning "an immense agitation for amnesty" that would stir dangerous passions of hatred and revenge in some American workers. Spargo was one of the few petitioners who based none of his appeal for amnesty on Debs's personal qualities. In fact, he thought Debs was emotional and erratic, too often drunk and too free with his incendiary rhetoric. Still, he told Wilson that "every day that Mr. Debs or Mrs. O'Hare remains in prison adds to the discontent."[37]

In reply, Wilson told Spargo that the amnesty question "concerns a matter that I have more nearly at heart, I think, than I have been able to make evident. I assure you that I am going to deal with the matter as early and in as liberal a spirit as possible." He forwarded Spargo's letter to Palmer for his consideration. While discounting the letter's "exaggerated feelings," the president told Palmer that "Spargo is right. . . . Our action ought to be promptly formulated and taken." For at least the second time in a month, the president pleaded to his attorney general, "Won't you advise me in the matter?"[38]

By the middle of September, Palmer's assistants completed a new review of the Espionage Act cases. Once again they argued against a general amnesty. The president probably never saw this report, however. A week earlier he had left Washington, embarking on his ill-fated national tour to rally public support for the League of Nations.

By the fall of 1919, the Justice Department attorneys in charge of the Espionage Act cases noticed an important change in the tone and char-

acter of the letters they were receiving. During the war they heard often from radicals whose petitions were part of various IWW and Socialist Party defense campaigns. But now they found a broader and "more
emphatic" demand for the release of the wartime prisoners coming
from people who "profess to have no sympathy even with Socialism."[39]

Many of these letters came from union workers, the first showers in
an impending storm of petitions stirred up by Lucy Robins. Robins
traced her involvement in the amnesty cause to a frigid winter night in
Emma Goldman's Greenwich Village apartment. Convicted of conspiracy for their opposition to the draft, Goldman and her lifelong comrade
Alexander Berkman were bound for prison the next day. Robins was
part of what she called a shivering band of forlorn "idealists and theo-
rists" who gathered to wish them farewell. As radicals were wont to do,
Goldman and her friends warmed their spirits that night by conjuring
up an impressive sounding new organization, the "League for Amnesty
for Political Prisoners."[40]

Though this "league" had no constituency and no budget, Goldman
chose wisely when she appointed Lucy Robins to take charge, a task she
was to share with Berkman's lover, M. E. Fitzgerald. Robins was a free-
spirited anarchist, but she had a keen sense of social justice and a knack
for organizational discipline. Before the war she had played key roles
in several national protest movements, including the campaign to keep
Tom Mooney out of the electric chair. Her new assignment, pressur-
ing the federal government to free hundreds of wartime prisoners,
would be the greatest organizing challenge she had ever faced. Robins
accepted the job reluctantly, and only out of respect for Goldman, her
departing friend and mentor. Taking her previous experience as a guide,
Robins expected that the work of this new "league" would be fleeting
and futile. Radicals usually preached to the converted, she had found,
and confused their immediate political goals with manic prophecies
of violent revolution that only convinced most American workers to
steer clear.[41]

As far as Robins was concerned, the Socialist Party's early efforts on
behalf of the political prisoners were a case study in what she was coming to think of as radical "farce." During the war, party leaders announced a campaign to raise a "Million Dollar Defense Fund," but

brought in less than twenty thousand dollars. Their journals were filled with crackpot schemes, like the proposal that twenty party members should each volunteer to serve six months of their leader's ten-year sentence. They had threatened a massive general strike on the day Debs went to jail, and another on the Fourth of July—but neither had materialized. When they did manage to get workers into the streets, Robins thought that the results were even worse. The May Day riots, along with the various real and rhetorical threats of general strikes and prison raids, only drove away the very people for whom the radicals presumed to speak, the working men and women of America.[42]

The only way to get Debs and others out of jail, Robins decided, would be to find a new way to reach the "conservative mass" of America's unionized workers and convince them that they had a stake in the amnesty fight. Toward that end, she traveled to Chicago in November 1918 to appeal for the support of Samuel Gompers, the powerful president of the American Federation of Labor.

When Emma Goldman anointed Robins to take charge of an amnesty campaign, she surely never anticipated that her young disciple would seek the help of Gompers. While the various factions of American radicals disagreed on many things, they shared contempt for the conservative trade union leader. He was a traitor to the true interests of the working class, they believed. Instead of demanding control of the means of production, Gompers and his followers wanted only "a fair day's wage for a fair day's work," a strategy that radicals believed put workers into the vest pockets of their capitalist masters. Over the years Debs had been as critical of Gompers as anyone, heaping scorn on labor's great "misleader." Gompers fought back with equal fervor, denouncing socialists as misguided utopians and using all of his considerable political skills to minimize their influence in the trade union movement.

The war only intensified this bitter split. As labor's most important representative in Wilson's war bureaucracy, Gompers had rallied union support for the war and denounced the anti-war radicals as traitors. As government prosecutors put pacifist radicals behind bars, he had publicly bid them good riddance. Because of his loyal service to the war effort, Gompers emerged from the war more powerful than ever. When

Robins arrived in Chicago not long after the armistice, she found that the city was in the midst of a three-day celebration honoring his "patriotic services." As she waited outside his office, martial music drifted up from army bands serenading him from the street below. A lifelong pacifist, Robins feared that she was about to deliver herself into the belly of the beast. "Here was militarism displayed in all its glory," she thought, "in honor of the very man whose assistance I was seeking to free prisoners who had opposed militarism."[43]

If Gompers was an unlikely ally in a campaign to free radicals, it was just as surprising that Robins should seek him out. Though she was half his age, the two had started life much the same way. Both were Jewish immigrants who entered the union movement through the cigar-makers' trade. But when Robins was still quite young, she heard Emma Goldman speak and was drawn into the world of radical ideals. Anarchism offered a path to true liberation, she decided then, a way to break free from the twin constraints of class oppression and her family's Jewish orthodoxy. While many Americans viewed anarchism as a dangerous doctrine imported from benighted Europe, Robins embraced it as the perfect expression of American individualism.

At the age of fifteen Robins eloped with a fellow anarchist, and the two set out to explore the country. Heeding Emma Goldman's warning that marriage was a bourgeois trap, Robins had insisted on an unusual set of marital vows. The couple agreed to a temporary marriage that would be open for reconsideration after five years. This innovation scandalized her family, and later the guardians of morality in San Francisco, where the couple settled. At the urging of Jack London, they started a vegetarian restaurant in that city's bohemian district. London soon converted to a diet of raw meat, but Robins never lacked for customers as her restaurant became a meeting ground for anarchists, Wobblies, socialists, and assorted California eccentrics.

There Robins discovered that she had a talent not only for vegetarian cuisine but also for political organizing. Though driven to the work by her anarchist idealism, she was also a born pragmatist. Tangible results mattered more than ideological purity, she decided. The campaign to save Tom Mooney gave her a first glimpse at the hidden levers of political influence, the tools for actually getting things done. In the Mooney campaign, radicals threatened general strikes they could never deliver, and tried without success to turn sympathy for Mooney into a recruiting device for the radical movement. In the end, Robins decided that all of this activity had not helped the prisoner one bit. The governor of California finally overturned Mooney's death sentence, she realized, because President Wilson had intervened. And he had done so not out of respect for or fear of radical protests, but thanks to the quiet persuasion brought to bear by Samuel Gompers.

And so, ignoring the disapproval of her husband Bob and her anarchist friends, Robins found herself in Gompers's office, face to face with "the man who was blessed and cursed by thousands of people during the war." To her surprise, Robins found that Gompers was sympathetic. "My girl," he told her, "I am not a man hunter. I believe that every man must have his liberty, and that right should be protected above everything else." Gompers gave her a written statement in support of a general amnesty for political prisoners and agreed to help her win a hearing for the cause within the AFL. He told her that he would not actively campaign for amnesty, however, until she convinced many more union members to back the idea. Here was a lesson that Robins would soon take as an axiom of democratic politics: leaders marshaled their influence carefully, preferring to negotiate behind the scenes, and speaking out for an idea only when it already enjoyed a visible momentum.[44]

When Robins set out to sell amnesty to the rest of the American Federation of Labor, she soon found that she had her work cut out for her. Armed with what she called a "carte blanche endorsement in writing from the Old Man," she presented her amnesty resolution at the AFL's 1919 convention, held in Atlantic City that June. Representatives from the more radical unions backed her, but many more denounced the idea as an insult to the country and a slight to the many working men who had done their patriotic duty during the war. "My own are still 'over there,'" one objected, "and I don't know whether I shall ever see them again. I shall be the last to join a movement to protect slackers!" While many agreed that the Espionage Act should be repealed once the peace treaty was signed, a strong majority thought that any expression of sympathy for "jail-birds" like Debs was an insult to "every man who wore the uniform." After a long afternoon of bitter debate, the resolution was soundly defeated.[45]

The news that the AFL leaders turned their back on Debs and the other jailed dissenters inspired a fresh round of denunciations in the radical press. John Reed charged that, while militant workers were marching toward revolution across Europe, the American labor movement was going "backward, hopelessly entangled in the mazes of its narrow craft unionism, corrupt and ignorant." For different reasons, Robins was stunned by this setback. Some of the country's most powerful union leaders had not only failed to support her call for a presidential pardon, but had declared these prisoners to be enemies to the nation. Robins believed that Eugene Debs was a noble martyr who was suffering in the service of working-class liberation. Now she realized with a shock that the "great mass" of workers spurned him as a coward and a traitor.[46]

Reed charged that Gompers had orchestrated the AFL's stand against amnesty, but Robins knew better. Still, she expected that, in the face of this rebuff from his fellow labor leaders, Gompers would silently withdraw his own support. She was surprised when, instead, he urged her to keep fighting. Although Gompers was America's most powerful labor leader, Robins concluded that he was eager to prove that he was not a traitor to his class. "He was bothered far more than he would ever admit by the attacks of the radicals," she thought. "Many of these radicals were his own people, the Jews of the East Side, and he was hurt. He wanted them to understand and admit that he had been true to his ideals."[47]

With his support and counsel, Robins tried a new approach to mobilizing what she called "the conservative masses of organized labor." Though a majority of the AFL leadership rejected her amnesty proposal, the more radical "Jewish Unions" on the Lower East Side of New York were eager to help. A local of the International Ladies' Garment Workers' Union provided a small office on Second Avenue, while other locals of the United Hebrew Trades donated enough funds to begin a grassroots campaign. Leaving the leadership of Emma Goldman's "league" to others, Robins added a new line to her résumé, as she became the secretary of the Central Labor Bodies Conference for the

Release of the Political Prisoners. There she established a beachhead for amnesty in the country's largest and most important working-class movement.[48]

Robins then set out to convince the "conservative masses" of America's union workers that they should care about the plight of America's imprisoned radicals. With the help of Morris Hillquit, she crafted an amnesty resolution that she hoped all four million AFL union members would debate, and ultimately support. Shunning the rhetoric of revolutionary radicalism, she tried instead to convince workers that they had a duty to protest against the government assault on America's Constitution. This "invasion of individual rights," as she put it, should concern all "true patriots of our country and lovers of liberty." In her resolution, Robins acknowledged that the Espionage Act might have been necessary as an emergency wartime measure. But keeping the "political offenders" in jail a minute longer, she contended, "is contrary to the democratic idealism and the traditions of freedom to which our country is committed." In short, Robins hoped to convince AFL workers that they should support amnesty not out of sympathy for the politics of the wartime prisoners but to defend American liberties threatened by the government's unprecedented exercise of its wartime powers. She would teach them to be radical, but hers was the old radicalism of the American Revolution.[49]

Acting through the Central Labor Bodies, Robins sent this amnesty resolution to each of the thirty-six thousand local unions affiliated with the AFL, asking them to endorse the measure. From experience Robins knew that each trade had "its own problems, its own terminology, its own folklore," and she tailored her requests accordingly, hoping to better command their attention. Some locals took one look at her proposal and rejected it. Debs and his kind were enemies of "this great country," one told Robins, who should "take what is coming to them." A carpenters' union from Delaware replied that their local was "absolutely opposed to your movement and will do all in its power to kill same." Across the country, however, many union locals began to debate the resolution, arguing over the meaning of the First Amendment in a way that up to that point had been the province of a handful of lawyers, judges, politicians, and journalists.[50]

No less than the justices of the Supreme Court, these workers found themselves struggling to clarify the murky line that divided legitimate protest from dangerous treason. One local decided that no American had a right to advocate assassination or "malicious destruction of property." An Arizona union had a similar idea. "We are not in accord with some of the acts of these so called 'Soviets' and Revolutionists," they resolved, "but we are for free speech and free Assembly and for the right of man to speak his mind as long as he does not advocate the overthrow of the Government by violence as we believe that we still have the ballot and if we do not like a person in office we can use our votes at the ballot box and therefore remove him." Just as Robins had hoped, many locals endorsed her petition and drafted their own resolutions calling on the government to repeal the Espionage Act, and to free those convicted for their "political beliefs."

Through the summer and fall of 1919, Robins kept up the pressure. Working on a shoestring budget from her tiny New York office, she badgered locals that dragged their feet, and orchestrated the delivery of thousands of resolutions and petitions to key figures in state and federal government—to governors and congressmen, and to Wilson, his attorney general, and his secretary of war. As these letters piled up in the mailbags of the mighty, Robins believed that she was at the center of a movement that was both quintessentially American and quite "radical." Instead of "the usual worthless methods that radicals employed," she found a way to promote the liberation of workers through the orderly and democratic structure of the trade union locals. In union halls across the country, working men and women were learning to think for themselves and to "ask questions, and pass criticism even upon their 'sacred' government officials." The leader of an ironworkers' union in Alabama captured this new spirit when he told President Wilson, "I do not wish to be considered anything but a Loyal American Citizen, but when my own Government is at fault, I have the right to protest, providing I do so in a proper way."[51]

After Debs had been in the Moundsville prison for two months, the superintendent of prisons in Washington ordered him to be transferred to the federal penitentiary in Atlanta. When Terrell broke the news, Debs "seemed to sag down completely and his face turned several colors." To soften the blow, Terrell promised to write to Atlanta, explaining that Debs was a model prisoner, and urging his new warden to be as lenient as possible.[52]

Hoping to deny his supporters the chance to organize protest rallies along the train route to Georgia, federal authorities ordered Debs to be moved quickly and secretly. He had an hour to gather his things and to change into civilian clothes. Accompanied by two federal guards, Terrell drove Debs to the railway station in Wheeling. The warden had heard a rumor that some influential socialists were trying to arrange a presidential pardon. Eager to offer his friend some hope, he asked Debs if he would agree to stop "preaching" socialism in exchange for his freedom. Debs replied that social revolution "is a life crusade with me and I cannot give it up, no matter what the cost." Shaking hands with the warden, he parted with what he later described as "real regret." "My stay with you at the Moundsville prison," Debs wrote to Terrell once he arrived in Atlanta, "will always be to me a source of satisfaction and inspiration."[53]

At the depot, a local reporter recognized Debs and asked him for a statement. Obeying orders from the federal guards, Debs said nothing. He seemed "deeply depressed," the reporter thought, "for he hung his head as he boarded the train." "No one in Moundsville will regret his going," he added, "for his presence there naturally had a tendency to bring to that city undesirable visitors from among his misguided worshippers." But at least one local resident was disappointed. "I am personally sorry to lose Debs," Terrell told Mabel Curry, "as I had formed rather an attachment for him."[54]

Across the country socialists expressed outrage when they learned that the federal government had once again "kidnapped" their leader. "No reason was assigned for this unusual proceeding," one editor wrote. "It was surmised, however, that the treatment accorded Debs at the Moundsville prison was not to the liking of his Democratic Party persecutors at Washington." Theodore believed that the Wilson administration was trying to "completely shatter his health in a hot southern hellhole and thus accomplish in that what they dare not in another." Karsner speculated that West Virginia's "coal kings" had driven him from the state, still angry over his work among the miners. Others assumed that Washington feared an attack on Moundsville, either by radicals who wanted him free or mobs who wanted him lynched. Years later, in fact, one radical claimed that John Reed and Jim Larkin had perfected their plot to break Debs out of jail, a scheme that was foiled because Debs was moved on the very day they planned to strike.[55]

Perhaps the government transferred Debs to avoid the wrath of John Reed and his co-conspirators, but a less dramatic explanation seems more plausible. The order was most likely prompted by a mundane bureaucratic wrangle over money. Debs had been sent to Moundsville because the federal system was unable to cope with the influx of wartime prisoners. Angling for a better deal, West Virginia's prison superintendent complained to federal authorities that the extra security that Debs required was costing his state five hundred dollars a month. At that point, the federal government no longer needed West Virginia's help in housing its prisoners, since the Atlanta penitentiary had just opened a new cell block. Instead of paying more to keep Debs in Moundsville, the federal superintendent ordered the state to send him to Atlanta, "in accordance with your request." Warden Terrell tried to prevent the move and regretted what he called a "misunderstanding."[56]

While many radicals denounced the transfer, a few of Debs's friends believed that the government had inadvertently opened a legal loophole that might be used to free him. Some socialist lawyers told Debs that because Judge Westenhaver had ordered him jailed in Moundsville, the transfer to Atlanta could be considered a "second sentence" imposed without due process of law. They urged him to take that argument to court, a maneuver that might win him a temporary reprieve or even "end his captivity for all time."[57]

Whatever the plan's legal merits or likelihood of success, it posed a moral dilemma for Debs. Though he longed for his liberty, escaping on a legal technicality seemed to him a selfish move, one that would put his own comfort ahead of the needs of the wider amnesty movement. "This is not the time for me to try to save myself," he concluded. He had been sent to prison, in part, for publicly defending the speech rights of the wartime prisoners. Now he realized that by standing "firm and unshaken" he could still serve that cause, ensuring that the public did not forget all those who were "suffering for opinion's sake." He told his lawyers he would win or lose this free speech fight on the basis of principles, not legal maneuvers.

Debs had never offered a sophisticated theory about the nature and limits of free speech, leaving the wrangling over such matters to his lawyers. But he had come to realize that prison afforded him a quite different forum to make his case, the wider court of public opinion. There he could defend his speech rights on the ground he knew best, ignoring fine legal distinctions and speaking instead in the broad gestures of political symbolism. Behind bars he would not be excluded from the national debate over the administration's war on radicals, but would turn his cell into a new stage, casting himself as the hero in a morality tale as old as democracy itself. Though silenced, he would embody the value of free speech, transforming himself into a potent symbol of intellectual liberty and the individual's power to resist government repression. Over time, his example would prove to be more persuasive than any legal argument, forcing many Americans to reconsider their government's war on dissent. Recognizing that the eyes of the nation were upon him, he told his comrades to look toward Atlanta. There, high above his prison cell, he said, "they will see my torch flaming in the sky!"[58]

Chapter 9

Atlanta Penitentiary

AFTER A LONG, HOT TRAIN RIDE south, Debs and his guards approached Atlanta's federal penitentiary, which loomed like a "vast sepulcher" of the "living dead." Debs silently resolved to face its trials with serene detachment, a stoicism that was soon put to the test. Guards took his clothes, his money, even a favorite quill toothpick. After a mandatory shower and physical inspection, he dressed in a rough secondhand denim suit and posed for a mug shot. Marched to the mess hall, he poked at a meal that "created nausea rather than appetite," while a club-toting guard reviewed the rules that would now govern his every hour, perhaps for the rest of his life. Waving to another prisoner was forbidden, as was putting his hands in his pockets. Inmates spoke to guards only when necessary, and had to stand at least six feet away, heads bowed. Those who broke the rules would be sent to "the hole," solitary confinement in a windowless room, on a diet of bread and water.

After a few days in a temporary cell, Debs was moved to what he called a "regular cage" that he would share with five others. They are "fine, bright fellows," he assured Theodore, "and they vie with each other in being kind to me." A German immigrant, convicted for providing alcohol to servicemen, not only gave Debs his coveted lower bunk but insisted on making his bed each day. Others soon risked the wrath of the guards to smuggle him a piece of pie or to wave a friendly greet-

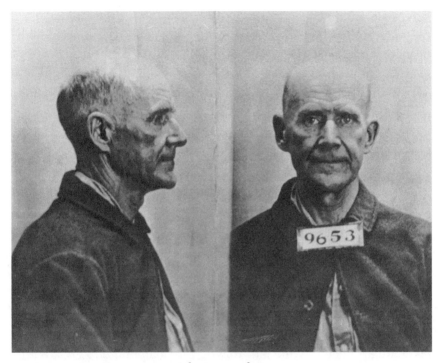

Atlanta mug shot.
David Karsner Papers, Manuscripts and Archives Division,
The New York Public Library, Astor, Lenox and Tilden Foundations.

ing across the prison exercise yard. Even among Atlanta's murderers and "rape fiends" Debs found things to admire, "magnificent qualities that sparkle in these men who are supposed to be the hopeless dregs of humanity."[1]

Assigned light clerical duties in the clothing room, Debs fell into lockstep with the prison's dreary routine. Roused at seven, the men worked from eight to four, exercised in the prison yard for twenty minutes before dinner, and were back in their cells by five, locked down for the evening. No longer under Warden Terrell's indulgent protection, Debs felt profoundly isolated. He could not receive radical literature, had limited visiting privileges, and was allowed to send only one letter a week to a family member. "I am treated the same as the common run of prisoners," he told Theodore in his first letter from Atlanta, though he was quick to add that he had "no complaint on that score."

A week later Debs was summoned to the office of Warden Fred Zerbst, who had by then read Terrell's letter praising him as a model prisoner. Once again, Debs was fortunate in his jailor. Since taking over in 1915, Zerbst had labored to make the Atlanta prison a showcase of what he called "uplift." He constructed new dormitories, expanded the prison library, and encouraged public concerts by the inmate orchestra. He broke ground on a prison farm to supply his men with more vegetables, prepared "scientifically." The first step in turning a criminal into an "upright liver," he believed, was to give him a "contented stomach." Zerbst even indulged his prisoners' request for a monthly allotment of candy—though he took precautions to make sure that no drugs were smuggled in with the bonbons and gum drops.[2]

The anarchist Alexander Berkman, who knew quite a lot about the inside of prisons, conceded that Zerbst was a good man who was trying to modernize an institution mired in the dark ages. Sent to Atlanta for obstructing the draft, Berkman was released in October 1919, a few months after Debs arrived, and would soon be deported to Russia for his anarchist beliefs. As he left Atlanta, Berkman praised Zerbst but issued a statement charging that the prison guards were "vulgar, brutal and dissipated men," morally inferior to those whom they guarded. All inmates suffered sadistic cruelty at their hands, he wrote, and political prisoners were treated particularly badly.[3]

Like Berkman, Debs came to admire Zerbst but found that the prison offered little in the way of "uplift." Many of the guards seemed "scarcely a degree above the brute," abusing the prisoners through "club rule and black-hole torture." Thanks to graft and mismanagement, the prison kitchen served up the "cheapest and stalest conglomeration of stuff that the market afforded." In the prison hospital, some doctors encouraged rather than cured addiction, providing drugs for a handsome profit.[4]

As far as Debs was concerned, the first and greatest scandal was the very existence of the prison as a capitalist institution. Since his 1894 stay in the rat-infested Cook County Jail during the Pullman strike, Debs had taken a personal interest in the penitentiary system, which he considered to be a device the rich used to control the poor. Few wealthy men could be found behind bars, he often observed, because prisons were designed to protect property. Debs thought most criminals were the victims of a society that forced them into a "bitter struggle for existence." He predicted that when the revolution banished poverty, prisons would also vanish, replaced by a smaller number of asylums and hospitals offering enlightened treatment for the addicted and the insane.[5]

To Debs, the sight of armed guards patrolling the prison walls above him perfectly expressed the inhumanity of the capitalist system. But down below among the inmates, he found glimpses of the better world to come. For decades Debs had dreamed of a society without greed, where people would live in the harmony that would come once the profit motive was banished. Ironically, he found hints of this utopia in prison, where men had nothing, could aspire to nothing, and dwelled in what he called a "perfect democracy." "I was in the midst of what are called the lowest types of criminals," he found, "flanked by Negro murderers, and yet, I never felt myself more perfectly at one with my fellow beings. We were all on a dead level there and I felt my heart beat in unison with the heartbeats of those brothers of mine."

Debs set out not simply to survive his prison stay but to reform the place from within. At his first meeting with the warden, he promised to abide by all prison rules but also declared his enmity to the penitentiary as an institution. To his credit, Zerbst listened receptively. Before long the two were discussing ways to improve the food and raise morale, and Zerbst trusted Debs to advise him on the problems of kitchen graft and guard brutality. Debs got the warden to provide more recreational time for inmates, and not long after his arrival he also won a small victory for religious freedom. Attending his first mandatory chapel service, he was offended by the presence of scowling, club-waving guards. Though he admired the prison's Protestant and Catholic chaplains, from that point on he refused to attend services that he considered to be a "ghastly travesty." Rather than force Debs to comply, Zerbst made worship services optional for all prisoners.[6]

Debs also worked to humanize the prison through personal example. Criminologists in his day often applied a crude biological determinism to the exploration of the "criminal type." Debs conceded that many of his fellow inmates had a "hunted look and wretched appearance," but he felt sure that these were not innate traits but the scars left on men battered by an inhumane economic system. Even the most hardened criminal, he believed, would respond to the healing force of kindness and respect. One of Debs's favorite books was Victor Hugo's *Les Miserables*, which told the tale of Jean Valjean, a wretched convict whose life was transformed by a single act of kindness. In Atlanta, Debs tried to do the same, and with remarkable results. Each evening in the exercise yard, he was surrounded by men who sought his advice and counsel, or just his kind words.

Before Debs had arrived, the political prisoners had been ostracized by the other inmates, dwelling at the very bottom of the institution's pecking order. Some of the "politicals" preferred it that way; they were religious or political idealists who considered the average criminal to be either a sinner or a social parasite. In turn, the regular prisoners were mostly enthusiastic patriots who had contempt for the conscientious objectors. These men were "crazy for war news," and clamored in vain for the chance to enlist. To ease their disappointment, Zerbst allowed them to form their own "U.S. Penitentiary Training Corps"; they drilled each week in the prison yard and longed for a shipment of wooden rifles. In spite of their different views on the war, Debs commanded their immediate respect. Before long, those few inmates who dared to call him anything other than "Mr. Debs" faced the wrath of their peers. The warden was amazed to find that the inmates even began to clean up their "foul language" after Debs told them that he found such coarse talk painful to hear, and beneath their dignity as men.[7]

Though such friendships made prison more bearable, the intense heat of an Atlanta summer, the poor food, and the harsh environment soon took a toll on his health. Debs lost the weight he had put on in Moundsville, and friends who visited him were shocked to find him looking "emaciated." His worn denim prison suit hung loose on his bony six-foot frame, one reported, and his pallid face showed signs that he was being poisoned by the "unsunned prison air." While Debs sent back cheerful reports, Mabel Curry heard from others that he was "visibly failing." Rumors that he was dying swirled through the press. "Of course he has made no such complaint," Curry fretted to Karsner, "and his wife doesn't dream this is the case. He always spares those who love him."[8]

Upton Sinclair seized on these rumors to make yet another appeal to President Wilson. Debs was "an old man weakening in health," he cabled, "confined fourteen consecutive hours daily in cell in midsummer of southern climate. This means practically death sentence inflicted upon a man of finest sensibility for indubitably sincere conscientious objections to war. . . . If Debs should be allowed to die in jail I believe that a peaceable solution of social problem would be impossible in America."[9]

Wilson did not share Sinclair's admiration for Debs's fine "sensibility" and once again ignored the pardon request. However, he did ask Palmer to investigate the rumors that Debs was ill and mistreated. Zerbst soon reported that Debs was "in fully as good health as when he came here." The charge that he was being kept in his cell for fourteen hours each day was true, he conceded. Due to a shortage of guards, all prisoners were locked down at 5 p.m., and Debs had specifically asked for no special consideration. Passing on a classic Debsism, Zerbst added that the prisoner told him "he had met more human kindness at Moundsville and here, than he ever found outside of prison."[10]

As his friends suspected, that was not the whole story. The prison doctor detected a "bilious murmur" in his heart that he thought could prove fatal at any time. When Marguerite Prevey visited in August, she was "greatly shocked" at the sight of him and pressured Zerbst to intervene. By that point, the warden realized that his famous prisoner was too proud and stoic to admit to his suffering. Though Debs protested, Zerbst moved him to a new job as a hospital assistant. As in Moundsville, the position provided easy work, a private room, and a bit more freedom to exercise.[11]

Realizing that Debs was a positive force at the prison, Zerbst loosened other regulations as well. He allowed Debs to have more visitors and adopted Terrell's system for handling his mail. Twice a week Debs forwarded a package of letters to his Terre Haute office, penciling his brief replies in the margins. The warden also allowed him to write an extra weekly letter to his "office manager," Mabel Curry. "I'm with you all the time," Debs told her. "God bless your wonderful devotion!—it keeps me strong and true." He sent her little lyrics about the power of love to conquer iron bars, picked violets in the prison yard to send her, and devised a new code to transmit sentiments more passionate than comradely. "I love you awfully, fiercely, terribly," he wrote, "and I am glad there is no remedy." Dropping the code name "Mrs. Wilson," he was now "Ura," a reverse acronym for the American Railway Union.[12]

Atlanta's prison censors worked overtime to review Debs's mail; many weeks he received twice as much as the rest of the prison combined. In Washington, the pardon attorneys at the Justice Department struggled to keep up with their own mountains of mail about Debs—petitions, resolutions, and personal appeals from citizens around the country. Some urged the Wilson administration to keep Debs in jail. The Citizen's Patriotic League of Covington, Kentucky, for example, told the president that "the American people will not favor pardon of men who endeavor to destroy their country in its hour of trial." Debs was a "lawless devil," another wrote, who should have been jailed long ago.[13]

Debs had often claimed that he was being punished for his socialism, not for obstructing the war effort. In the anxious summer of 1919, many Americans agreed but saw no problem with this. In peace no less than in war, they argued, a nation should not have to tolerate someone devoted to its destruction. Debs's speeches against the war, they thought, were just the latest chapter in a long career as a traitor. "Lenience to such as he," as one put it, "only encourages anarchists, I.W.W.s and other criminals of their stamp." When a reporter took the pulse of public opinion in Chicago, a law clerk told him that he opposed any pardon for Debs. "The party he heads and represents has caused too much trouble and havoc for our government already," he reasoned. "If he were released it would probably mean more trouble, and in the end putting him back in jail."[14]

Most writers pulled in the opposite direction, making a variety of arguments for amnesty. Sinclair had warned Wilson that leaving Debs in jail was stirring "deplorable bitterness" in the country, and many of these letters confirm this. "There are no courts for the underdog," one radical union wrote, "and the principle of the accused being given a fair trial by a jury of his peers is a huge joke. The extreme severity of the sentences imposed would lead us to believe that we are not on a par mentally with even Europe." Many of these letters were not requests, but threats. "Mr. Debs will not serve ten nor half of ten," one predicted. "I don't think he will serve one. The American working people have been easy but the time has arrived when the 85% are no longer to be ruled by the 15%. WE are going to give you some of your own medicine, as you sowed, so shall you reap." From Chicago, a working-class woman who described herself as a "natural born citizen" told the president, "For my part the Bolsheviki rule cannot begin any time too soon in this country. A government that will deliberately take away the inalienable rights of its natural born citizens, throttle free speech, confiscate personal property and even capitalize woman's labor, institute espionage and intimidation systems, cannot be held in low enough contempt by its subjects." Many of these letters threatening the "bone-heads of autocracy" with "eternal damnation" were forwarded by Justice Department attorneys to J. Edgar Hoover's new Bureau of Investigation, where they padded his growing files on "dangerous radicals."[15]

Through the fall of 1919, federal attorneys noted with evident surprise that many of the letters came from people with no connection to radicalism. "I am not a Bolshevist, but I am not a fool either," as one put it. Another demanded a Debs pardon, then added, "P.S. Our family have been Americans since 1630." Many petitioners proudly announced their union affiliation and were likely inspired by Lucy Robins's AFL campaign. A mine workers' local from Arkansas, for example, told "Brother" Wilson that their group was "composed entirely of Americans—White in Color—and Loyal in adherence to the Work You are doing for *World Peace.*" Others had no tie to organized labor but offered their middle-class professions as proof that they were reliable and reasonable patriots—they were journalists, lawyers, ministers and teachers, landed farmers, and small-town merchants.[16]

Often these petitioners urged amnesty for "safety valve" reasons. "This nation is like a rumbling volcano," a West Coast fruit grower warned his president. "If you are a wise man, you will let out some of the gas and steam before the explosion blows us all to H°ll." A Georgia poet warned that keeping men like Debs in jail "really acts as a hotframe, or fertilizer. I have been amazed at the beanstalk growth of radicalism . . . since the Espionage Act was passed. Everyone seems angered." A mayor and grain dealer from a small Ohio town warned Palmer that he risked "national calamity" by turning Debs into a martyr. "While at liberty he could address but a few thousand people. Now he addresses his millions, since his spirit prevails at practically all the labor meetings through the world." Amnesty would not be a victory for extremists, they contended, but the best way to defeat them.[17]

Others moved beyond from these pragmatic arguments, lecturing the president and his attorney general about the meaning of justice and the history of the First Amendment. Wilson was a former Princeton professor who had written many books on American history and politics, but some thought he had forgotten the lessons of his own writings. A Memphis war veteran reminded him that his own textbook on American history traced the rise of the Democratic Party to Jefferson's protest against the Alien and Sedition Acts of 1798. "Yet, notwithstanding this," he observed, "the Democratic Party is about to break its neck in attempt to destroy freedom of speech." Another group asked Wilson if he had forgotten the "noble and magnanimous attitude of Abraham Lincoln toward the insurgents" after the Civil War. Given the president's wartime attacks on "hyphenated Americans," he might have been surprised to hear such a history lesson coming from the Czechoslovak Workingmen's Council of Racine, Wisconsin.[18]

In the first months after the war, attorneys in the Justice Department labored to provide each of these petitioners with a firm but courteous rebuttal. Dozens of times each day, John Lord O'Brian, the special assistant in charge of wartime prosecutions, "respectfully informed" them that "there are no political prisoners in confinement." Sometimes the attorneys conceded that errors had been made due to the "excitement of the times." Still, they insisted that "men were prosecuted not for their opinions but for intentional obstruction of the government's war program." They acknowledged that many Americans believed the prisoners were being punished for their opinions, but insisted this was a "fallacy."[19]

Later, worn down by "innumerable" letters calling for amnesty, pardon attorneys in the Justice Department took a step down the slippery slope, referring to them as the "so-called 'political prisoners.'" This reluctant concession marked an important strategic victory for the amnesty movement. Through the alchemy of a concerted public relations campaign, those once derided as "slackers" and "traitors" were becoming "political prisoners" in many public forums, or even more grandly, "the prisoners of conscience." Journalists understood better than anyone the power of language to frame public debate, and some waged a futile counterassault, echoing the Justice Department's argument that, by definition, a democracy could not have "political prisoners." "There is a good deal of nonsense and hysteria going as to the case of Debs and his punishment," one commentator explained. "It is claimed he is a political prisoner. He is not. There is no such thing in the United States. Debs is in prison for the same reason his fellow convicts are in prison— for breaking the law. He is not there on account of his opinions. He is there for what he did."[20]

By the fall of 1919, however, Palmer's assistants in the Justice Department lost heart for that battle. As the flood of petitions continued to swell, their replies were often brief. "Your letter to the president has been referred to this department," they wrote, sometimes adding, "your suggestions have been noted." They filed this correspondence in folders marked "Political Prisoners."

As the sheer volume of these letters suggests, across the country Americans were forced by the events of the war to examine their ideas about free speech. A traveling salesmen observed that, everywhere he went, people were debating the fate of the political prisoners. Church groups and reading groups, mutual aid societies and community forums held meetings to discuss amnesty, and in a surprising number of cases felt strongly enough about the issue to petition their president. They did not generate new ideas about the value of free speech, but gave fresh consideration to the old ones. In their attempts to persuade Wilson to free Debs, they drew on arguments for liberty from Milton and Mill, Jefferson and Lincoln. As they did, they made these ideas their own, casting them in their own vernacular and applying them to their own moment in time.

Many of these letters show a remarkable faith not only in the value of free speech but in the power of their own words to influence government policy. Historians and many contemporaries of President Wilson remember him as an aloof personality, a grim Presbyterian who could be admired but never loved by his constituents. In contrast, many who wrote to him about amnesty seemed to feel that he was quite accessible, that he was a reasonable man who needed just one more heartfelt appeal to his sense of justice, one more clear and frank opinion from an American voter, in order to do the right thing. "I was astonished," a druggist from Colorado told his president, "upon returning home from my vacation, to learn that Debs and about five thousand [sic] other political prisoners were still in the penitentiary. . . . I felt sure you would lose no time in correcting what looks to me like a blunder."[21]

Others felt entitled to rage against their president, unfazed by the fact that many Americans had gone to jail for much less. They denounced him as a modern-day Pilate, a pious hypocrite, a moral weakling who had cynically deceived Americans in 1916 with his promise to keep the country out of the war. They felt personally betrayed by Wilson's policies, they wanted him to know it, and they assumed that he would read their letters.

In fact, the president most likely saw none of the bulging correspondence files, read none of these friendly and angry, inarticulate and profound reflections on the First Amendment that poured in from his fellow citizens. The White House forwarded them immediately to the Justice Department, "without any intention of calling the President's attention to them."[22]

Wilson was preoccupied that summer and fall, selling Americans on his controversial plan to join the League of Nations. Stymied by the Senate, the president set out in September to speak directly to the American people. Many radicals welcomed this chance—not to hear their president, but to force him to listen to their demands. Angered by his studied silence on the amnesty question, Theodore Debs hoped that the president would "meet this question at every point on his speaking tour."[23]

In fact, amnesty forces made no discernible impression on Wilson in the first weeks of his western tour. In the many long, impromptu speeches he gave across the Midwest he ignored the issue, while vowing to stand firm against those radicals who threatened to use violence to impose their will on the American people. The president who put so

many speakers in jail spoke earnestly about the importance of unfettered political debate. "We must have discussions," he insisted, "we
must have frank discussions."[24]

The amnesty movement finally got Wilson's attention, briefly, when
he arrived in Seattle on September 13. Confetti rained down on city
streets, and Boy Scouts had to be called in to help the police to restrain
a massive crowd. The president's triumphant march across the city
was marred, however, by what the *New York Times* called a "sinister
note." Thousands of Wobblies lined several blocks of the parade route.
Wearing hatbands that read "Release Political Prisoners," these long-
shoremen, miners, and lumberjacks looked on in a "sullen" silence that
spoke volumes. The president took no notice of the protest, continuing
to wave his silk hat from his touring car, but some of the protestors felt
sure that he looked "physically stricken." When the president fell sick a
few weeks later, some even took credit for slaying their persecutor with
a mighty moral blow.[25]

Upton Sinclair tried a more conciliatory approach. Since breaking
with the Socialists at the start of the war, he had periodically offered the
president unsolicited advice on a range of issues, particularly the administration's treatment of radicals. Wilson often sent brief but cordial
replies, enough to convince the novelist that he enjoyed a measure of
influence in the White House. Now, as the president's tour neared his
Pasadena home, Sinclair hoped for a chance to meet the president and
make a personal appeal for amnesty.

A savvy choreographer of democratic protest, Sinclair arranged a
mass amnesty meeting to coincide with Wilson's arrival in southern
California. This convention would draft a resolution that would get
some play in the newspapers, then Sinclair planned to lead a delegation to present their petition to the president while he was in Los Angeles. Leaving nothing to chance, he cabled Wilson, assuring him that
he would bring along only those who had proven themselves "loyal."
"Would be pleased to have intimation if you will grant ten minutes to
such committee."

Wilson met this modest request with stony silence. Tumulty told
Sinclair that the president's schedule was full, but he would be glad to
pass any petition on to Wilson "at the first free moment." The president

had ample reason to ignore Sinclair. He had already resolved to post-pone action on amnesty until the peace treaty was signed. Toward that end, he was engaged in an exhausting Western tour to rally public support for the League of Nations. Just as his doctor and family had warned, the trip was taking a frightful toll on his health, and he was suf-fering terrible headaches and exhaustion. Fighting a battle against con-servatives and isolationists who were bent on "breaking the heart of the world," Wilson saw the plight of several hundred political prisoners, many of them vocal critics of his administration, as a minor sideshow in the struggle to advance democracy around the world.

Sinclair was never one to be put off easily, however, and when the president arrived in Los Angeles, he sent another urgent note. He had gone ahead with the amnesty meeting, he told the president, but events had taken a troubling turn when he announced his plan to include only "loyal" Americans in the delegation. "I insisted that something might be gained by appealing to you in this way," he reported, "and I was ridi-culed by the radicals." He had almost lost control of the meeting, his voice drowned by a "murmur of distrust and bitterness" from the two thousand assembled.

The entire experience had shaken the almost unshakable Sinclair. "I don't want to admit that I failed utterly," he pleaded with the president, "and to be made ridiculous for my persistent faith in you. It is not any question of myself personally, either way, but because I know the bitter-ness is growing, down below the surface over which you move. And I am hoping that you will give me some sign, some hint that you do care about this matter. So it is that I am waiting at your door, and will wait till you either send me away, or grant me a few minutes."[26]

Wilson sent him away empty-handed.

As Americans debated amnesty in newspapers, union halls, and city squares across the country, Sinclair was not the only one waiting to hear more from the president. Yet through the fall of 1919 Wilson said sur-prisingly little about the subject. Faced with this void, friend and foe alike speculated about his thinking. Like Sinclair, many of his admirers on the left still assumed that Wilson regretted his administration's war-time repression, and hesitated to declare amnesty only for pragmatic political reasons. In vain they offered him plans to minimize the political damage that a general pardon might cause. Some thought Debs's illness offered a perfect excuse; Wilson could sidestep tricky political and constitutional questions by making a humanitarian gesture to save an old man. Others assumed that he welcomed their efforts to rally public support for amnesty, demonstrations that would allow him to deflect responsibility for the decision by seeming to bow to the public will. John Spargo, for example, offered to organize a delegation of distinguished public men who would call on the White House with an amnesty petition. In this way, the president could free the remaining prisoners without assuming the full political burden for the decision.

All of these suggestions were founded on a suspect premise, that Wilson wanted Debs to be freed, or at least that he wanted to be free of the controversy. In spite of his early enthusiasm for a general amnesty, by September Wilson seemed to change course, particularly about Debs. "Before the war he had a perfect right to exercise his freedom of speech and to express his own opinions," the president now decided, "but once the Congress of the United States declared war, silence on his part would have been the proper course to pursue." When his advisor Colonel House passed him an amnesty proposal drafted by Lincoln Steffens, Wilson reportedly threw it down in an angry tantrum. In cabinet meetings that summer, several of his advisors tried to revive his original plan for a general amnesty, but Wilson scuttled the suggestion. "Suppose every man in America had taken the same position Debs did," the president argued. "We would have lost the war and America would have been destroyed." Some of his friends feared that the embattled president was losing his perspective, consumed by a spirit of "malicious vindictiveness." Perhaps this brittle anger was a symptom of his impending stroke, as some historians have suggested. One of his advisors blamed it instead on Wilson's rigid Presbyterian soul.[27]

Whether the source of Wilson's stubborn anger was psychological or theological, Debs did nothing to soften the president's mood. On those rare occasions when he got a chance to talk with reporters, he told them that he would never ask the government for a pardon because he had done nothing wrong. "My attitude has not changed one whit since I came to prison. I would not take back a single word. I would not retract a single sentence. I will make no promises of any kind or nature to obtain my freedom. It would not be freedom if obtained by any retraction, promises or apostasy. To me that would be the worst slavery." Stretching the truth to underscore his defiance, he told reporters that he had given "no thought" to getting out. "I simply feel that I am continuing my work as usual. I feel like this prison is my office and that I am conducting my affairs uninterrupted behind prison bars."[28]

That fall Debs also poked his rhetorical knife in Wilson's most sensitive spot, attacking the League of Nations. When Wilson had first issued his Fourteen Points, Debs had praised them, but now he joined the many leftists who charged that the president had betrayed those ideals at Versailles, bringing home a treaty shaped less by internationalist idealism than by "greed, passion, and fear." At the *Liberator,* Max Eastman renounced his earlier support for the president, blaming his temporary lapse in judgment on the president's "blinding vapor of self-righteous emotion." Debs added a revolutionary wrinkle to the radicals' critique of the treaty. The whole idea of a League of Nations would be moot "within two years" anyway, he predicted, since the workers' revolution was about to eliminate nations. "The people have at last found out that they own the earth," Debs thought, "and they are getting ready to take charge of it."[29]

By September 1919, then, the amnesty question was bound up in an increasingly bitter and personal grudge between Wilson and Debs, the president and the prisoner of conscience. Wilson's silence masked a growing contempt for Debs, who in turn openly scorned the president. Debs now believed that Wilson had sent him to prison "to kill or break me," and he vowed never to yield.[30]

Instead, the president broke first.

Wilson had suffered his first stroke in 1906, and the challenges of his wartime presidency put enormous pressures on his health. That spring in Paris he showed alarming symptoms of an impending breakdown, sharp headaches, bursts of anger, erratic emotions. He may well have suffered a minor stroke then, and another in midsummer. The president's doctor, wife, and closest advisors all warned against the national speaking tour. Wilson ignored them, convinced that a direct appeal to the American people was the only way to salvage support for the

League of Nations. Believing that the League embodied the "essence of Christianity," he embarked on this last crusade with a martyr's stoicism. "Even though, in my condition, it might mean the giving up of my life," he told Tumulty, "I will gladly make the sacrifice to save the Treaty."[31]

Wilson collapsed after giving a speech in Pueblo, Colorado, on the night of September 25. As his train raced back to Washington that evening, the president told his doctor, "I seem to have gone to pieces." Less than a week later he suffered a massive stroke, from which he never fully recovered. This blow would have enormous consequences for the postwar peace, for the direction of the country for the next year and a half, and of course, for those men and women in prison still hoping for a presidential pardon.[32]

Chapter 10

An Amnesty Business
on Every Block

T HROUGH THE FALL, Woodrow Wilson remained secluded in his White House bedroom, access closely guarded by his wife and doctor. Even many in his own cabinet were not told that the president had suffered a cerebral thrombosis, that for the first month after his stroke he clung precariously to life, that much of his left side was paralyzed, and that he would most likely remain incapable of the sustained mental focus required to lead the country. Though a medical expert told them all this, the small band of loyalists who hovered over the fallen man told the public only that he was suffering a bout of "nervous exhaustion" brought on by overwork. Joseph Tumulty, the president's devoted secretary, scotched a move by some in the cabinet to turn over the reins of government to Vice President Thomas Marshall.

Even before the president's stroke, the administration had not dealt effectively with the rising levels of violence and unrest in the first year after the war—the bloody race riots, the thousands of strikes, the anger over rising prices, and the growing anxiety over the Bolshevist threat. Technically the country remained at war in Europe, while the domestic fight over the peace treaty ground on in bitter stalemate. And now the government was rudderless. The cabinet degenerated into a debating society, while Edith Wilson served as gatekeeper to the president, determined to protect him from all "nervous excitement." With little education and no authority under the Constitution, she became the president's "self-appointed censor," assuming the power to set the agenda for the executive branch.[1]

And so the president probably heard nothing that fall about the growing national debate over the speech rights of radicals. Many were clamoring for the administration to take stronger action to silence radicals and stamp out revolutionary threats. Lawmakers flooded Congress with plans to ban red flags, raise new barriers to immigration, and put those who had already arrived through a crash course in "Americanization." Impatient with the slow pace of federal action, dozens of states passed their own laws against sedition and revolutionary conspiracy, while New York launched a full-scale investigation of radicalism. And what federal and state prosecutors failed to accomplish was handled by vigilante groups who continued the wartime practice of breaking up meetings and ransacking offices. During an Armistice Day parade in Centralia, Washington, to take the most notable of many examples, marchers from the American Legion attacked a local IWW hall. The outnumbered Wobblies fired on them, killing several of the veterans. Enraged, the Legionnaires routed the radicals, hunted down one of their leaders, and lynched him.

Disturbed by signs that the nation was growing even more intolerant in this first year of "peace," a small but growing number of Americans began to pull the other way, rising to the defense of traditional American freedoms. And when they did, the cause of the political prisoners served as a rallying point, a concrete issue that embodied their wider concerns about the impact of war and revolution on civil liberties. From New York to Los Angeles, citizens organized a bewildering variety of new "amnesty" organizations and legal defense funds. Some evolved out of the legal aid organizations that sprang to life in 1917 to defend conscientious objectors. Others were formed by church groups that called for postwar reconciliation. Some groups defended one or a handful of jailed radicals from a particular city. Others, such as Kate Richards O'Hare's defense fund, were supported by thousands from across the country, all readers of a single newspaper.[2]

While many of the liberal amnesty organizations were modest in size, their letterheads bristled with the names of influential social gospel ministers, civil liberties lawyers, professors, settlement house progressives, feminists, and muckraking journalists. These men and women insisted that they were fighting to defend the principle of free speech, not any specific political program. For the same reason, they disavowed an interest in winning "special pardons for certain cases," even though many expressed a particular sympathy for Debs. Most of the wartime prosecutions had been a mistake, they insisted, and the best way to correct this error would be to convince the president to declare a general amnesty, establishing a precedent that would afford fuller protection for dissent in the future.

The most visible of these organizations was the National Civil Liberties Bureau, precursor to the ACLU. Organized in 1917 to help conscientious objectors, the NCLB expanded its role over the course of the war to defend those convicted under the Espionage and Sedition acts. The organization was led by Harvard-educated social worker Roger Baldwin. Like so many in the liberal intelligentsia, Baldwin began the war sure of his ability to persuade the president, and only gradually realized his error. Federal agents raided the NCLB office, Baldwin spent nine months in prison for refusing to register for the draft, and the group spent much of its energy defending itself from government charges of disloyalty. In spite of these setbacks, the NCLB served as a clearinghouse for information on the wartime cases, built alliances with other amnesty groups, and formed the Liberty Defense Union to provide legal aid to workers convicted under the wartime laws.[3]

In New York, a small group of philosophical anarchists and civil libertarians worked for the League for the Amnesty of Political Prisoners, the group christened by Emma Goldman on the eve of her departure for prison, and run initially by Lucy Robins and M. E. Fitzgerald. After moving to the AFL, Robins remained on the League's advisory board, which also included Helen Keller, Lincoln Steffens, and Roger Baldwin. Using funds drawn from Goldman's last lecture tour in the United States, the group emphasized the need for Americans to acknowledge the status of "political prisoner," pointing out that most European countries made a legal distinction between idealistic "non-conformists" and "so-called common criminals."[4]

The radicals behind the Tom Mooney "Defense League" expanded their mission to cover the new batch of "class war prisoners" produced by the Espionage and Sedition acts. The IWW formed its own amnesty organization, the Workers Defense League, run by labor activist Elizabeth Gurley Flynn. Though the group spent most of its time raising bail and paying for lawyers, they also held mass meetings to inform workers that the best way to free the prisoners would be to form one big union and bring the capitalist jailors down through a general strike.

While Lucy Robins and the civil libertarians believed that fighting for amnesty was a way to defend and restore traditional American rights, many radicals had a very different view of what was at stake. As one left-wing socialist put it, "The constitutionality or unconstitutionality of the law matters not." The wartime prosecutions seemed to confirm their view that the entire legal system was nothing more than an "act of aggression by the bourgeois class against the working class." If that was true, further appeals to the First Amendment were a waste of time.

The Greenwich Village radicals at the *Liberator* thought that Lenin had much to teach American workers about the true nature of free speech. As they consolidated their power, the Bolsheviks had ruthlessly denied speech rights to their "class enemies." "A dominant class will always suppress the propaganda that seriously threatens its dominance," the *Liberator* explained with a surprising cheerfulness. "There is in Russia no pretense at freedom of speech, no pretense that equality of rights between the two classes exists. The dominant proletariat is openly and boastfully stamping out the rights of the bourgeoisie." The lesson from Russia seemed to be that speech could never be truly free until workers united to create a classless society.[5]

The *Liberator* also pointed out that no one seemed more determined to exploit the revolutionary possibilities of his imprisonment than Debs himself. By refusing to ask for a pardon, and demanding to be released last of all, he had demonstrated a "true revolutionary attitude" that others should emulate. Locked in his cell, he had not been deprived of his place in the revolutionary movement, but had become its "rallying spirit." Many radicals were coming to the conclusion that the rising clamor over the political prisoners might be just loud enough to rouse American workers from their capitalist slumbers. When workers united to "demand" freedom for Debs, they would be learning how to liberate themselves.[6]

Surveying this fertile free speech debate that emerged after the war,

Walter Lippmann observed that the various organizations working for
amnesty did not offer a single, coherent defense of the First Amendment, but a tangle of competing theories. The one thing they shared in
common, he thought, was the fact that none embraced free speech as
an absolute value, a right due to everyone at all times. Ultimately,
Lippmann concluded, we never value free speech for its own sake, but
as a tool for achieving something we value more, our vision of a more
just and harmonious world. Some in the amnesty ranks, then, defended
free speech as a way to encourage wide democratic participation in progressive reforms; others saw it as a vital tool for organized labor to win a
greater share of the fruits of industry; and others saw little value in free
speech unless it contributed to the destruction of a capitalist system
that held workers in bondage. Those opposed to amnesty considered
themselves no less the champions of free speech, but believed that this
right should be denied to those who would use it to undermine the social order. In their view, those agitating for amnesty, and demanding
civil liberties for anarchists, Wobblies, and other malcontents, were
"free speech fakers" who were cynically using the First Amendment as a
shield to protect their efforts to destroy the American way of life. In this
sense, the amnesty debate that was emerging in the fall of 1919 ignored
the fine distinctions that were the province of judges and legal scholars.
The fight over the fate of the political prisoners was instead a debate
about the future direction of the country.[7]

As Lippmann saw, most branches of the amnesty movement offered
no new arguments about the value of free speech. These groups were
led by social activists, not lawyers and legal scholars, and their use of
free speech arguments was more pragmatic than precise. We should
not, for this reason, underestimate the impact that this protest movement had on Americans' growing concern for civil liberties. In the aftermath of the war, many thousands of Americans worried that patriotic
mobs and government prosecutors were doing serious harm to the
nation's democratic institutions. The various factions of the amnesty
movement helped people voice these fears, channeling their concerns
in a way that linked broad democratic ideals about free speech and fair
play to a more concrete and attainable political goal, the liberation of
wartime prisoners.

Many in the amnesty movement felt frustrated by their differences, feeling sure that their disagreements undermined their ability to bring pressure to bear on the president. However, civil liberties lawyer Harry Weinberger considered this diversity to be a strength. Each group knew how to reach a different segment of the public, he argued, crafting free speech arguments that were most likely to convince their own audience, and offering different ways to voice those concerns. Together, these groups helped many thousands of Americans rethink their ideas about civil liberties. At a time when war and revolution gave fresh energy to the nation's most reactionary forces, the amnesty movement provided a way to organize a counterreaction.[8]

Because so many of the prisoners were Socialists, the leaders who remained out of jail believed that their party had a particular obligation to lead this working-class battle for amnesty. Their efforts were hampered, however, by continuing harassment from government agents. Post Office censors still disrupted the circulation of party newspapers and either delayed or destroyed official correspondence. The Justice Department planted spies and provocateurs. Arrests continued and legal bills mounted, leaving many of the accused to face their trials without significant financial help. When party leaders asked for contributions to an amnesty fund, they raised only five hundred dollars, a reflection, they felt sure, not of apathy but of their members' dire economic troubles. The one bright spot was the "prison comfort club," a volunteer effort by Socialist women who provided sweets and socks to the prisoners, and winter clothing for their families. Mothers left destitute by their husbands' imprisonment pleaded for cash to cover the rent, but there was none to give.[9]

Under these difficult circumstances, the party decided that the best way to promote amnesty would be to organize an alliance, joining forces with liberals, church groups, and trade unionists who shared an interest in defending the free speech rights of American workers. Though the AFL's national convention rejected the amnesty cause, the Socialists knew that many of the more radical unions were supportive. In the summer of 1919 the party invited its amnesty allies to send delegates to an "American Freedom Convention" in Chicago. There the Socialists hoped to forge, and then lead, a movement powerful enough to send a "warning to the tyrants in authority."[10]

Along with government interference, amnesty organizers faced an even more formidable challenge from within the Socialist ranks. Since early 1919 tensions had been mounting between the party's militant "left wing" and its more moderate leadership. That spring the controversy spilled over into the amnesty work when spokesmen for the party's left-leaning foreign-language federations announced that their members refused to work with liberals and other "petit-bourgeois elements," on amnesty or any other cause. Convinced that all talk of American "rights" was a bourgeois fraud, they insisted that an alliance with liberals would distract the party from its proper task, winning the class war against capitalism. "The Socialist Party alone must gain the power," they insisted, "then the jail doors will open and our comrades go free."[11]

This skirmish over strategy reflected a much deeper ideological divide among Socialists that would soon erupt into a civil war and splinter the movement. From its birth, the party had been an uneasy coalition of reform-minded moderates who believed in the political process, and more revolutionary "reds" who pressed for "immediate action." Sparring between the "slow-shulists" and the "impossibilists" was a common feature of most party debates, and one of Debs's greatest contributions had always been his ability to mediate these tensions.[12]

During the war years, the balance of power in the party shifted sharply to the left. Many moderates abandoned the party, while those who remained were radicalized by years of government persecution. This leftward trend was accelerated by the massive influx of Russian and East European immigrants who joined after 1917, eager to emulate the militant example of the Russian Bolsheviks. By early 1919, leaders of the left-wing faction concluded that the Socialists' traditional program of democratic political action was not only too timid, but even "counter-revolutionary." Meeting on their own, they decided that the party's moderate leadership practiced a "perverted version of socialism" and "could not be trusted." Lenin himself had said as much. In spite of all that men like Morris Hillquit and Victor Berger had done for the party, and all they had suffered during the war years, the Soviets denounced them as "opportunists" and "social traitors." When the Socialists held their annual convention in Chicago in early September, the left wing was determined to seize control of the leadership and turn the party into a truly revolutionary force.[13]

The moderates considered themselves supporters of the Russian Revolution, but they felt sure that the left wing's dream of bringing a Bolshevik-style revolution to American shores was delusional. Entranced by Marxist theory, the left wing seemed out of touch with American reality. Capitalism was stronger than ever, while the radical movement was small, battered, and impoverished. If Debs and the other comrades had to wait in their cells until the Socialists somehow "gained the power," they would likely all die behind bars. Believing that the left wing's extremism would only destroy what remained of the party, the moderates managed to maintain control at the convention, but only through a series of unseemly parliamentary maneuvers and help from the Chicago police. Denouncing the party leadership, many of the leftists broke away to form two separate communist parties, each claiming to carry the true revolutionary gospel to America's working class.[14]

The party Debs had lived and gone to jail for, the party that stood by its principles for more than two years in the face of government prosecutions and mob attacks, now seemed bent on destroying itself. "How pathetic it is," Theodore complained to Karsner, "that just at this time when the plutocracy is straining every nerve to crush and silence us, . . . that we should be at each other's throats! It is surely a day of jubilation for our enemies."[15]

Three weeks after this disastrous party split, several hundred delegates arrived in Chicago for the American Freedom Convention. Although some of them came from labor unions and civil liberties groups, reporters noted that the gathering looked suspiciously like a Socialist meeting. And there in Chicago, the party's battle lines were once again evident. Many who took the podium demanded a "truly radical" amnesty program, one not aimed at restoring traditional American liberties but dedicated to the creation of a new and higher system of justice. One declared that he was ready to "strip the verbiage off" and be honest about the true stakes in the fight to free Debs. "It is time to quit talking about

American liberty," he argued, "and talk about workingmen's liberty. It is time to quit talking about restoring constitutional liberty and to talk about establishing an industrial republic."[16]

Moderates at the convention wanted to lobby Congress, but radicals declared that signing petitions and passing resolutions were acts of "utter futility." They were done with begging for favors from a government run by and for the capitalist class. Instead, workers needed to organize, using the "power of solidarity" in order to "demand" their rights. Fretting that the party's amnesty campaign was being hijacked by extremists, the moderates who ran the Socialists' amnesty committee tried to move the conversation away from plans for "conquest of the world" and on to a more practical program of action, but their pleas were in vain. One speaker after another demanded the creation of One Big Union, or a proletarian army strong enough to "break down the jails." In the end, the moderates complained that the party's amnesty program had been "sabotaged" by those who were more interested in advancing their revolutionary theories than they were in getting Debs and his comrades out of jail.[17]

The convention founded yet another amnesty organization, the American Freedom Forum, to carry out the directives of its militant manifesto. Though the Forum claimed to be a nonpartisan alliance, all of its small staff and most of its modest support came from the Socialists and the unions they controlled in Chicago and the surrounding region. Ignoring the convention's incendiary rhetoric, the Forum's staff pursued more modest and conventional goals, urging its affiliates to send letters to Washington, pass out leaflets, and talk about amnesty with "friends, neighbors and shopmates." Even these humble efforts were often stymied, as many of their amnesty meetings were either attacked by mobs or shut down by the police.[18]

In the charged atmosphere of late 1919, the Socialists were not the only ones who found that many Americans were determined to stop them from speaking about free speech. That Christmas morning, two hundred members of Emma Goldman's League for the Amnesty of Political Prisoners attempted to stage a protest march up New York's Fifth Avenue. Dressing in "manacles" and prison suits, they planned to sing carols and wave signs on the steps of city churches, stirring the consciences of worshippers as they left their morning services. Instead, they were scattered by the police, who tore their banners, threw some demonstrators in snowbanks, and chased the rest on what one reporter called a "songless scamper" through downtown streets. The *New York Times* gloated over the "theatrical realism" that the police added to the scene by arresting five who were already dressed like convicts. Afterward, some straggled back to their headquarters and made plans to file charges of police brutality.[19]

Stories of the Christmas morning "red parade" ran in papers across the country, and the protestors consoled themselves with the thought that they had given amnesty "enormous" publicity. Though editors denounced the group as "essentially absurd," the wire stories reminded readers across the country that several hundred of the wartime prisoners remained in jail that Christmas day.[20]

In the face of public ridicule and police nightsticks, amnesty organizations continued to spread across the country in the year after the armistice. As Lucy Robins put it, "every block had a little amnesty business." She did not mean this as a compliment. Like traveling salesmen for civil liberties, each group competed for the same customers, the small but growing number of Americans willing to stand up for the political prisoners. The liberals, Robins believed, lacked a serious commitment to what she conceived of as a working-class cause. Many of them were "young boys with floating Windsor ties and young girls with massy, bobbed hair" who took money in order to give "fat jobs to lawyers." She thought the radicals were even worse, alienating many by confusing the cause of amnesty with their wild schemes for a general strike, or the nationalization of industry, or the defense of two Italian anarchists arrested for shooting a Boston policeman, whose names were Sacco and Vanzetti. This approach, she felt sure, only alienated the "conservative masses," men and women who sympathized with Debs but had no interest in supporting the radicals' "latest fad."[21]

In turn, the radicals believed that Robins, as a "henchman" of Gompers, was bent on destroying the revolutionary possibilities of the amnesty cause. The charge was fair enough. She dreamed that amnesty would teach American workers to band together, not for a proletarian revolution, but for the progressive improvement of their society. And her more immediate goal was explicitly conservative, the restoration of what she called "a normal way of thinking and feeling" that had been lost during the war years. Robins believed that her approach valued meaningful results over empty revolutionary rhetoric, but many radical journalists denounced her as a "traitor, reactionary, and jingo."[22]

For Robins, this debate over the true meaning of the amnesty fight ran through the middle of her own home. Her husband Bob considered her alliance with Gompers to be a "betrayal of radicalism and a repudiation of our way of life." Robins was stung by the public attacks on her work, many from her former friends in the radical movement, but was even more hurt when Bob did not rush to her defense. He refused to even meet Gompers. The couple agreed to an uneasy compromise; she would not join the AFL, and he would not become a communist.[23]

Exasperated by this criticism, Robins decided to travel to Atlanta and put the matter to Debs himself. Though she had been working on his behalf for months, Robins never dreamed that she might actually meet the man she thought of as a working-class "messiah." Now she sat in the warden's office, her heart pounding, face to face with "the noblest man in America." She brought Debs tokens of esteem from unions across the country. Tears rolled down his cheeks as he examined a cane with an engraved silver head, an elaborately carved pipe, and silk pajamas monogrammed in red, all tributes from American workers. Then she brought him greetings from Gompers, his old nemesis, and laid out a handful of the thousands of letters and amnesty petitions she had been gathering from conservative AFL unions. She wanted him to see that he was "not only the martyr of a certain political party, or of a certain factional group," but that his imprisonment concerned "the entire labor movement."[24]

Debs seemed both surprised and moved by this support, and told Robins to send his thanks to Gompers. "Nothing troubles me more than the fratricide in our movement," he told her. Robins felt assured, believing that she had received Debs's blessing for her approach to amnesty. Of course, Debs would have been both ungracious and unwise to reject help from Gompers and Robins in winning freedom for himself and his comrades. Robins stretched things, however, when she

Debs and Lucy Robins at the prison farm.
Debs Collection, Indiana State University Library.

interpreted his remarks as a sign that her work was forging a new understanding between Gompers and Debs, the left and right pillars of working-class America.[25]

Few "messiahs" stand up to close personal scrutiny, but Debs more than met Lucy Robins's expectations. She was surprised, though, by

Warden Zerbst. Her old friend Alexander Berkman told tales about his Atlanta days that made the warden seem like a monster, but Robins found him to be considerate and charming. After bending prison rules by letting Robins meet privately with Debs, he offered to take her on a tour of Atlanta. Never one to hold back, she asked if Debs could come along as well, and to her delight Zerbst agreed.

The next day Debs, his jailor, and his would-be liberator drove through the streets of Atlanta. To avoid unwanted publicity, the warden asked Debs to hide himself under a long cape. Relishing his freedom, Debs pointed out landmarks as they drove along, recounting stories of the Civil War and the class war in Georgia. Zerbst was eager to show off the model prison farm that he was building in Decatur, just east of the city. For the rest of the afternoon, the group frolicked among the cows and chickens. No less than David Karsner, Robins felt in the presence of history, and eagerly recorded Debs's comments for posterity. When they found a cage where the inmates kept rabbits, she asked him why men who lived behind bars themselves would inflict the same pain on "poor little animals like these, just for the fun of it?"

"It is the same everlasting human weakness," Debs replied, sorrow in his voice. "The strong gloating over the weak. That, Comrade, is the evil root implanted in the human being, which we Socialists must eradicate by education." Inspired by Debs's "God-like soul," Robins vowed to re-double her devotion to winning his freedom.[26]

She kept a treasured memento from that day, snapshots of herself with Debs taken by Warden Zerbst. They show her beaming with delight, a spark plug of energy in a floppy hat. Looming over her in his convict denim, Debs wore the ambivalent smile of a prisoner on a picnic.

Chapter 11

Candidate 9653

THE SOCIALIST PARTY that gathered in New York for its annual convention in May 1920 was a remnant of the movement that had once inspired its followers and rattled its enemies. Though the communists had departed, the ideological power struggle continued to divide the party at a time when it desperately needed a united front. A third of the delegates came from what remained of the party's militant left wing. Embracing the Bolsheviks' methods, they wanted Socialists to organize American workers into soviets, preparing the way for a future dictatorship of the proletariat. The lesson of Lenin's success was obvious, they insisted—revolutions are won not through talking and voting, but through industrial organization and the canny use of brute force by a disciplined minority.

The moderate majority at the convention ridiculed such talk as a futile attempt to apply "Russian methods" where they did not belong. The great mass of American workers would either not understand Bolshevism, Morris Hillquit insisted, or would reject it soundly if they did. "We must discard phrases," he pleaded, "and talk sense for a while." In spite of all they had been through during the war, the moderates insisted that the democratic process remained the best tool for bringing socialism to America. Hillquit and his allies hoped to rebuild the party in 1920 by calling the nation's alienated but unorganized radicals and liberals to their banner, turning the election into a protest against an administration that had "overthrown the corner stone of the republic, the freedom of the press, speech and assemblage." In this way, Hillquit argued, Socialists would prove to the electorate that they were the most conservative party in the race, the only one devoted to preserving America's traditional democratic principles.[1]

Outside the hall, police guarded against an attack by the American Legion or some more impromptu vigilante swarm. Inside, delegates took turns attacking each other, particularly over Lenin's call for all socialist parties to join a Russian-led Third International. The Russians had not invited the entire Socialist Party to participate; only the left-wingers were considered revolutionary enough, the "tendency" that Lenin thought was epitomized by Debs. When Victor Berger announced that he had no more interest in living under a proletarian dictatorship than under any other kind of tyranny, angry leftists hissed and hooted. "The capitalists gave me twenty years," Berger shot back. "How many would you give me? I have faced patriotic mobs and I am not afraid of Communist mobs!" At one point, desperate to restore order, the moderator banged his gavel so hard that its head flew off, glancing off the skull of a hapless reporter in the audience.[2]

The Socialists did find one thing on which they agreed. When a delegate from Indiana nominated Debs for his fifth run for the presidency, the crowd erupted in a thirty-minute demonstration of "yipping yells, piercing cat-calls, feminine shrieks, stamping feet, clapping hands, and general shouting and cheer-leading." Chants of "Debs! Debs! We Want Debs!" were punctuated by choruses of the "Internationale" and the "Hymn to Free Russia." For three years these men and women had suffered humiliating defeats at the hands of what Hillquit called "all the powers of darkness and oppression in the country"—their meetings had been mobbed, their leaders jailed, their party infiltrated by government spies. Thanks in part to this pressure, only thirty thousand remained on the party's membership roles, and even they were splintered into embittered factions. Now the Debs nomination offered catharsis and a chance for the party to pull together in a gorgeous gesture of defiance. Delighted by this prospect, delegates joined hands to hips for a "snake-dance," their long line twisting through the hall as they chanted

"Eu-Gene Debs!" Leftists and moderates, staid lawyers and blue-collar activists paid giddy tribute to their leader, whose image looked down on them from a massive portrait hung on the podium.[3]

Even the journalists were swept up in the euphoria. Back home their editors thundered against the Debs nomination. "Mr. Debs's strength as a candidate," the *Times* fumed, "seems to rest mainly upon the fact that he is a lawbreaker and a revolutionist." Another called the entire party a "criminal conspiracy" to promote contempt for the law. Reporters in the convention hall were more sympathetic. When a rose landed on their table, these minions of the capitalist press plucked scarlet petals to wear in their lapels, grinning at their token gesture of rebellion. To them, the dancing Socialists seemed less like the vanguard of revolution than a hapless but incorrigible American underdog.[4]

Drunk on the symbolism of a convict candidate, the delegates sobered a bit when it came time to choose a running mate. While some lobbied for Kate Richards O'Hare, also still in prison, the convention decided that at least one member of the ticket ought to be at liberty to wage an actual campaign. Seymour Stedman, Debs's lawyer and long-time friend, got the nomination. One observer joked that only a seasoned lawyer like Stedman could campaign against Wilson's "new freedom" and manage to avoid arrest.[5]

David Karsner liked to take credit for being the first to suggest to Debs a "jail house to the White House" campaign. He had broached the idea a year earlier, during their long trolley ride to the Moundsville penitentiary. Back then, Debs showed no interest. "There is better timber in the woods than I," as he put it. However, through the fall of 1919, as the split in the radical movement widened into open warfare, friends from all sides of the conflict urged him to accept the nomination for his fifth run for the presidency.[6]

When Karsner visited him in Atlanta the following March, Debs reluctantly hinted that he would accept this "honor" if the party offered it. Karsner was ecstatic. Convinced that a Debs campaign would unite America's scattered radicals and send a "thrill and a throb through every lover of liberty" in the country, he pushed the idea in the pages of the *New York Call*. Through the spring, Karsner served as Debs's emissary to the various factions, appealing for a truce that would allow them to campaign "in solid formation and united phalanx, not in struggling squads battered and weakened by internecine warfare." In an open letter Debs pleaded that, since the two communist parties were outlawed, American radicals "either have to enter the campaign as the Socialist party or not at all. . . . Why not go into the fight with all our forces united?"[7]

But Karsner met a cold reception from communist leaders who rejected any overtures from the "stinking carcass that calls itself the Socialist Party." The time had come, they told Karsner, for Debs to choose sides. If he stayed with the Socialists, they would consider it their "duty" to oppose him in the name of the true worker's revolution. When Debs criticized their call for armed revolution and called the idea of American soviets "folly," the communists denounced his "milk-and-water" attitude. He was "a noble gent, but fooled," they decided, a true radical who was leading a party of self-aggrandizing dupes and reactionaries.[8]

Karsner had no better luck preaching tolerance to the leaders of the Socialist Party. They not only ignored Debs's request to invite a fraternal delegation of communists to the party convention, but they banned the distribution of their propaganda in the hall. "It is a hell of a situation," Karsner fumed after weeks of fruitless negotiation, "and the kind of one to give a person mental and spiritual nausea."[9]

For Debs, this blow was both political and personal. Some who now denounced him as a traitor to the revolution were comrades from more than two decades of socialist struggle. All through those years Debs had done much to hold the party together, embodying and containing its differences. Now, even the sympathy and respect he enjoyed from all sides was not enough to rebuild his party. Rebuffed by communist leaders, he could only take comfort in the fact that he still enjoyed the personal loyalty of many who had left the Socialist Party. At the *Liberator,* Max Eastman and his fellow Greenwich Village Bolsheviks scorned the Socialists for having no "real understanding of the revolution," but they put a portrait of Debs on their cover that spring and declared him to be "Our Candidate." Any communists who planned to vote that year would likely cast their lot with Debs, but what they did not do is return to the Socialist fold. In this sense, Debs lost the campaign of 1920 before he had even been nominated, failing in his primary goal of reuniting the factions of his beloved Socialist Party.[10]

Still, seeing Debs's name on the ballot breathed new life into the party faithful. As one comrade put it, "Nothing that has happened since the dark days of the war has so cheered and inspired us." For more than a year, while their comrades sat in jail, Socialists had been distracted by partisan warfare, their meetings degenerating into what one frustrated radical called "debating societies." As membership dwindled, concerted efforts toward amnesty ground to a halt. Time and again, the Socialists had announced plans for massive protests that never materialized and squabbled among themselves over tactics. With the Debs nomination, however, they enjoyed a renewed sense of mission, and a new vehicle to express their political passions. Though they still paid homage to the distant dream of building a cooperative commonwealth, they fought now for a more immediate goal, freedom for "our Gene."[11]

Eager to capitalize on the national interest generated by their unusual candidate, two hundred Socialists traveled to Washington after the convention to pressure the Wilson administration to release the "political prisoners." Newspaper editors across the country considered this "brazen effrontery." Debs remained unrepentant, the *Washington Post* reminded its readers, and if released he would "plunge immediately into a campaign of abuse and vilification of the government, and would do all in his power to bring about a red orgy of anarchy."[12]

Still, the mainstream press could not resist this vignette of political theater. Marching two abreast toward the White House, Socialists noted with delight the flock of cameramen on hand to record their protest for a national audience. As they filed by, a White House doorman muttered, "All kinds of anarchists and socialists are coming here to have their pictures taken." Within days, those photographs and newsreels spread the amnesty message across the country, and signaled to friend and foe alike that the Socialist Party had survived the war, battered but unbowed.

As the only man capable of granting amnesty, Wilson was the ostensible target of this demonstration, but an audience with the isolated and convalescing president was out of the question. Access was still closely guarded by his wife and his physician, and his only contact with the country came in a few brief and carefully scripted meetings with senators and foreign dignitaries, and sporadic messages penned by aides who spoke for, but rarely or never saw, the president. As the nation debated the terms of the armistice, struggled with the economic shocks of demobilization, and fought over the best way to deal with the communist threat, Wilson showed only slight signs of recovery in the early months of 1920. Confined to his bed or a wheelchair, he had great difficulty focusing his attention for long. That spring he spent his mornings touring Washington in an automobile, his afternoons watching movies at the White House. His favorites were the old newsreels of his triumphant reception in Paris, which he watched again and again.

The president's suffering in these months was both physical and political. Unwilling to compromise with his Republican opponents in the Senate, he seethed with contempt for those "Benedict Arnolds" who blocked ratification of his treaty. He further isolated himself by cutting all ties with his former friend and confidante, Colonel House, and firing his secretary of state, Robert Lansing, for a variety of betrayals, real and imagined. Scores of liberals and socialists who once believed they enjoyed influence over the president now found themselves shut out of his small and shrinking inner circle. Impotent but intractable, Wilson sometimes dreamed of running for a third term, fantasizing an impossible political comeback that would vanquish his foes and secure his plan for a progressive international order. More often he thought of resigning, moaning to Dr. Grayson that he "felt like going to bed and staying there."[13]

Standing in for the president, Joseph Tumulty met with the Socialist delegation. He listened respectfully as Seymour Stedman ran through arguments that were fast becoming familiar—that Debs, Kate O'Hare, and others were "political prisoners" who had been jailed for expressing legitimate dissent, that even if the government did have the right to silence them during the war, peace should bring their freedom, and that "civilized governments everywhere" had already freed their war prisoners. To this familiar litany the petitioners added a new twist. Since Debs was now their candidate, keeping him behind bars put their party at a decided disadvantage in the coming campaign. He should be free, they argued, as a matter of "simple political fairness."[14]

"These are serious matters," Tumulty told the petitioners as he ushered them to the door. "I am sure the President will give them conscientious consideration." In fact, Wilson had advised his secretary not to meet with the Socialists at all. More diplomatic than his petulant boss, Tumulty ignored this suggestion, but he surely saw no point in sharing the Socialist petition with the president.[15]

A smaller delegation also called on the man that some now dubbed "Pontius Palmer." As the Socialists rehearsed their plea, a reporter for the *Call* thought that the attorney general's mind was "disturbed by a glimmering appreciation of the issues involved." But others in the room saw no evidence that he was moved. In the midst of an hour-long conversation, Palmer suggested that if Debs and his fellow prisoners wanted their freedom, they should ask the president for a pardon. Frustrated by the administration's "gnawing hunger for apologies," the Socialists replied that Debs would rather die in jail than make any such admission of guilt. In turn, Palmer told his visitors that he would do nothing that might undermine the authority of the judiciary or imply that the government had jailed Americans unfairly. Faced with this stalemate, Palmer ended the interview with an evasive promise to take their request "under advisement." The road to a presidential amnesty led through the attorney general, and he seemed unwilling to budge.[16]

A few weeks later, the administration did commute the sentence of Kate Richards O'Hare, next to Debs the best-known Socialist in prison. Evidence suggested that O'Hare had been the victim of perjured testimony inspired by a local political feud in the North Dakota town where she had been arrested. In releasing her, Palmer acknowledged none of this, but claimed instead that, because she was a wife and mother, a year in prison had been sufficient punishment.[17]

While Socialists greeted the O'Hare pardon as a sign that their pressure tactics were working, the Wilson administration made no further pardons and said little about the amnesty controversy that spring. "Official Washington is an enigma," Theodore Debs complained. Rumors swirled that Wilson's cabinet was deeply divided over the issue, but the president's only public comment on the matter that spring was a claim that he "did not know that there was any demand for the release of political prisoners." This lie seemed artfully designed to infuriate the radicals. Some took it as proof of the president's mental incompetence—as Theodore put it, Wilson was "running with the squirrels." Others, still trusting in the president's liberal sympathies, suspected that Tumulty, Palmer, and Edith Wilson were shielding the fragile president from the rising public protest.[18]

In the face of this stonewalling from the White House, the Socialists had little choice but to speak louder, ratcheting up public pressure on the administration. The strategy was risky, even likely to be counterproductive, since the administration wanted to avoid the appearance of yielding to the radicals' demands. Still, the Socialists saw no alternative. Appeals through the courts had been exhausted, the president ignored amnesty petitions, if he heard them at all, and though the tide of public opinion seemed to be turning gradually in their favor, most of the mainstream press remained hostile. Their only hope, Theodore Debs now believed, would be to use the election campaign as a tool for rallying public support for amnesty. "If our showing in the fall election is such as to merit contempt," he predicted, "that is what we will get. A large vote will not only restore the freedom of the press, the right of assemblage, but it will open the doors of every prison and liberate the hundreds of comrades inside the walls."[19]

In search of this "large vote," the party had to pursue new and creative channels to reach the American public. The war and the battle over communism had reduced their membership by two-thirds, and their once vibrant independent press was decimated. Even the *New York Call*, the party's strongest surviving voice, was riven by factionalism and teetered on the verge of bankruptcy. Socialists needed to reach beyond the party faithful to the wider mass of discontented voters, and toward that end they orchestrated an irresistible media moment, a nomination ceremony at the Atlanta penitentiary. However much mainstream newspaper editors thundered against the Debs nomination, few could deny that such a scene radiated human interest. As one conceded, "Nothing in the history of American national elections has presented a situation so unique." At a time when politicians, war propagandists, and soap salesmen were all experimenting with powerful new strategies of mass persuasion, the Socialists showed that they were keeping pace in the modern art of media manipulation.[20]

On May 29, a half-dozen Socialist leaders drove to the gates of the prison, joined by as many journalists and photographers. Emerging from the prison gates, Debs greeted each of his comrades with a bear hug and a kiss on each cheek, and accepted a bouquet of crimson carnations. A local reporter thought the delegation looked suspiciously un-American, their accents Old World, and their complexions "swarthy" behind "thick-lensed spectacles." Most of Debs's friends had not seen him since he left for Moundsville a year earlier, and they were surprised to find him looking healthy, his blue eyes flashing behind steel spectacles, his skin "tan as an Indian." Tall and bony in his prison denim, he loomed over them, a comfortable and genial host greeting old friends on the porch of his penitentiary.[21]

After Debs introduced his friends to Warden Zerbst, the group repeated the ceremony of kissing and carnations for the benefit of the newsreel cameras. The convict-candidate waved to America as one photographer called out, "You're a fine actor, Mr. Debs . . . a bully actor!"[22]

Gathered in the warden's office, the group listened to party spokesman James Oneal formally offer Debs the nomination, praising him for combining the virtues of Jesus, Socrates, and John Brown. Debs replied with a forty-five-minute acceptance speech. In four previous runs for the White House Debs had launched his campaigns with fiery speeches before adoring crowds. Now he spoke quietly and deliberately to a handful of comrades and reporters—and to Warden Zerbst, who smiled as he surveyed the unlikely scene unfolding in his office.

Most journalists showed little interest in what Debs had to say about the issues of the 1920 election. Their editors sent them to gather a human interest story, not a serious profile of a viable third party. The candidate's pink flannel socks and prison slippers seemed more worthy of note than his position on the nation's unemployment crisis. The reporters perked up, though, when Debs announced that he was still a Bolshevik, "never more so than now." He scolded his comrades for cautiously chasing votes when they should be organizing workers for

The nomination committee greets
Debs on the steps of the Atlanta penitentiary.
Debs's lawyer and running mate, Seymour Stedman, is in the front,
to Debs's immediate left.
Debs Collection, Indiana State University Library.

revolution. Still searching for an elusive middle ground, Debs also challenged the party's left wing and the communist sectarians. "I am not
a Russian bolshevik in America," he explained, "but an American
bolshevik—fighting here for what they are fighting for in Russia." As
such, he rejected violence and "dictatorship of every form," even in the
name of the worker's revolution. "We stand for freedom, equal rights,
and justice for all."[23]

Many papers ignored Debs's speech and concentrated instead on the
fact that he had greeted the Socialist delegation with a kiss. The wire
service provided its customers with a close-up of Debs and Stedman,
locked in comradely embrace. "He Kisses the Committee," the *Times*

noted in its headlines. The sight of Debs "actually kissing" his comrades, another editor noted, sent a "shiver of repugnance" down his newspaper's metaphorical spine. The Terre Haute paper quipped that the ceremony looked suspiciously French, while the Atlanta reporter also mocked these public displays of affection. The Socialists found it easier to get into America's newspapers than they did to control the message.[24]

While the nation's editors scoffed, they also worried. Sensing the public's deep dissatisfaction, many predicted that the Socialists would make impressive gains in the 1920 election. By running Debs from prison, the party would appeal to many who had little or no interest in socialism but wanted to protest against the Espionage Act, Palmer's raids on radicals, the country's economic slump, or any number of other issues in those troubled first months of peace. A vote for Debs, in short, seemed a fine way to vote against Wilson, Palmer, and Burleson, and many editors believed that a growing number of Americans would jump at the chance.[25]

In their coverage of the Debs nomination, a few papers praised the Socialists for their moderation and their continued commitment to the democratic process. The party had driven off its Bolshevik extremists, after all, and drafted a platform that included strong calls for civil liberties, and a host of reforms that once sounded radical but had since become common progressive causes. The Socialists were chasing after votes, as one editor saw it, and posed no threat to American democracy. Most editors disagreed, insisting that the Socialists were as unpatriotic and dangerous as ever. Putting Debs on the ballot was an insult to the legal system, they argued, and a slap on the Supreme Court's face. "The day will come," the *Houston Post* warned, "when the people of America will have to deal with these radicals, and from this time on they require more and more the attention of the people and the Department of Justice."[26]

Thousands of Americans were keeping an eye on Debs that month, watching the newsreels of his Atlanta nomination ceremony that flickered on screens across the country. Distributed by the Labor Film Service, the radicals' answer to the emerging corporate film distribution networks, the film explained that "Debs is serving a prison term, for he loved liberty too well when there was no liberty." In New York the movie shared the vaudeville stage with Helen Keller, who peppered her appearances with an appeal for the political prisoners. As part of her act, Keller fielded questions from the audience, and she was often asked which living American she most admired; that gave her a perfect chance to sing Debs's praises. Socialists across the country found the newsreel "an inspiring and touching sight." Some viewers hissed, and others complained that the film was a "rank piece of seditious propaganda," but many more cheered. "Better propaganda," an English reporter observed, "than most Socialist speeches."[27]

The *New York Times* was incensed by the public's enthusiasm for what it called a "fraudulent melodrama." "It is not a genuine scene," the paper complained. "It is a performance carefully planned with a view to creating sympathy among the unthinking." Manipulating "mob psychology," the newsreel ignored the fact that Debs had been duly convicted for undermining the war effort, and played instead on the "pathos of old age in distress." In spite of this bad review in the *Times*, the Socialist strategy seemed to be working. A smiling old man in prison garb, clutching carnations and kissing his friends, Debs looked less like a threat to his country than its victim.[28] By the spring of 1920, a growing number of liberals felt that Debs was winning the moral high ground in his standoff with the Wilson administration. As war passions cooled, Debs looked to many like a martyr for the cause of free speech, the embodiment of a sacred right of patriotic dissent.[29]

Chapter 12

The Trials of A. Mitchell Palmer

O N JANUARY 2, 1920, the Wilson administration's long war on
radicalism reached its dramatic crescendo. Under the direction
of J. Edgar Hoover, Justice Department agents launched a nationwide series of "raids" that rounded up more than six thousand men
and women suspected of being communists. Lacking the legal authority
to detain American citizens, Palmer went after immigrants, intending
to deport them under a 1918 immigration law that targeted aliens who
belonged to any organization that preached hate against America or
promoted the doctrine of violent revolution. Because noncitizens enjoyed no right to a trial, Palmer planned to give each detainee a quick
hearing in front of Immigration officials, and predicted that the government would soon deport over three thousand of them. He had already
given this strategy a successful test run in December, when he expelled
Emma Goldman, Alexander Berkman, and 247 others to Russia aboard
a ship that the press gleefully dubbed the "Soviet Ark."[1]

While some objected to the Justice Department's "czarist" tactics,
most congressional leaders and newspaper editors praised Palmer for
this bold move against the enemy within. "There is no time to waste," as
the *Washington Post* put it, "on hairsplitting over infringement of liberty." In the face of public pressure for action, and the bombing of his
own home, Palmer had joined the fight against radicalism only slowly.

By that winter, however, his public statements became increasingly pugnacious. Bolshevism was simply another word for "robbery," he explained, an assault on property, religion, and the sanctity of marriage that the government had an obligation to stamp out. In the face of this international conspiracy, he reasoned, "there could be no nice distinctions drawn between the theoretical ideals of the radicals and their actual violations of our national laws." The attorney general claimed that his raids had already broken the back of American communism, but he promised more dragnets in the months ahead.[2]

For months Palmer had been criticized for not moving more aggressively against the radicals. Now his "fruitful intelligent vigor" against the red menace made him one of the most visible and popular members of the Wilson administration, and a likely prospect for the Democratic nomination.[3]

The Palmer raids were only the most spectacular of many attacks on radicals in the 1919 "Red Scare." State and city governments, in fact, led this war on communism. State police arrested many of the party leaders, including Rose Pastor Stokes and Big Bill Haywood, for violating freshly minted laws against sedition or criminal conspiracy. Several dozen legislatures banned the display of red flags, while one even outlawed red neckties. In New York, the socialist Rand School was invaded and closed down during a legislative investigation, while around the country school boards imposed loyalty oaths and fired those suspected of teaching Bolshevism to the young. Many commentators declared that colleges had become Leninist "hotbeds," while a number of clergymen lost their pulpits, accused of being "parlor pinks." Industrialists funded various patriotic societies that flooded the country with anti-radical propaganda. "When you hear a man tryin' to discredit Uncle Sam," one of their pamphlets warned, "that's Bolshevism." Those who tried to defend the free speech rights of communists found themselves denounced as red sympathizers. The National Civil Liberties Bureau came in for particular attack, slandered by government officials as an "actively disloyal" organization that was guilty of "developing sympathy for the Bolsheviki movement."[4]

As the term *Red Scare* suggests, historians describe the postwar assault on radicals as a brief but intense period of irrational emotion, a spasm of national "hysteria." Robert Murray, for example, thought that this flagrant disregard for basic civil liberties was best explained as the symptom of "a tremendous social delirium." Some blamed this on the unspent emotions of a brief war, others on the "nativist" fear of foreigners that often erupts in times of economic stress. Of course, the threat of foreign subversion was not simply the figment of the fevered imaginations of American bigots. During the war German agents did sabotage American facilities; unknown anarchists did plant bombs, more than once targeting American judges, politicians, and business leaders; in 1919 governments across Europe were rocked by communist revolutions. Though the danger of this happening in America was slight, tens of thousands in the country, mostly recent immigrants, had organized parties that embraced Lenin's call to arms, in rhetoric if not in reality.[5]

Clearly, Americans exaggerated and overreacted to this threat, often in ways that undermined the very democratic institutions they hoped to defend. From lynch mobs to congressional committees, people lost patience with the restraints imposed by the Bill of Rights. As a journalist at the time put it, the country defended its Constitution in unconstitutional ways, fought lawbreakers using illegal tactics, and attacked those who advocated violence by introducing their very own "reign of terror."[6]

And yet, even as the national campaign against radicals reached its peak in the first months of 1920, a growing number of Americans began to speak out against the state-sponsored war against radicals. This change in public mood became obvious when, soon after the raids, Congress took up Palmer's request for a peacetime sedition law. On the grounds that the nation was still technically at war, federal prosecutors had continued to arrest radicals using the Espionage Act, punishing them for obstructing a draft that was no longer in effect. Palmer warned Congress that once the treaty was signed, his prosecutors would be left "helpless," lacking any legal authority to fight the spread of communist doctrine. He estimated that sixty thousand radicals would be free to lay the groundwork for a proletarian revolution. Lawmakers responded to Palmer's request with enthusiasm, drafting seventy different proposals that would give the government the power to silence, deport, and in some instances execute those who advocated violent revolution. One senator suggested making it a felony to "entertain a disbelief in organized government," while another wanted to ban from the mail anything written in German. A Florida senator proposed turning Guam into a penal colony for political extremists.[7]

When Congress opened hearings on two draft sedition bills, however, they faced a deluge of public criticism. Dozens of newspaper publishers challenged the plan to give the postmaster permanent authority to ban from the mail any literature that advocated "insurrection." Samuel Gompers warned that a new sedition law would give Palmer a powerful weapon that he would use to stifle organized labor, and all progressive political movements. A "reign of terror" would sweep the country, he declared, and "heresy hunting would quickly become a national industry." Francis Kane, a federal prosecutor from Pennsylvania, resigned in protest against the January raids and testified against the sedition bill. Palmer's dark warnings about communist conspiracies were "ridiculous," he scoffed, and a permanent law would "breed suspicion among honest, law-abiding citizens." Harvard professor Zechariah Chafee warned that the law would set a dangerous precedent, giving the government a power to regulate speech that might one day be used "against the most conservative of us."[8]

Even Palmer refused to testify on behalf of the congressional versions of the sedition bill, which were so extreme that they made him "shudder a little." He insisted that he was an earnest guardian of free speech rights and had no interest in stifling even the angriest diatribes against the government. He told lawmakers that all he wanted was a "simple" bill that would give his office the authority to arrest those who published writings that advocated "the threat, or promise, or necessary implication of the use of force." People should be free to propose any plan to reform society, he argued, but when they urged others to use violence to achieve their goal, they should not expect the Constitution to protect them.[9]

A month earlier many lawmakers had criticized Palmer for not drafting a tough enough sedition bill. From every corner of the country, people were "clamoring" for the attorney general to use "all the power of the Federal Government" to protect the country from the red threat. Many editors continued to insist that the government needed new laws to punish what the *Post* called "any outrage of speech attacking the integrity of the Government or advocating violation of any law." Lawmakers, however, found it difficult to agree on a plan that would not give the government too much power to stifle legitimate speech, infringing on traditional American liberties. Faced with widespread protest from liberals, labor leaders, publishers, and church organizations, Congress quietly dropped the idea of a sedition bill entirely.[10]

While public protests helped kill the sedition bill, Congress was also influenced by revelations that spring that exposed the dark side of the Justice Department's war on red terror. Hundreds had been arrested without warrant, including American citizens, and many were brutally beaten by the police. Offices had been not only searched but mindlessly vandalized. Through an administrative order the detainees had been denied the right to counsel, and some were held for months without charges, unable to contact family or friends. Packed into overcrowded and unheated cells, sometimes denied food, some had committed suicide, while others went insane. At the time of the arrests, Palmer described the detainees as men with "sly and crafty eyes" of the "unmistakable criminal type." Of the more than six thousand rounded up, however, most were innocent, the victims of faulty intelligence or overzealous agents who simply swept into jail anyone in the vicinity of a raid. Some did belong to communist organizations that advocated violent revolution, but most denied knowing much about their group's politics; on closer examination, some of the "Bolshevist cells" proved to be little more than social clubs for Russian immigrants. In raids that spanned twenty-three states and more than thirty cities, agents found only three pistols, no bombs, and no proof that radicals had done anything more dangerous than talk about armed revolution.[11]

Faced with this evidence, Wilson's labor secretary, William B. Wilson, halted the immigration hearings and released more than 70 percent of those scheduled for deportation. When Congress investigated the matter, the Labor Department's assistant secretary Louis Post charged that the Justice Department had "broken all rules of law in its activities against the Reds," and had done so with Palmer's full knowledge and approval.[12]

Public reaction against the Red Scare was further galvanized by the

New York legislature's decision, in January 1920, to prevent five of its members from taking their seats because they were Socialists. Across the country, liberals and conservatives condemned what Walter Lippmann called the "frenzy in Albany." Warren Harding joined other senators in denouncing the New York legislature, and even Palmer distanced himself from this flagrant violation of democratic principles. Former Republican presidential candidate Charles Evans Hughes protested on behalf of the New York Bar Association. A year earlier, Hughes had pressured those same legislators to investigate the Bolshevik threat. Now he concluded that the New York legislature posed a greater risk to democracy than the radicals, and he offered his own services to defend the barred Socialists. Americans "have passed beyond the stage in political development," he declared, "when heresy-hunting is a permitted sport." As one historian of the Red Scare describes it, "Citizens could now see their own exaggerated fears mirrored in those of the New York legislators, and the reflection appeared ridiculous."[13]

As Red Scare fears subsided that spring, many now charged that the whole thing had been an illusion, a "paper dragon" stirred up by big business and political reactionaries in order to discredit organized labor and distract the country from the scandals of war profiteering. Newspapers began to investigate the huge and sometimes illicit profits reaped by some American corporations during the war; their stories added weight to the radical charges that American soldiers died in France to protect the interests of J. P. Morgan and his cronies. Some companies took advantage of government contracts in ways that one federal auditor described as "inordinate greed and barefaced fraud." A Senate investigation revealed "startling profits" for millers and meatpackers. Bethlehem Steel enjoyed an 800 percent increase in profits, and some coal companies fared even better. These stories appeared at a time when consumers struggled with inflation and many returning veterans struggled to find work. As William Jennings Bryan put it, "The bleeding overseas halted, but the bleeding here has continued." Newspapers that had enthusiastically pulled the nation's patriotic bandwagon during the war began to run editorial cartoons that juxtaposed fat and free capitalist profiteers with lean and lonely war prisoners, still languishing behind bars.[14]

ON THE OUTSIDE
—Williams, Washington Times.

By 1920 many concluded that the wrong people were behind bars.
From *Public Opinion: Where Does It Stand on the Question of Amnesty of
Political Prisoners?* [Chicago?] Printing and Publishing Workers Industrial
Union No. 450 [1923]. Courtesy of Debs Collection, Indiana State University Library.

This change in public mood found encouragement from an unlikely
source, the same Supreme Court that only months before had given
unanimous support to several Espionage Act convictions. After Oliver
Wendell Holmes Jr. issued his decision in the Debs case in the spring of
1919, he was surprised to find the opinion criticized from a variety of
quarters, including liberals at the *New Republic,* the more conservative
Harvard law professor Zechariah Chafee, and his fellow judge Learned
Hand. As Chafee summarized their complaints, Debs had been convicted of obstructing recruiting, "yet no provocation to any such definite
and particular act was proved. . . . If all verbal or written opposition to
the war furnishes a basis for conviction, because it is dangerous under
the circumstances and indicates a criminal mind, then none but the
most courageous will dare speak out against a future war."[15]

At first Holmes dismissed this criticism as "a lot of jaw about free speech." Through the summer and fall of 1919, as public debate raged over the political prisoners and Palmer's war on reds, Holmes and his colleague Louis Brandeis reconsidered their position. This remarkable intellectual turnabout became apparent in early November, when the court ruled on the Abrams case, another test of the wartime speech laws. Once again a majority of the court upheld the conviction, this time of five Russian anarchists who had been sentenced to twenty years in prison for publishing a leaflet calling workers to protest America's military intervention in Russia. In this case, however, Holmes reversed course and offered an eloquent dissent. "I think that we should be eternally vigilant," he wrote, "against attempts to check the expression of opinions that we loathe and believe to be fraught with death, unless they so imminently threaten immediate interference with the lawful and pressing purposes of the law that an immediate check is required to save the country." Holmes's dissent did nothing to keep Abrams and his friends from jail and eventual deportation to Russia, but it marked the first step in a new direction for the court, one that would eventually produce much greater protection for the rights of dissenters.[16]

Reflecting this growing interest in protecting and expanding First Amendment rights, the National Civil Liberties Bureau announced plans in January 1920 to reorganize itself as the American Civil Liberties Union (ACLU). While the NCLB had taken particular interest in the defense of conscientious objectors and pacifists, the ACLU planned a broader mission, the formation of a permanent organization devoted to the protection of free speech, press, and assembly. In addition to continuing its work as a publicity agency and source of legal aid, the group planned to take the offensive, initiating a "dramatic campaign" of test cases that would expand the rights of working people to organize, and keep First Amendment issues on the national agenda.[17]

In the name of fighting Bolshevism, Walter Lippmann declared, federal agents had slandered innocent people, "doctored" the news, stirred up unfounded fears of terrorist conspiracies, launched a network of government spies, and "violated every principle of fair play." But in the spring of 1920 he noted with evident relief that the days of "red hysteria" were over. Oswald Garrison Villard agreed that the country seemed to be snapping out of its five-year "patriotic trance." Though Palmer continued to insist that tens of thousands of dangerous radicals remained at large, "the country no longer lies awake o'nights from fear." Villard welcomed what he called "the return of reason."[18]

Under these circumstances, some in Congress became more receptive to amnesty, at least the "constructive" version of it presented by the AFL. In addition to piling up petitions in the White House, Lucy Robins pressed the amnesty case in Congress, forwarding petitions by the thousands to legislators and sending personal delegations to meet with representatives. She also polled congressmen, asking each to take a stand on the issue. Some remained "dead set" against amnesty, but by early spring 1920 Robins found that a growing number were ready to publicly support her resolution, even some who acknowledged that the cause remained unpopular with their constituents. Progressive Republicans took the lead. Robert La Follette, who had weathered intense criticism for his stand against the war, was joined by Hiram Johnson of California and William Borah of Idaho, both outspoken opponents of the Espionage Act. Most Democrats remained loyal to the president, though many hoped that some compromise solution could be found to "wipe out old war animosities."[19]

Robins chose Senator Joseph France, an unassuming Republican from Maryland, to be her organization's voice in Congress. During the war, France felt growing alarm over what he called the administration's "bureaucratic and autocratic" assault on free speech. In 1918 he led a futile attempt to moderate the Sedition Act. A year later, with more than a hundred wartime prisoners still in jail and Palmer escalating his attacks on radicals, the senator decided that the time had come to rally "the great liberal spirit in the country." After consulting with Robins, he introduced a version of her amnesty resolution to the Senate Judiciary Committee in March 1920. There France asked Congress to endorse his claim that "the further prosecution and imprisonment in the United States of such a body of political offenders is contrary to the democratic idealism and traditions of freedom to which our country is committed."[20]

Through this "France Resolution," Robins succeeded in drawing the country's most powerful and visible debating society directly into the controversy. And since many who backed amnesty also opposed Wilson, the cause would tap into the energy of partisan politics at the start of a crucial election year. "After the introduction of the resolution, we never let go of Congress," Robins recalled. "Daily we interviewed, debated, and argued with Congressmen, and they in turn discussed it with their friends and colleagues, until Washington became permeated with the talk about political prisoners and the war-time laws."[21]

The one place in Washington where no one seemed to be discussing amnesty was the White House. Behind the scenes, however, several of the president's advisors worried that the controversy was becoming a political liability for the administration, one that might hurt the Democrats' chances in the 1920 election. Liberals and pro-war socialists had been saying as much for more than a year, and that spring the White House was getting the same message from Democrats across the country. An Oklahoma judge, for example, warned Tumulty that Republicans in his district were promising to "free the political prisoners if given the power." If Debs and others were not released before the election, he warned that his state would be "sure lost to the Democrats."[22]

Thus, when Wilson showed signs of improving health that spring, Joseph Tumulty seized the chance to put amnesty back on the president's agenda. He reminded Wilson that when he returned from Paris ten months earlier, he had considered making an amnesty declaration and had delayed only at Palmer's insistence. Perhaps now, Tumulty hinted, "the time is ripe for action." Acting on his secretary's suggestion, Wilson again asked Palmer and Secretary of War Newton Baker to advise him on the idea of declaring a general amnesty. Wilson had not taken the initiative on the issue, but he seemed ready to be led.[23]

Baker replied first, and seemed to question Palmer's claim that no American had been punished for "mere expressions of opinion." He agreed with the attorney general, however, that a general amnesty was a blunt legal instrument that might only cause more confusion and resentment, and undermine the integrity of the law. While some had gone to jail for harmless remarks, Baker thought that others were truly dangerous, and he put Debs in that category. The man got what he deserved for throwing "intellectual dynamite," mixing "falsehood and passion" to convince his followers to break the law. Baker also worried that amnesty would allow a few of the most "notorious cases of disloyal propagandists" to escape all punishment; Victor Berger, Bill Haywood, and Rose Pastor Stokes, for example, were still free on appeal, and an amnesty proclamation might allow them to stay that way. For these reasons, Baker thought that the government should take each case on its own merits, the approach long endorsed by the attorney general.[24]

However, Baker urged the president to issue a strong public statement in favor of free speech. "In the interests of a fresh start under peace conditions," he thought Wilson should "call a halt to all further arrests for expressions of opinion" and order a further review of the wartime cases to ensure that no person had been unjustly punished. In this way, the president might placate his liberal allies by making a long-awaited gesture of respect for civil liberties, while avoiding the legal complexities posed by a general amnesty. Baker's own department had already set such an example. Responding in part to pressure from Lucy Robins, the War Department had moved quickly after the armistice to pardon all but the most defiant conscientious objectors, and had absolved many soldiers convicted of minor violations while in the service. In his memo to the president, Baker said nothing about Palmer's crusade against radicals, but he clearly hoped that the president would rein in the attorney general and encourage him to adopt a similarly lenient approach.

Wilson liked the idea so much that he asked Baker and Palmer to draft amnesty proclamations—Baker's to cover the remaining military prisoners, and Palmer's for civilian convicts—so that he could hold them "in readiness." That same week, Wilson presided over a brief cabinet meeting, the first time most of his advisors had seen him in eight months. Shocked by his appearance, Palmer noted that his boss spoke with difficulty, remained paralyzed on his left side, and looked and acted "like an old man." Wilson made no mention of amnesty during a meeting cut short by the hovering presence of his wife and Dr. Grayson, but he did cryptically advise his attorney general "not to let the country see red." Struggling through the fog of his illness, the president seemed poised to make a gesture of national reconciliation that his liberal supporters had been pleading for since the armistice.[25]

Once again, Palmer stymied this plan. For a second time ignoring

Wilson's request for a draft amnesty resolution, he instead sent the president a long letter defending his campaign against America's "enemies within" and criticizing Baker's proposal as "entirely futile." Palmer complained that a proclamation against future arrests for "mere expressions of opinion would imply that such arrests and prosecutions had been made in the past and that others are contemplated." Once again, he denied that that there had been a "single instance" of government disregard for the First Amendment. The Supreme Court, he reminded Wilson, had unanimously rejected the free speech claims of those convicted under the Espionage Act.

Palmer also denied Baker's insinuation that the speech law prisoners had been unfairly tried or harshly punished. Of the two thousand arrested under the Espionage Act, half had escaped conviction entirely, and hundreds of those sent to jail had already been pardoned. Warming to his theme, he called those who remained behind bars "enemies fighting in the rear against the courageous men and women who by the million supported the country's cause in as righteous a war as ever was fought by any nation." Granting freedom to Debs, the most notorious of these traitors, would "shock the sense of justice of our people," Palmer concluded, and would undermine the government's ability to recruit soldiers and build civilian morale in future wars.[26]

This disagreement between Baker and Palmer reflected wider divisions among Wilson's advisors over the amnesty issue, and the Justice Department's ongoing war on radicalism. As might be expected, Postmaster Burleson stood with Palmer. So did Bainbridge Colby, the new secretary of state; inexperienced and obsequious, he was fast becoming one of Wilson's favorites. Baker's more liberal approach was backed by Secretary of Labor William Wilson, who had done much to stymie Palmer's plan to deport the aliens rounded up in the January raids. Interior Secretary John Barton Payne also favored amnesty, as did Secretary of the Navy Josephus Daniels. Tumulty wavered, supporting his friend Palmer but fretting over the political ramifications for his president and his party. He said that he favored a general amnesty, but only if and when it could appear to be motivated by Wilson's high-minded generosity, not by his fear of the radical threat.

In this clandestine amnesty debate, the coming election played an

A. Mitchell Palmer on the campaign trail in 1920.
Library of Congress, Prints and Photographs Division.

unspoken but important role. That spring, Palmer had been touring the country, campaigning for the Democratic presidential nomination. The attorney general tied his political fortunes to his reputation as the scourge of radicalism, billing himself as the "Fighting Quaker—Laying Down the Law." Not far from the Atlanta penitentiary, he stumped for the votes of Georgia Democrats by telling them, "I am myself an American and I love to preach my doctrine before undiluted one hundred percent Americans, because my platform is, in a word, undiluted Americanism." At a time when the country remained anxious about Bolshevism and labor unrest, Palmer cast himself as the champion of law and order, and such talk won him second place in the Georgia primary. More troubling for the attorney general and for the administration, he lost the race to native son Tom Watson, who called Palmer a "one hundred percent idiot" and demanded "Debs in the White House and Wilson in Prison."[27]

Wilson's advisors might well dismiss Watson as a crackpot, but some of them continued to worry that Palmer's raids, and the growing agitation over political prisoners, were alienating "the great mass of men and women in the country of liberal thought and tendencies." That concerned William McAdoo, Wilson's son-in-law, who had served as the president's first secretary of commerce. Like Palmer, McAdoo wanted the Democratic nomination and longed for the president's endorsement. With an eye on the November election, he urged Wilson to defuse the controversy by declaring amnesty that spring. He did so, however, with pathetic caution, raising the matter in a telegram that he sent from a train "speeding westward" as he left Washington for several weeks of vacation.[28]

In their conflicting views on amnesty, Palmer and McAdoo embodied the warring halves of the president's paradoxical personality, his unstable blend of liberalism and intolerance, democratic idealism and authoritarianism, Christian charity and pious wrath. A more flexible and politically astute leader might have navigated these conflicting currents in the nation and in his own psyche, finding a compromise to defuse the controversy, and shore up left-wing support in the coming election. After his stroke, Wilson was no longer that man. Bitter toward both friend and foe, his attention wavering and inconsistent, he refused to acknowledge, let alone to lead, the growing national debate over the right of free speech in times of war.[29]

Thanks in large part to the growing concern over civil liberties among liberals and labor leaders, Palmer's bid for the nomination collapsed at the Democratic convention that June. In the spring Palmer had embarrassed himself by making dire predictions that American Bolsheviks would launch a wave of revolutionary violence on May Day. Across the country, police and state militias mobilized, bomb squads and machinegunners watched city squares, and guards surrounded the homes of public leaders whose names were on the communists' alleged "death list"—but the red terror never materialized. A few months earlier, mainstream papers had praised Palmer for his "resolute will." Now they blamed him for stoking irrational fears. He was, as one commentator put it, full of "hot air."[30]

Making matters worse for Palmer, a group of distinguished legal

scholars issued a report weeks later that sharply criticized his department's use of domestic spies and its brutal tactics in the winter raids.
They charged that the Justice Department had been guilty of "continued violation" of the Constitution. Congress launched an investigation
of their charges that Palmer's agents had arrested immigrants without
due cause, detained them illegally for long periods of time, searched
homes without warrant, stolen private property, forged evidence, and
"shamefully abused" their prisoners, many of whom were later proven
to be innocent. At these hearing, Palmer remained unapologetic, insisting that he had done what was necessary to avert a serious national
threat. "I point with pride and enthusiasm to the results of that work,"
he insisted. "I glory in it."[31]

By the summer of 1920, many Americans felt differently. Just before
the convention, a *Literary Digest* poll showed the attorney general
"only slightly ahead" of Debs in a presidential race.[32]

McAdoo, who represented the more liberal impulses of the Wilson
White House, fared better at the convention, but his candidacy was undermined by the president's failure to endorse him. Befuddled by his
illness, or blinded by what some described as his messianic egotism,
Wilson dreamed to the end that his party would beg him to accept a
third term—an illusion maintained by his wife and closest advisors, who
feared that a harsh dose of reality might endanger his recovery. To his
doctor, he confessed that he was fully prepared to sacrifice what remained of his life, if the country should call on him to "lead them out of
the wilderness."[33]

Instead, the Democrats nominated an administration outsider, Ohio
governor James Cox. Though Cox and his running mate Franklin D.
Roosevelt vowed to run as champions of Wilson's League and his legacy,
the convention's choice was an unmistakable repudiation of the president and his policies. Every opinion poll that summer showed that,
thanks to widespread discontent with the administration, the Democrats were headed toward a crushing defeat in November.

The mood was grim, therefore, when Wilson convened a cabinet
meeting on August 10, and the group took up the issue of amnesty for
what would prove to be the last time. Once again, Debs did nothing to
encourage the better angels of Wilson's nature. Just that week, radical

papers published an interview with Debs that made it clear that fifteen months in prison had failed to rehabilitate his respect for authority. "I do not think there is any man in history who will be visited with more permanently enduring contempt than Woodrow Wilson," Debs reportedly said, adding that he had "absolutely nothing to ask at the hands of the Wilson-Palmer-Burleson Administration." Some evidence suggests that these comments, picked up by mainstream papers across the country, were actually concocted by Debs's Socialist supporters, who felt entitled to put words in the mouth of their censored candidate.[34]

Whatever their source, they accurately reflected Debs's growing contempt for the president. Wilson felt the same way about Debs, a man who was fast becoming a political anchor around his neck. Drawing on an irrelevant precedent from his days as governor of New Jersey, the president announced to his cabinet that he would grant a pardon only if the idea received their unanimous support. Palmer, the man who had done more than anyone to postpone Debs's freedom, now switched sides to support a pardon. Burleson, however, stood fast, and Secretary of State Bainbridge Colby still "doubted." With evident regret, Josephus Daniels noted in his diary that this "ended hope for Debs and the others."[35]

In addition to her campaign to win congressional support for amnesty, Lucy Robins continued to cultivate the support of labor's "conservative masses." She moved "grasshopper-like" from one union meeting to another, making impassioned and sometimes tearful speeches. A few influential AFL leaders still resisted. A general amnesty was not "sufficiently discriminating," a head of the powerful United Mine Workers argued, while the editor of an important labor journal criticized Robins for asking patriotic union members to defend the rights of assassins and saboteurs. Some locals continued to reject her petitions, warning that "any more literature of this nature will not be given any notice whatever." Robins ignored them, and her consciousness-raising publicity "machinery" continued to grind out correspondence to more than thirty thousand union locals. By the spring of 1920, as unions responded with a steady flow of resolutions, letters, and small donations, Robins believed that her months of work were paying off. "Our principles," she found, "nearly always conquered our opponents in the end."[36]

The greatest test of her progress came in June, when she traveled to Montreal for the AFL's national convention. A year earlier this gathering of the nation's most powerful labor leaders had rejected her amnesty resolution in a storm of patriotic contempt. Now she trembled as she mounted the podium and described for the delegates her meetings with the political prisoners. "Most of them are old men, or very young men, or women," she explained with more pathos than precision. "Some of them did very little. If you were to meet those boys and girls you would know that they certainly were harmless, that they did not intend to overthrow the government, as stated by the Department of Justice."

Robins tugged on their sympathies but did not ignore their self-interest. She reminded them that, months after the armistice, Palmer had invoked his wartime powers to break strikes and pushed for a sedition bill that would give the government a permanent tool for stifling the voice of organized labor. By standing for the rights of the political prisoners, Robins argued, unions would be protesting the use of federal power to control all dissent, protecting speech rights that were essential in their own fight for economic justice.[37]

This time the delegates agreed, giving her amnesty petition a ringing endorsement. Even some who had been amnesty's harshest critics now changed their minds. For Robins, this victory was a milestone, the culmination of months of persistence. The nation's largest body of organized workingmen, more than four million mostly conservative and patriotic workers, now stood up for those jailed radicals they had once denounced as traitors.

The mainstream press wondered what Gompers hoped to gain by standing up for "the egregious Mr. Debs," but the radicals thought they knew. They charged that AFL leaders were joining the amnesty cause "at last" because rank-and-file workers had demanded it. Though Gompers now claimed to sympathize with the political prisoners, his "hidden motivation" was a desire to prevent workers from realizing the revolutionary possibilities in the amnesty fight. If Gompers truly wanted Debs out of jail, they charged, the administration would quickly oblige—a charge that vastly overestimated the old labor leader's waning influence in the White House. Socialists published a picture of the Atlanta penitentiary, claiming that "this is the Federal prison where

Eugene V. Debs will close his life, if Capitalists and Gompersites have their way." In other radical papers, cartoons depicted Gompers dressed as a guard.[38]

The civil libertarians offered a more astute criticism of the AFL's contribution to the amnesty campaign. Lawyer Harry Weinberger told Gompers that he considered their resolution to be "satisfactory in its conclusion" but "wrong in its premises." The goal of amnesty should be not simply to free the prisoners, he argued, but to overturn the legal principles that put them in jail in the first place. The AFL petition asked Wilson to declare amnesty in order to soothe "wartime animosities" but did not challenge the administration's right to jail dissenters. Weinberger insisted that no person "guilty of mere words" had been "properly sent to jail during the war, in view of the Constitutional guarantees." The Supreme Court disagreed, but Weinberger countered that this only proved that the legal system was "human" and fallible. He warned Gompers that unless the amnesty battle could be won on First Amendment grounds, the government would retain the right to silence speech in the name of public safety and would make all of organized labor its next victim.

Robins scarcely paused to consider these criticisms, convinced as she was that the AFL represented the only "constructive" approach to amnesty, and the only one likely to wield enough influence to actually achieve the goal of getting Debs out of jail. Recognizing all that Gompers had done to nurture her amnesty work, she seethed at the radicals' "poisonous misinterpretations." More than ever she felt sure that the Socialists had no understanding of the way power actually worked in America. She felt a similar contempt for people like Weinberger, the liberals and radical intellectuals allied with the Civil Liberties Union. Though they claimed to fight for the interests of the working class, she decided that they cared more about abstract principles than they did the flesh-and-blood men and women who languished in jail.

She, on the other hand, now carried with her a resolution that expressed the collective will of more than four million American workers, and she was eager to use this to pry her way into the attorney general's office. Twice Palmer denied her request to bring a delegation to his office to present the AFL petition. For the past year Gompers had been a thorn in Palmer's side, denouncing his use of injunctions, rallying opposition to his sedition bill, and helping to kill his bid for the Democratic nomination. Palmer was in no mood to hear a lecture from Gompers about the political prisoners. Exasperated by Palmer's stonewalling, Robins sent him a "scathing missive." He was a heretic to his Quaker faith, she told him, and if he only knew what the American people really thought about him, he would kill himself. She punctuated these insults with a fresh barrage of telegrams from union leaders across the country. In the end, these "hammer blows on his conscience" seemed to hit their mark. On September 14, Palmer met with an amnesty delegation, orchestrated by Robins and led by Gompers and New York's Socialist congressman Meyer London.

After reading the AFL resolution, Gompers waved his finger in the attorney general's face. "Our country is safe," he insisted. "Our territory and our freedom are not in danger, the institutions of our country are as unshaken as the rock of Gibraltar. There is not anything that can overturn them except our own consciousness." Palmer listened glumly, reviewed his usual objections to a blanket amnesty, and agreed to share the AFL's concerns with the president. A Socialist delegation called on Palmer that same day, and much to Robins's chagrin they took a more confrontational approach, telling him that "no sane person considers Debs a criminal." Privately, she had just told Palmer much worse, but she cringed when she heard her amnesty rivals say such things in public, sure that they were doing more to antagonize than to persuade the attorney general. The next day, in fact, headlines across the country announced that Palmer was still "Determined to Keep Debs."[39]

Two days later a massive bomb exploded at a busy Wall Street intersection, killing over thirty and wounding more than two hundred. Police found a note nearby, misspelled in red ink, and signed by a group that called itself the "American Anarchist Fighters." "We will not tolerate any longer," the note threatened. "Free the political prisoners or it will be sure death for all of you." The Justice Department's chief investigator told the press that the bombing was not an assassination attempt on Morgan, who was out of the country at the time. Rather, the bombers aimed at "the financial heart of America as a defiance against the American people and the American government." In cities across the country, police guarded banks and public buildings against a second attack that never came.[40]

Racing to New York to lead the investigation, Palmer announced that the bombing vindicated his claim that America faced a serious and imminent threat from violent revolutionaries. In that election season he also blamed the Republican Congress for cutting his department's budget. The national press followed this sensational story with interest, but the attack failed to produce a new wave of anti-radical paranoia. "There must be no yielding to panic fear," the *Times* asserted. "That would be to make the assassins believe they had half succeeded." Other papers around the country agreed that the bomb was probably not part of a vast revolutionary conspiracy, but the work of a handful of deluded criminals. "The public is merely shocked," a Cleveland paper asserted, "not terrorized."[41]

Though Palmer was distracted by the bomb investigation that fall, Robins continued to pressure him, sensing that he was wavering. As the only anarchist in the country who enjoyed the privilege of scolding Palmer to his face, she told him that his raids, deportations, and injunctions were "terrible crimes against our Country." Everywhere she went, Robins said, his name was met with "bitterness, satire and hatred." He could change all this, she suggested, by convincing Wilson to liberate the political prisoners. "You would help to restore in the hearts of millions of citizens the trust and confidence to the present administration and to the United States government as a whole. Can any man ask for more?" Reminding him of the obvious, she confessed in one of these letters that she was "blest with . . . oh! so much impudence."[42]

A few weeks later Palmer agreed to meet privately with Robins. There he sounded like a beaten man. For more than a year, he had done more than anyone to scuttle the amnesty idea, but now he confided that he no longer had any "personal objection." He told her that he had already changed his mind on the Debs case. The only roadblock that remained was the president himself. But Palmer told Robins not to get her hopes up because Wilson had "closed his mind" on the subject. Further public appeals would mean little to the president, he warned her, because Wilson had grown bitter, convinced that "the people have rejected him." In a confessional and self-pitying mood, Palmer also confided to Lucy Robins that being a prosecuting attorney was a "tragedy."[43]

Palmer's tragedy was laced with irony. His stand against amnesty and his raid on radicals ruined his career, and forever marked this moderate progressive as a symbol of government repression. Quite unintentionally, Palmer also helped stimulate a new public concern for civil liberties. As long as American soldiers risked their lives in France, many liberals and pro-war socialists had accepted the federal government's campaign against dissent as an unfortunate but necessary expedient. If Palmer had not discouraged Wilson from offering a broad amnesty after the armistice, the postwar debate over civil liberties might have been quite different. For many liberals, objections to the administration's wartime repression would have been tempered by praise for the president's willingness to forgive. Some probably would have accepted the government's prosecution of dissenters as just one more price the country had to pay to win a modern war.

Instead, when Palmer convinced Wilson to keep Debs in jail, he gave the amnesty forces a potent symbol around which they organized a broad national protest against the government's program of repression. After the armistice, Palmer's heavy-handed attacks on radicals only helped the amnesty cause make its case that the war had undermined traditional liberties. While many Americans applauded Palmer for his actions, he also faced stiff, immediate, and well-organized opposition, much of it from those already galvanized into action by the amnesty movement. The longer Palmer continued to insist that America had no political prisoners, the more his fellow citizens came to believe that he was wrong.[44]

Chapter 13

The Last Campaign

I N THE SPRING OF 1920, Clyde Miller met privately with Warren
Harding, the Ohio senator who had recently thrown his hat in the
ring for the Republican nomination. Two years earlier the *Cleveland
Plain Dealer* reporter had done more than anyone to get Debs arrested.
Now he came on a mission of penitence, hoping to convince Harding
that Debs was an innocent man. Miller had already been rebuffed by
another Ohio politician, Secretary of War Newton Baker. To his surprise, Harding was more receptive. "Why should we kid each other?" he
conceded off the record. "Debs was right. We shouldn't have been in
that war." Harding told Miller that if he ever got into the White House,
he would release Debs—not immediately, but "by the Fourth of July."[1]

In public opinion polls, Harding ran at the back of the Republican
pack that spring, and few pundits expected him to win the nomination. Many favored General Leonard Wood, who was Theodore Roosevelt's partner in the preparedness crusade and the leader of the federal
troops who put down Seattle's general strike in 1919. Campaigning in
his army uniform and flanked by fellow officers, Wood promised to restore law and order across the country, vowing to hunt and kill America's communists like "rattlesnakes." Illinois governor Frank Lowden, a
more moderate and accomplished politician, also ran strong, though
his campaign bogged down in a fund-raising scandal. No Republican

stirred more passion among voters, however, than Hiram Johnson, the former governor of California. In 1912 Johnson had left his party to join the Bull Moose revolt, running as Roosevelt's vice president. After Wilson's victory, Johnson returned to the Republicans but remained determined to wrest control of the party from conservatives. While supporting the war, he often led the Senate's opposition to what he called the president's "autocratic leadership and inept following." He helped to kill the press censorship clause of the Espionage Act and vainly fought against the 1918 Sedition Act, which he called a "war upon the American people." He denounced war profiteering, opposed Palmer's raids and America's military intervention in Russia, helped kill the peacetime sedition law, and joined other progressives in backing Senator France's amnesty resolution.[2]

Campaigning in Republican primaries that spring, Johnson warned time and again that the recent war had spawned two fundamental threats to the Constitution. In foreign affairs, he argued, joining Wilson's League would undermine national sovereignty and strip Congress of its right to declare war. And at home, Johnson charged, the administration had manipulated "war psychology" to justify the unprecedented expansion of executive power. In the Committee on Public Information, the government had forged dangerous new tools to create the public opinion it was supposed to serve, spreading propaganda and disinformation in a way that Johnson described as "picking our pockets to poison our minds." He agreed with the old socialist charge that most newspapers did the bidding of big business, and he denounced Burleson for using the war as a pretext to silence the media's few dissenting voices. "In these days," he insisted," we have come perilously near losing a free press."[3]

Johnson's program—rejection of the League, a slate of progressive reforms, and a defense of the First Amendment—hit a responsive chord, at least among those described by one reporter as "the dissatisfied elements, the seekers for change." Running with little money and a skeletal organization, he made a surprisingly strong showing in many primaries, winning more votes than any of his rivals. Johnson was a charismatic speaker—some thought the best of his day—and across the country his rallies had all the emotional fervor of Billy Sunday revival meetings. In packed halls from San Francisco to Philadelphia, he called voters to unite in defense of American sovereignty and free speech. "You and I must zealously guard these fundamental principles," he urged. "The difficulty with our present situation," he continued, "is that some of those who talk of law and order most eloquently do so with a mental reservation. They mean law of their own interpretation to regulate other men's opinions, and order then, under the stern repression of that law. Opinions at variance with theirs seem to them not only sacrilegious but unlawful. They think in terms of prisons and machine guns and fondly hug the delusion that by jailing men's bodies they forever imprison their opinions."[4]

As Republicans gathered in Chicago that summer for their nominating convention, Johnson's progressive faction urged their party to make the defense of free speech a campaign issue, part of a broader assault on the president's wartime record of "autocratic" rule. Such a move, they hoped, might even help win labor voters away from the Democrats, since Palmer's policies had clearly alienated Gompers and many rank-and-file union members. Eager to court the AFL, Senator France arranged for Lucy Robins to address the Republican platform committee, where she urged them to turn her amnesty resolution into a platform plank that would make the political prisoners an issue in the 1920 campaign.[5]

For Robins, that speech capped a remarkable political journey. As a young Jewish immigrant she had once rolled cigars in a factory not far from the hall where she now gave a lecture on liberty to those whom she called America's "economic royalists." Out in the hotel lobbies, radicals confronted Republican delegates with their picket signs, but inside the convention hall Robins enjoyed a private audience with Harding's wife, Florence. When Robins tried to interest her in the wartime prisoners, however, she discovered that "humanitarian causes had little appeal" for Mrs. Harding. The woman whom Harding liked to call "The Duchess" preferred to talk about her husband's chance for the nomination.[6]

Robins was enthralled by this glimpse behind the curtain of political power, but Gompers warned her not to expect too much. "We shall accomplish nothing here," he predicted. Continuing his tutorial on the art of pragmatic politics, he advised her to "take all you can get from politicians, but never assume that they are altruists." Events soon confirmed his skepticism. In their platform, the Republicans declared themselves in favor of the "ancient and constitutional right of free speech, free press and free assembly," but steered clear of a more controversial stand for amnesty.[7]

Likewise, Hiram Johnson fell short in his bid to turn the Republican Party into the vanguard of progressive reform. In spite of his strong showing in many state primaries, thanks to party rules he came to Chicago with only a handful of committed delegates, and his campaign died in the convention's legendary "smoke-filled room." Faced with a deadlock between Wood, Bowden, and Johnson, the party's power brokers settled on Warren Harding as a compromise candidate, a result shrewdly engineered by Harding's campaign manager, Harry Daugherty. Johnson left the convention in a huff, vowing to expose the leadership's "cynical and contemptuous regard of the expressed will of the people." "The bosses believed that any man could be elected this year," one of his supporters complained, "and so believing they picked the man most completely in harmony with their own views." Liberals around the country ridiculed Harding as a party hack, a mediocrity, and an "errand boy for the old guard politicians and the business interests they serve."[8]

Warren Harding was a distinguished-looking man with an undistinguished record in the Senate. Though he had accomplished little, he had likewise alienated few. As one historian summarized his legislative career, "He carried his committee load, stayed out of trouble, and generally followed the lead of older, conservative Republicans." Good looks, sociability, and rhetorical ambiguity had carried Harding far, and they would serve him well in the 1920 campaign. At a time when many Americans were eager to repudiate Wilson, Harding seemed the perfect antidote. Wilson appeared remote, self-contained, and rigidly ideological—traits only heightened by his illness. Harding, by contrast, was a gregarious harmonizer who had good friends on both sides of the political aisle; none ever suspected him of intellectual superiority, least of all himself. With disarming humility, he offered Americans "not heroics, but healing; not nostrums, but normalcy; not revolution, but restoration."[9]

At a time when many political observers believed that the nation faced stark and momentous choices, Harding offered voters comforting ambiguities. Though he adopted the campaign slogan "Let's Be Done With Wiggle and Wobble," both his supporters and his opponents had a hard time pinning him down on the issues, and in fact his campaign managers urged him to say as little as possible. On the most pressing question of the day, America's role in the League of Nations, he straddled in a way that offered comfort to both sides. While rejecting "Wilson's League," he promised to support an ill-defined "association of nations." On the controversy over civil liberties, he praised the sanctity of free speech while vowing to stand firm against radicalism. As one disappointed progressive put it, Harding seemed to say, "Free speech is sacred, except for those who use it to oppose what we approve." Privately, Hiram Johnson denounced his rival as a political animal who was "devoid of principles."[10]

Such a judgment, however, seems unfair. Harding's claim to be a "champion" of free speech was more than political opportunism. Like other former newspaper men who held seats in Congress, he had opposed the press censorship provision of the Espionage Act and had joined the chorus of protests when the New York legislature barred the Socialist assemblymen. Harding was no red-baiter, and during the campaign he downplayed the threat posed by radicalism. "Too much has been said about Bolshevism in America," as he put it, and his appeal to "normalcy" included a calmer approach to the issue. Though he was no leader on this or any other question, he had reason to think of himself as a tolerant conservative and a friend of the First Amendment. He valued free speech as a hallowed tradition, a founding principle, a noble abstraction, while giving little thought to some of the hard questions it provokes. In this, as in so many other ways, Harding embodied a yearning for a simpler prewar past that soon proved to have enormous appeal to voters in 1920.[11]

As the campaign began, Harding was pressed to take a more definite stand on the amnesty question, and as usual Debs served as the symbolic center of the controversy. Parley Christensen, presidential nominee for the fledgling Farmer-Labor Party, enjoyed a brief moment of national media attention when he sent an open letter to Harding and his

Democratic rival James Cox, asking them to join him in petitioning for Debs's release. Christensen "disliked utterly" to start a campaign "while one of my opponents is in prison, and especially while he is in prison for no crime other than an honest public expression of his political views." Even if Debs was mistaken on the war, as an American he enjoyed "the right to think wrong." Christensen called on his unjailed rivals to join his call to free Debs, in the name of democratic "sportsmanship."[12]

Harding refused, but he could not afford to ignore Christensen entirely. Eager to keep Johnson and his progressives from once again bolting the party, he expressed some sympathy for the amnesty cause. "I believe as heartily as you do in freedom of thought and speech and press," he told Christensen in an open telegram, and he promised, if elected, to offer a "generous amnesty" to the political prisoners, though not a general one. A few civil libertarians cheered Harding's use of the term "political prisoners." Though not known for his linguistic precision, the nominee seemed to concede that Debs and others had been jailed for their opinions, a point doggedly denied by Wilson's Justice Department. Beyond this, however, Harding offered nothing that had not already been promised many times by A. Mitchell Palmer—a timely review of individual cases, with no concession that the government had wrongly jailed these men and women during the war. Harding tried to close the door on the matter by insisting that each case must be considered "on its merits." Until he could review the privileged information available only to a president, he declared, it was "impossible to utter an opinion" on any individual case.[13]

Democratic nominee James Cox, like Harding a former newspaper editor from Ohio, ignored Christensen's telegram. When Cox agreed to carry the torch of "Wilsonism," he inherited the liability of the amnesty controversy, and he had even more reason than Harding to avoid the subject. Denouncing his Republican rival as a reactionary, Cox urged progressives to flock to his banner, but he said little to ease their concerns about the administration's record on civil liberties. The Democrats had assumed a defensive tone on the issue from the very start of the campaign. "We resent the unfounded reproaches," their platform complained, "for alleged interference with the freedom of the press and freedom of speech." The Wilson administration had "assailed no utterance" that had not been "animated by treasonable purposes." Christensen sent Cox a second public telegram asking him to join the call to free Debs, but got no response.[14]

However, on the campaign trail Cox found that hecklers would not allow him to dodge the issue. During a speech in Madison Square Garden, for example, he was interrupted by a man who demanded to know what he would do about Debs. As the hall erupted in cheers and catcalls, another spectator mocked the candidate by shouting, "On the advice of counsel, don't answer." After settling the crowd, Cox said he supported the immediate repeal of all wartime measures that curtailed "individual liberty." However, he insisted that "what happened during the emergency of war is another matter." In short, Cox chose to stand by Wilson's war record, while disowning Palmer's postwar attack on radicals. Only in the race's last desperate days would Cox ask Palmer to campaign for the party he once dreamed of leading.[15]

Cox's position disappointed the administration's left-wing allies, who continued to plead for a stronger stand on civil liberties. After failing to found a "patriotic" socialist party, John Spargo had been writing and speaking against Bolshevism, a crusade that further alienated many of his former comrades. Though he remained an admirer of Wilson, Spargo continued to argue that leaving Debs in jail mocked America's "best traditions." Giving up on his attempt to reach the president, he turned instead to Cox, who promised that he was making a thorough review of the case. Cox ultimately concluded, however, that Debs was a dangerous man who got what he deserved for speaking "against the Government." Such talk, he told Spargo, was not only illegal during wartime but probably "a violation of Peace regulations." Spargo gently urged Cox to put more faith in the power of truth to drive out error. "You, my dear Governor, could easily enough answer and defeat Debs's advocacy of a Soviet Government (should he advocate it) but you cannot answer and defeat his martyrdom. The prison cell magnifies his voice and lends it additional authority." Others joined Spargo in warning the administration that keeping Debs and the others in jail was alienating many liberals and bringing the Democrats ever closer to electoral annihilation.[16]

These appeals did not free Debs, but they may have forced the prison door open just a crack. The White House announced in August that it would suspend prison rules during the fall campaign, allowing Debs to issue a series of messages to the voters, one each week until Election Day—an awkward compromise that straddled Debs's dual identity as a convict-candidate. Where Debs had once stormed the country in a verbal torrent, he would now have five hundred words a week, forwarded to his brother and then distributed through the wire services. Publication, of course, remained at the discretion of newspaper editors. The *Call* and the nation's few other surviving radical papers ran them, while in New York campaign workers passed them out as broadsides. "They have the snap and tingle of his good old self," an old friend told Theodore. "The hunger of the masses for our messages is insatiable." A few major papers ran all or parts of these brief articles, but many editors would not touch them. Back in Terre Haute, Theodore eagerly scanned the Indiana papers that fall, but found no sign of Debs's prison messages. In fact, he saw nothing about socialism at all, "unless it be the arrest of a red with a couple hundred pounds of dynamite concealed under his coat. That gets a front page with a two inch line across the sheet."[17]

Still, Debs made the most of this limited opportunity to speak to American voters. As usual, he attacked his rivals in the dominant parties as twin lackeys of the master class. "They are stuffed people, not real," he wrote in his first address. "They have not a single idea for a man who is alive. They get their inspiration from the tombs." He denounced Wilson's clandestine military campaign against the Soviet Union, blamed the government for rising prices and a coal shortage that winter, and even waded into some local issues in Georgia, condemning state policies that had somehow produced a "wastage of watermelons." In the first national election after ratification of the Nineteenth Amendment, Debs made a particular appeal to women voters, reminding them that Socialists had supported female suffrage well ahead of the mainstream parties.[18]

Much to Lucy Robins's chagrin, Debs devoted one of his messages to an attack on those "misleaders" who distracted American workers from their historic struggle against capitalism, a group headed by that "chief betrayer of labor," Samuel Gompers. Still dreaming that her amnesty fight was building common ground between radical and conservative workers, Robins felt sure that Debs was too wise and too kind to attack a man who was doing so much to win his release. In her view, the statement was not only ungrateful but politically stupid, bound to alienate the rank-and-file union members she had been cultivating—the very men and women that Debs needed in order to win both votes and his freedom. Hoping that this was the handiwork of misguided zealots at Socialist headquarters, she sent Debs an urgent letter, warning him about the "statement given out under your name."[19]

In reply, Debs claimed full ownership of this attack on Gompers and other conservative union leaders. Theodore relayed his message to Robins. "He wants his liberty bad enough, God knows," he explained, but he would rather stay in prison than "keep silent when he sees hard-working rank and file betrayed and delivered like sheep at the shambles by crooked leaders to get juicy jobs from the greasy politicians themselves." Robins no doubt took little comfort in Theodore's assurance that the attack was not "personal."[20]

Surprisingly, Debs said nothing about his own case, or the wider question of civil liberties, even though the administration claimed to place no restrictions on the content of his weekly messages. Perhaps he believed that the odd circumstances of his campaign spoke eloquently enough about the Socialist stand on free speech. More likely, he wanted to avoid the appearance of special pleading and the charge that his campaign was nothing more than a publicity stunt to win his personal freedom. While his friends in the various amnesty factions understood that Debs was their movement's most compelling symbol, the one prisoner not likely to be forgotten behind bars, he felt ambivalent about the role. Time and again he told amnesty leaders not to single him out, but to wage their fight on behalf of all of the wartime prisoners. "If I should be freed before the others," he argued, "then the poor unknown boys, also political prisoners, will remain living corpses."[21]

And yet, for most Americans Debs embodied the entire controversy. He was the only prisoner who had a public face and voice, the one who provoked citizens to either defend or oppose their government's prosecution of wartime dissenters. By the fall of 1920, as war passions cooled and his sentence dragged on, many began to see him in a new light—no longer as an object of scorn, but now as an interesting and even sympathetic figure. When a *Chicago Tribune* reporter asked five random pedestrians their views on Debs in the month before the election, only one of these "men on the street" wanted him kept in jail. The other four thought Wilson should free Debs. Several charged he was being punished for his political beliefs, one woman worried that he was an old man who might die behind bars, and all thought that it made little sense to punish a man for opposing a war long after the conflict itself had ended.[22]

Much of the mainstream press also began to change its mind about Debs that fall. While many continued to denounce him, others decided that the time had come to free the prisoners and put the issue to rest. Unable to resist the human interest story of a presidential campaign waged from a prison cell, reporters dunned the Justice Department for permission to visit Debs. Palmer faced a dilemma. As a prisoner Debs had presumably forfeited his right to address the public. However, as the chosen candidate of a legitimate, if suspect, political party, he seemed entitled to meet with reporters, speaking through them to voters about the issues of the day. In the first months after Debs's nomination, the government chose to limit press access, telling most reporters that the prisoner owed all his "time and energies" to the penitentiary and that publicity would be "subversive of good discipline." By the fall, as more editors clamored for the story, Palmer relented, and many papers and magazines ran profiles.[23]

Debs made great copy. He was a saint in denim, a stoic philosopher who befriended murderers and thieves, a kindly old man who remained an "untamed revolutionist" but had to be admired for the courage of his convictions. Reporters flocked to Atlanta not to record his political views but to capture his prison *"experience."* One thought Debs, though dressed in frayed denim, looked like "a college professor and a dreamer," his gestures graceful and "his language precise and cultivated." Forced to share a cell with slack-jawed bootleggers and worse, this "truly remarkable man" seemed to accept his lot philosophically. Debs told a *New York World* reporter that his stay in Atlanta had become nothing less than a spiritual sojourn. After months of legal wrangling, he had arrived at Moundsville feeling harried and distracted, his heart failing and his body "worn out." Prison stripped life to its essentials, he found, returning him to the fundamental truth that had motivated his entire career. "There is only one thing in life that matters," he learned all over again. "That is service to our fellow men."[24]

Reporters were fascinated by the story that Debs changed bad men into good. Many papers mentioned his relationship with Sam Moore, a black man jailed for robbery, who was later sentenced to life in prison for murdering a prison guard. For years the guards considered Moore incorrigible and both provoked and punished his rage by chaining him, flogging him, and locking him for long weeks in the prison's isolation tank. When Moore ended up in the prison hospital, broken in body and spirit after another beating, Debs befriended him. This simple gesture of kindness and respect transformed Moore's character. He became nonviolent and followed Debs around the prison whenever he could, like a loving disciple. With help from socialist friends in New York, Debs eventually helped Moore win parole. Though the Socialists usually initiated these stories about Debs, they were quickly confirmed by the prison's Catholic chaplain, and even the superintendent of prisons in Washington praised Debs as a "splendid prisoner."[25]

As Debs's self-appointed Boswell, David Karsner took the lead in embellishing this chapter of what biographer Ray Ginger called the "Debs Legend." Nine months after dropping Debs off in Moundsville, Karsner rushed into print an "authorized life" of his hero that circulated in 1920 as a semi-official campaign biography. In the book, Karsner included a transcript of the Canton speech. For those who cared to look, this was the first chance to see what Debs actually said that fateful day; until then, even radical publications had offered only brief summaries, fearing that publishing the full transcript might itself be a criminal act.

The rest of Karsner's *Debs* was a loose compilation of his stories on the Cleveland trial and the ride to Moundsville, some letters Debs had written since then, and a review of highlights from his long career. Throughout the book, Karsner portrayed Debs as a lover of humanity, a peaceful friend of children, a homespun philosopher with a "merry twinkle" in his eye. People might hate his politics, Karsner concluded, but none could deny that he was "honest, kind, sincere, loyal, devoted, true, lovable and loving, always doing what he could in rain or shine, in prison or at home, to make this world a brighter place for the people who inhabit it."[26]

Some eagle-eyed citizens brought Karsner's biography to the attention of the federal authorities, urging them to arrest a writer who dared to lionize America's most infamous traitor. The left-wing literati at the *Liberator* objected for quite different reasons. "I cannot say that I like the Gospel according to St. David Karsner," Floyd Dell complained, "nor the gentle Debs, meek and mild, who is therein presented." Offering a new twist on the now familiar theme, Dell suggested that Debs was like Jesus in another way that Karsner and other writers had missed—his "kind sayings" were remembered, while his stern revolutionary principles were too quickly forgotten. "Jesus wasn't crucified for being nice to people," Dell preached, "nor Debs put in prison for being the kindest man alive." Beneath drifts of sentimental prose about the saintly socialist, Dell and many other radicals struggled to uncover an angry and uncompromising revolutionary, an icon for their own, harder-edged political religion. Their Debs wanted none of the maudlin sympathy that might inspire an act of government clemency; he was a militant whose martyrdom stoked the fires of working-class resentment, leading the way toward revolution.[27]

Once again, the amnesty campaign had become an intramural battle among the radicals, a struggle to define what Debs stood for, what his imprisonment meant for the future of the entire movement. Karsner and many moderate socialists wanted to use the fight to free Debs as a tool to rebuild the party, restoring the momentum it enjoyed before the war. Robins dreamed of an even wider coalition of working-class Americans, a movement that yoked Debs's idealism and Gompers's political pragmatism. Dell and his fellow Greenwich Village Bolsheviks insisted that Debs was not a harmless humanitarian, a vote-getting politician, or mainstream labor leader, but a working-class warrior. The amnesty drive, they insisted, had become a key front in the wider war against capitalism, and the time had come to abandon the failed tactics of politicking and compromise.

What Debs thought about these conflicts is not entirely clear. Isolated behind bars, he was deprived of regular access to news, particularly from the radical press, and his mail was censored. Only rarely did a fellow inmate snatch scraps of newsprint from the censor's office and smuggle them to him. Much of what he knew about the volatile political landscape of postwar America was filtered through messengers who traveled to Atlanta, each shading the facts from their distinctive vantage point. In turn, Debs spoke through these visitors, who carried back pronouncements from prison that were colored by the same biases. And more than once, these friends conjured statements on his behalf, putting words in the mouth of their leader, assuming that they knew best what Debs would say if he could. The result was a frustrating chaos of mixed signals, mutual recriminations by various allies of Debs who felt sure that others were manipulating and misquoting him.

In later years, Karsner came to regret his biography of Debs as a hasty work of propaganda. But in 1920 he was by no means the only writer eager to wring political advantage out of the pathos of the Debs story. Dozens of writers in America and Europe paid homage to the convict candidate, producing a stream of testimonials, morality plays, songs, and protest lyrics. A sampling of this work was hastily gathered and published by Upton Sinclair, with editorial help from another California radical, Ruth Le Prade. While the contributions to *Debs and the Poets* varied in style and quality, the muse inspired all of these radical writers in much the same way.[28]

Most argued, for example, that putting Debs in jail was itself a criminal act, that history's judgment would fall not on the prisoner but on his persecutors. Feminist author Charlotte Perkins Gilman denounced the nation's "historic mistake," while Carl Sandburg thought the sight of Debs locked away in the "national hoosegow . . . draws commentary not so much on the plight of Debs—he can stand it—as on the nation." From across the Atlantic, Britain's radical writers chimed in, including H. G. Wells, George Bernard Shaw, and the socialist and scientist Alfred Russell Wallace. None knew Debs personally, and most confessed ignorance about the details of his case. Still, they agreed with soldier-poet Siegfried Sassoon, who wrote of Debs, "I honor his name, and loathe the system which has persecuted him."

Most radical writers also agreed that, by facing his imprisonment with stoic dignity, Debs had joined the elite ranks of the world's democratic martyrs—"another God in jail," as poet Witter Bynner put it. He was a "bald, lone, tall man of the plebs," one wrote, the nation's misunderstood dreamer, and as Max Eastman put it, "the sweetest strong man in the world." Several authors conjured late-night visits to the Atlanta penitentiary from the spirits of Jesus, Lincoln, John Brown, and Walt Whitman. Sinclair's co-editor, Ruth Le Prade, put the theological proposition most baldly. "To the millions who have called 'Gene comrade," she wrote, "he has become holy and apart. They no longer dare to clasp his hand, but kneel in adoration at his feet."

Never missing a chance to move the merchandise, Sinclair billed these volumes as perfect Christmas gifts for every radical's list, with profits going to support the amnesty movement. Palmer granted Sinclair permission to send five hundred copies to Atlanta, so that Debs could autograph them, adding to their value as mementos. Some papers rejected Sinclair's request to buy ad space, however, fearing that even this might bring down the wrath of a post office censor.

Debs and the Poets reached only a handful of true believers; in fact, in spite of his best efforts Sinclair found himself stuck with a number of copies on his hands. During the fall campaign, however, millions of Americans read about Debs from a more unlikely source, the powerful newspaper chain of William Randolph Hearst. Ever on the lookout for a human interest story with a populist edge, especially one that would embarrass the president, Hearst editors sent their liberal pundit Norman Hapgood to Atlanta. A former editor of *Collier's* and *Harper's Weekly*, Hapgood was a moderate progressive whose loyal support of the president had been rewarded with an ambassadorship to Denmark. Though he had made no objection to Debs's arrest in 1918 or his imprisonment in 1919, Hapgood now declared that keeping him in jail was "one of the outstanding governmental crimes of modern times."[29]

Like so many liberals, Hapgood still found it inconceivable that Wilson bore any personal responsibility for this alleged "crime." The fallen president's only flaw, he insisted, was his single-minded devotion to the cause of world peace, a lofty detachment that left the rough job of American justice in the hands of misguided subordinates like Palmer and Burleson. Hapgood also blamed this setback for civil liberties on "public apathy and newspaper apathy." On speaking tours around the country, he met many Americans who supported amnesty; even conservative businessmen conceded that it was time to put the entire controversy to rest. But Hapgood believed that, after a double dose of war propaganda and Palmer's fear-mongering, many Americans remained "drugged," too sluggish to mount an energetic defense of their own liberties. As a result, they complacently allowed their own government to keep punishing Debs, a "rare spirit, so courageous and so good." "Now, gentle reader, stop and think," he lectured. "It makes little difference perhaps whether this one noble American dies in a prison cell. It may make a great difference that we are a reactionary, intolerant nation, and that the love of justice is not in us, rather the cowardice that brings the very evil it would escape."[30]

Hapgood published a five-part profile of the prisoner-candidate that probably enjoyed more readers in a week than the socialists toiling in their propaganda mills could hope to reach in years.

Though battered, the Socialist Party worked hard that fall to win votes for a ticket they described as "Eugene Debs and your constitutional rights." They wore campaign buttons featuring a photo of "Convict No. 9653" in his prison garb, and passed out broadsides that asked, "Do Cox and Harding Present Issues for Which They Would Go to Prison?" Seymour Stedman, Scott Nearing, and Kate Richards O'Hare held rallies across the country, while some high-flying radicals dropped thousands of pounds of Debs leaflets from airplanes over Toledo. Rejoining the Socialist Party, Upton Sinclair ran for Congress in his southern California district, using the platform to call for amnesty and to push his plan for public ownership of the press. Stedman sent Debs encouraging news from the campaign trail. "Countless hundreds" had asked him "when will Brother Debs be out, some with tears." In spite of all the party had been through, Stedman thought it was "astounding to see the rebounding of the movement." Debs even enjoyed an endorsement from beyond the grave when the ghost of Susan B. Anthony appeared to a suffragist and sent a message to American women to cast their first presidential ballot for him.[31]

In many places, however, the party limped where it once had bounded. Socialists were active and organized in only seven states and had a "paper" presence in another nineteen. Local chapters had been

SOCIALIST PARTY
FOR PRESIDENT

EUGENE VICTOR DEBS

Debs campaign postcard.
Eugene V. Debs Foundation.

decimated by attacks during the war, and vigilantes continued to break up meetings in many places. The party also continued to suffer from the self-inflicted wound of the communist split. In the Socialist stronghold of Ohio, for example, Bolshevik defectors captured the Socialists' state treasury, several party newspapers, and a number of the locals. Only what one survivor called "a pitiful little remnant" still remained to stump for Debs in Ohio.[32]

In spite of these liabilities, many editors predicted that Debs would do very well at the polls that year. Most added, however, that much of this support would come from voters who were looking for a convenient way to register their disapproval of the status quo. A *Times* reporter noted that it was a "common thing" to meet both Republicans and Democrats who declared, "I'm going to protest, and as Debs can't be elected, I'll vote for him, though I don't give a damn for Socialism." Backing Debs seemed a good way to express a variety of frustrations. The *Nation* summed up the electoral options as "Debs or dubs," while one jaded citizen captured the mood by asking aloud, "Vote for Debs? Why Not?" Some wanted to honor his personal courage, others wanted to protest government repression, but only a fraction signed on to the party's wider goals.[33]

Though Harding waged much of his campaign from the relative safety of his front porch, he found the Debs question thrust upon him "many times," whenever he ventured out in public. By the end of the campaign, no longer fearing a defection by the party's progressives, he took a tougher line. Though he still called the wartime dissenters "political prisoners," Harding now decided that this was not a point in their favor. Attempting to speak "as plainly as I can," he first claimed to see no difference between political and "ordinary" crimes, and then added that thieves and gangsters were, if anything, less dangerous than those radicals who had tried to "destroy our American institutions." Pressed yet again on another campaign stop, he elaborated on this comparison. "A grant of amnesty to political prisoners," he reasoned, "is no more justified than a general grant of amnesty to yeggmen [i.e., burglars]. If there is any difference between the danger of yeggmen and political prisoners, I believe most Americans will uphold me when I say that it is the political conspirator who is the greater menace to the United States."[34]

Well before Election Day, the candidate who compared Debs unfavorably to thieves seemed headed for a landslide victory. When Maine held its early election in September, Harding trounced Cox by a wide margin. (Only a couple thousand Mainers, just over 1 percent, backed Debs.) All political observers saw trouble ahead for the Democrats, and Wall Street speculators favored the Republicans by seven-to-one odds. Cox's running mate, Franklin D. Roosevelt, countered that every opinion poll was wrong, and that his party would sweep to victory thanks to a "silent vote" that expressed America's "silent thoughts." Only Wilson seemed to share Roosevelt's optimism. Shielded from discouraging news by advisors worried about his health, Wilson assured Tumulty that "the hearts of the people are right on this issue and we can confidently look forward to a triumph." While Harding waged a well-funded campaign using the latest innovations in public relations, Cox spent weeks on old-fashioned barnstorming, traveling more than twenty thousand miles and speaking himself hoarse. On election eve, exhausted and embittered by the futile ordeal, he charged that anyone who voted for Harding the next day was a "traitor" to America.[35]

On November 2, 1920, Mabel Curry cast her first presidential vote ever, and spent the rest of the day as a poll watcher for the Socialist local in Terre Haute. In the cells in Atlanta, inmates prayed for a Debs victory, some believing that his first act as president would be to throw open the prison gates. On the streets of the capitol that evening, thousands braved a heavy downpour to follow the returns as they flashed from scrolling billboards outside the city's newspaper offices. Secluded in the White House, Wilson sat with his wife and doctor, awaiting the people's verdict. As the returns came in by telegraph, Tumulty brought the president bulletins that confirmed their greatest fear. Cox was going down to a humiliating defeat. Wilson retired early, leaving Tumulty alone to reckon the full extent of what he gradually realized was a political "earthquake."[36]

Warren Harding and his supporters gathered that night in his home in Marion, Ohio, where they read dispatches out loud and cheered the good news pouring in from every part of the country. When victory seemed certain, Harding issued a statement to the press. "It is all so serious," he declared with appropriate humility, "the obligations are so solemn that instead of exulting I am more given to prayer to God to make me capable of playing my part."[37]

James Cox found himself on the losing end of what one editor called "the greatest landslide in political annals." Even his home precinct went for Harding. Reporters noted that he still wore a smile, one calling him "the gamest of losers." He conceded defeat in a private telegram to Harding, but refused to make a public statement.[38]

The mood was more festive that night in the Atlanta penitentiary, where Zerbst invited Debs to his office to follow the returns along with Mrs. Zerbst, some prison officials, and a local reporter. Through the evening, they called the *Constitution* office for updates, and at first things looked promising for the Socialists. Debs ran even with Cox in a few New York districts, and a party spokesman telegraphed that their vote was "up to expectations." As they waited for the news to trickle in, Debs entertained the group, joking and reminiscing about better days when he had stormed the country on the Red Special. Fully enjoying this brush with history, Zerbst passed out "campaign cigars" to his guests. The group stayed up until Harding declared victory, and Debs could, as he put it, "once more breathe a sigh of relief as a defeated presidential candidate."[39]

In a press release that the warden allowed Debs to release earlier in the day, he predicted that American voters would once again be cheerfully "jumping from the frying pan into the fire and back again. They seem to enjoy the diversion." Though isolated behind prison walls, Debs claimed that he could read the political winds. As always, they whispered to him that socialism was on the rebound. In four years, he predicted, the party would win "an overwhelming victory," if only his splintered comrades would set aside their differences and work together for the revolution.[40]

Across the country, editors tallied up an amazing Republican victory. Harding won 404 of the 531 electoral votes, the most lopsided margin to that point. Republicans enjoyed similar success in congressional races, and the party tightened its control of both houses. For the first time since Reconstruction, they even won in the "Solid South," taking Tennessee and Oklahoma. Some read this as a victory for Harding's hazy pledge to put "America first." Many more agreed with the *New York Post* that the vote was a "colossal protest against Woodrow Wilson and everything from every conceivable angle that might be attached to his name." Even some Democratic victories were embarrassments for the administration. In the Georgia race for U.S. senator, voters elected Tom Watson, a candidate who led what historian C. Vann Woodward called "as plain-spoken a fight for freedom of speech and press as was being waged anywhere." On the campaign trail Watson had defied the red-baiting threats of the American Legion, ridiculed his own party's "perjured president," and promised to bring the amnesty fight to the floor of the Senate. Free speech liberals took scant comfort from Watson's victory, however, since he was a Klan supporter who also vowed to fight against the Pope's minions and the international cabal of Jewish bankers.[41]

Socialists felt vindicated by Wilson's humiliation. "The gentlemen who trafficked in our liberties," one wrote Debs, "have earned a well-deserved rest and they will get it in oblivion." But as the final tally rolled in over the next week, party leaders were disappointed by their own showing. At the start of the campaign they had predicted that Debs would win three million votes, the first step in Socialism's postwar resurgence. Instead, the final tally was 913,664. Debs won almost as many votes in 1920 as he had in 1912, a considerable improvement over Alan Benson's tally four years earlier. Because of women's suffrage, however, the total number of votes cast had more than doubled. As a percentage of the electorate, then, support for Debs had dropped about half since 1912, to about 3.5 percent of the voters, and all agreed that many of them voted for free speech, not for socialism. The *New York Call* conceded that the Debs vote "fell far short of the general expectations, which were shared by friend and foe alike." Karsner tried to console Debs by suggesting that the success of his campaign could not be measured by counting ballots. "You have won the hearts of the people," he said, "whose heads do not yet respond to their best and noblest impulses."[42]

Other Socialist candidates had not fared much better. In New York voters reelected four of the five socialist assemblymen who had been expelled from Albany. However, Victor Berger was defeated in his Wisconsin stronghold, and after predicting that they would capture a dozen congressional seats, the party found it would have one lone voice in Washington, New York's Meyer London. Socialists could take some small comfort in the fact that their third-party rival, Christensen's new

Farmer-Labor Party, had fared even worse. Their attempt to build a new political coalition of workers, farmers, and discontented liberals had garnered only 200,000 votes, further evidence of America's conservative turn.

Though dismayed by the Republican victory, the *New York Times* found a silver lining in the radicals' "meager" showing, in spite of all the discontents and "nervosities" caused by the war. The *Washington Post* was likewise relieved to discover that "the Socialist revolution which the radicals predicted to be imminent was a figment of the imagination. One red-badged fire eating radical makes more noise than a thousand respectable law-abiding Americans, and thus the number of radicals is greatly exaggerated. . . . America is sound at the core."

In the mainstream press, only Norman Hapgood insisted that a million votes for a jailed radical was an impressive showing, especially in light of the government's three-and-a-half-year campaign of "scare-propaganda." The men and women from all political persuasions who cast a ballot for Debs not only ignored the pressure of government propaganda, but seemed in many cases to understand their votes as a gesture of protest against the administration's war on dissent.[43]

Over the years many commentators and historians have described the 1920 election as further evidence of a conservative reaction in the postwar decade, linking Harding's victory to the return of pro-business policies in Washington, the death of progressive reform, and the emergence of the Klan and other reactionary movements. But historians also note a counterreaction against what one has called the decade's "culture of conformity"—a quickened interest in civil liberties that is sometimes described as a new "rights consciousness." Americans had always prided themselves on their respect for free speech, but in the postwar years those pressing for greater speech protections forced the issue onto the national agenda in a variety of forums. While the origins of this new and distinctively modern interest in free expression are diverse, one could not find a better moment to mark its birth than November 2, 1920, the day that almost a million Americans cast their ballot to protest the imprisonment of Eugene Debs.[44]

Chapter 14

Lonely Obstinacy

I N THE WEEKS AFTER THE ELECTION, Debs fell into a deep malaise. He often suffered bouts of exhaustion after the physical and emotional stresses of a campaign. Though he had been spared the travails of a national tour, he was no doubt discouraged by the Republican triumph and his own lackluster showing, in spite of his public claim that there was "no reason for gloom." Now a conservative pro-business administration was coming to power, one supported by a vast majority of Americans, and led by a man who seemed to have little political or personal incentive to worry about the fate of imprisoned radicals. The mail brought more bad news. In late October Debs learned that his friend John Reed had died of typhus while in Russia; his brother Theodore was suffering serious eye problems; and he continued to yearn for Mabel Curry.

Prison life put great emotional strain on him as well. Debs derived much comfort from his radical ministry to those he called "Les Miserables," but he was exhausted by the daily exposure to human despair and degradation. For a year and a half, he had suffered being "isolated, cramped, watched day and night, counted at regular intervals, and dwarfed and dulled by the daily deadly routine." Thanks to graft the food was often stale and unappetizing. Many of the guards were brutal and depraved, their characters poisoned by unrestrained power. Deprived of normal sexual outlets, many inmates sank into "abysmal depths of depravity that the lower animals do not know," while Debs watched young men being schooled by their elders in every form of crime and vice. In this great "deformatory," as Debs called it, both guards and inmates were reduced to inhuman caricatures. Debs's life work was fueled by moral outrage, but the cruelty and waste he saw around him now were making him sick.[1]

Working and living in the prison hospital added to the heartache. Debs watched a friend die from a botched operation and many men suffer lonely deaths, ending in paupers' graves on the prison grounds. One in every five of his fellow inmates was infected with syphilis, while several hundred passed through the hospital ward each year suffering from drug addiction, mostly under the sway of morphine and heroin. At night his sleep was often shattered by the shrieks of men suffering "cold turkey," pleading for death or begging for another fix. He was not well himself, and some nights his heart troubles kept him awake, gasping for air, and unable to sleep lying down.[2]

Visiting Debs to review the election results, David Karsner sensed a change in his hero's mood and physical condition. "His face was drawn," Karsner reported to his comrades, "and I thought he was panting a bit, as though he might be out of breath. His eyes were not as clear, either, as I had seen them before in our prison talks." Though Debs continued to send reassuring letters home to Terre Haute, Mabel Curry sensed the change in her beloved. "I *knew* when the election was over and the pressure was removed he would go to pieces and he *did*. . . . But he has fooled his family all right." Fearing that her "great man" was dying, she sent a desperate letter to Norman Hapgood, pleading with him to do something to save Debs. In a comment ripe with double meaning, Curry added, "I know what a very tricky heart he has."[3]

Through the megaphone of the Hearst newspaper chain, Hapgood warned Americans that their government was about to commit a "perfectly legal murder." He followed this with a private note to Wilson, suggesting that Debs's poor health offered the president a "good way out of a bad mess." Why not pardon him on humanitarian grounds, Hapgood suggested, as a gesture of kindness to a sick old man? In this way, the president could defuse this standoff against Debs in a way that would sidestep the legal and political issues at stake, and remove a stigma that had already driven some of Hapgood's "best and most influential friends" away from the Democrats. Ignoring all evidence to the contrary, Hapgood still assumed that Palmer was to blame for the administration's intransigence and that the president was searching for some face-saving "way out."[4]

At the same time those who wanted Debs kept behind bars stepped up their pressure on the White House, fearing that Wilson was about to give in to the mounting public pressure. Many editors urged the president not to read the election results as a mandate for amnesty, and warned him not to turn "every traitor . . . loose with a leather medal." They were delighted when the White House tersely announced that the president still had "no intention" of pardoning Debs. Unnamed White House officials explained that the president believed that clemency would "set a bad precedent and would encourage others to oppose the Government in the event of another war." The American Legion praised the decision as a noble defense of "the fundamental doctrines of the Constitution" and a blow to "the enemies in our midst."[5]

As Christmas season approached, some of Wilson's old friends and advisors made yet another attempt to convince him to free Debs. In the season of goodwill toward men, the president traditionally pardoned some federal prisoners, and radicals across the country swapped rumors that Wilson would use the occasion to free a "big batch of politicals," including Debs. Gompers sent a public letter to the president, urging his wartime ally one last time to grant amnesty, in the name of the "kindly and considerate spirit of Christmastide." "To open the gates to these prisoners now will be no less an example of our moral strength and self-reliance than was their imprisonment in the hour of danger." Wilson made no response to this call for Christian charity.[6]

As usual, appeals for mercy were undermined by Debs himself, who preferred the role of revolutionary martyr to that of a sickly saint. He told reporters that he wanted to be liberated "last of all," only after all of the other political prisoners were freed. "Really I would rather that it come not at all under the present administration," he added, "because I would be ashamed to be at large under the chaotic conditions of society."[7]

Even as Debs needled the president from afar, many expected that Wilson was about to give in at last. Lucy Robins was ecstatic when Warden Zerbst confided to her that officials in Washington had ordered him to weigh Debs, a standard preliminary for prisoners about to be released. Karsner was so sure that the great moment had come that he headed to Atlanta to greet his hero as he walked through the penitentiary gates. Reporters hung near the White House, expecting the president's announcement at any time. Only Theodore seemed unwilling to get his hopes up; disappointed so many times before by similar rumors, and carrying his own grudge against Wilson, he told friends, "I shall refuse to enthuse until the confirmed word is at hand."[8]

That Christmas season was the second that Debs was spending behind bars. Though no conventional Christian, he treasured the holiday as a family celebration, and in all his years traveling on the lecture circuit he had taken great pains to be back in Terre Haute on Christmas Eve. He observed the season this year by issuing a public Christmas message, reflecting on the way prison had deepened his admiration for Jesus. "I can feel his majestic presence in my prison cell on this anniversary of his birth," he wrote, "and the glowing spirit of him possesses me and lights up and leads the way to victory, and to Peace and Brotherhood for all Mankind! I can feel the world-shaking influence of that class-conscious carpenter, that heroic Jewish Rebel, that glorious Proletarian Revolutionist across twenty centuries, as I hail his Martyr Spirit as the spirit supreme and triumphant now sweeping over the earth with majestic strides and keeping step to the heart-beats of the Revolution that is conquering capitalism and emancipating the race!"[9]

Debs had paid such a tribute to Jesus many times before, but during his stay in prison his ideas about religion had been evolving. In his isolation, he had taken the time to read more about spirituality, and talked about his search for religious meaning with some of his fellow political prisoners. Debs was no longer an atheist, one of them concluded, but had become a Tolstoyan, skeptical of organized religion but "inclined to believe that there is some supernatural power—God—that inspires us, actually dwells in us."[10]

On Christmas Eve, two prisoners approached Debs in his cell, a sol-

emn Irishman and a grinning "Chinese," who ushered him to the base-
ment of the prison hospital. There a gathering of inmates surprised him
with a special holiday feast, treating him as their honored guest. They
had decorated the room with flowers and homemade ornaments, and
each prisoner donated the contents of his Christmas packages to the
communal supper. The radicals had most to offer, thanks to the gift
packages of food and clothing sent by the women of the Socialist Prison
Comfort Club. The convicts took turns serving each other, and called on
Debs to honor the occasion with a speech. "In every eye there was an
expression of delight and kindness," he later recalled. "If I had never
before understood the meaning of human happiness and the radiant
heights to which it may ascend, I perceived it that night in the faces of
my fellow prisoners who had in this loving and simple way translated
the thought of 'good will among men' into kindly deed." The steel bars
seemed to melt away, and Debs felt that "Jesus Christ was in the prison
that night."[11]

The mood was more somber in the White House that evening. That
day the president had announced his long-awaited decision on a Christmas pardon. He granted freedom to 180 prisoners, including two dozen
"politicals," but Debs was not among them. Releasing the "unrepentant" radical, the president had decided, would be "a breach of faith
with the American boys who went to France." Christmas dinner at the
White House had been disrupted, rumor had it, when Wilson's daughter clashed with her stepmother over the decision to keep Debs in jail.[12]

In spite of his illness and his bitter disappointments, Wilson had not
lost his capacity for both personal empathy and political pragmatism.
With Palmer's blessing, he had commuted sentences for hundreds of
wartime prisoners, called off the prosecution of Rose Pastor Stokes and
many others who still awaited trial, and backed Newton Baker's decision
to free all conscientious objectors held in military prisons. But in Wilson's mind, Debs was different. The aged radical was no martyr and innocent idealist, he decided, but an unredeemed traitor who continued
to mock the noble sacrifice made by the thousands of American soldiers
who had died on the battlefields of Europe. They were the true saviors
of Mankind, willing to spill their blood in defense of democracy, and
Debs was their Judas. For the embittered president, Debs came to em-

body all who had betrayed the nation's ideals, undermined its crusade for democracy, and smashed the president's hopes.

Socialists were disappointed, then outraged, by the president's decision, and pointed out that he had pardoned "murderers, bank robbers, burglars . . . dope dealers, and other choice criminals." They were particularly galled by Wilson's decision to free Frank Von Rintelen, a German officer caught during the war trying to firebomb American cargo ships. When Rintelen walked out of the Atlanta penitentiary just weeks before the president denied Debs a Christmas pardon, the liberal minister John Haynes Holmes sputtered that no further proof was needed that Debs was the victim of the president's "wanton persecution." "Patience has ceased to be a virtue," Holmes declared, "And the time has come to denounce it with the unmeasured wrath which it deserves."[13]

The usually optimistic Upton Sinclair also abandoned all hope that Wilson could be reached, a bitter conclusion shared by many radicals and disillusioned liberals. Two months remained in his term, however, and Lucy Robins pressed on, desperate to succeed before Harding took office. A few days before Christmas, a Senate Judiciary subcommittee finally began consideration of her amnesty resolution, introduced by Senator France back in March. Robins hoped that this hearing, the culmination of long months of careful politicking, would legitimate the amnesty cause before a national audience and raise the pressure on Palmer and Wilson to free Debs in the last days of their administration.

Though they represented a range of political opinions, most senators at the hearing sympathized with the practical goal of the "France resolution"—the release of those who had been imprisoned for criticizing the war, as long as they had not intended to provoke insubordination, undermine morale, or incite draft-dodging. All agreed that determining a speaker's intent could be a tricky business, and that under wartime pressures judges and juries had suspected the worst of the defendants, sending to jail some who were probably only exercising their right to speak. Witnesses at the hearing underscored the point with jarring examples—a California filmmaker imprisoned for three years for making *The Spirit of '76,* a feature film about the American Revolution that a jury decided might sap Americans' will to fight by casting the British allies in a bad light; a deaf and bewildered old man who was still in the Atlanta penitentiary for suggesting to members of the local draft board that the country could not afford the economic costs of sending an army to Europe; men arrested years after the armistice for passing out leaflets promoting an amnesty meeting. Montana's senator Walsh conceded that he had "no doubt at all that, in the hysteria in which the people were, quite naturally and quite reasonably during the war, some people were actually tried and convicted who, upon calm consideration of the case, never should have come within the provisions of the act."

While the senators acknowledged these miscarriages of justice, most had no intention of now accepting any blame for passing the Espionage and Sedition acts, forging the blunt instrument that federal prosecutors had used to create these political prisoners. Several worried out loud that endorsing the amnesty resolution might imply a criticism of Congress or a judgment that the Espionage Act was unconstitutional. They believed that they had only been doing their "simple duty" when they passed the laws needed to unify the country in its hour of peril.

Among the senators on the panel, only Joseph France offered a dissenting view, insisting that the amnesty debate raised fundamental questions about the constitutionality of the wartime laws. While most lawmakers still maintained that many of the convictions had been justified, France said that he "never shared that view." In his opening remarks, he argued that the government had been wrong and "unwise" to try to "preserve our constitutional Government by a flagrant violation of constitutional principle."[14]

Those testifying at the hearing divided along similar lines. Speaking for the AFL, Gompers thought that the Espionage Act "grated on the man who is a real American believing in American principles," but he conceded that it may have been necessary to meet the national crisis. When asked if he sought pardons for those "draft-dodgers and slackers" who fled to Mexico rather than fight, Gompers balked, and then confessed, "I haven't given the matter the consideration it deserves." Robins likewise avoided a direct attack on the senators and their Espionage Act, and skirted the legal complexities posed by a general amnesty. Playing on emotion rather than principle, she told the senators about her visits with Eugene Debs and repeated tales of his benevolent influence on the murderers around him. "He surely could never propagate crime, he could not propagate violence," she told the panel. "He can only say good things; and he can bring out the best that is in the worst kind of a criminal." After the hearing, Senator France complimented Robins for her moving testimony, provoking a wave of jealousy in Gompers, who feared that his young protégé had found herself a new mentor.[15]

The Socialists who testified at the hearing took a quite different approach. Robins had done all she could to keep them from appearing, fearing that they would grandstand, threaten revolution, and generally confirm the public suspicion that radicals were not responsible stewards of the right of free speech. Learning about the hearing only at the last minute, party leaders insisted on their right to testify, if only to force their point of view onto the pages of the "capitalist press." They hastily arranged for Algernon Lee, a socialist educator from New York, to lead a small delegation to Washington. Far from sidetracking the deliberations with revolutionary theatrics, Lee presented the most informed and principled testimony at the hearings, offering the senators a history lesson designed to convince them that the Espionage Act was not a harmless and justifiable act of national self-preservation, but a violation of America's long tradition of tolerance for dissent. He reminded them that Daniel Webster and Abraham Lincoln had spoken against the Mexican War, and that Lincoln had exercised his power over northern critics during the Civil War with comparative restraint and pledged a generous amnesty to confederate rebels, binding the nation's wounds rather than punishing his political foes. While Lee conceded that the Senate Judiciary Committee could not rule on the constitutionality of the Espionage Act, he refused to accept the senators' contention that the question was moot.

Senators listened respectfully to Lee's testimony but had no interest in using the amnesty resolution to force their colleagues to rethink, and maybe even recant, their decision to pass the wartime speech laws. They were not there to put themselves on trial, after all. The person they wanted to bring before their bar of justice was Attorney General Palmer, who was called to testify at the hearing on January 19, just weeks before Harding's inauguration. Everyone in the hearing room that day understood that, even then, Palmer was preparing a final list of pardon recommendations for the president.

This was not the first time Congress had tried to put the unpopular attorney general on the hot seat. Palmer complained, in fact, that since Republicans had taken control in 1918, he had been "the subject of numerous and almost constant investigations by the committees of an unfriendly Congress." During another afternoon of "grilling" before the Senate subcommittee, Palmer apologized for nothing. He repeated his arguments against a general amnesty and insisted that most who had been convicted under the Espionage Act were already free. Palmer was somewhat embarrassed to confess that, thanks to faulty record keeping, he was not entirely sure how many Americans remained in jail for violating the wartime speech laws. He could only say that his office was currently reviewing 130 cases. Pressed by the senators, he acknowledged that a pardon for Debs was still a possibility, in spite of the president's earlier statements opposing his release.[16]

A couple of weeks later, in the waning days of the Wilson administration, Palmer made the announcement for which Robins had long worked. While he had privately supported clemency for Debs since at least August, he now went public with his change of heart, telling reporters that he would recommend this in his final report to the president. In this letter, Palmer reminded Wilson that Debs had been a "model prisoner," and that many thousands of Americans had petitioned for his release. After long reflection, Palmer had decided that keeping him in prison much longer would "invite criticism of a discriminating character." He concluded by noting that the prisoner was old, and though he might not be "punished adequately, he has at least been severely punished."[17]

Privately, many of Wilson's advisors urged him to accept Palmer's recommendation. They enjoyed no influence, however, over a man who had spent his last months in office stewing over grudges, petty and great, against those he perceived as his political foes. After reviewing Palmer's report, the president told Tumulty that he would "never consent to the pardon of this man." He acknowledged that "in certain quarters there is popular demand" for clemency, but he felt a greater obligation to "the mothers of this country who sent their boys to the other side. . . . While the flower of American youth was pouring out its blood to vindicate the cause of civilization, this man, Debs, stood behind the lines, sniping, attacking and denouncing them." The president understood that if he stood firm against Debs, his critics would call him "cold-blooded and indifferent," but he said this would make "no impression" on him.[18]

At least that is how Tumulty later recalled the president's thinking. All the public knew was that Wilson wrote "Denied" across Palmer's request and sent it back to the Justice Department without further comment—a blow to the amnesty cause, and a parting humiliation for his beleaguered attorney general. Stunned by the public repudiation, Palmer went home sick that day.[19]

Robins was equally devastated. "My mind is in a whirl," she told Theodore when she heard the news. "I do not know just what we ought to do next." Every lever of political influence had been pulled, and to no avail. In a few days the power to pardon would pass into the hands of Warren Harding, a man who had little incentive to please liberals and labor leaders, much less anarchists and socialists. Drained of her formidable supplies of energy and confidence, she thought of resigning, though both Gompers and Debs talked her out of it.[20]

When the news of the president's decision reached Atlanta, Debs denounced Wilson as "the most pathetic figure in the world." In a statement smuggled out of prison by a friend, Debs said, "It is he, not I, who needs a pardon. Woodrow Wilson is an exile from the hearts of his people. . . . No man in public life in American history ever retired so thoroughly discredited, so scathingly rebuked, so overwhelmingly impeached and repudiated as Woodrow Wilson."[21]

Though the president claimed to dwell in a lofty realm above the influence of public criticism, those barbs seemed to hit their mark. The superintendent of prisons ordered Debs's visiting and mailing privileges suspended, on the grounds that he had violated prison rules by providing an interview without permission. Though the superintendent denied that Debs was being punished specifically for "assailing" the president, he added that the new restrictions would be lifted if Debs apologized—which he would not do. Already denied regular commerce with the world outside the prison walls, Debs was now plunged into even greater isolation.[22]

Wilson's decision won praise from many, while critics like Tom Watson called the suspension of Debs's privileges a "Russian barbarity." For many of the president's liberal supporters, the move to punish Debs seemed like the final act of a great political tragedy, as they watched the great leader's "world-shaking idealism" fade away into a "lonely obstinacy."[23]

Chapter 15

Free Speech and Normalcy

O N THE MORNING of March 23, 1921, hundreds of Shriners milled around the Atlanta train station, in town for their annual convention. Through their midst walked Eugene Debs, the nation's best-known prisoner and five-time presidential candidate. Brass bands played, photographers snapped pictures of the conventioneers, and a few local reporters even hailed Warden Zerbst—but none noticed Debs as he took leave of the warden and boarded a train headed for Washington, D.C. Debs had been summoned to a secret meeting with Harry Daugherty, the nation's new attorney general. The friends and foes of amnesty were stunned when they learned that this convicted felon, so often described as a dangerous revolutionary, had been trusted to leave prison and travel hundreds of miles without guards. Harding's plan to restore "normalcy," all now realized, would include a fresh approach to the controversy over America's wartime prisoners.

Harding signaled that intention in his first weeks in office, ordering Daugherty to begin yet another review of the status of political prisoners. Daugherty professed a strong personal and "technical" interest in the Debs case, and called Zerbst from Atlanta to get a first-hand account of the prisoner. After singing Debs's praises, Zerbst suggested, "half in jest," that Daugherty ought to meet him to judge for himself. To his surprise, Daugherty agreed and told him to sneak Debs out of prison for a secret conference at the Justice Department.[1]

Blustering and insecure, Daugherty was one of the least qualified men ever entrusted with the job of directing the nation's legal system. A machine politician, he knew much more about the bare-knuckle skills of Ohio's partisan politics than he did about the intricacies of federal law and the challenges of running a major government bureaucracy. When Daugherty's critics heard about his decision to grant Debs a secret furlough, they took this as confirmation of his incompetence. When reporters asked him whether he had the power to let a federal prisoner roam free across the country, he replied, "I am satisfied there is full authority. I have not looked it up, but I am satisfied it exists." Asked to cite the precedent for such an action, he joked, "Now there is."[2]

To Daugherty, the controversy over Debs was more a political problem than a legal one. "The Debs case stands alone," as he put it, a frank recognition of the obvious but a point long denied by Palmer, and by Debs himself. Debs was different from the hundred or so other remaining "politicals," Daugherty thought, because he was the leader of a political party, because his age and health made him a prime candidate for martyrdom, and because public agitation over his imprisonment was stirring working-class resentment at a time when the new president promised to restore domestic tranquility. In spite of some tough remarks on the campaign trail, Harding had privately confided to several people that he wanted Debs out, if only to shed the political baggage that had weighed so heavily on his predecessor. As Daugherty saw it, the challenge was to find a way to accomplish that without giving comfort to the radicals, without embarrassing the president or making him appear soft on Bolshevism, and without outraging the many Americans who still saw Debs as an impenitent traitor.

Such a resolution could not be teased out of law books or imposed on the country by executive proclamation. Rather, Daugherty felt, it demanded careful political calculations—something he understood better than the fine points of his new job description. Toward that end, he decided that he needed to look Debs in the eye, in order to find out how cooperative he was willing to be in this scheme for his own liberation.[3]

On March 23, Warden Zerbst announced that he was taking Debs to spend the day on the prison farm, a ruse to avoid the prison's six daily roll calls. After driving in that direction a few blocks, he detoured back to his own home. There Debs changed into a prison-tailored civilian suit and picked up a lunch specially prepared by Mrs. Zerbst. At the station the two men felt like mischievous boys as Debs hid in plain sight, skirting a crowd of unsuspecting reporters, passengers, and Shriners. After a night on the train, Debs appeared at Daugherty's office by ten the next morning.

The nation's chief law officer and its most notorious political prisoner talked for several hours. Few details about their conversation were disclosed. Daugherty made Debs take a vow of silence at the time, and they said little about the meeting later. Lucy Robins, who talked with both men soon after their meeting, reported that Debs stood firm before the man who controlled his fate, repeating his "demands"—that he wanted no special consideration, but expected freedom for all of his fellow political prisoners, and that he would not apply for or accept any pardon that implied acceptance of his guilt. Both conditions troubled Daugherty, who would not accept any arrangement that might allow the radicals to declare victory in this standoff. Perhaps hoping to charm Debs into softening his position, Daugherty told him he was a "wonderful man" who could be of great service to America "if you made up your mind to be loyal." Debs countered that "it may be possible to help the country more by not being loyal in your sense of the word."[4]

Robins reported that Daugherty was moved to tears by this encounter with her working-class hero. Perhaps. Years later, after his own scrapes with the law, Daugherty did write a self-justifying memoir that included some warm words for Debs. However, evidence from the time suggests that he found Debs to be personally appealing but also a dangerous and disloyal fanatic. In spite of these misgivings, Daugherty gave the prisoner good reason to hope that his days in prison would soon be over when he asked him if he would mind returning within a month for a personal meeting with the president. Driving Debs back to the train station that afternoon, a Daugherty aide considerately offered to buy him a small "memento" of his trip to the capital. Debs requested some new quill toothpicks, replacing the ones that guards had taken from him the day he arrived in Atlanta.[5]

Though Daugherty made Debs promise to keep their meeting secret, he could not resist telling reporters about the story. The attorney general suffered a difficult relationship with the press, and he clearly enjoyed the fact that he had put one over on them. At a routine press conference that afternoon, he startled his audience by announcing, with studied nonchalance, that there was "not much in the way of news—except that I wanted to tell you about Debs coming to Washington today."

The reporters gasped, then dashed for the phones to break this "stunning" story. The news soon sparked across the telegraph wires, leaping ahead of the train that carried Debs back to prison. Stepping onto the platform in Atlanta, he was greeted by Zerbst, and a crowd of reporters, photographers, and newsreel cameras. "I'm mighty glad to see you again, Mr. Warden," he said as they shook hands. Zerbst granted reporters a few minutes with the prisoner, but Debs honored his promise not to reveal any details about his conference, except to say, "I appreciated the confidence shown in me, by letting me go alone and on my honor to Washington, and I enjoyed the trip." He joked that he was "going back to be a good convict again," and then Zerbst whisked him away.[6]

Daugherty's odd decision to reveal this "secret" meeting suggests that he hoped, in a blundering way, to test public opinion about the prospect of a Debs pardon. Amnesty forces were jubilant, of course. One socialist told reporters that the meeting could only mean one thing—that Harding was getting ready to release Debs. The opponents of amnesty agreed, and Daugherty soon found himself the object of their wrath. The *New York World* called the secret meeting a "disgraceful act," while the *Times* seethed against this "official tenderness of treatment and coddling of this impenitent criminal." A number of Democratic papers charged that Daugherty, the slick political operator, had flaunted the law in order to court labor votes in 1924. Across the country, state chapters of the American Legion fired off telegrams of protest, while a South Carolina congressman took to the floor of the House to denounce this special treatment for a traitor. When someone pointed out that

Debs had been "man enough" to return to jail as promised, he countered that he could "bring plenty of moonshiners from Atlanta that will
do the same thing and who would bring you something good if you
would let them come up here."[7]

More poignantly, Daugherty heard protests from citizens who felt betrayed. "Speaking as a father whose only son lies buried in France," a
California businessman wrote, "it if should be during this administration that such despicable criminals as Debs should again be turned
loose, I, in common with hundreds and thousands of other parents will
feel that our sacrifice has been in vain." Harding's office was likewise
deluged with complaints from those who feared that their vote for "One
Hundred Percent Americanism" had been wasted. Claiming to speak
for "tens of millions of Americans," an influential Cleveland Republican
told Harding he was shocked by news that he was considering letting
"the most dangerous man in America" out of jail. As head of his city's
chapter of the American Protective League, this man had followed the
Debs case closely, spying on his Ohio meetings and attending his trial.
"In my opinion," he told Harding, "the release of *Debs* will be the first
great blow against the safety of America. A blast which will shatter the
very foundation of our patriotism, and will lower the morale of our people in the reverence for our Government."[8]

The president stood by his attorney general, announcing that he had
approved his unorthodox methods. This storm of criticism convinced
the two, however, to set the issue aside for the time being. A week
earlier, Daugherty had told reporters that he would make his recommendation on Debs in a few days. Now he announced that the case
was more complicated than he had thought, and he would need more
time to craft his report.[9]

Eager to press their advantage, Robins and her allies on the Senate
Judiciary Committee arranged several meetings with Daugherty during the early weeks of the Harding administration. After the election
Robins had dreaded the prospect of working with the new administration, assuming that the pro-business conservatives would be unsympathetic and intractable. In her meetings with Daugherty, however,
she sensed immediately that this "paunchy and genial businessman"

would be easier to work with than the prim and principled Palmer. Her hunch was confirmed when Daugherty let her bring an amnesty delegation to meet the president, access that the gatekeepers in the Wilson administration had never granted. On April 4 she guided the near-blind Gompers into Harding's office, accompanied by a dozen other delegates, mostly leaders from various AFL trade unions. In a gesture of solidarity, Gompers once again shared the role of spokesman with Socialist congressman Meyer London.

These men, assembled on the pinnacle of American power, clearly felt unnerved by Lucy Robins's presence, and treated her with a condescending chivalry. Harding insisted that she be seated in his chair, while he stood with his male visitors. London joked weakly that "women are disturbers at all times. Their place is in the home." Harding countered, "Bless them, I love them," and handed Robins a rose from a nearby vase. "I sat there with the flower in my hand," Robins recalled, "like a dunce in the corner."[10]

Her humiliation was outweighed by her excitement as she watched Harding, the man who held the key to the prison doors, give the group a cordial and sympathetic hearing. Ever the harmonizer, Harding urged everyone to set aside their political differences and "work together." The delegation left the White House charmed and reassured. Though Harding only promised to act "as favorably as possible," Robins felt sure that Debs would be free in a matter of weeks.[11]

The day after Harding took office, the Socialists announced their own plans to bring pressure to bear on the new president. The lesson of the past few years, they now decided, was that principles mean little in Washington. Wilson's cabinet had been stocked with high-minded idealists, after all, but under the pressures of war they had cast aside their values and "destroyed the freedom of America." Harding's men, by contrast, were mostly "colorless nonentities and vicious reactionaries." Less encumbered by the pretense of idealism, they seemed even more likely to yield to the external demands of political expedience. The time had come, Socialists resolved, to take the offensive, trying new ways to force the president to free Debs and the others. They would make the issue a "front page story" in every capitalist newspaper, raising a clamor that the Harding administration could not ignore and reestablishing their party as the vanguard of American radicalism.[12]

Meeting in Boston that spring, Socialists unveiled their new "Let's get them all out" campaign. They appointed Harriet Stanton Blatch to work as full-time amnesty lobbyist in Washington. Daughter of feminist Elizabeth Cady Stanton, Blatch was a veteran activist in the suffrage movement, the avant-garde in the evolving art of mass-mediated political protest. After leading the successful campaign to win the vote, Blatch joined the Socialist Party, declaring civil liberties and economic justice to be her next battleground. Drawing on her organizing skills, the Socialists announced plans for a nationwide petition campaign, a "massive" demonstration in Washington on April 13 to mark Debs's second full year in jail, and a picket line in front of the White House. Echoing the suffragists' strategy, the party decided that these picketers would all be women.[13]

Upton Sinclair applauded the party's new militancy. Still frustrated by his failure to persuade Wilson, he felt sure that Harding would be even harder to reach, only responding to extreme political pressure. Months before the Socialists unveiled their plans, he used his weekly column to call for fifty volunteers willing to march on the White House and face "jail and the hunger strike." When only two readers signed up for such a mission, he quietly dropped the matter. "It is a little embarrassing," he confided to Theodore, "to call on others for martyrdom when you do not offer to lead them." Sinclair had gone to jail before, and would again, but for now he decided that he was more useful to the amnesty cause as a propagandist than as a prisoner.[14]

Having already wiled her way into Harding's office, Lucy Robins was horrified by these plans for noisy and aggressive demonstrations at the White House gates. She had no objections to the Socialists' "monster petition." Such gestures were "valueless," she thought—much less effective than her own strategy for creating working-class solidarity and building alliances with Washington insiders. But she saw little harm in the project, and even agreed to help the Socialists distribute their petition through the AFL's vast network of locals. However, she dreaded the party's plan to descend on Washington en masse and to antagonize Harding with a picket line. Such theatrics, she felt sure, would only alienate the public opinion she had so patiently nurtured, stiffen resistance to amnesty in and out of Washington, and make it politically difficult for Harding to release Debs. She was particularly incensed when the Socialists announced that Debs himself would be the keynote speaker at their demonstration, a grandiose promise that she feared would discredit the entire movement. As she put it, the dramas staged by American radicals too often turned into tragedies.[15]

Norman Hapgood, Robins's ally in the mainstream press, shared her concerns and publicly warned the Socialists, *"Don't do it."* He sensed that, in spite of some intemperate remarks on the campaign trail, Harding was sympathetic and hovered on the verge of making a "Lincolnesque" decision to set Debs free. Angry confrontations and groundless boasting from the nation's radical fringe would only delay, even derail, this result. The new president deserved a "reasonable time" to act on his own, Hapgood argued. The Socialists replied that the path of moderation had been tried and had proven futile. After all, they countered, Hapgood and his fellow liberals had not even been able to persuade Wilson, their political ally. What hope did they have of reaching a conservative administration? The only way to move Harding, they insisted, was to badger and embarrass him until he could stand it no more.[16]

Once again Debs had to mediate this conflict between various amnesty factions. He agreed with Robins and Hapgood that the new president had shown a "decent disposition" to act soon, and urged his comrades to postpone their demonstration. Public sympathy for the prisoners was swinging their way, Debs sensed, but this support was fragile and might evaporate if the party seemed unreasonable. Further, Debs worried that the demonstration would flop. His usual optimism tempered by a steady stream of bad news about the party's fortunes, as well as feuds within the amnesty ranks, he feared that "division and dissension" would "breed indifference or disgust, and the affair will be nothing compared to what it should be, and its influence for good will be perhaps negligible or of a questionable nature." A poor showing in Washington would mock their claim that amnesty sentiment was powerful and growing across the country.[17]

Party leaders were aghast. After announcing such bold plans, they feared that calling them off now would further demoralize the comrades and undermine the party's credibility. More was at stake, they believed, than the fate of Debs and his fellow prisoners. The amnesty fight was an integral part of the struggle to save their entire movement, providing valuable publicity and a renewed sense of purpose that they needed desperately. Party secretary Otto Branstetter told Debs that the membership already seemed "largely indifferent and lukewarm" about the amnesty campaign, willing to let Robins and Gompers, Hapgood, the ACLU and Senator France fight what should be the party's own battle. Thus, with misgivings, Debs authorized his fellow Socialists to go ahead with the petition drive and the amnesty demonstration, while the party agreed not to confront Harding with a picket line.[18]

Even this more cautious plan began to fray when Lucy Robins convinced many AFL leaders to avoid the Washington rally. Her allies on the Senate Judiciary Committee canceled their plans to attend, lest the public mistake their support for free speech with sympathy for socialism. Unable to muster the "thousands of workers" they had first predicted, the Socialists had to settle for sending two hundred "delegates" to Washington, mostly party leaders with a smattering of representatives from the ACLU, the Farmer-Labor Party, and some of the more radical AFL unions. On April 13, the second anniversary of Debs's imprisonment, this group observed "Political Amnesty Day" by marching down Pennsylvania Avenue toward the Capitol. Though few marched, many across the country had been willing to sign, and the focal point of the parade was an open touring car carrying the "monster petition." Two strong men were needed to hoist the four-foot-high scroll, said to contain "more names than any other petition ever presented in the history of the nation." Among them were the signatures of Helen Keller, novelist Booth Tarkington, and various college presidents, progressive reformers, and retired politicians.[19]

At the end of the parade the delegates split up. Armed with swaths of signatures carved from their massive petition, smaller groups called on Harding, Daugherty, Vice President Calvin Coolidge, and various congressmen. Harding treated the lead delegation respectfully, and they were delighted to find him "highly sympathetic" to their cause. The petitioners left the White House, however, with little more than they had

The Socialists bring their "monster petition" to Washington.
Courtesy of the Abraham Lincoln Presidential Library.

ever received from the Wilson administration. Still opposed to a general amnesty, Harding only agreed to decide each case on its merits. And he added what would prove to be a troublesome new condition; any action on the wartime prisoners would be delayed until the war was officially over, the treaties with the Central powers finally resolved. For his part,

Daugherty assured the petitioners that he would approach the matter with what he ambiguously called "a growing leniency."[20]

On that same day, the amnesty cause suffered a new setback when the Supreme Court declined to review an appeal by forty-six Wobblies who had been convicted in the mass trial in Chicago. Facing the prospect of ten years in a federal prison, Big Bill Haywood and nine others jumped bail and fled to Russia. The rest now swelled the ranks of the nation's "political prisoners."[21]

In spite of this setback, party secretary Otto Branstetter was relieved to report to Debs that the demonstration had been "quite successful in all respects." Overcoming the "intrigue and double-dealing" of Lucy Robins and Samuel Gompers, the party had mounted a dignified and respectable protest. Robins and her AFL allies fired back that the demonstration had accomplished little for Debs and the other prisoners, and was motivated more by the party's hunger for publicity. In turn, Socialists attacked Robins for the "nightmare hallucination" that she was the only one capable of liberating their leader. For weeks, both sides exchanged bitter letters and barbed editorials, while the communists heaped scorn on them both for begging favors from a "capitalist government." Again, from his cell Debs pleaded with his rescuers to set aside their "small differences."[22]

In spite of their feuds, the amnesty factions did succeed in keeping the plight of political prisoners on the nation's agenda. As long as Debs remained in jail, Daugherty and Harding could expect that the issue would dog them. Harding heard appeals from a stream of visitors, including Mae West and one of his own nieces. When he attended the funeral of Champ Clark, the former Senate leader, Clark's widow urged him to free Debs. Clyde Miller, still working to redeem himself for sending Debs to jail, wrote that he had some "facts not in print" that the president might want to consider. The Unitarians sent an amnesty resolution to the president and a convention of Universalists almost came to blows over a similar proposal. Jacob Coxey, leader of the 1894 poorman's march on Washington, volunteered to personally carry the news of Harding's pardon to Debs in Atlanta.[23]

From Europe, intellectuals and writers continued to plead for Debs. Taking Socialist propaganda at face value, H. G. Wells thought Debs was a bit too saintly for his taste but declared that his only crime had been "a premature craving for universal peace." Villard tried to recruit George Bernard Shaw to cross the Atlantic to lecture Americans on the virtue of political tolerance, an offer he declined. "Come to America!" he replied. "No thank you. If they put E. V. Debs in prison for an extraordinarily mild remark, what would they do to me, who never opens his mouth in public without saying things that would shock E. V. Debs to the bottom of his too tender heart?"[24]

Poets also stepped up the war of words, publishing variations on the now common theme that Debs was, as Witter Bynner put it, America's "Last Christian." During the war Bynner had lost his teaching post at the University of California, in part for expressing his support for amnesty. When his poem appeared in the *New Republic* in August, Mabel Curry thanked him for sending literary "smelling salts to revive the Christian principles in the hearts of *cowards in high places!*" Bynner's verse probably had no such effect on Harding and Daugherty, who devoted their leisure hours to golf and poker, not poetry.

By the summer of 1921, however, Daugherty complained that journalists never asked him about anything but the political prisoners. As public interest intensified, Theodore felt sure that his brother would be out soon, not because Harding had any desire to make "restitution for the outrage," but thanks to an "irresistible pressure which is increasing with the passing days and which can no longer be stayed."[25]

As support for amnesty continued to grow, some organized an increasingly effective counterattack, bringing concerted pressure to bear on Harding and Daugherty to keep Debs and the others in jail. The editorial pages of many major newspapers insisted that amnesty was demanded only by a noisy and suspect fragment of the public, and that in America there was "no such thing as a political prisoner." As the *New York Times* put it, "the proposal to turn loose on the community dangerous criminals is almost fantastically preposterous." Through 1921, grim reminders of the sacrifice of war no doubt strengthened the resolve of those not ready to forgive men and women who had been convicted of trying to undermine the nation's will to fight. Coffins bearing the remains of soldiers killed in France continued to arrive at the docks, wounded veterans were a common sight on American streets, and for months Washington solemnly prepared for the unveiling of a new memorial to honor the "unknown soldier."[26]

The American Legion took a lead role in organizing the opposition to amnesty, treating the Debs case as a litmus test to distinguish true patriots from dangerous radicals and deluded liberals. Founded just months after the armistice by Teddy Roosevelt's son and some of his fellow officers, the Legion could mobilize more than a million veterans across the country and wield considerable power in national politics. The group lobbied Washington on a variety of issues, including universal military training, better services for disabled soldiers, accelerated bonuses, and jobs programs for returning servicemen. In its early years the organization was best known, however, for its devotion to "one hundred percent Americanism," a program that included protecting the nation's schools and public squares from the subversive influence of political radicals. The Legion proposed a new federal law to bar "un-American" literature from the mail and pushed for schools to add a "morale hour" to the curriculum. "If the American Legion is unanimous in just one thing," its commander Alan Owsley told Daugherty, "it is in opposition to the pardoning or releasing of Eugene Debs."[27]

When Owsley claimed that "all ranks" of veterans "without exception" opposed freedom for the "insidious Debs," he was clearly wrong. Two rival veterans groups formed at the same time, both claiming to better represent the views of the average soldier and determined to rally ex-soldiers to "progressive" causes, including amnesty. In a letter to Harding, the head of the Private Soldiers and Sailors Legion protested the "amazing insolence and effrontery" of the American Legion's claim that it spoke for all veterans, while some Legion members resigned rather than support what one called a "childish grudge" against Debs. By 1921, however, the Legion emerged as the largest and best organized veterans' group, and Harding and Daugherty understood that they ignored the organization's stand against amnesty at their peril.

Faced with this conflicting clamor, Harding decided to set the matter aside for a time. Averse to conflict, the president often handled contentious issues in this way, preferring to postpone difficult decisions, hoping that partisan tempers might cool and that time might reveal some way forward. Theodore Debs described the president's leadership style less charitably. "Harding, being a politician—likewise a coward, seeking to offend neither, drifts with the tide in the vain hope that something will turn up." And so, a month after the Socialist visit, Daugherty announced that he was still reviewing the "numerous facts" of the case and his report would be delayed indefinitely.[28]

Through the summer of 1921, rumors swirled that Debs was about to be set free, news that Daugherty sometimes denied and other times seemed to encourage. "These are wearisome days of waiting," Theodore complained. When no action was taken by late June, Socialists protested that they had been misled. "In all courtesy," they wrote Daugherty, "we demand from you a definite decision. . . . Many months have passed and the men and women still languish in prison, separated from their families, in all the stifling, sultry heat of midsummer." A month later Daugherty promised to give his recommendations to Harding in ten days, but then he predicted that his "comprehensive study" would not be ready till summer's end.[29]

Each new pronouncement reached Debs, mingling disappointment with fresh hope. "I thought surely I would see you before this time," he wrote Curry in mid-July. "It seemed to me the extreme limit had been reached and that I could wait no longer to keep my sanity." Curry was terrified to learn that Debs's health took another turn for the worst. His heart condition kept him up many nights, while his weight slipped to a scant 158 pounds. For Debs, the travails of these long summer months were made worse by the departure of Warden Zerbst. In early July, Harding gave the job to J. E. Dyche, an Oklahoma insurance salesman who had produced a big Republican vote in his state in 1920. With regret, Zerbst moved on to become the new warden at Leavenworth. Dyche did not share his predecessor's interest in reform, and like many of Harding's cronies he soon proved to be affable but less than competent. Still, Dyche and Debs became friends, and the new warden continued to grant him the small privileges that made prison life more bearable.[30]

In spite of his personal sympathies for the prisoner, Dyche also maintained the gag order on Debs that had been imposed after he gave an interview attacking Wilson at the end of his term. The Justice Depart-

ment denied visitor passes to anyone connected to a newspaper, a group
that included most of his propagandizing friends. The few personal visits allowed were closely monitored by guards. As the nation continued
to debate Debs's crime and his punishment in 1921, he grew further out
of touch with the world outside of Atlanta's prison walls. One visitor that
summer was shocked to find Debs looking "thin, extremely pale and
listless." He seemed a broken man, losing his grip on reality and growing careless about his fate.[31]

In his isolation, Debs drew consolation from the small community of
his fellow "politicals," a mix of Socialists, Wobblies, anarchists, and
Christian pacifists whose political differences seemed trivial in light of
their common burden. They held regular meetings in the prison yard at
exercise time and shared the shreds of news they had gleaned from the
outside world. On May Day 1920, they honored the red holiday by gathering at the edge of the yard around a picture of a waving flag that
someone had etched in the sand, the word REVOLUTION written across
its center. As a Russian anarchist played his violin, the group sang the
words to the radical anthem "Red Flag." Debs smiled as they sang the
chorus:

> Then raise the scarlet standard high:
> Within its shade we'll live and die,
> Tho' cowards flinch and traitors sneer
> We'll keep the red flag flying here.

"We were happy," Debs's friend Joseph Coldwell later reminisced.
"We felt the solidarity of comradeship."[32]

Debs also continued to find comfort from the letters he received
from friends and admirers who assured him that he was not forgotten. Johns Hopkins historian Broadus Mitchell, for example, wrote
that "every man with a social conscience and an historical sense ought
to express his indebtedness to your courage." Some comrades sent
him veiled references to political developments, ambiguous enough to
evade the watchful but overtaxed eye of the prison censor. Debs also
heard faithfully from Hattie Norris, a teenager from Monroe, Louisi-
ana, who was her high school's only socialist. He treasured these cheery

notes in which she described her attempts to stir class consciousness among her schoolmates and expose the capitalist bunk spread by her teachers. Sprinkled within these heaps of fan mail were sputtering angry notes from those who hoped the guards would "throw the whip" into him daily.[33]

Debs also heard from various religious enthusiasts who sent him advice about how to free his soul, if not his body. Some counseled a closer relationship with Jesus, while others urged "Love Dynamics," astral projection, and other experiments with spiritualism. "Believe me," Thorstein Veblen's ex-wife assured him, "we live in a stranger world than we know."[34]

When Debs did imagine his soul flying free of prison bars, it traveled straight to the side of Mabel Curry. "Don't you hear me treading in your footsteps," he wrote her, "and whispering my love to you many times each day?" At other times Curry made the "mystical nocturnal migration" to Atlanta, appearing to him in his dreams. Debs seemed to enjoy more success in sneaking out private letters to her in these months. No longer forced to cram his love into cryptic notes, he filled pages with sentimental lyricism and deep longing. "It is not yet time for us," he wrote, "but the day is on the way, and we have to be patient yet awhile. It seems very hard at times, almost unendurable, and it is then we have to assert our mastery over self to escape madness and despair."[35]

Though prison censors continued to bar radical literature, Debs also pieced together the news that his beloved Socialist Party continued to struggle. That spring party leaders unveiled a new membership drive, promising a shiny new car to the state organization that signed up the most recruits. By summer they abandoned the campaign "owing to the apathy and indifference of the membership." The party dwindled to ten thousand or so dues-paying members and bankruptcy loomed, prompting desperate pleas to save the Chicago headquarters from the auction block. At the same time the communists continued to attack the party for its "compromising and cowardly" dealings with capitalist politicians. Many communists still hoped to recruit Debs once he was free, but after his meeting with Daugherty others wrote him off as a lost cause. "Poor old Debs," one communist editor scoffed, "straining his weak eyes in the direction of the red vanguard of the revolution, sinks deeper and deeper into the swamp of social-democratic reform." With Socialists under attack from the left and the right, Meyer London considered it a "miracle" that the party remained alive in the summer of 1921.[36]

The most formidable challenge they faced came from patriotic mobs, many organized by the local chapters of the American Legion. While the Legion's bloody clashes with the Wobblies drew the most attention, the Socialists also found that the armistice brought little relief from threats and intimidation. The Legion's national officers disavowed these attacks, but they could not control their "impulsive" young members, many of whom liked to brawl with Socialists, as one historian put it, "whenever the opportunity arose." Many meetings were canceled in the face of these threats, and public gatherings were often broken up by patriot gangs.[37]

In early July, in Twin Falls, Idaho, Debs's old friend Kate Richards O'Hare was kidnapped by a vigilante mob that was led by the local Legion commander and apparently condoned by the town's "most prominent business men." O'Hare had come to Twin Falls to deliver a speech on "Crime and Criminals," a reflection on prison reform inspired by her recent stint at Leavenworth. When she ignored police warnings to leave town, she was kidnapped by three carloads of men who took her in the middle of the night. Only half dressed, she was pinned to the floor of a car as it sped through town. After they drove more than an hour across mountainous terrain, the car broke down, and in the confusion O'Hare escaped into the night. She followed a rail line back to a tiny station in Montello, Nevada, where railroad agents offered her protection. Even then the frustrated kidnappers threatened to kill her if she returned to Twin Falls.[38]

Drawing national attention, the incident seemed to confirm the Socialists' charge that the American Legion posed a serious threat to their First Amendment rights and was "with the possible exception of the Ku Klux Klan . . . the most lawless and potentially the most dangerous organization in the country." Three years after the armistice, the Legion seemed determined to preserve the white-hot fervor of wartime and perpetuate one of the war's dubious legacies, a nationwide vigilante campaign to silence those suspected of insufficient patriotism. While the Espionage Act convictions focused public concern on the threat of expanding federal power, these outbreaks of vigilantism demonstrated that the greatest threat to free speech came not from government prosecutors or FBI spies but from spontaneous expressions of mob violence. Progressive intellectuals like John Dewey, who had once welcomed the war as an opportunity to forge national unity, now worried about the dangers to liberty posed by the tyranny of the majority, especially when it came in the form of a self-righteous mob.[39]

None made the point more forcefully than Oswald Garrison Villard. Through the summer of 1921, the *Nation* ran a series of articles exposing the threat to free speech posed by the American Legion. "Elsewhere," the journal declared, "we are slowly yet noticeably demobilizing our intolerant 100 per centism, deflating our hysterical super-patriotism. Not so the American Legion, which is attempting to perpetuate the war psychology as its contribution to peace." At the same time Villard ran exposés on the Ku Klux Klan, which was emerging as a powerful force in many parts of the country. While the Legion and the Klan were not allies, Villard warned that they each preached a populist militarism, and an irrational patriotism, that posed a serious threat to American liberty. Both were, he argued, America's version of the fascists just then coming to power in Europe.[40]

Villard used his pages to catalog the evidence, much of it gathered by the fledgling branches of the ACLU—editors whipped for publishing critical stories about the Legion, a fresh wave of attacks on the Wobblies and the communists, race riots and Klan-inspired lynchings, Socialists hauled off their soapboxes, and even a riot in Los Angeles when Legionnaires prevented the showing of the German film *The Cabinet of Dr. Caligari*. In addition to this "long, long trail of lawlessness," the Legion, the Klan, and other vigilante groups pressured local officials to ban socialist meetings and forced school boards to drive "disloyal" teachers out their classrooms.[41]

Faced with what Villard called an "American Inquisition," many liberals concluded that much more was at stake in the amnesty fight than the fate of a hundred or so men and women. Freeing the prisoners not only would make amends for past wrongs, the excesses of wartime persecution, but would make a powerful statement against the nation's current spirit of intolerance. For this reason, the ACLU pressed Harding to declare a general and immediate amnesty, abandoning his plan to pardon each one individually as their cases were reviewed. "You are thinking of pardoning a few men," Lincoln Steffens told the president. "I am asking you to break the hate; and the war psychology; do the free, uncalled for, magnificent Thing."[42]

That summer Villard led a delegation of liberals who called on the president to once again make the case for a general amnesty. Flanked by Kansas editor William Allen White and Monsignor John Ryan, Villard rehearsed his arguments in favor of the unconditional release of all prisoners, but the conversation turned inevitably to the singular case of Eugene Debs. Harding told the group that Debs seemed like a "kindly and good man" and assured them that "no one in the administration had any feeling against him whatever." He added, though, that he had not expected the "tremendous storm" of criticism over Debs's trip to Washington. At that meeting, the president got a glimpse of the anger and frustration that was also growing among amnesty supporters. After Harding told his visitors that he would act soon, one of his petitioners interrupted. "Mr. President, that's no way to answer us," she declared. "We demand a yes-or-no answer now!"

Straightening, Harding replied, "My dear woman: You may demand anything you please out of Warren Harding. He will not resent it. But the President of the United States has a right to keep his own counsel, and the office I occupy forbids me to reply to you as I should like to if I were elsewhere!"[43]

Some in the group nervously applauded the president's rejoinder, but Villard warned Harding that many more were reaching "the end of their patience." Villard told the president that radicals had lost patience and were planning a march on Washington that would be "no 'pink tea affair.'" Harding warned that such tactics would be "the very worst thing that could happen for Debs." True to the peculiar logic of power, he would not act if it might look as if he was being forced to act.[44]

At the same time, the American Legion issued its own threats against the president. Responding to reports that Harding continued to welcome amnesty delegations, Legion commander John Emery took a remarkably belligerent tone in a public telegram he sent to the White House in late July. The Legion was already angered by Harding's veto of an accelerated bonus for veterans—a stand for fiscal responsibility that the president had taken in the face of enormous pressure from veterans, who had successfully pushed the measure through Congress. Now Emery warned that a pardon for Debs would "draw the fire of ex-service men" and force the Legion to engage in a "fight to the finish." Letting Debs out of jail, the commander wrote, "would do more to license a wholesale disregard of law and order than any one act the President might take."[45]

Radicals threatened to send pickets if Harding did not free Debs, while the Legion promised vague but ominous retaliation if he did. Through the early fall, the administration continued to offer assurance to both sides while postponing any decision. Joining a Socialist delegation to the White House, Samuel Castleton expected a heated exchange with the president, but found the group entirely "disarmed" by Harding's sympathy and goodwill. Treating them like allies in a common cause, Harding urged them to continue their efforts to rally public support for amnesty, in order to create "the appearance that the American people are for Gene's release and he is carrying out a mandate." After leaving the meeting, Castleton wrote to Theodore that, "if Gene is not out very, very shortly, then there is something rotten in Denmark."[46]

Just weeks later, however, Daugherty offered comfort to those opposed to amnesty. In a speech to the American Bar Association, he scoffed at the claim that the wartime offenders were in any sense "political prisoners" who deserved special consideration. Those calling for amnesty, he went on, were either dangerous radicals or naive but "very well meaning people, among whom are ministers of the gospel, teachers, editors and college professors, to say nothing of that vast number of sentimentalists who always stand ready to make heroes out of criminals, whenever opportunity offers."[47]

And yet Daugherty continued to dangle the prospect of freedom for Debs and his fellow radicals. As September neared, papers reported that his "exhaustive study" was "virtually ready" for the president's consideration. Three weeks later, he announced that the recommendations "may" be ready at any time; he only needed to "go over them again and make some changes." Two weeks later, he told reporters he was still tinkering with the "phraseology."[48]

"Oh you 'phraseology'!" Debs protested to Theodore when he heard that the attorney general planned to postpone his report for "about the thirty-ninth time in the last seven months." When Daugherty announced plans for further "important changes" a couple weeks later, Norman Hapgood ridiculed this "tortured sifting of the relevant law." The attorney general's "futile imaginary researches," he charged, "could not occupy 10 hours of a good lawyer's time." Though Hapgood once counseled patience, he was beginning to lose his own. In the Hearst papers he wondered aloud if the radicals had been right all along when they claimed that the president would act only if he was forced to by angry protests.[49]

While Daugherty dithered over this report, Harding used some delaying tactics of his own, continuing to insist that he would take no action on amnesty until the peace with Germany was finalized, a formality that had been delayed by partisan wrangling over the Versailles Treaty. In March, when Harding first laid down this condition, none considered this a significant barrier. After all, the president put the matter at the top of the national agenda when he called Congress into special session that spring. However, lawmakers remained divided over America's role in postwar Europe and took three months to hammer out a joint peace resolution. On July 2, Harding declared the war with Germany officially over.

Amnesty forces rejoiced at this otherwise anticlimactic news, believing that the last barrier to presidential action had been removed. Instead, Harding announced that he did not consider America to be truly at peace until an actual treaty was negotiated with Germany and ratified by the Senate, effectively postponing an amnesty decision for several months, and possibly much longer. Enraged by these delays, Socialists and civil libertarians denounced this as nothing more than presidential pettifogging. The war had ended almost three years earlier, they pointed out, and the treaty was only a diplomatic formality that had no obvious bearing on the justice or mercy due to the wartime offenders still behind bars. Exasperated by the president's "latest reason" to delay, Theodore scolded the man who held his brother's fate in his hands, writing to him that his decision was "not only silly and disgusting, but cowardly. You may think you are fooling the people. So thought the unlamented Wilson, which accounts for your present occupancy of the White House."[50]

Hopes for amnesty were revived when the Senate finally ratified the treaty in mid-October. David Karsner was so sure that the president was about to act that he made travel plans for Atlanta, eager to see Debs walk through the prison gates a free man. "I look forward to this as one of the big events of my life," he wired to Debs. Instead, Harding delayed once more, announcing that he would review amnesty requests only after he issued a formal proclamation of the peace, as part of the national observance of Armistice Day in mid-November. Their hopes raised and dashed once again, amnesty supporters greeted this announcement as another arbitrary delay, further proof that Harding was desperately buying time, buffeted as he was by growing pressure from both the friends and foes of amnesty. "I think the 'powers' are shaking in their boots over the disposition of this man," Mabel Curry told a friend. "They can't hold him indefinitely and they can't seem to find a time to release him."[51]

Clearly Harding let the moment pass when amnesty supporters might have hailed him for making a "Lincolnesque" gesture of postwar reconciliation. Even as the president continued to assure them of his good intentions, many grumbled that he was a moral coward. Instead of taking a bold and principled stand for free speech and national reconciliation, he seemed blown along by "the shifting breezes of popular opinion," timidly waiting for a politically safe time to release Debs, one that never seemed to arrive.[52]

This interpretation of Harding's actions is supported by the common historical assessment that he was a weak leader whose talents and temperament were better suited to the social club of the Senate than to the lonely responsibilities of the presidency. However, this underestimates the effectiveness of Harding's strategy for handling a controversy that stirred the passions of a divided country. He sensed that Americans would more readily accept freedom for Debs and his comrades if this was presented as part of his administration's wider program to restore "normalcy." By linking amnesty to the peace treaty, Harding set the issue in a new context, treating the liberation of political prisoners as the final act in a month-long pageant of postwar reconciliation.[53]

These ceremonies began on November 10, when many thousands of Americans passed through the Capitol rotunda to pay their respects to the remains of the Unknown Soldier. The next morning Harding led the funeral procession to Arlington Cemetery. In a speech carried by wire from New York to San Francisco, he said, "I can sense the prayers of the people, of all peoples, that this Armistice Day shall mark the beginning of a new and lasting era of peace on earth, good will among men." As the nameless hero was interred, Harding led the vast crowd in a spontaneous recitation of the Lord's Prayer.[54]

The following day, Harding linked respect for the sacrifices of the past to hopes for a more peaceful future when he opened the ceremonies at the Washington Disarmament Conference. At this summit of the world's great military powers, the president claimed that all Americans wanted "less of armament and none of war." Secretary of State Hughes then unveiled a dramatic proposal for reductions in naval power, one that would ultimately be embodied in the Five-Power Naval Treaty.

In late November, as the disarmament conference drew to a close, the press reported that Harding was ready to take up the petitions for amnesty. He had used the power of his office to frame this decision as one more act of postwar healing. While Harding had good reason to believe that many Americans shared his view that the time had come for some form of amnesty, he also knew that others remained bitterly opposed. That month the American Legion's national convention passed another resolution "demanding the continued incarceration of Eugene V. Debs," and they published an open telegram to the president, arguing that a pardon would mean that "the lives of those American boys who lie on the fields of France and those who lie broken in the hospitals and the homes of this country have been uselessly sacrificed, and our service has indeed been given in vain." As Harding put it, the Legion had once again given him a "panning," and this clearly troubled him.[55]

On the other side, some in the amnesty camp chose this moment to put new pressure on the president. Disregarding Harding's frequent warnings against picketing, the ACLU's Roger Baldwin announced in early November that the time had come for "vigorous and dramatic work." During the Armistice Day ceremonies, four winners of the Congressional Medal of Honor confronted the president in front of a national audience, petitioning him for a general amnesty; another veteran's group published an open letter asking him to restore "that condition of goodwill and love of neighbor which obtained throughout our beloved country before the war." For the next two weeks, these veterans joined forces with ACLU volunteers to picket the disarmament conference. Hoping to embarrass Harding during his moment in the international spotlight, they waved banners that declared "Allied Nations, We Congratulate You for Releasing Political Prisoners. The United States Alone Keeps Them in Prison." Lucy Robins dismissed what she called a "picketing comedy," while the Socialists refused to participate, fearing to antagonize the president just as he seemed ready to decide Debs's fate. Though Harding had long warned that such a confrontational demonstration would make it impossible for him to act, when the picketers finally arrived at his gates he chose instead to neutralize their impact by meeting with them, hearing their grievances, and then announcing to the press that such protests would have no influence, one way or another, on his decision.[56]

At the same time, other branches of the amnesty movement gave the president just what he asked for, a respectful but visible show of public support for amnesty that would allow him to claim that, in liberating Debs, he was only yielding to the sovereign will of the American people. Particularly valuable in this regard was a change of sentiment in what Robins called the "bourgeois press." A columnist who had once denounced Debs now decided that he "never ought to have been imprisoned." Debs was a "perpetual minority report," as he put it. "We need him and his kind." The influential Hearst columnist Arthur Brisbane had a similar change of heart, and even the *New York Times* conceded that none would become "violently excited" if Harding freed the political prisoners. "Most of them probably are misguided rather than really vicious folk," the paper reasoned, "victims of a congenital inability to understand what is meant by 'freedom of speech.'" The remnant of the Socialist press devoted all its energy to this final push for amnesty. Karsner reported every rumor in the *Call*, the revived *Appeal* ran amnesty updates in every issue, and in Chicago socialists launched a new journal that called itself *Debs Freedom Monthly.*[57]

Nowhere was the cause taken up more enthusiastically than in Terre Haute. At a downtown booth people stood in line to sign an amnesty petition, and copies also circulated in local coal mines, banks, and Knights of Columbus meetings. The *Terre Haute Post*, which had once

recommended the firing squad for wartime dissenters, now ran a series of editorials from Robert La Follette, Alice Paul, economist Basil
Manly, and others, each calling on readers to support the amnesty campaign "if you feel that free speech is worth preserving in America." The
mayor told Harding that his town had decided that their notorious
neighbor had been sufficiently punished. They now wanted him home
to spend Christmas with his good and long-suffering wife. Sixty percent
of the town's residents signed the petition, sent to Harding in Christmas
wrapping. Eager not to antagonize the president, the petitioners made
sure the holiday bow did not have "too much red in it."[58]

When Harding canvassed his advisors on the amnesty question, he
found that they were as divided as the country itself. James Finch, the
pardon attorney in charge of reviewing the Debs case, considered this
"a subject upon which a person might change his mind every ten minutes." Postmaster General Will Hays and Secretary of State Hughes
supported a pardon for Debs; both had criticized the excesses of the
Red Scare, and they advised the president to free everyone who had
been jailed during the war just for "talking." Others were less enthusiastic, including Secretary of Commerce Herbert Hoover. No one in the
White House was more adamantly opposed to a Debs pardon than Mrs.
Harding.[59]

Daugherty's own, long-awaited report did little to resolve the disagreement. The attorney general was deeply troubled by the fact that
Debs showed no sign of remorse. He still refused to ask for a pardon,
still insisted that his free speech rights had been violated, and still
claimed that he had been right to oppose the war. Daugherty decided
that Debs suffered from a "mental obsession" that prevented him from
accepting the Supreme Court's "final decision . . . respecting the limitations of freedom of speech." Debs was an "impressive personality,"
Daugherty conceded, but that only made him more dangerous in his
ability to "lead the unthinking." "Upon what possible ground," he asked
Harding, "can clemency be granted without placing a premium upon
disloyalty, lawlessness and defiance of the authority of the Government?"

After building this case against Debs, Daugherty reluctantly gave the president what he wanted, a recommendation based on mercy rather than justice. He pointed out that Debs was an old man, in fragile health. And he argued that, after almost three years behind bars, Debs had probably been punished enough to vindicate the government's power and send a clear warning to dissenters in future wars. The Debs case taught Americans a lesson that, as he put it, "will never be eradicated from the pages of history."[60]

Of course, not everyone had derived the same moral from this story, and Daugherty acknowledged that hundreds of thousands of citizens were petitioning their government to release Debs. He warned Harding that, if he ignored these appeals, many would accuse him of "extreme and unjustifiable severity," and the law itself would lose some of its moral authority. In a roundabout way, Daugherty acknowledged that the meaning of free speech was determined as much by public opinion as it was by the Supreme Court. Heeding the twin demands of mercy and political expedience, Daugherty advised Harding to commute Debs's sentence, making him eligible for release.

After reviewing this report, Harding decided in early December that he would free Debs by Christmas, along with two dozen of his fellow political prisoners. He rejected Daugherty's suggestion that the prisoners should be granted their freedom only if they promised to "lead an upright life and obey and respect all the laws of the United States." Debs had already made it clear that he would accept no such conditions for his release, and Daugherty was willing to make an exception in his case. "He might go on his honor," he grumbled, "if he has any."[61]

Harding also overturned Daugherty's plan to hold Debs until New Year's, a delay that the attorney general argued would help preserve the sanctity of Christmas. This was an unusually pious concern for a cigar-chomping, whiskey-drinking poker player whose corrupt dealings would soon bring him within a hair's breadth of federal prison himself. In a more generous holiday spirit, Harding insisted that Debs should be able to "eat his Christmas dinner with his wife."[62]

A week before Christmas, Atlanta's Piedmont Hotel filled with journalists and amnesty supporters, eager to witness the historic moment when Debs would walk free. Karsner had been in the city for more than a month. Theodore arrived several days before Christmas, and in the warden's office he embraced his brother for the first time since Debs left for Moundsville. Lucy Robins arrived bearing gifts for the political prisoners and shooting hostile glances at Karsner and Castleton, men she held responsible for some of the Socialists' blundering tactics and slanders against herself and Gompers.

For days, all looked to Washington for the telegram that would confirm Harding's decision to release Debs. Rumors incubated in this anxious environment—that Debs would be smuggled out of prison in the dead of night, that mobs of Klansmen or Legionnaires might try to lynch him at the prison gates, that communists had convinced Debs to stay in jail, rejecting any offer from Harding short of a complete pardon and the liberation of all the political prisoners.

After a final meeting with Daugherty on the evening of December 23, Harding issued a press announcement that he would commute Debs's sentence, effective on Christmas Day. Though the decision had long been expected, some of Harding's close friends and supporters were still shocked. The president assured them that it was "the right thing to do." "The spirit of clemency," he told a friend, was a key part of what he was "trying to do here in Washington." Across the country amnesty forces cheered wildly, while the telegraph office in Terre Haute was soon jammed with messages of congratulations—from Helen Keller, Charlie Chaplin, George Bernard Shaw, and hundreds more. But in Atlanta Debs's closest supporters refused to trust these news dispatches. So often disappointed by false rumors, they waited anxiously for official confirmation of Harding's decision. Robins called the warden every hour, but the government's order did not arrive until 11:30 the next day, the morning of Christmas Eve. Warden Dyche carried the news to Debs, who accepted it quietly and asked for an hour to decide whether or not to accept the president's offer.[63]

Clearly Debs longed for his freedom, but the presidential commutation presented him with a moral dilemma. If he accepted, he would walk out of prison the next day having accomplished a great personal victory; he had survived the ordeal with his dignity intact, his spirit unbroken by the humiliation and loneliness of three years in prison. But Debs had endured all this suffering for the sake of the radical movement, and a commuted sentence was no clear-cut victory for that cause. In announcing his decision, Harding had insisted that Debs had been fairly tried and justly punished. After three years of bitter conflict, the fundamental issues at stake in the Debs case would remain unresolved, with no concession on either side about the nature of the war or the right to free speech in times of national emergency.

Even more troubling for Debs, the president offered individual acts of clemency for two dozen prisoners, leaving more than a hundred still behind bars, and ignoring the call for a general amnesty. Debs had often insisted that he would only leave prison after all his fellow comrades were released, and if he accepted his freedom now, he would break that promise. In spite of all he had endured, he might seem in the end to be putting his personal comfort ahead of his commitment to the move-ment. At least one of his fellow prisoners was whispering such things in his ear. This cellmate insisted that a true revolutionary would reject Harding's offer, escalating the conflict in order to stir radical ferment. Outside of prison, Robins, Karsner, and Clarence Darrow feared that Debs would agree, and they urged him to accept the commutation. Once he was free, they insisted, he could work more effectively to liber-ate the others. In that hour alone in his cell, Debs weighed these choices. As a tired and lonely man, he desperately wanted his freedom; as a self-described "uncompromising revolutionist," he felt it his duty to stay. After thinking this over, Debs told Warden Dyche that he was will-ing to leave prison the next day.[64]

When the warden went home that evening, he advised reporters that Debs would not be released until the following morning. Suspecting a government plot to slip the prisoner out in the night, the press spent Christmas Eve camped out in front of the prison. The next morning they were jolted awake by the sight of Debs strolling out of the prison gates in his prison denim, but they soon learned that he was only headed to the warden's house for a farewell breakfast. Returning to his room, Debs dressed in his prison-tailored civilian suit and felt hat, and pocketed the five-dollar bill issued to all convicts to help them make their way in the world. After a tearful farewell to some of his friends, including the "lifetime negro murderer" Sam Moore, Debs walked out

Debs acknowledges the convicts' applause.
David Karsner Papers, Manuscripts and Archives Division,
The New York Public Library, Astor, Lenox and Tilden Foundations.

of the Atlanta penitentiary for the last time. Newsreel photographers cranked their cameras madly as Debs strolled across the wide lawn, flanked by Warden Dyche and his assistant.

Halfway to the street, Debs was stopped in his tracks by a roaring tribute from his fellow inmates. In Debs's honor, the warden had loosened prison regulations that holiday morning, and the prisoners pressed against all three stories of barred windows, craning for a last look at their beloved cellmate. Most of the two thousand convicts cheered, hollered, and called his name. Debs turned to face them, and for half a minute he held his hat aloft as their applause grew louder. Finally overcome, he bowed his head and wept. This was, he later wrote, "the most deeply touching and impressive moment and the most profoundly dramatic incident in my life." The prisoners' ovation continued, still

Christmas morning, 1921.
David Karsner Papers, Manuscripts and Archives Division,
The New York Public Library, Astor, Lenox and Tilden Foundations.

audible a half-mile away, as Debs rode in the warden's car to the train station.[65]

After witnessing what one reporter called "the most unique demonstration in American history," the press got another surprise when they arrived at the train depot. Debs announced that, instead of heading back to Terre Haute for Christmas dinner with his wife, he had a government-issued ticket to Washington, D.C. The president had "invited" Debs to come to the capital for a brief interview. While Daugherty insisted that this visit was voluntary, and not a condition of his release, Debs seemed to consider this a command appearance. Adding to the mystery, he told reporters that he would honor Harding's request not to make any statement to the press until the two had a chance to talk things over.[66]

And so Debs spent Christmas Day on the train to Washington, accompanied by Theodore, Lucy Robins, David Karsner, and an entourage of reporters. Since they never mentioned it, one can only imagine the awkward silence, the chill stares that must have passed between Robins and Karsner, archrivals in this common cause. Perhaps they set aside their differences in the spirit of the day, but neither one ever acknowledged the other's contribution. In fact, the two soon published accounts of the amnesty campaign that denigrated the other, missing the fact that the two movements had, in fact, worked together to put pressure on the president. The Socialists' threat of a general strike, and later a picket of the White House, helped Robins make the case that the AFL offered a more "reasonable" approach to the issue. And both groups developed distinctive methods of social organizing that mobilized different constituencies. Along with the elite liberals in the ACLU, the anarchists in Emma Goldman's League, the progressive Republicans in Congress, and countless grassroots movements that sprang up to demand amnesty, they created a clamor of protest that Harding could not ignore.

As the train rolled toward Washington, Socialists and other admirers boarded in order to ride a few stops with their hero, and the day passed with much laughter and backslapping. True to his word, Debs said little to the reporters about his case or his plans, but he found other ways to spread the socialist message during this rare moment in the national media spotlight. He announced that, instead of riding in the expensive Pullman car provided by the government, he would travel in a more humble coach and donate the difference to Russia's famine victims. And at Karsner's suggestion, he also gave his prison-issued five-dollar bill to the legal defense fund for Sacco and Vanzetti. The *Call* ran a photograph of Debs's receipt for this donation and advised readers to clip the image for their socialist scrapbooks.

On the morning of December 26, Debs paid his second visit to the attorney general's office, still wearing the cheap suit, baggy overcoat, and "gawky prison-made shoes" that marked him as a recent convict. Afterward Daugherty expressed satisfaction with the visit, though he had been unimpressed by Debs's plan to devote himself to liberating all of the Atlanta prisoners. Those men were "no more guilty than I," Debs insisted. The attorney general urged his visitor to find a more "useful purpose" and to abandon his "erroneous ideas."

Debs then walked to the White House for his appointment with Harding. Along the way, many greeted this gaunt, smiling man as if he were a returning war hero. Some women kissed him, others "called down the blessings of God upon him." Though most of the White House was closed for the Christmas holiday, Harding waited for him in his office. Rising to shake Debs's hand, he said, "I have heard so damned much about you, Mr. Debs, that I am now very glad to meet you personally."[67]

Afterward Harding issued no statement about their half-hour conversation. Some speculated that the meeting had been arranged to satisfy the president's simple curiosity about this man, so beloved and so hated; others suggested that Harding tried to persuade Debs to abandon his radical views, or at least to tone down his revolutionary rhetoric in the name of national harmony. If so, the president was no doubt disappointed when Debs emerged from the White House and told reporters that, though he found Harding to be a "very kind gentleman," he had informed the president that he planned to pick up where he left off in 1919, fighting for his "principles, convictions and ideals." "As for the White House," the five-time presidential candidate concluded, "—well, gentlemen, my personal preference is to live privately as a humble citizen in my cottage in Terre Haute."

In Union Station, as Debs prepared to leave for Indiana, he stopped to thank a throng of his admirers for their support. When reporters asked him how he felt about losing his American citizenship rights, he parried that it was "a citizenship I was not very proud of. Now I am only a citizen of the world." He maintained his silence on the radical split, saying that he needed time to study the "changed conditions." "I cannot foretell my future activities," as he put it. "I must first find myself."[68]

In this, his first public address in years, he tossed out grand plans, caressing all the possibilities opened by his new freedom. He would consider Lenin's offer to take a tour of Russia, he would work to liberate all the political prisoners and reform the penal system, he would start a drive to have every man, woman, and child take a pacifist pledge, first in America and then around the world. He knew that many still hated him, but he told the crowd that he felt no "bitterness or hatred," even for those who had jailed him. As Debs finished with a tribute to the value of free speech and the power of love, he was confronted by a policeman who demanded to see his speaking permit. When Debs confessed that he had none, the officer told him he had taken "a great liberty." Shaking the man's hand, Debs apologized and boarded the train home to Terre Haute.[69]

Chapter 16

Last Flicker of the Dying Candle

B Y THE TIME Debs arrived in Terre Haute on the evening of December 28, excitement had been building in town for days. Socialists came from across the country, but most of the twenty-five thousand who gathered to meet his train were Debs's neighbors. An FBI informer reported that dozens waved banners welcoming "DEBS THE HUMANITARIAN" and "DEBS THE LOVER." As his train arrived, cheers were punctuated by church bells, fire whistles, and the music of three brass bands, but the scene grew eerily quiet when Debs emerged onto the platform. After shaking hands with the mayor, he was lifted into a baggage truck and pulled slowly through the crowd, his path lit by torch flames and the flash of camera bulbs. "Now and then an eager hand would stretch out to touch 'Gene's garments," Kate O'Hare reported, "a choked word of blessing trembled from time to time from some old comrade's lips, but for the most part it was a silent homage paid." As a black band played "Swing Low, Sweet Chariot," his escort delivered him to his porch a few blocks from the station. There he embraced his wife, their first meeting since he left the Moundsville penitentiary years earlier. In brief, emotional remarks Debs thanked his comrades and neighbors, then closed the door.[1]

Across the country, many papers expressed their disgust at this display of affection and respect for Debs. "A shallow, howling minority has had its way," the *Times* fumed. Some have forgotten, another editor wrote, that Debs had blood on his hands for undermining the war effort. Others focused their anger on Harding for making a "farce of the law," and even worse, honoring Debs with an invitation to the White House.[2]

Still, the administration was relieved to find that public outcry was, as Daugherty put it, "one hundred percent less than was anticipated." Many had been convinced by some of the amnesty movement's various arguments, while others no doubt welcomed an end to the debate that had consumed so much of the public's attention in the postwar years. Papers that had once opposed amnesty now expressed a grudging admiration for Debs—more for his courage than for his principles. He was still a dangerous man, one Philadelphia editor conceded, but he had proven himself a "gallant enemy." A fuller tribute came from H. L. Mencken. Though he considered Debs to be "unquestionably wrong" in his devotion to pacifism and "the Marxian rumble-bumble," Mencken declared him a democratic hero for refusing to "grovel" for his freedom. "Is his release denounced by the New York Times, the Rotary Clubs and the idiots who seem to run the American Legion?" Mencken asked. "Then it is precisely because he is fair, polite, independent, brave, honest and a gentleman."[3]

Pausing only briefly to admire what Debs had done, socialist and communist leaders were more interested in what he would do next. Though Debs was out of touch with the complex political changes since 1919, his years in prison reinforced his stature as the nation's best-known revolutionary. He enjoyed a fame and moral authority that were rare commodities in the American radical movement. Ignoring his request to be left in peace while he recovered from his ordeal, partisan delegations arrived in Terre Haute over the next few weeks, each vying for his support. "When I went into prison the party was united," he complained to a friend, "and when I was released it was torn into warring factions."[4]

Too exhausted to wade into these "party broils," Debs chose to retreat. Prison had taken its toll on his fragile health, and his doctor warned that, without extended rest, he would not live long. He announced that, though he remained a Socialist, he would make no decision about his political future until he had ensured his physical survival. He spent much of the winter of 1922 in bed, but in spite of his wife's efforts to drive visitors away, comrades continued to knock at his door, and hundreds of telegrams and letters arrived each day. "My friends are killing me," he groaned, and in July he tried to escape by checking himself into Lindlahr, a health spa outside of Chicago that specialized in the "nature treatment." The resort served as a congenial prison of sorts, reimposing on his life some of the isolation and routine that had shaped his days as an inmate. Before long Debs was raving to Theodore about the revitalizing power of nuts and raw vegetables, warning him to avoid ketchup and caffeine, and advising him to sleep with his head facing north in order to enjoy the healing properties of the earth's magnetic field.[5]

Back in Terre Haute, Theodore did all he could to protect his brother, turning away countless requests for speaking engagements, book deals, and even several lucrative offers to appear on the vaudeville stage. Meanwhile, he worried about well-founded rumors that the comrades in Chicago could not bear to leave Debs alone. Among his many visitors were two young literary rebels, Sinclair Lewis and Carl Sandburg. Living nearby, they broke Debs out of the sanitarium for folk song fests, serious discussions, and high-minded drinking sprees. Lewis, who had just won fame with *Main Street,* was deeply touched by these conversations and vowed to the old radical that he would stop lampooning the middle class and devote himself to writing a great proletarian novel—a promise he proved unable to keep.[6]

In spite of these interruptions to his treatment, or perhaps because of them, Debs did gradually recover that summer. As he turned his attention to the hard choices that faced him once he returned to public life, he found few good options. The Socialists were in desperate straits, their numbers still dwindling, their headquarters sold, their press devastated. Even the *New York Call* was on its way to collapse, the victim of diminishing subscribers and party factionalism. Upton Sinclair tried in vain to rally support for a new "fighting socialist weekly." The party abandoned its use of soapbox oratory and street meetings, and found it could no longer afford to send organizers into the field. While Milwaukee, Chicago, New York, and Pennsylvania remained Socialist strongholds, in much of the country the once-vibrant national movement was dead or dying.

Since the party split in 1919, many of the most energetic young Socialist leaders had defected to the communists. Even as the passions of the Red Scare faded, they continued to face the threat of arrest, usually for violating state "syndicalism" laws that outlawed membership in any organization advocating the overthrow of the government by force. Though communists remained a small and despised group in America, the government's campaign to stamp them out strengthened their sense of destiny, their faith that they were the vanguard of a "world-historic" mission that would one day bring down capitalism. The success of the Russian Bolsheviks, themselves a small but disciplined minority, convinced their American counterparts that anything was possible, a view that was evidently shared by the Justice Department.[7]

Most Socialists bitterly resented the communists for splintering their party, harassing and heckling their meetings, and doing little to help in the amnesty campaign. Debs shared these misgivings, but he also admired the communists' revolutionary spirit, sympathized when they were jailed, and longed for reconciliation. While many Socialist leaders concluded that the Bolsheviks had perverted the ideals for which they fought, to the end of his life Debs continued to praise Russia's "sublime experiment" in creating a workers' republic.[8]

However, when he returned to public life in late 1922, Debs refused to join the communists. While he was in prison, troubling reports had reached him about the Bolsheviks' use of terror against their enemies and their heavy-handed attempts to impose their will on the international socialist movement. In the early years of the revolution, Debs had dismissed stories about Soviet tyranny as capitalist propaganda—and the American press did provide its readers with an abundance of disinformation. By 1921, however, some former supporters of the revolution began to change their minds, offering firsthand accounts of life in Russia that Debs could not ignore. He read Emma Goldman's articles on her disillusionment with Lenin's regime, and in Atlanta was visited by an old Socialist friend, just back from Russia, who told harrowing stories about the fate of the Bolsheviks' political prisoners that made the Atlanta penitentiary seem like a citadel of reason.[9]

Lucy Robins, who distrusted the Bolsheviks from the start, may well have told Debs about her own experience. In the midst of the amnesty fight, her marriage had fallen apart, as she and Bob proved unable to reconcile their growing political differences. While he resented her work with Gompers, she believed that he was being seduced by the "self-deception and fanaticism" of communism. Hoping to straighten his wife's politics and save their marriage, Bob asked her to drop her amnesty work and escape with him to Russia, where they could roll up their sleeves and help build the new workers' republic. Robins was shocked. "I could scarcely believe," she later recalled, "that Bob seriously expected me to forsake my country." When she refused, he went ahead without her, a "temporary separation" that both knew would be permanent. When Bob arrived in Russia, he soon found that his life was endangered by the Bolsheviks' secret police, who were suspicious of his anarchist past. Only with difficulty did he manage to escape back to America, his marriage over and his political ideals in tatters.[10]

Debs considered the Bolsheviks' tactics to be "cruel and reprehensible." He was horrified by the news that the czar and his family had been murdered, and in the summer of 1922 he sent an open telegram to Lenin, objecting to his government's plan to execute two dozen socialists from a rival faction who had been convicted of treason in a show trial. Pleading in the name of "our common humanity," Debs told Lenin that killing these men would leave a "foul and indelible spot" on the Bolsheviks' reputation, and urged him to show the world that working-class revolutionaries offered a more enlightened form of justice than their capitalist enemies.

Karsner, who actually wrote the text of Debs's telegram to Lenin, praised it as "the Sermon on the Mount . . . condensed and brought up to date." Lenin, however, ignored this plea for mercy, while American communists attacked Debs for what they now considered his naive pacifism and faith in bourgeois notions of justice and fair play. Violence, they insisted, was a necessary evil, the birth pang of a new socialist order. Debs heard such arguments, for example, from Lincoln Steffens, the muckraking journalist who had visited him in Atlanta just days before his release. After returning from a tour of the Soviet Union, Steffens had famously proclaimed, "I have been over into the future, and it works." When Debs shared his concerns about Bolshevik terror, Steffens blithely assured him that in revolutions "some things happen that we don't expect." Debs conceded the point, though privately he continued to have his doubts.[11]

Steffens was merely a fellow traveler, a sentimental liberal who was content to watch the Russians build the future from a safe distance. But many American communists, including his old friend Rose Pastor Stokes, now accused Debs of lacking sufficient revolutionary zeal. He clung to a false faith in "bourgeois democracy," they charged, and failed to grasp Lenin's great insight that the proper path to socialism was the "dictatorship of the proletariat," a disciplined revolutionary party that was prepared to fight capitalism unencumbered by concerns about free speech, the democratic ballot, and the rule of law. The ACLU lawyers who often defended the free speech rights of communists were dismayed to find that their clients had no compunctions about breaking up Socialist meetings and vowed to do the same to capitalists when they got the chance. As one American communist explained it, the truly "modern materialist revolutionary will do the things not that are metaphysically moral, but the things that work, and he will take a position for free speech when it is the bourgeois dictatorship that is on top, and he will take a position against free speech for the bourgeoisie, when it is the workers that are on top." In his brief infatuation with Bolshevism in the early 1920s, Max Eastman likewise concluded that he no longer believed in free speech. "So long as our civilization consists in its economic essence of a war between two classes, Free Speech will exist only at such times, or to such extent as may be harmless to the interests of the class in power." Once the left's charismatic champion of free expression, Eastman now declared that nothing would please him more than the chance to "suppress" the *New York Times*.[12]

Of course, critics called the communists hypocrites for claiming rights that they would deny to others. The communists replied that America's ruling class had done the same. When opposition to the war threatened the capitalists' economic interests, hadn't they quickly dispensed with free speech, jailed their enemies, refused seats to duly elected representatives, and hounded their class enemies with spies, mob attacks, and illegal deportations? The principles of democracy, as they put it, were "artificial rules devised by [our] mortal enemy, but not observed by the enemy." As far as America's Bolsheviks were concerned, the wartime persecutions had ripped the mask off American democracy, proving once and for all that the government, the press, and the legal system were only tools of class domination. Under such a system, they insisted, further attempts to win socialism through peaceful democratic methods were a fool's errand. "We are not distinguished by freedom," Eastman wrote as he surveyed America, "but by the sanctimoniousness with which we institute the grossest forms of tyranny."[13]

Fresh from jail, Debs had every reason to agree, but in the end he could not follow communism down this road. "I am not a communist and I don't want to be one," he told a delegation when it knocked on his door. "I do not believe in MINORITY RULE." While he continued to admire the Bolsheviks for their accomplishments, he still believed that, in America at least, the democratic process afforded the best path to radical social and economic change. The cooperative commonwealth that he had devoted his life to building would offer "tolerance of opinion to the fullest extent," he insisted, "if I have any understanding whatever of what would be the meaning of socialism in power." Instead of joining the communists, he agreed to serve on the board of the American Civil Liberties Union.[14]

While Debs pulled back from Bolshevist methods, he still considered himself a determined enemy of capitalism, and so he showed little interest in Lucy Robins's dream of using the amnesty cause to build a new alliance between socialists and the conservative unionists of the AFL. During the campaign, Robins had arranged two meetings between Debs and Gompers, hoping to reconcile their bitter rivalry. In the fall of 1921, she escorted Gompers to Atlanta, where the old foes faced each other for the first time in decades. During their brief conversation in the warden's office, they reminisced, and Debs thanked Gompers for his work on behalf of the political prisoners, but only Robins left Atlanta convinced that the gulf between the two men had been bridged.[15]

After his release, Debs showed no interest in building an alliance with Gompers. He agreed with Lucy Robins that American workers needed to join forces; the choice, as he put it, was "solidarity or slaughter." But he urged them to rally behind policies that were opposed by the AFL leadership—support for the Socialist Party, recognition of the Soviet Union, the creation of industrial rather than craft unions, and continuing agitation on behalf of the political prisoners. However grateful Debs was for Gompers's help in winning his personal freedom, nothing had changed his mind about the true path to working-class liberation. A shared commitment to amnesty did not provide much common ground, and the campaign had done little to resolve the long-standing animosity between conservatives and radicals in the labor movement.[16]

Robins brooded, convinced that her rivals among the Socialists had seduced Debs back to a dead-end radicalism. Gompers agreed, claiming that Debs had squandered his last chance to make a meaningful contribution to labor's struggle against capital. In order to maintain his stature in the dwindling radical movement, Debs had resumed what Gompers called a "twisted" obsession with destroying capitalism. Debs and Robins remained friends, but her idea of a grand working-class alliance was dropped.[17]

Rejecting communism on the left and the AFL on the right, Debs chose instead to remain with the Socialist Party, devoting his last years to a frustrating and futile attempt to revive the movement that was his life's work. In November, eleven months after leaving prison, he felt strong enough to return to the platform. Speaking to large and adoring crowds, he enjoyed sparks of the old revolutionary flame. Even as organized labor suffered staggering declines, and conservative pro-business politicians ruled in Washington, Debs sensed once again that Socialists were on the move, and that the revolution was just around the corner.[18]

In these speeches Debs took up where the police had interrupted him in 1918. Vowing that he would go to the gallows before retracting a word of his Canton speech, he blasted the now-decrepit Wilson for taking America to war, and heaped fresh scorn on profiteers. Sixty thousand American boys had died, he charged, only to produce "thirty thousand new millionaires." He declared that he owed Harding "nothing" for setting him free. The president had kept him locked up "as long as he dared," he told his audiences. "It was you who opened the doors of the prison for me."[19]

FBI agents monitoring these speeches complained that they contained many "mis-statements, half truths and catch phrases," but concluded that nothing he said was now "actionable." In fact, by 1923 Debs's analysis of the war sounded much less scandalous to many Americans, as public opinion grew increasingly cynical about the war. Similar charges could be heard in some of the mainstream press, among the jaded young writers of the "Lost Generation," and even in the halls of Congress. Wilson's crusade for democracy had been a cruel illusion, a growing number now believed. The administration had lied about the causes and likely consequences of the war, big business had fattened itself while families sacrificed, and much of the patriotic fervor that gripped the country in the war years had only been froth churned by the government's propaganda machine. With a conservative Republican president leading an international drive for disarmament, newspapers attacking Daugherty for failing to arrest corrupt wartime contractors, and many thousands of Americans now declaring themselves pacifists, much of what Debs had to say about the war seemed like old news.[20]

In addition to demanding amnesty for the remaining "politicals," Debs also denounced what he called the "vicious influence and debauching results" of the penal system. He wove a call for prison reform into his speeches and worked with Karsner on a series of magazine articles about his sojourn in the Atlanta penitentiary, published by a national press syndicate eager to cash in on his recent celebrity. Debs needed the money; he had not earned an income in almost five years. But as always, reaching a large audience through the mainstream press came with a price. Interested only in Debs's personal story, editors cut out most of his socialist analysis and refused to run several columns devoted to his belief that prisons are instruments of class warfare. His complete work, gathered in *Walls and Bars,* was not published until after his death.

Like the magazine editors, many who flocked to hear Debs speak in his final years were more interested in his legend than in his solutions to the world's ills or his analysis of a war that was receding into the past.

Even in the rousing meetings he held in his first tour after prison, few in the audiences were converted to his cause, and party membership continued to stagnate. Debs could "galvanize a corpse," as one party diehard put it, but he could not revive the entire movement on his own. Over the next few years, as his health wavered and people grew tired of hearing his "old story" about the war, he spoke to dwindling and apathetic crowds. He found the experience painful and humiliating, and in dark moments conceded that there would be no socialist revival.[21]

Making matters worse, Debs watched helplessly as more of his old friends abandoned the party. Scott Nearing, the man Debs praised as America's greatest teacher, decided by 1923 that the Socialists were "near extinct." Like so many other young radicals, his encounter with wartime repression had convinced him that American democracy was hopelessly corrupted by capitalism. Nearing abandoned his faith in pacifism and the political process, spent a few brief and intellectually tumultuous years as a communist, then turned to homesteading in the mountains of Vermont. His quest to live a life of honest toil, unstained by exploitation, led him to become a prophet to many in the 1960s counterculture, a hero to young people who knew more about his solar greenhouses than they did about his free speech fights in a forgotten war.[22]

Even David Karsner, Debs's loyal young friend, left the party and gave up radical politics altogether. In the first year after Debs's release, the two had worked together more closely than ever. In addition to co-authoring the prison articles and drafting many of Debs's public statements, Karsner published a series of "talks" with his hero. Though he never lost his faith that Debs was one of the great idealists in American history, by 1924 Karsner decided that the Socialist Party was dead, "stalking the graveyard of current events seeking respectable burial." In the end he concluded that the whole movement had been nothing more than a "one-man organization." For decades millions of Americans were inspired "now and then" by Debs, but the party had no practical accomplishments to show for it. Though Socialists proclaimed themselves the friends of the working class, Karsner now argued that only the mainstream parties had actually produced meaningful reforms. And the movement's ultimate goal of slaying capitalism and replacing it with a "cooperative commonwealth" was, he bitterly concluded, "the dream of a vain utopia." After years of service to the cause, the young, chain-smoking idealist now found socialism "preposterous. . . . It promises what it cannot deliver, human nature being what it is."[23]

Though Karsner's loss of faith must have hurt, Debs assured his "dear little great-souled David" that their political differences would never undermine their friendship. "It does not matter about the mutations of life," he assured his friend. "I could never cease to love you." Their correspondence grew thinner, though no less warm, as Karsner moved on to write for the *New York Herald,* a "capitalist" paper that had often attacked Debs. Disillusioned with the failed crusades of his own day, Karsner devoted the rest of his short life to writing biographies of the heroes of an earlier freedom fight—Andrew Jackson, John Brown, and Ulysses S. Grant. He wrote them all on a desk that Debs had used in prison, a treasured relic of his own brush with greatness.[24]

In these years Debs also abandoned any hope of uniting with Mabel Curry. In the first flush of their love, and then through years of separation, they both took comfort in the thought that "our day must come." After his release they continued to exchange long, affectionate letters. "You are an angel, Mabel," he told her, "and on my lips there trembles a prayer to the God I love and worship to bless and keep you forever!" Well aware of Kate Debs's disapproval, they used Karsner as their courier and arranged to meet outside of Terre Haute. In the end, however, they chose to avoid the scandal and heartache of two broken marriages, a decision that was probably more his than hers. In 1925 Curry moved with her husband to Chicago, though she treasured Debs's letters for the rest of her life. Debs remained loyal, in his way, to his more proper but less passionate bond with Kate. A new life with Mabel Curry remained one more of his unfulfilled prophecies.[25]

Adding to his woes, as Debs toured the country he was harassed by vigilantes who did their best to disrupt his meetings. The problem appeared in his first week of freedom. While the residents of Terre Haute were preparing to give Debs a hero's welcome, Indiana governor Warren McCray declared that he was "extremely sorry that the one arch traitor of our country should live in the state of Indiana." Speaking to a state meeting of the American Legion, McCray suggested that they should march on Terre Haute and teach Debs "a lesson," an idea promptly seconded by the group's commander. Debs ridiculed the governor's threat as "the bombast of a posing nut." Daring them to show their faces in Terre Haute, he added, "I fear no man and no mob." The Legionnaires never did appear at his home, and by a twist of fate the pugnacious governor was soon on his way to the Atlanta penitentiary himself, sentenced to ten years for mail fraud. As Debs traveled, however, he often faced such threats and relied on the protection of some strong-armed socialists.[26]

And in many cities Debs now found that halls were closed to him. In Cleveland, civic groups pressured the City Club to withdraw its invitation, while the Chamber of Commerce blocked his visit to Columbus. After being denied the use of auditoriums in Los Angeles, Debs resorted to an open-air meeting at the zoo. In Cincinnati, the Music Hall bowed to demands from Legionnaires, the Kiwanis, and the Chamber of Commerce. Turning Debs away, the board announced that the auditorium was open to "all parties, creeds and people, but not to any person convicted of disloyalty who justifies such disloyal action." Surrounded by a volunteer bodyguard of striking steelworkers, Debs spoke instead at the city's largest union hall, where he gave three speeches in an afternoon, daring both the mayor and the assembled police force to arrest him. Soon after, he faced a similar challenge from the Legionnaires in Everett, Washington. "They said if I said anything radical they would stop it," Debs wrote Theodore, "but by God, I changed their mind. I cut loose and gave them hell from start to finish."[27]

Everywhere Debs traveled he ignited fresh debate over his free speech rights, an argument that divided communities, civic groups, labor unions, and churches. Although the country no longer faced the perils of war, many still considered him a traitor, an enemy to the country and its Constitution who had forfeited any claim to the free speech protections afforded to loyal citizens. These critics were often countered, however, by others who were determined to defend the right of free speech, even for those with unsavory views. Recoiling from the abuses of wartime patriotism and the intolerance of postwar vigilantes, these men and women concluded that the true lesson of the war was not the need for greater vigilance against internal enemies but the importance of providing better safeguards for civil liberties. Arguments for free speech first marshaled in the amnesty campaign now found a wider application. Preachers sermonized on the value of tolerance, labor unions found places for Debs and other radicals to have their say when they were turned away from city auditoriums, student groups defied their deans by inviting radicals to speak on campus. In many states voters backed candidates who declared their commitment to civil liberties, and in other places politicians stood firm against public pressure to ban unpopular speakers, and pardoned some convicted under state sedition laws. In 1923 Upton Sinclair was arrested by Los Angeles police for speaking on behalf of striking dockworkers, pulled from the platform while reading the text of the First Amendment. The incident prompted hundreds of Californians to join him in founding a state chapter of the ACLU.[28]

Still a small and suspect organization, the ACLU offered advice and limited financial support in many of these controversies. In the early 1920s the group expanded its focus beyond the defense of conscientious objectors and other war prisoners, working to protect the rights of labor to speak and organize on a variety of fronts. The group did not forget, however, the more than one hundred wartime prisoners who remained in jail. As some in the ACLU had feared, putting pressure on the government became more difficult once Debs left prison, because public interest in amnesty waned. Those still behind bars were more anonymous and less appealing to public sympathy—they were rebellious tenant farmers from Oklahoma, foreign-born anarchists, and defiant Wobblies who refused to ask for a pardon or accept anything short of a general amnesty for all of their comrades. "The average American," as one paper noted, "doesn't care whether these prisoners are in or out, and certainly wouldn't lift a finger to help them get out."[29]

Some in the amnesty movement felt much the same way. Considering her job finished when Debs left prison, Lucy Robins closed her office and went into real estate sales, while continuing to work as an AFL organizer. She remained a disciple of Gompers, though she turned down more than one marriage proposal from the homely old labor leader in the last years of his life. Socialists still pushed for amnesty, but focused more energy on rebuilding their party once their leader was liberated. The Senate Judiciary Committee dropped plans to introduce an amnesty resolution, and when Meyer London introduced a similar bill in the House, he met stiff criticism. Harding, who considered most of the remaining prisoners to be a public menace, refused to meet any new amnesty delegations.[30]

The ACLU would not let the matter drop, hoping not only to free the remaining prisoners but also to force the government to admit it had been wrong to jail these men and women in the first place. As Oswald Garrison Villard stated their position, when Harding liberated Debs he had done the right thing for the wrong reasons. "Amnesty as an act of mercy has little social value," he wrote, but "as an act of justice it is invaluable." If the friends of civil liberty failed to press this point, Villard feared that they would miss a vital opportunity to defend and clarify the First Amendment questions raised by the war. "To be unconcerned for the fate of our political prisoners," he wrote in 1922, "is to invite the settlement of all questions not by discussion but by relentless conflict between groups which will use their control of the political machinery remorselessly against their opponents. It is to invite also the death of that regard for personality which is imperative if we are to escape a mechanized society and a servile state."[31]

William Borah, the maverick Republican senator from Idaho, took a lead role in sustaining the drive for amnesty. Weeks after Debs left Atlanta, Borah pressed Daugherty to accelerate his review of the remaining cases and toured the country rallying public support for an immediate amnesty and U.S. recognition of Soviet Russia. Beginning with a massive meeting in Chicago, the senator was joined on stage by Jane Addams and Clarence Darrow, who applauded his declaration that the Espionage Act convictions had violated the nation's most cherished principles. "It seems to me that a vicious doctrine has grown up," Borah charged, "that when war comes the constitution is for the time suspended. This is indeed a vicious and treasonable doctrine." When he mentioned Debs, the five thousand in the hall erupted in several minutes of applause.[32]

Another effective attempt to keep pressure on the president came from Kate Richards O'Hare. In April 1922 she led a dozen wives and eighteen children of political prisoners in a cross-country march to the

Kate Richards O'Hare leads the Children's Crusade.
Library of Congress, Prints and Photographs Division.

gates of the White House. Where principled arguments and democratic petitions had failed, she hoped to shame Harding into action with her "Children's Crusade." Stopping at cities along the way, this "living petition" proved to be an irresistible magnet for press attention. They spent their first night in Terre Haute, where Debs left his sickbed to share a meal with the young crusaders and to offer them his "blessing."[33]

When the group arrived in Washington, Harding's deft political instincts seemed to fail him. For a month he ignored O'Hare's daily requests for an interview, dismissing the "theatric parade" as a manipulative publicity stunt. Supported by donations from the ACLU, the crusaders settled in for a long siege, establishing a picket line at the White House gates. Every day for seven weeks, solemn children held signs that read "Debs is Free—Why Not My Daddy?" while their mothers declared themselves "Innocent Victims." O'Hare issued press releases reporting that the president had plenty of time for golf, as well as meetings with a parade of lobbyists, movie stars, and Babe Ruth, and yet refused to meet with "twenty-seven little children." At last Harding flinched, inviting them to his office and vowing a speedy review of the remaining cases. That summer he commuted the sentences of fifty more prisoners, including those related to the protestors. Once their husbands and fathers were free, the White House picketers melted away.[34]

Working with church, veteran, and labor groups, the ACLU continued to send amnesty petitions and picketers to the White House, and by the spring of 1923 Harding announced that he was eager to resolve the matter once and for all. Over months he gradually released many of the seventy-six remaining prisoners, a few each month. He freed any alien willing to submit to immediate deportation and revived a plan he had rejected in the Debs case, offering freedom to those who would pledge to be law-abiding. Insisting on their innocence, several dozen of the IWW prisoners refused any such compromise.

After Harding's untimely death in August 1923, amnesty forces feared that his successor, Calvin Coolidge, would have little sympathy for these last holdouts. Once again a conservative Republican president surprised his liberal petitioners. Though known as a flinty opponent of radicalism, Coolidge appointed a special commission to review the remaining thirty-six cases, choosing members who were known to favor a wholesale pardon. On December 15, 1923, more than five years after the armistice, America's domestic fight over the political prisoners finally ended when Coolidge commuted the sentences of the remaining prisoners.[35]

"I am delighted," Senator Borah told the press, "that a President of the United States has discovered the First Amendment to the Constitution and has had the courage to announce the discovery." Once again, Daugherty hotly denied that free speech was the issue. Charging that the amnesty movement was led by a group of "rabid, lawless" agitators who had misled the country, he insisted one last time that the prisoners had been convicted not for their opinions but for their "deliberate and damnable attempt to retard the Government of the United States in the prosecution of a great war."[36]

True to his reputation, "Silent Cal" did not elaborate on his reasons for the pardon. Like Harding, he objected to the term *political prisoner* and never questioned the government's actions during the war. He did, however, share his predecessor's interest in restoring the country to what he called "the old and normal habits of thought." The war was long over, he told a convention of the American Legion in 1925, and the country needed "intellectual demobilization as well as military demobilization."[37]

Coolidge may also have been motivated by a desire to distance his new administration from scandals brewing in the Justice Department. Public criticism of Daugherty had been building since the day Harding had appointed him, much of it for his heavy-handed attacks on labor and his failure to prosecute war profiteers. His downfall came, however, when a congressional investigation implicated him in tawdry schemes involving kickbacks, influence peddling, and illegal liquor licenses. The man who had once advised Debs to use his talents for the public good narrowly avoided his own stay in a federal penitentiary. Though Daugherty protested that he was the victim of perjury and a communist conspiracy, Coolidge fired him in March 1924. Attempting to clean house after this and other Harding scandals, he put Harlan Fiske Stone in charge of the Justice Department. Declaring that the government's "secret police" could become "a menace to free government and free institutions," Stone stopped the FBI's program of anticommunist propaganda and its surveillance of labor, radical, and civil liberties groups.[38]

A final skirmish remained to be fought. Many of the prisoners had been deprived of their citizenship as a result of their felony convictions. Though Debs boasted publicly that he preferred to think of himself as a citizen of the world, his identity as an American citizen concerned him. After leaving Atlanta he made several inquiries but remained unsure about his status. Determined at last to test his case, he left his sickbed, and with Theodore's help walked to Terre Haute's city hall and successfully registered to vote.[39]

A month later he suffered a heart attack. With his brother Theodore by his side, he died on October 20, 1926. When his old comrades gathered in Terre Haute to pay their respects, many suggested that his life had been cut short by the three years that he had spent in prison. While the Socialist party lived on, it was also in some respects a victim of wartime repression. By the time Debs died, the party had dwindled to less than ten thousand members. Though the movement enjoyed a brief revival under Norman Thomas during the Great Depression, it never recovered its prewar vitality and mass appeal. Looking back, Morris Hillquit wrote that Debs's 1920 campaign had proven to be "the last flicker of the dying candle."[40]

A decade of war and revolution had also taken its toll on all of America's radical and working-class movements. The IWW was broken and bankrupted by years of mob violence, deportation, and imprisonment. Emma Goldman, the guiding spirit of American anarchism and perhaps the country's greatest defender of free speech, was living in permanent exile. Even Gompers's conservative union movement was suffering "lean years," hurt by the corporate campaign for the open shop and the government's pro-business policies.

Because the threat of proletarian revolution was a fading memory in 1926, many eulogists in the mainstream press could afford to remember Debs fondly. "As a national force in politics, socialism will be felt no more," one wrote. "The heart of its 'cause' has ceased to function." Papers that had once denounced him as a traitor now concluded that the old radical had been misguided but also quintessentially American—a democrat, a humanitarian, and an individualist who had the courage to stand by his convictions. Some took one last chance to denounce him as a "tragic misfit" and a "weird prophet in a land of common sense." But to many, Debs no longer seemed like such a "dangerous man." They remembered him instead as one of America's "great dreamers."[41]

Epilogue: Amnesty and the Birth of Civil Liberties

D EBS NEVER FOUND the words to convince most Americans to cast their lot with the socialist revolution. But his unflinching stand for his principles, even in the face of government persecution, had an unintended consequence, provoking a national debate about the meaning of the First Amendment at a crucial time in the country's history. As the Wilson administration prepared to send American troops into a world war, it tried to impose unity on a divided country by claiming unprecedented powers to shape public opinion and stifle dissent. Once war passions cooled, the danger this posed to democratic traditions was made starkly visible by the sight of Debs behind bars.

Long before the war, American radicals had tried to defend their First Amendment rights in state and local courts, though rarely with much success. The excesses of the federal government's campaign against war protestors brought these free speech arguments to the attention of a much wider circle of Americans. From the congressional debate over the Espionage Act to the final push for amnesty, radicals and civil libertarians engaged a national audience in ideas that they had been working out for decades—about the role of free speech in the fight for social justice, the value of dissent as an instrument of progress, and the danger to democracy when the wealthy and powerful control the channels of communication.[1]

Fewer Americans would have listened to these arguments if Eugene Debs had not gone to jail. Most of the hundreds of other political prisoners were anonymous and comparatively inarticulate, their stories less likely to win a sympathetic hearing from the press and the public. The image of Debs in prison garb was more difficult to ignore. To be sure, many Americans had no qualms about the government's attempt to punish those who refused to support their country in its hour of need. But after the armistice, a growing number of men and women had second thoughts, and many came to see Debs and his comrades as the victims of government tyranny. In letters to the editor and to the White House, in union halls and church conventions, in political campaigns and congressional hearings, those who fought to free Debs provoked a remarkably broad national debate over the meaning of the First Amendment.

In the end this massive protest movement not only liberated the prisoners but pressured the government to moderate its postwar campaign against radicals. Those working for amnesty rallied public opposition to Palmer's raids, helped kill his plan for a permanent sedition law, and contributed to the national repudiation of the Wilson administration in the election of 1920. This political lesson was not lost on Wilson's successor. As Warren Harding moved to restore prewar "normalcy," he reduced the federal government's power to control individual expression, correcting the worst abuses of Wilson's wartime administration. Harding released Debs and most of the remaining wartime prisoners, while his new postmaster, Will Hays, repudiated Burleson's censorship campaign and restored mailing privileges to all radical publications. After Harding's death, Calvin Coolidge continued this process, supporting Attorney General Harlan Stone's decision to suspend the FBI's surveillance of political radicals. Most Americans applauded Stone's announcement that the Justice Department would no longer be "concerned with political or other opinions of individuals."[2]

With characteristic exuberance, Lucy Robins surveyed all that the amnesty campaign had accomplished and declared it "one of the most important" social movements in the nation's history. Though proud of the role she had played in liberating her hero, she thought that the amnesty crusade had accomplished something even grander. She felt sure that America's conservative union workers had been radicalized by the experience of fighting to free Debs. By this Robins did not mean that they had embraced the socialists' war on capitalism. Rather, she believed that, as working-class Americans of various political persuasions joined together for amnesty, they gained a new appreciation for the older revolutionary principle on which their country had been founded—the belief in free expression as the bedrock of democratic self-government. Oswald Garrison Villard put the same point another way. Those working to liberate Debs and his comrades were engaged in "a new fight for old liberties."[3]

Touring the country in late 1921, British author H. G. Wells was impressed by what he called "the struggle that's going on over here for free speech and free discussion." As he observed the amnesty movement's final push to win Debs's freedom, Wells thought that the young republic had finally "grown up." Americans seemed ready to acknowledge that "the attempt to shout down and suppress unpopular opinions and to create panics of hostility against minority views is unworthy of the general greatness of American life."[4]

Many who continued to fight for civil liberties in the 1920s were less optimistic about what the amnesty movement had accomplished, and about the country's level of tolerance for free speech. When Harding released Debs and his comrades, he insisted that this was an act of mercy, not justice. Congress repealed the Sedition Act in March 1921, but the Espionage Act remained on the books, ready for use when the next war came along. A solid majority on the Supreme Court remained unsympathetic to civil liberties arguments through most of the decade and supported the convictions of radicals under state conspiracy and sedition laws. The federal government abandoned the heavy-handed tactics of Burleson and Palmer, but supported corporations who used quieter and more informal ways to stifle labor radicalism. Organized labor's fortunes continued to decline through the decade, as the courts issued injunctions against strikes and local governments supported capital's drive to break unions.[5]

As Debs's experience makes clear, free speech rights were also threatened by vigilante violence long after the passions of war had cooled. Across the country, Klansmen, Legionnaires, and dozens of other "patriotic" organizations continued to intimidate speakers and block their access to local platforms. Other groups drew up blacklists of those suspected of promoting un-American ideas, and never failed to include the leaders of the ACLU. Norman Hapgood published an exposé of these "professional patriots," showing that many of the country's self-appointed censors enjoyed the financial backing of business and civic leaders. In mid-decade, the ACLU's Roger Baldwin noted bitterly that the country was experiencing fewer free speech violations, but only because so many rebellious voices had already been silenced.[6]

Historians often agree with Baldwin's assessment that the 1920s was a decade of oppressive conformity. The era of "normalcy," as one put it, "was no golden age of political liberty." However valid, this generalization obscures an important development in the postwar years, an emerging commitment to individual rights that Eric Foner has recently described as "the birth of civil liberties." The years of war and revolution pushed the country in a conservative direction, but also prompted a small but growing number of Americans to organize to defend the rights of radicals, minorities, artists, and other dissenters. While debates about the proper interpretation of the First Amendment continued, in the aftermath of World War I the right to free expression moved to the very center of the way Americans thought about democratic liberty, where it has remained ever since.[7]

This shift was reflected in the thinking of many of the nation's progressive reformers and intellectuals. Before the war, most of them showed little interest in civil liberties, in part because conservative judges had used traditional notions of individual freedom to block reform, shielding corporate power behind the doctrine of "liberty of contract." At the start of the war, few progressives expressed sympathy for the victims of the Espionage Act; no less than corporate leaders, the radical dissenters seemed to value their own rights more than the public interest and the will of the majority. As progressives saw it, people like Debs were interfering with the efficient prosecution of a noble national cause, a "people's war" that promised to advance democratic reforms at home and around the world. Most of these progressives were disillusioned by the results of Wilson's crusade. The years of state-sponsored repression and mob violence led many to temper their faith in government, and their trust in the wisdom and benevolence of a democratic majority. They came to agree with Randolph Bourne that the state "represents all the autocratic, arbitrary, coercive, belligerent forces within a social group." After the war, these chastened progressives developed a new appreciation for the values of pluralism, and the promotion of "rights, checks on state power, and individual autonomy." For many of these men and women, the amnesty movement afforded the first opportunity to articulate and defend these new concerns.[8]

While some intellectuals took a new interest in minority rights, others turned their attention to understanding problems that the war had exposed in democracy's bedrock principle of majority rule. In addition to silencing critics, the Wilson administration had used war propaganda to "manufacture consent," as Walter Lippmann put it. Whatever its intentions, this propaganda fueled a mob spirit that proved more effective in silencing radicals than any federal or state law. A string of academic studies and popular articles dissected the administration's "war lies," while others took a new interest in mass psychology. As sociologist Harold Lasswell put it, Americans had the unsettling feeling that they had been duped, dragged into war by the "silver chains" of propaganda.[9]

A leader in this new field of propaganda studies was Clyde Miller, the reporter who had repented his role in sending Debs to jail. Believing that he had been fooled by the government's patriotic disinformation campaign, he earned a doctorate, taught at Columbia Teachers College, and in 1937 helped found the Institute for Propaganda Analysis, the first such institution in the country. Ironically, this work brought him under the scrutiny of the House Un-American Activities Committee for, among other things, expressing a suspicious pacifism before America's entry into World War II and failing to be sufficiently critical of Soviet propaganda. Called to testify before HUAC, the star witness against Debs now became the defendant.[10]

The postwar decade was also marked by a gradual but crucial shift in the Supreme Court's thinking about the First Amendment. After Holmes issued his opinion in the Debs case, friendly critics pressed him to reconsider, urging him to abandon the traditional "bad tendency" test in favor of a new doctrine that would be clearer and more protective. As

Zechariah Chafee put it, the time had come for the court "to determine the true limits of freedom of expression, so that speakers and writers may know how much they can properly say, and governments may be sure how much they can lawfully and wisely suppress."[11]

At first Holmes resisted, declaring such criticisms "rather poor stuff." Months later he relented, perhaps influenced by the growing public clamor over the political prisoners and the Palmer raids. Guided by Chafee, Holmes found the precedent for a new free speech test in an unlikely place, his own opinion in the Schenck case. In the Supreme Court's first ruling on an Espionage Act conviction, Holmes had spoken for a unanimous court in upholding the law and sending Schenck to prison. In that opinion, he had written that the government could punish speech if it posed a "clear and present danger" to the public. In his Abrams dissent in the fall of 1919, Holmes began the process of turning this chance phrase into a new legal test, suggesting that the government should interfere with speech only when it posed "the present danger of an immediate evil."[12]

In a series of dissents over the next decade, Holmes and Brandeis elaborated on this idea, offering eloquent pleas for greater free speech rights. By the 1930s, a majority of the court came to accept this "clear and present danger" test. As a result, Justice Holmes, the man who wrote the decision sending Debs to prison, is often remembered as a prophet of modern free speech doctrine. Though Holmes never repudiated his decision in the Debs case, legal scholars today agree that if Debs had been tried under a "clear and present danger test," he would not have been convicted.

Guided by the postwar dissents of Holmes and Brandeis, the Court would emerge over the course of the century as a much more effective guardian of the speech rights of dissenters. However, as Zechariah Chafee pointed out, the surest protection for free speech comes not from lawyers' briefs and judges' rulings, but from public opinion. "The ultimate security for free and fruitful discussion," as he put it, "lies in the tolerance of private citizens." Debs and his fellow radicals went to jail not simply because judges had embraced the traditional "bad tendency" doctrine; their right to challenge the will of the majority was limited as much by the fear-mongering of government propagandists, the indignation of newspaper editors, the threat of patriotic mobs, the personal ambitions of prosecutors and politicians, and the prejudices of citizens in the jury box.[13]

If public opinion did all this to put Debs in jail in 1919, it also played an important role in getting him out three years later. As the history of the amnesty campaign makes clear, the mounting protest was neither the spontaneous expression of Americans' democratic instincts nor the natural reaction of a society recovering from a bad case of war fever. Rather, the demand for amnesty was both stimulated and organized by political activists who effectively framed the controversy in a way that appealed to many Americans' sense of empathy and fair play. Because the government had silenced the radical movement's presses and platforms, many of these activists had been forced to develop new ways to reach the public, building on techniques pioneered by the abolitionists, the suffragists, and the labor movement. Lucy Robins forced a free speech debate in the AFL locals; Kate O'Hare staged a "children's crusade"; the ACLU and war veterans picketed the disarmament conference; the Socialists hauled their "monster petition" to Washington and, most importantly, pressed voters to send Debs from the jailhouse to the White House. All of these strategies forced the plight of the political prisoners onto the front pages of mainstream newspapers, no matter how hostile their editors might have been to that cause. At a time when commercial advertisers and government propagandists were creating powerful new techniques of mass persuasion, amnesty leaders were learning to practice a form of free speech politics that has since become a familiar part of the American political conversation.

Over the course of the decade, the ACLU continued to build on some of the organizing strategies developed in the amnesty campaign. Finding little sympathy for their cause in the courts, they tried instead to raise public concern for free speech through a series of protests and dramatic test cases. Even before the wartime prisoners had all been released, the ACLU and its allies in the labor and radical movements joined forces to defend two new "political prisoners," the anarchists Sacco and Vanzetti. In these early years the ACLU also helped communists convicted under state sedition laws, labor leaders who made free speech arguments against court injunctions, teachers who were forced to take loyalty oaths, and artists whose work upset government censors. Though civil libertarians won few of those cases, they succeeded in keeping First Amendment questions on the nation's agenda, contributing to a gradual but profound change in American ideas about the value of free expression.[14]

In the decades since Debs was arrested for his Canton speech, the right to dissent in America has expanded dramatically. Those who protest wars in our own day can do so with far less risk of facing a long jail term or the wrath of an angry mob. And yet, in times of national crisis, we find that some of the important questions raised by the Debs case are still with us, as we struggle to define the proper balance between free speech and national security.

Then and now, many Americans have argued that, during wartime, speech rights should be reserved for those who use them responsibly. Then and now, some have defended this position with emotional appeals to "true Americanism," while others have made compelling arguments about society's right to limit personal freedoms for the sake of national survival. They insist that speakers who try to undermine the nation's resolve in times of war endanger the very source of American liberty, claiming the protection of a freedom that they would recklessly destroy. For those who take this view, Debs ended his public life where he had begun, as a "dangerous man" who could perhaps be tolerated in times of peace, but who was justly punished for failing to support his country in a time of national peril.

The fight to free Debs convinced many other Americans that their society should offer greater protection for those who refuse to support the majority, even in times of war. Today civil libertarians return to many of the same arguments employed by the amnesty movement almost a century ago, arguing that democracy is strengthened by diversity of opinion, that the freedom to speak is a right undermined by social and economic inequality, that suppression of dissent is often counterproductive, and that the First Amendment's guarantees should apply equally in times of war as in times of peace.

In the end, our country's perennial debate over the rights of war protestors reminds us that "free speech" is no one thing, but the crossroads for competing claims about the relative value of individual liberty and public order, and the freedoms and responsibilities of democratic citizenship. The amnesty movement got Debs out of jail but never resolved this fundamental conflict over the terms of our democratic social contract, and nearly a century of battles, legal and military, has expanded the freedom of dissent but produced no consensus. We find in the story of Convict 9653 an important chapter in our own, ongoing arguments about the limits of free speech in times of war, but no last word.

Notes

Abbreviations

AC	*Atlanta Constitution*
AMP	A. Mitchell Palmer
ATR	*Appeal to Reason*
CSM	*Christian Science Monitor*
CT	*Chicago Tribune*
DK	David Karsner
DKP	David Karsner Papers, New York Public Library
DP	Eugene V. Debs Papers, Indiana State University
DPT	Eugene V. Debs Papers, Tamiment Library
EVD	Eugene V. Debs
MC	Mabel Curry
NYT	*New York Times*
RG 60	Department of Justice Papers, National Archives, College Park, MD
RG 204	Pardon Attorney Papers, National Archives, College Park, MD
RPS	Rose Pastor Stokes
RPS-Yale	Rose Pastor Stokes Papers, Sterling Library
SPP	Socialist Party Papers, Duke University Special Collections
SR	*Social Revolution*
TD	Theodore Debs
U.S. v. Debs	Case File, National Archives, Chicago
US	Upton Sinclair
USL	Upton Sinclair Papers, Lilly Library
WP	*Washington Post*
WW	Woodrow Wilson
WWP	Woodrow Wilson Papers, Library of Congress, published in *The Papers of Woodrow Wilson,* ed. Arthur S. Link (Princeton, 1966–1994)

1. Dangerous Man

1. *New York Times* (hereafter *NYT*), 5 Oct. 1908.
2. Ray Ginger, *The Bending Cross: A Biography of Eugene Victor Debs* (New Brunswick, 1949), 267.
3. *Appeal to Reason* (hereafter *ATR*), 28 Sept. 1912; Nathan Fine, *Labor and Farmer Parties in the United States, 1828–1928* (New York, 1928), 241.
4. Ernest Poole cited in Ginger, *The Bending Cross*, 282.
5. Max Ehrmann, "Eugene V. Debs as an Orator," *ATR*, Aug. 1907; *Brooklyn Eagle*, 27 Oct. 1912.
6. Eric Foner, *The Story of American Freedom* (New York, 1998), 142–144.
7. *The Outlook*, 20 Mar. 1909.
8. Examples of the Socialist Party platform are taken from the 1904 convention, cited in H. Wayne Morgan, ed., *American Socialism, 1900–1960* (Englewood Cliffs, 1964), 46–48.
9. For the history of American Socialism, see David A. Shannon, *Socialist Party of America: A History* (New York, 1955); James Weinstein, *The Decline of Socialism in America, 1912–1925* (New York, 1967); James Weinstein, *Long Detour: The History and Future of the American Left* (Boulder, 2003); Seymour Martin Lipset and Gary Marks, *It Didn't Happen Here: Why Socialism Failed in the United States* (New York, 2001); Irving Howe, *Socialism and America* (New York, 1986); James Green, *Grass-Roots Socialism: Radical Movements in the Southwest, 1895–1943* (Baton Rouge, 1978). A work that emphasizes the value of free speech in the wider radical movement is Christine Stansell, *American Moderns: Bohemian New York and the Creation of a New Century* (New York, 2000).
10. *Brooklyn Daily Eagle*, 27 Oct. 1912; Lincoln Steffens, "Eugene V. Debs on What the Matter Is in America and What to Do about It," *Everybody's*, Oct. 1908; Ginger, *The Bending Cross*, 270–272.
11. *Commonwealth*, 6 Sept. 1912; *NYT*, 5 Oct. 1912.
12. See, for example, Alan Trachtenberg, *The Incorporation of America: Culture and Society in the Gilded Age* (New York, 1982); Alan Dawley, *Struggles for Justice: Social Responsibility and the Liberal State* (Cambridge, 1991); David Montgomery, *The Fall of the House of Labor: The Workplace, the State, and American Labor Activism, 1865–1925* (New York, 1987).
13. Almont Lindsey, *The Pullman Strike* (Chicago, 1942).
14. On Debs's role in the Pullman strike, see Nicholas Salvatore, *Eugene V. Debs: Citizen and Socialist* (Urbana, 1982), chap. 5.
15. Melvyn Dubofsky, *Labor in America: A History* (Wheeling, 1999), 161.
16. Eugene V. Debs (hereafter EVD), "How I Became a Socialist," *Comrade*, Apr. 1902, 48–49; H. Wayne Morgan, "The Utopia of Eugene V. Debs," *American Quarterly* (Summer 1959): 127. Salvatore makes a convincing case that Debs became a socialist more gradually, drawn first to the Populist movement.

17. Francis Robert Shor, *Utopianism and Radicalism in a Reforming America, 1888–1918* (Westport, 1997), chap. 5; Bernard Brommel, *Eugene V. Debs, Spokesman for Labor and Socialism* (Chicago, 1978), chap. 4.

18. *ATR,* 5 Oct. 1912; for Debs on Gompers, see *ATR,* 18 Jan. 1908.

19. *Terre Haute Post,* 10 Nov. 1911.

20. Elliott Shore, *Talkin' Socialism: J. A. Wayland and the Radical Press* (Lawrence, 1988).

21. *Brooklyn Eagle,* 27 Oct. 1912; *NYT,* 30 Sept. 1912; Ginger, *The Bending Cross,* 274; *ATR,* 31 Aug. 1912.

22. "Impossiblism in the Economic Field," *Chicago Socialist,* 22 Sept. 1911; EVD to J. Mahlon Barnes, 31 May 1912, Eugene V. Debs Papers, Indiana State University (hereafter DP); Weinstein, *Decline of Socialism,* 1; James Chace, *1912: Wilson, Roosevelt, Taft and Debs—The Election That Changed the Country* (New York, 2004), 185–186.

23. Undated clipping in DP; Ginger, *The Bending Cross,* 279.

24. *Los Angeles Herald,* clipping in DP.

25. *Chicago Daily World,* 17 June 1912; *NYT,* 18 June 1912; Kirby cited in *Chicago Socialist,* 29 Jan. 1912.

26. *ATR,* 7 Sept. 1912; *NYT,* 23 July 1912; "Mad Dog" comment cited in *Christian Socialist,* 16 May 1912, DP.

27. "Firemen Rout Socialist," *NYT,* 31 July 1912; Ginger, *The Bending Cross,* 279; A. M. Simons, "An Incredible Story," *Coming Nation,* 30 Nov. 1912; Shore, *Talkin' Socialism,* 216–218.

28. *Springfield Illinois Republican,* 7 Nov. 1912; John A. Gable, *The Bullmoose Years* (Port Washington, 1978), 84–85; *NYT,* 3 Sept. 1912.

29. *A Crossroads of Freedom: The 1912 Campaign Speeches of Woodrow Wilson,* ed. John Wells Davidson (New Haven, 1956), 335; *NYT,* 24 Sept. 1918.

30. *NYT,* 14 Aug. 1912.

31. *ATR,* 26 Oct. 1912.

32. *Duluth Evening Herald,* quoted in *ATR,* 27 May 1910.

33. *The International* (Dec. 1912); *NYT,* 7 Nov. 1912.

34. *NYT,* 30 Sept. 1912, *New York Call,* 7 Nov. 1912.

2. Never Be a Soldier

1. John Reed, *Insurgent Mexico* (New York, 1914); Robert A. Rosenstone, *Romantic Revolutionary: A Biography of John Reed* (Cambridge, 1975).

2. James Weinstein, *The Decline of Socialism in America, 1912–1925* (New York, 1967), 119–120; Morris Hillquit, *Loose Leaves from a Busy Life* (New York, 1934), 148; David A. Shannon, *The Socialist Party of America: A History* (New York, 1955), 80–82; Nicholas Salvatore, *Eugene V. Debs: Citizen and Socialist* (Urbana, 1984), 274–275.

3. Meyer London, "There Must Be an End," *The Masses,* May 1915; Hillquit, *Loose Leaves,* 151–153.

4. Carl D. Thompson, "Liebknecht's Stand against Militarism," 1915 n.d.,

Socialist Party Papers, Duke University Special Collections (hereafter SPP); Alexander Trachtenberg, ed., *The American Socialists and the War: A Documentary History of the Attitude of the Socialist Party toward War and Militarism since the Outbreak of the War* (New York, 1917).

5. Eugene V. Debs (hereafter EVD), "Peace on Earth," *Miami Valley Socialist*, 15 Jan. 1915.

6. John Work, "Our German Comrades," 18 Sept. 1914, SPP; John Spargo, "Socialism and the War," *Ford Hall Folks*, 21 Mar. 1915; George Herron to A. M. Simons, 28 Sept. 1916, George Herron Papers, Tamiment Library; Hillquit, *Loose Leaves*, 159.

7. *NYT*, 21 Sept. 1914; Arthur Link, *Wilson* (Princeton, 1947), 3:25–30, 66–67.

8. Thomas J. Knock, *To End All Wars: Woodrow Wilson and the Quest for a New World Order* (New York, 1992), 44–47; Charles Catfield, "World War I and the Liberal Pacifist in the United States," *American Historical Review* (Dec. 1970), 1920–37; Donald Johnson, *The Challenge to American Freedoms* (Lexington, 1963), 2–4; Ernest McKay, *Against Wilson and War* (Malabar, FL, 1996), chap. 6; Knock, *To End All Wars*, 51.

9. Merle Curti, *Peace or War: The American Struggle, 1636–1936* (New York, 1936), 225; Michael Kazin, *A Godly Hero: The Life of William Jennings Bryan* (New York, 2006), 217–218; Bryan cited in Link, *Wilson*, 3:45; *NYT*, 19 Aug. 1914.

10. Link, *Wilson*, 5:12–15, 3:64.

11. Kazin, *A Godly Hero*, 237; *Terre Haute Post*, 11 May 1915; *National Rip-Saw*, June 1915; EVD in *Terre Haute Post*, 11 May 1915; *New York Sun*, 30 Nov. 1915; Trachtenberg, *American Socialists and the War*, 14.

12. Alan Dawley, *Changing the World: American Progressives in War and Revolution* (Princeton, 2003), 110; *NYT*, 22 July 1915.

13. Curti, *Peace or War*, 235; David Kennedy, *Over Here: The First World War and American Society* (New York, 1980), 146; General Leonard Wood quoted in Walter Millis, *Road to War: America, 1914–1917* (Boston, 1935), 95; Jeanette Keith, *Rich Man's War, Poor Man's Fight: Race, Class and Power in the Rural South during the First World War* (Chapel Hill, 2004), 18–20.

14. Knock, *To End All Wars*, 59; Wilson cited in John Patrick Finnegan, *Against the Specter of a Dragon: The Campaign for American Military Preparedness, 1914–1917* (Westport, 1974), 28; Tumulty, 247; WP, 30 Jan. 1916.

15. Oswald Garrison Villard to WW, 14 Aug 1912; undated letter Oswald Garrison Villard to Wilson, Oswald Garrison Villard Papers, Houghton Library.

16. Link, *Wilson*, 18; Kazin, *A Godly Hero*, 247–248; Curti, *Peace or War*, 235–237; C. Vann Woodward, *Tom Watson, Agrarian Rebel* (Savannah, 1973), 453; Johnson, *Challenge to American Freedoms*, 6–7; Knock, *To End All Wars*, 63–67.

17. George Herron to EVD, 24 Jan. 1916, Eugene V. Debs Papers (hereafter DP); EVD to *New York Sun*, 29 Nov. 1915, DP; EVD, "Never Be a Soldier,"

Appeal to Reason (hereafter *ATR*), 28 Aug. 1915; see also EVD, "'Prepared-ness' I Favor," *ATR*, 11 Dec. 1914.

18. Correspondence between Acting Secretary of War Henry Breckenridge and Assistant Attorney General William Wallace Jr., 14 Sept. 1915, 17 Sept. 1915, 22 Sept. 1915, Department of Justice Papers, National Archives, College Park, MD (hereafter RG 60), Central File 77175; Kennedy, *Over Here,* 24–25.

19. *ATR,* 9 Dec. 1916; EVD to Max Ehrmann, 21 Jan. 1916, DP, 2:235; Debs's critique of the film can be found in *Terre Haute Post,* 8 Jan. 1916.

20. Hillquit, *Loose Leaves,* 160–162.

21. Weinstein, *Decline of Socialism,* 121–124; EVD to Walter Lanfersiek, 24 Dec. 1915, DP; James Maurer, *It Can Be Done: The Autobiography of James Hudson Maurer* (New York, 1938), 215–216; Dawley, *Changing the World,* chap. 4; Knock, *To End All Wars,* 53–55; Curti, *Peace or War,* chap. 8, provides a fuller account of the debt Wilson owed to various peace organizations who developed plans for an international body to promote or enforce peace.

22. *NYT,* 9 May 1916; Eastman, "The Masses at the White House," *The Masses,* July 1916; Knock, *To End All Wars,* 66–67.

23. Upton Sinclair (hereafter US) to the Committee of the Anti-Enlistment League, 27 Sept. 1915, Upton Sinclair Papers, Lilly Library (hereafter USL).

24. EVD to US, 12 Jan. 1916, USL.

25. "Russell Plan, Says Debs, Invites War," *New York Sun,* 30 Nov. 1915; "Russell Leads Poll, But May Lose Race," *New York Sun,* 1 Dec. 1915.

26. Algie Simons to EVD, 21 Nov. 1915, DP; Shannon, *Socialist Party of America,* 85.

27. *American Socialist,* 27 Nov. 1915.

28. J. Robert Constantine, ed., *Letters of Eugene V. Debs* (Urbana, 1990), 2:131 n. 6; C. E. Russell to Carl Thompson, 15 Jan. 1915; Hillquit to Thompson, 20 Jan. 1915, SPP; Allan Benson to Carl Thompson, 19 Jan. 1915, SPP.

29. Knock, *To End All Wars,* 94.

30. Eastman cited in Link, *Wilson,* 125; John Spargo, "My Association with Woodrow Wilson, to 1917," unpublished (ca. 1960), in Spargo Papers, University of Vermont; Knock, *To End All Wars,* 94.

31. *NYT,* 15 June 1916; Harry Schreiber, *Wilson and Civil Liberties, 1917–1921* (Ithaca, 1960), 6–10.

32. Curti, *Peace or War,* 236; Walter Lippmann, "Poltroons and Pacifists," in *Force and Ideas: The Early Writings,* ed. Arthur Schlesinger Jr. (New Brunswick, 2000), 56.

33. Shannon, *Socialist Party of America,* 92; Scott Nearing, *Great Madness* (New York, 1917), 11; *ATR,* 11 Sept. 1915.

34. Wilson cited in Robert H. Ferrell, *Woodrow Wilson and World War I, 1917–1921* (New York, 1985), 10.

35. Kennedy, *Over Here,* 5; Knock, *To End All Wars,* 116–117.

36. *Social Revolution,* Apr. 1917.

37. *CSM*, 6 Mar. 1917; *NYT*, 8 Mar. 1917.
38. Shannon, *Socialist Party of America*, 89–90.

3. War Declarations

1. Robert H. Zieger, *America's Great War: World War I and the American Experience* (Lanham, 2000), chap. 3.
2. John Dewey, "Conscription of Thought," *New Republic* 12 (1917): 128–130.
3. *New York Times* (hereafter *NYT*), 2 Apr. and 3 Apr. 1917; David Kennedy, *Over Here: The First World War and American Society* (New York, 1980), 14–15.
4. Kennedy, *Over Here*, 22–23; David Thelen, *Robert M. LaFollette and the Insurgent Spirit* (Boston, 1976), 133–135.
5. Kennedy, *Over Here*, 24.
6. James Weinstein, *The Decline of Socialism in America, 1912–1925* (New York, 1967), 126–128; Eugene V. Debs (hereafter EVD), "On the Emergency Convention," *Social Revolution* (hereafter *SR*), May 1917.
7. Alexander Trachtenberg, ed., *The American Socialists and the War: A Documentary History of the Attitude of the Socialist Party toward War and Militarism since the Outbreak of the War* (New York, 1917), 38–45.
8. Paul L. Murphy, *World War I and the Origin of Civil Liberties in the United States* (New York, 1979), 54–55; Harry Schreiber, *Wilson and Civil Liberties, 1917–1921* (Ithaca, 1960), 11; James R. Mock and Cedric Larson, *Words That Won the War: The Story of the Committee on Public Information, 1917–1919* (Princeton, 1939), 22; Homer Cummings and Carl MacFarland, *Federal Justice* (New York, 1970), 414.
9. Schreiber, *Wilson and Civil Liberties*, 19.
10. *NYT*, 11 Apr. 1917; *Kansas City Star*, 21 Apr. 1917; *New York World*, 21 Apr. 1917; *NYT*, 4 May 1917, *Chicago Tribune* (hereafter *CT*), 10 Apr. 1917.
11. *NYT*, 15 and 20 Apr. 1917.
12. *NYT*, 19 Apr. 1917; 55 Cong. Rec., 2 May, p. 1701; *NYT*, 21 Apr. 1917.
13. *NYT*, 24 May 1917; *NYT*, 27 Apr. 1917; *New York Evening Journal*, 26 Apr. 1917; *NYT*, 23 May 1917.
14. *NYT*, 25 May 1917.
15. Murphy, *World War I*, 80–81.
16. According to David Rabban, Congress supported the mailing provision because it was better suited to attacking material with a certain tone. He suggests that lawmakers assumed that it would be desirable to root out "horrible" examples of unpatriotic publications, including those produced by the Socialists. Under the press censorship provision of the Espionage Act, Wilson's censorship powers would rest on a specific list of information deemed of use to the enemy. Burleson's powers were more vaguely defined, allowing him to go after works based on a subjective judgment about their "tone." Geoffrey Stone has a different view. He suggests that the strong support for the First Amendment voiced in the debate over censorship suggests that the Congress did not intend to attack free speech, and that the loopholes were

exploited, under pressures of war, in ways not anticipated in the debate. David Rabban, *Free Speech in Its Forgotten Years* (New York, 1997), 253; Geoffrey Stone, *Perilous Times: Free Speech in Wartime from the Sedition Act of 1798 to the War on Terrorism* (New York, 2004).

17. *Hearings on H.R. 291,* 21, Dyer paraphrasing the president and the attorney general; Rabban, *Free Speech,* 254–255.

18. *Hearings on H.R. 291,* 12

19. Ibid., 42.

20. *NYT,* 7 May 1917; Rabban, *Free Speech,* 254. On violations of free speech, see Harry Weinberger, *Free Speech and Free Press,* ACLU pamphlet (New York, n.d.).

21. Donald Johnson, *The Challenge to American Freedoms* (Lexington, 1963), 63–64.

22. Woodrow Wilson (hereafter WW), *Public Papers of Woodrow Wilson* (New York, 1925–1927), 3:67; Gregory cited in H. C. Peterson and Gilbert C. Fite, *Opponents of War, 1917–1918* (Seattle, 1968), 14.

23. Clipping in Eugene V. Debs Papers, Indiana State University (hereafter DP), 1 May 1917; *Terre Haute Star* cited in EVD, "The Plutocratic Press and Its Prostitutes," *SR,* July 1917; *NYT,* 30 May 1917.

24. Undated clipping in ACLU papers, New York Public Library.

25. Kennedy, *Over Here,* 150; Jeanette Keith, *Rich Man's War, Poor Man's Fight: Race, Class and Power in the Rural South during the First World War* (Chapel Hill, 2004), 43.

26. *SR,* April and June 1917.

27. Rabban, *Free Speech,* 255–256; Peterson and Fite, *Opponents of War,* 24; Stephen M. Kohn, *American Political Prisoners: Prosecutions under the Espionage and Sedition Acts* (Westport, 1994), 9–10.

28. Robert H. Ferrell, *Woodrow Wilson and World War I, 1917–1921* (New York, 1985), 17.

29. James Weinstein, "Anti-War Sentiment and the Socialist Party," *Political Science Quarterly* (June 1959): 217; Weinstein, *Decline of Socialism,* 136–137; Jim Bissett, *Agrarian Socialism in America: Marx, Jefferson, and Jesus in the Oklahoma Countryside, 1904–1920* (Norman, 1999), 149–150.

30. Kennedy, *Over Here,* 163; Kohn, *American Political Prisoners,* 27–29; in this period, the Jehovah's Witnesses were referred to as Russellites, the followers of Charles Taze Russell. I use the more recent appellation for the sake of clarity.

31. C. Vann Woodward, *Tom Watson, Agrarian Rebel* (Savannah, 1973), 455–457; Weinstein, *Decline of Socialism,* 138–140; Peterson and Fite, *Opponents of War,* 40–41; Keith, *Rich Man's War,* chap. 4; Bissett, *Agrarian Socialism in America,* 150–151.

32. Stephen J. Whitfield, *Scott Nearing: Apostle of American Radicalism* (New York, 1974), 77–80.

33. *NYT,* 10 Sept. 1917; Kennedy, *Over Here,* 72.

34. *Rip-Saw,* July 1917.

35. Burleson cited in Murphy, *World War I,* 98; "Socialist Press Throttled by the Postal Censorship," *SR,* Aug. 1917. Some months later, Burleson did offer to clarify what was unmailable. He would stop any publication that might "impugn the motives of the Government" or make the nation's allies look bad. "For instance," he offered, "papers may not say that the Government is controlled by Wall Street or munitions manufacturers, or any other special interests." That, of course, placed out of bounds what Debs and many other socialists and liberal pacifists thought about the war. A few papers managed to survive these restrictions, but only by adopting an explicit policy to express no opinion on the war at all. *NYT,* 10 Oct. 1917

36. Murphy, *World War I,* 100; Upton Sinclair to WW, 22 Oct. 1917, Upton Sinclair Papers, Lilly Library.

37. Rabban, *Free Speech,* 259–261; Walter Nelles, *Espionage Act Cases, with Certain Others on Related Points* (New York, 1918); Shawn Francis Peters, *Judging Jehovah's Witnesses: Religious Persecution and the Dawn of the Rights Revolution* (Lawrence, 2000), 30–31.

38. People vs. Sam Abels (1917), details in Harry Weinberger Papers, Sterling Library, Yale; many of these examples are drawn from Murphy, *World War I,* 126–132. See also Rabban, *Free Speech.*

39. Peterson and Fite, *Opponents of War,* 20; Murphy, *World War I,* 87–90.

40. "Anti-Sedition Work Is Planned," unidentified clipping in ACLU papers, New York Public Library; *NYT,* 25 Feb. 1918.

41. Peterson and Fite, *Opponents of War,* 45; Weinstein, *Decline of Socialism,* 161.

42. Peterson and Fite, *Opponents of War,* 19; John Lord O'Brian, "Civil Liberty in Wartime," 62 *Rep. N.Y. St. Bar Association* 275 (1919), 5; Schreiber, *Wilson and Civil Liberties,* 49; Gregory cited in Kennedy, *Over Here,* 81–82; Murphy, *World War I,* 95; William Preston Jr., *Aliens and Dissenters* (Cambridge, 1963), chap. 4; Thomas A. Lawrence, "Eclipse of Liberty: Civil Liberties in the United States during the First World War," *Wayne Law Review* 21 (1974): 50–51, 58–59.

43. Theodore Debs (hereafter TD) to George Bicknell, 13 Apr. 1917, DP; J. A. Poetz to EVD, 9 July 1917, DP; O'Neill, 64; Woodward, *Tom Watson,* 457.

44. *SR,* July 1917; Nicholas Salvatore, *Eugene V. Debs: Citizen and Socialist* (Urbana, 1984), 288;

45. EVD to TD, 11 and 12 Aug., 1917, DP; *SR,* Oct. 1917.

46. EVD to Mabel Curry, Aug.–Sept. 1917, in J. Robert Constantine, ed., *Letters of Eugene V. Debs* (Urbana, 1990), 2:326–329.

47. Weinstein, *Decline of Socialism,* 148.

48. *NYT,* 10 Nov. 1917.

49. Weinstein, *Decline of Socialism,* 152–159; Debs comments in *Eye Opener,* 1 Dec. 1917; *New York Call,* 23 Jan. 1918.

50. *Miami Valley Socialist,* 23 Nov. 1917; *NYT,* 30 Oct. 1917.

51. *NYT,* 2 Nov. 1917; *Eye Opener,* 24 Nov. 1917.

52. Adolph Germer to TD, 19 Nov. 1917, DP; EVD to Phil Wagner, 1 Feb. 1918, DP; EVD to Frank O'Hare, 2 Jan. 1918, DP.

53. *SR*, Mar. and Apr. 1918; Stone, 171–172; EVD, "Indicted, Unashamed and Unafraid," *Eye Opener*, 16 Mar. 1918.

4. Canton Picnic

1. *Social Builder*, May 1918. The *Rip-Saw* was briefly renamed the *Social Builder* in this period. To avoid confusion, in this chapter I have used the title *Rip-Saw* to identify the paper owned and edited in these years by Frank and Kate Richards O'Hare.

2. George Goebel quoted in Bernard J. Brommel, *Eugene V. Debs: Spokesman for Labor and Socialism* (Chicago, 1978), 151; Debs's statement that he felt "ashamed" not to be indicted is in the Socialist Party's *National Office Review*, Mar. 1918.

3. Speech as reported by E. R. Sterling, Canton, in the trial transcript, *U.S. v. Debs;* Debs's anticipation of his own arrest is suggested by Shubert Sebree in *Debs Remembered: A Collection of Reminiscences*, ed. J. Robert Constantine, Eugene V. Debs Papers, Indiana State University (hereafter DP). The version of the trial transcript used for this chapter can be found in U.S. v. Debs, RG 21, U.S. District Court, Northern District of Ohio, Eastern Division (Cleveland), Criminal Records, 1855–1977, Criminal Case Files, 1912–1977, Criminal Case #4057.

4. Ray Ginger, *The Bending Cross: A Biography of Eugene Victor* (New Brunswick, 1949), 353–355. Salvatore suggests that Debs was "fully expecting, even anticipating, his arrest" (Nicholas Salvatore, *Eugene V. Debs: Citizen and Socialist* [Urbana, 1984], 29).

5. Brommel, *Eugene V. Debs*, 150.

6. Clyde Miller, "The Man I Sent to Jail," *Progressive*, Oct. 1963. On Miller's relationship to Debs, see John Sproule, *Propaganda and Democracy: The American Experience of Media and Mass Persuasion* (New York, 1997), 1–7.

7. H. C. Peterson and Gilbert C. Fite, *Opponents of War, 1917–1918* (Seattle, 1971), 214–221; Geoffrey Stone, *Perilous Times: Free Speech in Wartime from the Sedition Act of 1798 to the War on Terrorism* (New York, 2004), 188–191.

8. Harry N. Schreiber, *The Wilson Administration and Civil Liberties, 1917–1921* (Ithaca, 1960), 22–24.

9. *Social Builder (Rip-Saw)*, May 1918.

10. *Social Revolution* (hereafter *SR*), Apr. 1918.

11. *Miami Valley Socialist*, 14 June 1918; Eugene V. Debs (hereafter EVD), "The Socialist Party and the War," *Social Builder (Rip-Saw)*, May 1918; EVD, "A Personal Statement," typescript copy, DP; Salvatore, *Eugene V. Debs*, 289; EVD to Adolph Germer, 8 Apr. 1918, DP.

12. *CSM*, 6 June 1918; James Weinstein, *The Decline of Socialism in America, 1912–1925* (New York, 1967), 165.

13. The version of the Debs speech used in this chapter can be found in the Socialist Party pamphlet *Debs and the War* (Chicago, 1920); *Marguerite Prevey: In Memoriam* (Akron, n.d.); Karl H. Grismer, *Akron and Summit County* (Akron, 1952), 366–373.

14. Clyde Miller, *How to Detect and Analyze Propaganda* (New York, 1939), 9.

15. *Washington Post,* 17 June 1918; *Butte Miner,* clipping in DP; *Terre Haute Tribune,* 20 June 1918; *Cleveland Plain Dealer,* 21 June 1918; Miller, "The Man I Sent to Jail."

16. Salvatore, *Eugene V. Debs,* 294.

17. *Indianapolis News,* 19 and 24 June 1919.

18. Reminiscence of Shubert Sebree in "Debs Remembered," ed. J. Robert Constantine, DP.

19. *New York Times,* 2 July 1918.

20. John Reed, "With 'Gene Debs on the Fourth," *Liberator,* Sept. 1918.

21. Robert A. *Rosenstone, Romantic Revolutionary: A Biography of John Reed* (Cambridge, 1975), 329–331; William O'Neill, *The Last Romantic: A Life of Max Eastman* (New York, 1978), 64–65.

22. Art Young, *Art Young, His Life and Times,* ed. John Nicholas Beffel (New York, 1939), 340; Ginger, *The Bending Cross,* 361.

23. Ginger, *The Bending Cross,* 351–352, 348; *Terre Haute Post,* 31 May 1917; Salvatore, *Eugene V. Debs,* 288; Reminiscence of Shubert Sebree, in Constantine, *Debs Remembered.*

24. James Lyon, Mayor, undated clipping, Eugene V. Debs Papers, Tamiment Library; Herman Hulman to EVD, n.d. June 917, DP.

25. *Terre Haute Tribune,* clipping in DP; *Terre Haute Post,* 4 July 1918.

5. Cleveland

1. *Indianapolis News,* 24 June 1918.

2. *New York Times* (hereafter *NYT*), 9 Sept. 1918; Scott Nearing, *The Debs Decision* (New York, 1919).

3. *Christian Science Monitor* (hereafter *CSM*), 10 Sept. 1918; *New York Tribune,* 5 Sept. 1918.

4. Art Young, *Art Young, His Life and Times,* ed. John Nicholas Beffel (New York, 1939), 331.

5. Max Eastman, *The Trial of Eugene Debs: With Debs' Address to the Court on Receiving Sentence* (New York, 1918), 9; see also Eastman, "The Trial of Eugene Debs," *Liberator,* Nov. 1918.

6. Eastman, *Trial of Eugene Debs,* 12. Baker took a comparatively lenient approach to the problem of conscientious objectors, a policy that Westenhaver warmly endorsed (Westenhaver to Newton Baker, Westenhaver Papers, 3 Jan. 1921, Western Reserve Historical Society).

7. *Miami Valley Socialist,* 13 Sept. 1918. On similar grounds, Stedman filed a motion on Aug. 6 to quash the indictment, claiming that the grand jury that indicted Debs held its hearing in secret, contrary to law, and was chosen from an unrepresentative section of the district's population. No members of the Socialist Party and no members of the "laboring class" were included on the grand jury, Stedman protested. The request was denied. (Ray Ginger, *The Bending Cross: A Biography of Eugene Victor* (New Brunswick, 1949), 364.

8. This account is based on the trial transcript found in the National Archives and Records Administration, Great Lakes Division (Chicago). US v Eugene V. Debs, RG 21, U.S. District Court, Northern District of Ohio, Criminal Case Files, 1912–1977, Criminal Case #4057.

9. *NYT,* 10 Sept 1918.

10. Eastman, *Trial of Eugene Debs,* 13; Rose Pastor Stokes quoted in *NYT,* 23 Sept. 1918; David Karsner, *Debs: His Authorized Life and Letters* (New York, 1919), 17.

11. William Ganson Rose, *Cleveland: The Making of a City* (Cleveland, 1990), 755–766; Thomas F. Campbell, "Mounting Crisis and Reform," in *The Birth of Modern Cleveland, 1865–1930* (Cleveland, 1988), 315; Eastman, *Trial of Eugene Debs,* 8.

12. Donald Johnson, *The Challenge to American Freedoms* (Lexington, 1963), 196–210.

13. Carl Sandburg, in *Chicago Daily News,* 19 Feb. 1918; Karsner, *Debs: . . . Life and Letters,* 44; Landis cited in unidentified clipping, Debs scrapbooks, 13 Sept 1918, Eugene V. Debs Papers, Indiana State University.

14. *NYT,* 10 Sept. 1918; Karsner, *Debs: . . . Life and Letters,* 18.

15. A typescript portion of Stedman's speech is found in SST.

16. Ginger, *The Bending Cross,* 365; Eastman, *Trial of Eugene Debs,* 10–11.

17. *Herald,* 9 Oct. 1918; Arthur Zipser and Pearl Zipser, *Fire and Grace: Life of Rose Pastor Stokes* (Athens, GA, 1989), 160–161.

18. Zipser, 166–171, 172–192.

19. Eastman, *Trial of Eugene Debs,* 10.

20. Nearing, *The Debs Decision,* 15.

21. *NYT,* 11 and 23 Sept. 1918.

22. Karsner, *Debs: . . . Life and Letters,* 21.

23. Karsner was convinced that Sterling did this as a tribute to Debs, while Eastman believed he was trying to help the jury understand the scandalous nature of some of the passages.

24. Ginger, *The Bending Cross,* 366. Debs did accept that, with minor exceptions, the Sterling transcription was a reasonable facsimile. Ever after, he regretted the errors that had been introduced by the stenographers into what became his most famous speech.

25. *Debs v. US,* 249 U.S. 211 (1919), hereafter *Debs v. US.*

26. *Debs v. US,* 219; *New York Call,* 11 Sept. 1919.

27. Karsner, *Debs: . . . Life and Letters,* 21; Clyde Miller, *How to Detect and Analyze Propaganda* (New York, 1939), 10.

28. Clipping, 12 Aug. 1918, Department of Justice Papers, National Archives, College Park, MD (hereafter RG 60), Central File 77175; *Debs v. US,* 222.

29. David Kennedy, *Over Here: The First World War and American Society* (New York, 1980), 165–167; Peterson and Fite, *Opponents of War,* 231–233; Murphy, *World War I,* 222–225.

30. *Chicago Tribune* (hereafter *CT*), 14 Sept. 1918.

31. *Debs v. US,* 217.

32. Nearing, *The Debs Decision*, 15.
33. Karsner's account suggests that they left for lunch instead. Karsner, *Debs: . . . Life and Letters*, 22
34. *Debs v. US*, 236.
35. Eastman, *Trial of Eugene Debs*, 16; *Debs v. US*, 242.
36. Eastman, *Trial of Eugene Debs*, 16.
37. *CSM*, 12 Sept 1918; *Debs v. US*, 237.
38. *CT*, 12 Sept. 1918.
39. *Debs v U.S.*, 241.
40. Westenhaver to Palmer, 21 Mar. 1919, RG 60, Central File 77175.
41. Eastman, *Trial of Eugene Debs*, 19.
42. *Debs v. U.S.*, 243–244
43. *Debs v. U.S.*, 244.
44. *Debs v. U.S.*, 249
45. *Debs v. U.S.*, 252
46. *Debs v. U.S.*, 254, 262.
47. Eastman, *Trial of Eugene Debs*, 20; Ginger, *The Bending Cross*, 372.
48. *Call*, 13 Sept. 1918.
49. Nearing, *The Debs Decision*, 31.
50. Ibid., 34.
51. *NYT*, 13 and 15 Sept. 1918.
52. *New York Herald*, 15 Sept. 1918; *NYT*, 15 Sept. 1918.
53. *Cleveland Plain Dealer*, 13 Sept. 1918; *Los Angeles Times*, 16 Sept. 1918; *CSM*, 13 Mar. 1919.
54. *New York Herald*, 14 Sept. 1918; *NYT*, 23 Sept. 1918.
55. David Karsner, "Verdict Reached after Six Hours," *New York Call*, 13 Sept. 1918.

6. Appeal

1. John Reed, "With Gene Debs on the Fourth," *Liberator*, Sept. 1918.
2. "Eugene V. Debs," *Class Struggle*, Dec. 1918, 622–623.
3. Horace Traubel to Eugene V. Debs (hereafter EVD), 24 Oct. 1918, Eugene V. Debs Papers, Indiana State University (hereafter DP).
4. Upton Sinclair, *Jimmie Higgins* (New York, 1919); W. F. Palmer to Upton Sinclair (hereafter US), 10 and 14 Sept. 1918; US to Frank Harris, 2 Aug. 1919, Upton Sinclair Papers, Lilly Library (hereafter USL).
5. EVD to US, 19 Sept. 1918, USL; W. F. Palmer to US, 10 and 14 Sept., 1918; US to Frank Harris, 2 Aug. 1919 USL; EVD to Algernon Lee, 10 Oct. 1918, Eugene V. Debs Papers, Tamiment Library (hereafter DPT).
6. EVD to Max Eastman (hereafter ME), 23 Sept., 16 Dec. 1918, Max Eastman Papers, Lilly Library; EVD to Algernon Lee, 10 Oct. 1918, DPT.
7. *Toledo Times*, 28 Dec. 1918.
8. Richard Polenberg, *Fighting Faiths: The Abrams Case, the Supreme Court, and Free Speech* (New York, 1987), 38–42; *Ohio Socialist*, 8 Jan. 1919; *Indianapolis News*, 24 June 1918.

9. Lenin, "A Letter to the American Workingmen from the Socialist Soviet Republic of Russia," reprinted in *Class Struggle,* Dec. 1918; James Weinstein, *The Decline of Socialism in America, 1912–1925* (New York, 1967), 186–187.

10. *Washington Post* (hereafter *WP*), 27 Feb. 1919. Consul Robert Treadwell was released by the Bolsheviks in May 1919. *WP,* 6 May 1919; *Terre Haute Tribune,* 26 Mar. 1919.

11. "Send Him to Russia," *Kokomo Dispatch,* 19 Jan. 1919; Theodore Debs (hereafter TD) to Seymour Stedman, 30 Nov. 1918, DPT.

12. EVD to Horace Traubel, 6 Dec. 1918, DP; *Cleveland Plain Dealer,* 10 Jan. 1918.

13. TD to US, 16 Nov. 1918, USL; Mabel Curry to Rose Pastor Stokes, 18 Nov. 1918, Rose Pastor Stokes Papers, Sterling Library.

14. Laurence Hoffman to ME, 23 Dec. 1918, Max Eastman Papers, Lilly Library.

15. Scott Nearing, *The Great Madness: A Victory for the American Plutocracy* (New York, 1917); *Free Speech and Free Press Go to Trial with Scott Nearing* (New York, 1919).

16. EVD to Shubert Sebree, 20 Sept. 1918, DP.

17. EVD to Algernon Lee, 10 Oct. 1919, DPT; *Call,* 4 Nov. 1918.

18. Weinstein, *Decline of Socialism,* 170, 178–179; Robert H. Ferrell, *Woodrow Wilson and World War I, 1917–1921* (New York, 1985), 208; *Call,* 24 and 31 Oct., 6 and 13 Nov. 1918.

19. David Kennedy, *Over Here: The First World War and American Society* (New York, 1980), 232–233, 242–244.

20. *The Nation,* 2 Nov. 1918, 502; Kennedy, *Over Here,* 245. George Creel expressed a similar view; see Paul L. Murphy, *World War I and the Origin of Civil Liberties in the United States* (New York, 1979), 269 n. 34; "Socialists of World, Not Plutocrats, Uphold Wilson, Says London," *Call,* 24 Oct. 1918.

21. Frank Harris to US, USL.

22. Sinclair cited in Leon Harris, *Upton Sinclair, American Rebel* (New York, 1975), 159; telegrams, 25 Oct. 1917, USL.

23. Wilson to Burleson, cited in Murphy, *World War I,* 102–103.

24. US to Frank Harris, 29 Oct. 1918, USL; *Upton Sinclair's,* Sept. 1918; Mencken cited in introduction to Greenwood Reprint Corp.'s reprint of *Upton Sinclair's* (Westport, 1970), n.p.

25. *Upton Sinclair's,* Nov. 1918.

26. Louise Bryant to US, 1 Dec. 1918; US to Albert Rhys Williams, 3 Dec. 1918, USL.

27. *New York Times* (hereafter *NYT*), 18 Nov. 1918; *Upton Sinclair's,* Jan. 1919.

28. Murphy, *World War I,* 254.

29. Holmes cited in Geoffrey Stone, *Perilous Times* (New York, 2004), 200–201; G. Edward White, *Justice Oliver Wendell Holmes: Law and the Inner Self* (New York, 1993), chap. 12; Albert Alschuler, *Law without Values: The Life, Work and Legacy of Justice Holmes* (Chicago, 2000), 68–71.

30. David Rabban, *Free Speech in Its Forgotten Years* (New York, 1997), 272–273.

31. Rabban, *Free Speech,* 55–57

32. Gilbert Roe to Seymour Stedman, 30 Dec. 1918, DPT.

33. Stone, *Perilous Times,* 159–160.

34. Holmes in *Patterson v. Colorado* (1907) cited in *Eugene V. Debs, Plaintiff in Error, vs US, October Term 1918, Brief for the United States, In Reply to Brief of Gilbert E. Roe, as Amicus Curiae,* no. 714, pp. 69–70, 2 (hereafter U.S. Brief), 81; Polenberg, *Fighting Faiths,* 209; Stone, *Perilous Times,* 159–160.

35. *Eugene V. Debs, Plaintiff in Error, vs US, Brief of Gilbert E. Roe, as Amicus Curiae,* no. 714, October term, 1918, 22–24 (hereafter Roe Brief).

36. Roe Brief, 28.

37. Story, cited in *U.S. v. Debs,* U.S. Brief.

38. Roe Brief, 17, 48.

39. Stone, *Perilous Times,* 164–168; *Eugene V. Debs, Plaintiff in Error, vs. US, Brief of Seymour Stedman,* no. 714, 79; Rabban, *Free Speech,* 273.

40. U.S. Brief, 72, 74; Hall, 531; Rabban, *Free Speech,* 277.

41. U.S. Brief, 79–80; Roe Brief, 71.

42. *Debs v. United States, Supreme Court of the United States,* 249 U.S. 211, 10 March 1919; Rabban, *Free Speech,* 283–284.

43. Rabban, *Free Speech,* 285.

44. White, *Justice Oliver Wendell Holmes,* 419–421.

45. *WP,* 18 Apr. 1919; *NYT,* 12 Mar. 1919.

46. Zechariah Chafee, "Freedom of Speech in War Time," *Harvard Law Review* (June 1919): 944.

47. Ernest Freund, "The Debs Case and Freedom of Speech," *New Republic,* 3 May 1919.

7. Long Trolley to Prison

1. *Washington Post* (hereafter *WP*), 11 Mar. 1919.

2. *CSM,* 26 Mar. 1919; *The Papers of Woodrow Wilson,* ed. Arthur S. Link (Princeton, 1966–1994) (hereafter *WWP*), 25 Mar. 1919.

3. John Blum, *Joe Tumulty and the Wilson Era* (Boston, 1951), 191.

4. L. L. Bowman to A. Mitchell Palmer (hereafter AMP), 4 Apr. 1919; Senator Pomerene to AMP, 3 Apr. 1919, RG 60, Central File 77175, National Archives, College Park, MD (hereafter RG 60).

5. Alfred Bettman to AG, 25 Mar. 1919; Alfred Bettman to AG, 10 Feb. 1919; both RG 60, Central File 77175.

6. On clemency for other prisoners, see AMP to Woodrow Wilson (hereafter WW), 4 Apr. 1919, *WWP.* Palmer's statement to Wilson on the Debs petition is included in Joseph Tumulty to WW, 4 Apr. 1919, *WWP; WP,* 4 Apr. 1919.

7. D. J. Pickle to AMP, 10 Apr. 1919, RG 60, Central File 77175.

8. Palmer statement, 7 Apr. 1919, RG 60, Central File 77175. Cable including

the petition is Tumulty to Wilson, 24 Mar. 1919, *WWP*; *WP*, 9 Apr. 1919; *New York Times* (hereafter *NYT*), 12 Apr. 1919.

9. Clyde Miller, *The Progressive*, Oct. 1963.

10. Helen Keller to Debs (hereafter EVD), 11 Mar. 1919, Eugene V. Debs Papers, Indiana State University.

11. *The Call*, 11 Mar. 1919; James Weinstein, *Decline of Socialism* (New York, 1967), 177, 171; *NYT*, 1 Apr. 1919.

12. *NYT*, 15 Mar. 1919.

13. Theodore Draper, *The Roots of American Communism* (New York, 1957), 161–163; "Meeting in Honor of Martens at Labor Lyceum," 11 Apr. 1919, War Department RG 165, pp. 1011–1194, War Department Papers, National Archives, College Park, MD.

14. C. Vann Woodward, *Tom Watson, Agrarian Rebel* (Savannah, 1973), 451–458, 476.

15. Watson's editorial is included in a letter to AMP, 14 Apr. 1919, RG 60, Central File 77157; *ATR*, 26 Apr. 1919.

16. David Karsner, *Debs Goes to Prison* (New York, 1919), 9.

17. Mabel Curry (hereafter MC) to Rose Pastor Stokes (hereafter RPS), 19 Apr. 1919, Rose Pastor Stokes Papers, Sterling Library (hereafter RPS-Yale).

18. *WP*, 9 Apr. 1919.

19. RG 60, Central File 77175; *WP*, 31 Mar. 1919.

20. Karsner, *Debs Goes to Prison*, 33.

21. Bernard J. Brommel, *Eugene V. Debs* (Chicago, 1978), 150; Karsner, *Debs Goes to Prison*, 20, 18.

22. Karsner, *Debs Goes to Prison*, 15, 13.

23. MC to RPS, 19 Apr. 1919, RPS-Yale.

24. Karsner, *Debs Goes to Prison*, 35.

25. Karsner, *Debs Goes to Prison*, 37; *New York Call*, 19 Apr. 1919.

26. Karsner, *Debs Goes to Prison*, 40.

27. "Debs in Prison!" *Justice, Official Organ of the International Ladies Garment Workers Union*, 19 Apr. 1919.

28. Karsner, *Debs Goes to Prison*, 4.

8. Moundsville

1. Karsner, *Debs Goes to Prison* (New York, 1919), 50.

2. *Wheeling Intelligencer*, 13 Apr. 1919.

3. Joseph Terrell, "The Imprisonment of Eugene V. Debs," unpublished typescript in Eugene V. Debs Papers, Indiana State University (hereafter DP).

4. Karsner, *Debs Goes to Prison*, 49. In fact, Karsner had threatened as much, telling the warden that "tens of thousands of Debs's friends and followers on the outside" would be watching him. Terrell, "Imprisonment," 4.

5. Eugene V. Debs (hereafter EVD) to Theodore Debs (hereafter TD), 16 Apr. 1919, DP; Terrell, "Imprisonment," 7.

6. EVD to TD, 4 June 1919, DP.

7. EVD to David Karsner (hereafter DK), 22 Apr. 1919, David Karsner Papers, New York Public Library (hereafter DKP).

8. Terrell to Karsner, 6 June 1919, DKP.

9. Karsner, *Debs Goes to Prison*, 80.

10. Mabel Curry (hereafter MC) to Rose Pastor Stokes (hereafter RPS), 14 June 1919, Rose Pastor Stokes Papers, Sterling Library (hereafter RPS-Yale).

11. Terrell, "Imprisonment," 6.

12. MC to RPS, 16 May 1919, RPS-Yale.

13. Karsner, *Debs Goes to Prison*, 95.

14. EVD to DK, 14 June 1919, DKP.

15. EVD to Helen Keller, in *Letters of Eugene V. Debs*, ed. Robert Constantine (Urbana, 1990), 2:515; MC to RPS, 16 May 1919, RPS-Yale.

16. Joseph Terrell to A. Mitchell Palmer (hereafter AMP), 16 Apr. 1919, Department of Justice Papers, National Archives, College Park, MD (hereafter RG 60), Central File number 77175; Terrell, "Imprisonment," 5.

17. Robert H. Ferrell, *Woodrow Wilson and World War I, 1917–1921* (New York, 1985), 211.

18. Robert K. Murray, *Red Scare: A Study in National Hysteria, 1919–1920* (New York, 1955), 42–45; James Weinstein, *Decline of Socialism* (New York, 1967), 181–182; N. Lenin, "A Letter to American Workingmen," 20 Aug. 1918, *Revolutionary Radicalism* (Albany, 1920), 1:657–675; "Manifesto of the Third International," in *Revolutionary Radicalism*, 1:476–492 (Lusk Committee Report).

19. Melvyn Dubofsky, *We Shall Be All* (Urbana, 1988), 258–259.

20. Adolph Germer to EVD, 19 Mar. 1919, DP; *Liberator*, Sept. 1919.

21. *Wheeling Intelligencer*, 2 May 1919; Stanley Coben, *A. Mitchell Palmer: Politician* (New York, 1963), 203–204; Murray, *Red Scare*, 70–71.

22. *Christian Science Monitor* (hereafter *CSM*), 3 May 1919; *Washington Post*, 2 May 1919.

23. Paul L. Murphy, *The Meaning of Freedom of Speech* (New York, 1972), 33–36.

24. John Dewey, "The Cult of Irrationality," *New Republic*, 17 (1918): 34–35.

25. Darrow to Woodrow Wilson (hereafter WW), 29 July 1919, *The Papers of Woodrow Wilson*, ed. Arthur S. Link (Princeton, 1966–1994) (hereafter *WWP*); for Darrow's views during the war, see *The War, Address by Clarence Darrow, under the Auspices of the National Security League* (New York, 1917).

26. WW to Joseph Tumulty, 28 June 1919, *WWP*.

27. Palmer's views are relayed in Joseph Tumulty to WW, 28 June 1919, *WWP*.

28. Coben, *A. Mitchell Palmer*, 200–201.

29. *Wheeling Intelligencer*, 19 June 1919; David Kennedy, *Over Here: The First World War and American Society* (New York, 1980), 288–289.

30. Coben, *A. Mitchell Palmer*, 203.

31. WW to AMP, 1 Aug. 1919, *WWP*; Wilson told Palmer, "I entirely agree with

your judgment about the suggestion with regard to Debs and shall hope to consult with you later as to the policy we ought to adopt."

32. *Nation*, 16 Aug. 1919; *CT*, 30 Oct. 1919.

33. NCLB, "Memorandum to the President of the United States as to Persons Imprisoned for Violation of the War Laws," RG 60, Central File 197009-1.

34. John Nevin Sayre to WW, 1 Aug. 1919, with enclosure Walter Nelles, "Memorandum to the President of the United States as to Persons Imprisoned for Violations of the War Laws," *WWP*.

35. WW to AMP, 4 Aug. 1919, *WWP*.

36. Thomas J. Knock, *To End All Wars: Woodrow Wilson and the Quest for a New World Order* (New York, 1992), 255–257.

37. Spargo to WW, RG 60, File 197009-1-3.

38. WW to Spargo, 29 Aug. 1919, *WWP*; WW to AMP, 29 Aug. 1919, RG 60, Central File 197009-1-3.

39. "Memorandum for the Attorney General," 5 Sept. 1919, RG 60, Central File 197009-1.

40. Frances Early, "Feminism, Peace, and Civil Liberties: Women's Role in the Origins of the World War I Civil Liberties Movement," *Women's Studies* 18 (1990): 95–115. Robins shared Goldman's charge with M. Eleanor Fitzgerald, Alexander Berkman's lover, who led the League for much of its existence. Early provides a fuller account of the League's work than the one offered here.

41. Lucy Robins, *War Shadows* (New York, 1922), 15.

42. *Ohio Socialist*, 12 Nov. 1919; *CSM*, 3 July 1919; Robins, *War Shadows*, 45.

43. Robins, *War Shadows*, 13–14.

44. Ibid., 16.

45. Ibid., 30.

46. *Liberator*, Aug. 1919.

47. Robins, *Tomorrow Is Beautiful* (New York, 1948), 135.

48. Robins, *War Shadows*, 380; Robins, *Tomorrow Is Beautiful*, 144; Kathleen Kennedy, "In the Shadow of Gompers: Lucy Robins and the Politics of Amnesty, 1918–1922," *Peace and Change*, Jan. 2000. Outside of Robins's own works, Kennedy provides the best summary of her usually overlooked role in the development of the civil liberties movement, including a clear-eyed summary of her shortcomings.

49. Robins, *War Shadows*, 47.

50. Ibid., 50; Robins, *Tomorrow Is Beautiful*, 156.

51. Robins, *War Shadows*, 48, 53, 59.

52. Terrell, "Imprisonment," 8

53. Terrell, "Imprisonment," 8–9; EDV to Joseph Terrell, 18 Mar. 1919, DP.

54. *Wheeling Intelligencer*, 14 June 1919; J. Terrell to MC, 13 June 1919, copy in Bernard Brommel Papers, Newberry Library.

55. J. Louis Engdahl, *Debs and O'Hare in Prison* (Chicago, 1919), 1; Robins, *Tomorrow Is Beautiful*, 169; Benjamin Gitlow, *I Confess* (New York, 1940), 42.

56. State Board of Control to F. H. Duehay, 2 June 1919; F. H. Duehay to E. B. Stephenson, 5 June 1919, typescript copy in DKP; EVD to J. Z. Terrell, 27 June 1919, DKP.

57. Joseph Sharts, "Debs's Renunciation," *Miami Valley Socialist*, 29 Aug. 1919; Prevey to TD, 20 Aug. 1919, DP.

58. *The Bulletin*, 18 Oct. 1919.

9. Atlanta Penitentiary

1. Eugene V. Debs (hereafter EVD), *Walls and Bars* (Chicago, 1973), 62; *Miami Valley Socialist*, 26 Sept. 1919; on life in the Atlanta penitentiary at this time, see also Julian Hawthorne, *Subterranean Brotherhood* (New York, 1914).

2. *Atlanta Constitution* (hereafter *AC*), 22 July, 1 Sept., 28 Mar., 30 Nov. 1915.

3. *AC*, 2 Oct. 1919; *Socialist Party Bulletin*, 25 Oct. 1919.

4. EVD, *Walls and Bars,*

5. Ibid., 173.

6. Ibid., 57–58, 86, 73–74.

7. H. Park Tucker, *A History of the Atlanta Federal Penitentiary, 1901–1956*, unpublished, pp. 86–89; EVD, *Walls and Bars*, 59; see also the wartime issues of *Good Words: A Paper Dedicated to the Welfare of the Men in Prison*, published in Atlanta.

8. Mabel Curry (hereafter MC) to David Karsner, 7 Sept. 1919, David Karsner Papers, New York Public Library.

9. Upton Sinclair (hereafter US) to Woodrow Wilson (hereafter WW), 10 Aug. 1919, *The Papers of Woodrow Wilson*, ed. Arthur S. Link (Princeton, 1966–1994) (hereafter *WWP*).

10. WW to A. Mitchell Palmer (hereafter AMP), 11 Aug. 1919, *WWP*; Fred Zerbst to AMP, 20 Aug. 1919, *WWP*.

11. EVD, *Walls and Bars*, 79.

12. EVD to MC, "Armistice Day," and EVD to MC, n.d., Mabel Curry Papers, Lilly Library.

13. Citizens Patriotic League to WW, Department of Justice Papers, National Archives, College Park, MD (hereafter RG 60), Central File, Box 2991.

14. H. Cooley to AMP, 10 Apr. 1919, RG 60, Central File, Box 77175; *CT*, 1 Oct. 1920.

15. Federated Trades, Duluth, Minn., 2 May 1919; unsigned, Allentown, PA, to AMP, 9 Apr. 1919, RG 60, Central File 77175; Loretta Merrick-Pease to Joseph Tumulty, 14 Apr. 1919, RG 60, Central File 77175; S. Garbourg to AMP, 28 Oct. 1919, RG 60, Central File 197009.

16. Dorvin Dueck to Gregory, 18 Mar. 1919, and W. M. Garrettson to WW, n.d., both RG 60, Central File 197009.

17. Sarah Cleghorn to WW, n.d., *WWP*; A. L. Detrick to AMP, 26 Oct. 1919, RG60, Central File 197009.

18. George Wallace to WW, 23 May 1919, Pardon Attorney Papers, National Archives, College Park, MD (hereafter RG 204), EVD Pardon Case File.

19. John Lord O'Brian to John F. McGarvey, RG 204, EVD Pardon Case File; John Lord O'Brian to Mr. Darvin Udkeck, 25 Mar. 1919, RG 60, Central File 77175.

20. Dr. Frank Crane, in *Review* (Spokane, WA), clipping in RG 60, Central File 77175.

21. J. T. McDill to WW, 22 Sept. 1919, *WWP.*

22. Alfred Bettman, "Memorandum to the Attorney General," 5 May 1919, RG 60, Central File 77175.

23. Theodore Debs to Joseph Cohen, 31 July 1919, Eugene V. Debs Papers, Tamiment Library.

24. *New York Times,* 14 Sept. 1919.

25. Louis Adamic, "The Assassin of Wilson," *American Mercury,* Oct. 1930, 138–146; *Chicago Daily Tribune,* 21 Sept. 1919. Some Wobblies, in fact, claimed that their protest had so disturbed Wilson that this caused his subsequent stroke a few weeks later. Wilson's doctor tells the story differently. Riding in the car with the president, he saw no discernable reaction from the president and believed that, contrary to several newspaper accounts, many of the Wobblies clapped in admiration for the president as he rode by.

26. US to WW, 21 Sept. 1919, Upton Sinclair Papers, Lilly Library.

27. Josephy Tumulty, *Woodrow Wilson as I Know Him* (New York, 1921), 504–505; Henry Turner, "Woodrow Wilson and Public Opinion," *Public Opinion Quarterly* (Winter 1957): 505–520; Josephus Daniels, *The Wilson Era: Years of War and After, 1917–1923* (Chapel Hill, 1946), 365; Lucy Robins, *Tomorrow Is Beautiful* (New York, 1948), 157.

28. *Call,* 20 Oct. 1919; *Truth,* 3 Oct. 1919.

29. Socialist Party platform, as noted in *CSM,* 8 Oct. 1919; *The Truth,* 3 Oct. 1919 (dateline Atlanta, Sept. 24), in Debs scrapbook, Eugene V. Debs Papers, Indiana State University; *Liberator,* June 1919.

30. *Miami Valley Socialist,* 26 Sept. 1919; *Call,* 20 Oct. 1919.

31. Tumulty, *Woodrow Wilson,* 435.

32. Robert H. Ferrell, *Woodrow Wilson and World War One, 1917–1921* (New York, 1985), 168–170.

10. An Amnesty Business on Every Block

1. Phyllis Lee Levin, *Edith and Woodrow* (New York, 2001), 375; John Milton Cooper, *Breaking the Heart of the World* (Cambridge, 2001), 203–205.

2. *Survey,* 20 Sept. 1919.

3. Donald Johnson, *The Challenge to American Freedoms* (Lexington, 1963), chap. 3. Frances H. Early, *A World without War: How U.S. Feminists and Pacifists Resisted World War I* (Syracuse, 1997) offers a detailed look at the role of the New York Bureau of Legal Advice, including its contribution to many of the activities more often credited to Baldwin's NCLB.

4. *New York Times* (hereafter *NYT*), 17 Dec. 1920; League for Amnesty for Political Prisoners, "Dear Friend," May 15, 1918, Socialist Party Papers, Duke University Special Collections (hereafter SPP).

5. *Liberator,* May 1919.

6. Ibid., Sept. 1919.

7. Paul L. Murphy, *The Meaning of Freedom of Speech* (New York, 1972), 25–27.

8. Harry Weinberger to Political Prisoners Defense and Relief Committee, n.d., Harry Weinberger Papers, Sterling Library.

9. James Weinstein, *The Decline of Socialism in America, 1912–1925* (New York, 1967), 229–230;

10. J. Mahlon Barnes, mass mailing letters, 16 Sept. and 8 Oct., 1919, SPP.

11. "Memorandum," 30 Aug. 1919, SPP; Weinstein, *Decline of Socialism,* 191.

12. Weinstein, *Decline of Socialism,* 208–209.

13. "Manifesto of the Left Wing Section Socialist Party Local Greater New York" and "Appeal of the Moscow International of Sept. 1, 1919," both in *Revolutionary Radicalism: Its History, Purpose and Tactics, with an Exposition and Discussion of the Steps Being Taken and Required to Curb It; Being the Report of the Joint Legislative Committee Investigating Seditious Activities, Filed April 24, 1920, in the Senate of the State of New York* (Albany, 1920), 1:706–708, 1:468–469.

14. Harry Laidler, "The Socialist Convention," *Socialist Revolution,* June 1920, 29; Nicholas Salvatore, *Eugene V. Debs: Citizen and Socialist* (Urbana, 1982), 317–320. I offer here a simplified account of the complex ideological and political struggles that caused the left-wing split. For a fuller discussion, see Weinstein, *Decline of Socialism,* chap. 4.

15. Theodore Debs to David Karsner, 26 Apr. 1919, David Karsner Papers, New York Public Library.

16. *Christian Science Monitor* (hereafter *CSM*), 26 Sept. 1919.

17. *Survey,* 22 Nov. 1919; Lucy Robins, *War Shadows* (New York, 1922), 105, 102. They told Robins they had the "monopoly" on Chicago and the Midwest, and "that they would not give up the territory"; for a fuller account of this group, see late summer and fall issues of the *New Majority* and the *Milwaukee Leader.*

18. J. Mahlon Barnes, 31 Oct. 1919, SPP; Otto Branstetter to Kate Richards O'Hare, 14 Feb. 1920, SPP.

19. Associated Press report, 26 Dec. 1919, clipping in Eugene V. Debs Papers, Indiana State University.

20. *NYT,* 26 Dec. 1919, 25; Robins, *War Shadows,* 97. Lucy Robins dismissed the League's protest as amateur theatrics, just the sort of thing that tended to discredit the radical cause in the eyes of the public. Allowing her pragmatism to trump her feminism, she dismissed the group, which included many of her anarchist friends, as "mainly organized by women, upon the emotional spur of the moment." As Robins had predicted on the night she agreed to Emma Goldman's request to work for the League, the group disbanded soon after its Christmas march.

21. Robins, *War Shadows,* 21, 95–96. Robins saw them as "opportunists." Describing their meetings, she wrote, "Resolutions of every description, in the interests of every new fad, were adopted, and money was collected." San

Francisco activists created the Political Prisoners Defense League of America (see *Mother Earth,* Nov. 1917); Chicago anarchists founded the International Defense League (*Mother Earth,* Jan. 1918), alternately called the Non-Partisan Radical League; in Detroit the Campaign for Amnesty for the Political Prisoners in America on conclusion of Peace (*Mother Earth,* Jan. 1918); Mooney Defense League of Chicago (*CSM,* 1 Sept. 1919).

22. Robins, *War Shadows,* 11.
23. Lucy Robins, *Tomorrow Is Beautiful* (New York, 1948), 46, 153, 161.
24. Robins, *War Shadows,* 118. The delegation included Jerome Jones, AFL leader in Georgia; John Fulton of the International Brotherhood of Electrical Workers; and Lang, a socialist journalist whom Robins later married.
25. Robins, *War Shadows,* 122; *Tomorrow Is Beautiful,* 170.
26. Robins, *War Shadows,* 129; Robins, *Tomorrow Is Beautiful,* 167–169.

11. Candidate 9653

1. Harry Laidler, "The Socialist Convention," and David Karsner (hereafter DK), "Debs in 1920," both in *Socialist Review* (hereafter *SR*), June 1920.
2. *The Independent,* 29 May 1920; *Chicago Tribune* (hereafter *CT*), 10 May 1920.
3. *New York Tribune,* 15 May 1920; W. Harris Cook, "We Want Debs," *SR,* June 1920; *Call,* 9 May 1920; *Christian Science Monitor* (hereafter *CSM*), 20 May 1920; *New York Times* (hereafter *NYT*), 14 May 1920.
4. *NYT,* 14 May 1920; *New York Tribune,* 15 May 1920.
5. Laidler, "The Socialist Convention."
6. DK, "Debs in 1920."
7. DK to Theodore Debs (hereafter TD), 16 Mar. 1920, David Karsner Papers, New York Public Library (hereafter DKP); 22 Mar. 1920; *Call,* 15 Apr. 1920; Eugene V. Debs (hereafter EVD) to DK, 30 Apr. 1920, DKP.
8. *Literary Digest,* 22 May 1920; *NYT,* 16 May 1920; DK to EVD, 27 Apr. 1920, Eugene V. Debs Papers, Indiana State University (hereafter DP).
9. DK to TD, 20 Apr. 1920, DKP. Both sides accused Karsner of fabricating Debs's call for unity. On the ban on propaganda, see *CT,* 10 May 1920.
10. *Liberator,* Apr. 1920.
11. Joseph Cohen to EVD, 26 Mar. 1920, DP.
12. *Washington Post,* 16 May 1920.
13. "A Memorandum by Cary Travers Grayson," 20 Mar. 1920 and 13 Apr. 1920, *The Papers of Woodrow Wilson,* ed. Arthur S. Link (Princeton, 1966–1994) (hereafter *WWP*).
14. *Atlanta Georgian,* 16 May 1920; Socialist Amnesty Petition, 14 May 1920, typescript copy in DKP; *Call,* 16 May 1922.
15. *NYT,* 16 May 1920; John Morton Blum, *Joe Tumulty and the Wilson Era* (Boston, 1951), 320; Woodrow Wilson to Joseph Tumulty, 12 May 1920, *WWP.*
16. *NYT,* 15 May 1920; *Call,* 15 May 1920; *New York Tribune,* 15 May 1920.
17. Sally Miller, *From Prairie to Prison: The Life of Social Activist Kate Richards*

O'Hare (Columbia, MO, 1993), 190–191. On the O'Hare imprisonment, see also Philip S. Foner and Sally M. Miller, *Kate Richards O'Hare: Selected Writings and Speeches* (Baton Rouge, 1982).

18. Wilson cited in TD to DK, 4 May 1920, DKP; TD to Joseph Cohen, 22 May 1920, Eugene V. Debs Papers, Tamiment Library.

19. TD to DK, 30 Mar. 1920, DKP.

20. Undated clipping, DP.

21. *Atlanta Constitution* (hereafter *AC*), 29 May 1920; *Atlanta Georgian*, n.d., clipping in DP.

22. *NYT*, 29 May 1920.

23. *CSM*, 31 May 1920

24. *Terre Haute Post*, 8 June 1920; *AC*, 30 May 1920.

25. *Literary Digest*, 29 May 1920.

26. *Reedy's Mirror*, 20 May 1920; *Literary Digest*, 29 May 1920.

27. Letter to the editor, *NYT*, 12 June 1920; P. W. Wilson, "The Presidential Election from a European Standpoint," *Outlook*, 11 Aug. 1920.

28. NYT, June 12, 1920; *CSM*, 4 Sept. 1920.

29. Charles Erskine Scott Wood, "Woodrow Wilson," *Reedy's Mirror*, 25 Mar. 1920.

12. The Trials of A. Mitchell Palmer

1. Stanley Coben, *A. Mitchell Palmer: Politician* (New York, 1963), 220–221; Robert K. Murray, *Red Scare: A Study in National Hysteria, 1919–1920* (New York, 1955), 207–209; Donald Johnson, *The Challenge to American Freedoms* (Lexington, 1963), 138–143; *New York Times* (hereafter *NYT*), 3 Jan. 1920.

2. A. Mitchell Palmer (hereafter AMP), "The Case against the 'Reds,'" *Forum*, Feb. 1920.

3. Johnson, *Challenge to American Freedoms*, 152–153; the *Washington Post* is cited in Murray, *Red Scare*, 217; *NYT*, 5 Jan. 1920; Coben, *A. Mitchell Palmer*, 221–222, 230.

4. Murray, *Red Scare*, 85–86; *CT*, 23 Aug. 1919; Johnson, *Challenge to American Freedoms*, 126.

5. Murray, *Red Scare*; John Higham, *Strangers in the Land: Patterns of American Nativism, 1860–1925* (New York, 1967); William Preston Jr., *Aliens and Dissenters: Federal Suppression of Radicals, 1903–1933* (New York, 1966).

6. Frederick Lewis Allen, *Only Yesterday: An Informal History of the Nineteen-Twenties* (New York, 1957), 39.

7. *Survey*, 7 Feb. 1920; *Chicago Tribune* (hereafter *CT*), 9 Jan. 1920.

8. *NYT*, 7, 19, 23 Jan. and 7 Feb. 1920; *CT*, 22 Jan. 1920; Lippmann and Chafee quoted in *NYT*, 29 Feb. 1920.

9. Coben, *A. Mitchell Palmer*, 243; *NYT*, 24 Jan. 1920; Johnson, *Challenge to American Freedoms*, 134–136.

10. Murray, *Red Scare*, 245–246; Paul L. Murphy, *The Meaning of Freedom of*

Speech (Westport, 1972), chap. 6; *Literary Digest,* 6 Mar. 1920 and 7 Feb. 1920.

11. Murray, *Red Scare,* 219; Coben, *A. Mitchell Palmer,* 228; Johnson, *Challenge to American Freedoms,* 140–145; Allen, *Only Yesterday,* 48.

12. Post cited in Johnson, *Challenge to American Freedoms,* 157; Coben, *A. Mitchell Palmer,* 231–233.

13. Todd J. Pfannestiel, *Rethinking the Red Scare: The Lusk Committee and New York's Crusade against Radicalism, 1919–1923* (New York, 2003), 20–21; *NYT,* 11 Jan. 1920; *Survey,* 7 Feb. 1920; Charles Solomon, *The Albany "Trial"* (New York, 1920).

14. *NYT,* 18 Jan. 1920, 6 July 1918; Geoffrey Stone, *Perilous Times: Free Speech in Wartime from the Sedition Act of 1798 to the War on Terrorism* (New York, 2004), 23; Meirion Harries and Susie Harries, *The Last Days of Innocence: America at War, 1917–1918* (New York, 1997), 285; John Milton Cooper, *Pivotal Decades* (New York, 1990), 321; Bryan quoted in *NYT,* 19 Jan. 1920.

15. Zechariah Chafee, *Freedom of Speech* (New York, 1920), 85; Louis Menand, *The Metaphysical Club: A Story of Ideas in America* (New York, 2001), chap. 15.

16. Richard Polenberg, *Fighting Faiths: The Abrams Case, the Supreme Court, and Free Speech* (New York, 1987), 236–242.

17. Johnson, *Challenge to American Freedoms,* 146–148.

18. *NYT,* 29 Feb. 1920; "Vigilance," *Survey,* Feb. 1920; *NYT,* 29 Feb. 1920; *Nation,* 24 Apr. 1920.

19. *NYT,* 19 Jan. 1920.

20. 66 Congress, 2d Session, S.J. Res. 171, 10 Mar. 1920.

21. Lucy Robins, *War Shadows* (New York, 1922), 208.

22. Department of Justice Papers, National Archives, College Park, JD, RG 60, Central File 77175.

23. Joseph Tumulty to Woodrow Wilson (hereafter WW), 23 Mar. 1920, *The Papers of Woodrow Wilson,* ed. Arthur S. Link (Princeton, 1966–1994) (hereafter *WWP*).

24. Newton Baker (hereafter NB) to WW, 26 Mar. 1920, *WWP;* Baker's views on the Debs case can be found in NB to Norman Hapgood (hereafter NH), 29 Nov. 1920, Norman Hapgood Papers, Library of Congress.

25. WW to White House Staff, 12 Apr. 1920, and Diary of Robert Lansing, 14 Apr. 1920, both in *WWP.*

26. AMP to WW, 19 Apr. 1920, *WWP.*

27. Murray, *Red Scare,* 251; Coben, *A. Mitchell Palmer,* 250, 257.

28. McAdoo to WW, 15 May 1920, *WWP.*

29. Tumulty, who had provoked the amnesty debate in the first place, was having second thoughts. As the cabinet debated the amnesty issue, railroad workers launched a series of strikes that threatened an already struggling economy. Mistakenly believing that radicals were behind this and other labor unrest

that spring, Tumulty worried that an amnesty proclamation might look like a concession motivated by fear, rather than an expression of the administration's high-minded liberalism. "The time when you ought to do it is most important," he advised the president, "and I am afraid this is not the psychological moment." Tumulty to WW, 15 Apr. 1920, *WWP.*

30. Murray, *Red Scare,* 252–253; Coben, *A. Mitchell Palmer,* 230, 235.

31. Murray, *Red Scare,* 255; Coben, *A. Mitchell Palmer,* 239; *NYT,* 28 May 1920; Palmer cited in Stone, *Perilous Times,* 225; David Williams, "The Bureau of Investigation and Its Critics, 1919–1921: The Origins of Federal Political Surveillance," *Journal of American History* (Dec. 1981): 560–579.

32. *Literary Digest,* 5 June 1920, 21; Coben, *A. Mitchell Palmer,* 259.

33. Coben, *A. Mitchell Palmer,* 253.

34. *Butte Bulletin,* 26 Aug. 1920, clipping in Eugene V. Debs Papers, Indiana State University. Believing that these provocative statements undermined Debs's chances of winning a presidential pardon, Warden Zerbst denied further visiting privileges to Samuel Castleton, the socialist attorney from Atlanta who had often visited Debs and was the presumed source of these statements. Castleton told Robins that he acted at the direction of Otto Branstetter, who told Castleton that Debs "can't possibly know what is good for the Party at this time" (Robins, *War Shadows,* 190, 192).

35. *The Cabinet Diaries of Josephus Daniels* (Lincoln, 1963), 545–546. Daniels records Baker as supporting the amnesty proposal. Not long after, however, Baker outlined strong opposition to a general amnesty, and to a pardon for Debs, in a letter to Norman Hapgood. NB to NH, 13 Dec. 1920, Norman Hapgood Papers, Library of Congress.

36. Robins, *War Shadows,* 50–58.

37. *NYT,* 19 Jan. 1920, 9 Feb. 1920.

38. Robins, *Tomorrow Is Beautiful* (New York, 1948), 160; David Karsner in Robins, *War Shadows,* 183.

39. Robins, *War Shadows,* 180. Gompers on Debs: "We have had our differences with Mr. Debs, and very serious differences, before the war and during the war, but we have never held that Mr. Debs was a traitor to his country or was untrue to his own honor. But it is not for Mr. Debs that we are appealing; we are appealing for all the political prisoners." *NYT* cited in Robins, *War Shadows,* 187.

40. *NYT,* 18 Sept. 1920; Murray, *Red Scare,* 257–259.

41. Murray, *Red Scare,* 257–259.

42. Robins, *War Shadows,* 199.

43. Coben, *A. Mitchell Palmer,* 259; Robins, *Tomorrow Is Beautiful,* 180.

44. Murphy, *Freedom of Speech,* 78.

13. The Last Campaign

1. Clyde Miller, "The Man I Sent to Jail," *Roosevelt University Alumni Bulletin,* 1954.

2. Wesley Bagby, *The Road to Normalcy: The Presidential Campaign and Election of 1920* (Baltimore, 1962), 28; Richard Coke Lower, *A Bloc of One: The Political Career of Hiram W. Johnson* (Stanford, 1993), chap. 3.

3. Hiram Johnson, New York speech transcript, undated, in Hiram Johnson Papers, Bancroft Library, University of California, Berkeley (hereafter Johnson Papers).

4. *New York Times* (hereafter *NYT*), 1 June 1920; *NYT*, 8 Apr. 1920; Bagby, *The Road to Normalcy*, 50.

5. Lucy Robins, *Tomorrow Is Beautiful* (New York, 1948), 173.

6. Ibid., 173–175.

7. Ibid., 174.

8. John Dean, *Warren Harding* (New York, 2004), chap. 4; Michael Weatherson and Hal Bochin, *Hiram Johnson: A Bio-Bibliography* (Greenwood, 1988), 34–35; Bagby, *The Road to Normalcy*, 97; W. F. Fitzgerald, "Fatal Reactionary Step," 30 June 1920, Johnson Papers; *New Republic* and *Nation* cited in Bagby, *The Road to Normalcy*, 100. For an alternative account of the politics of the convention, see James Giglio, *H. M. Daugherty and the Politics of Expediency* (Kent, OH, 1978), 109–111.

9. John Morello, *Selling the President, 1920: Albert D. Lasker, Advertising, and the Election of Warren G. Harding* (Westport, 2001), 38.

10. Robert K. Murray, *The Harding Era: Warren G. Harding and His Administration* (Minneapolis, 1969), 54; "Harding's Speech," 23 July 1920, Johnson Papers; on Harding's ambiguous approach to most issues, see Andrew Sinclair, *The Available Man: The Life behind the Masks of Warren Gamaliel Harding* (New York, 1965), 165–167.

11. Robert K. Murray, *Red Scare: A Study in National Hysteria, 1919–1920* (New York, 1955), 260–261.

12. *NYT*, 22 July 1920

13. *NYT*, 25 July 1920.

14. *NYT*, 23 July 1920.

15. *NYT*, 24 Oct. 1920; Stanley Coben, *A. Mitchell Palmer: Politician* (New York, 1963), 262.

16. John Spargo to James Cox, 12 Aug. 1920, John Spargo Papers, University of Vermont.

17. Joseph Cohen to Theodore Debs (hereafter TD), 13 Sept. 1920, Eugene V. Debs Papers, Indiana State University (hereafter DP); TD to David Karsner (hereafter DK), 17 Sept. and 15 Oct. 1920, David Karsner Papers, New York Public Library.

18. *Literary Digest*, 29 May 1920; *Atlanta Constitution* (hereafter *AC*), 24 Aug. and 15 Sept. 1920.

19. *NYT*, 10 Oct. 1920; Lucy Robins to Eugene V. Debs (hereafter EVD), 19 Oct. 1920, DP.

20. TD to Lucy Robins, 27 Oct. 1920, DP.

21. Lucy Robins, *War Shadows* (New York, 1922), 123.

22. *Chicago Tribune* (hereafter *CT*), 1 Oct. 1920.

23. *Literary Digest,* 2 Oct. 1920.

24. *Baltimore Sun,* 17 Mar. 1920; *Literary Digest,* 23 Oct. 1920.

25. *New York World,* 5 Oct. 1920.

26. DK, *Debs: His Authorized Life and Letters from Woodstock Prison to Atlanta* (New York, 1919), 226.

27. *Liberator,* July 1920.

28. *Debs and the Poets,* ed. Ruth Le Prade (Pasadena, 1920), introduction by Upton Sinclair; *Boston Evening Transcript* to Upton Sinclair, 7 Oct. 1920, Upton Sinclair Papers, Lilly Library.

29. *Washington Times,* 7 and 12 Oct. 1920. On Hapgood's career, see Michael Marcaccio, *The Hapgoods: Three Earnest Brothers* (Charlottesville, 1977).

30. Marcaccio, *The Hapgoods,* 136–138. During his ambassadorship, Hapgood had been denounced by conservative Republicans as a Bolshevik sympathizer. Wilson had stood by him. *Washington Times,* 11 Oct. 1920.

31. *NYT,* 1 Nov. 1920; Martin Zanger, "Upton Sinclair as California's Socialist Candidate for Congress, 1920," *Southern California Quarterly* 56, no. 4 (1974): 359–373; David A. Shannon, *The Socialist Party of America* (Chicago, 1967), 157; Stedman to EVD, 29 Sept. 1920, copy in Brommel Papers, Newberry Library.

32. Joseph Sharts to EVD, 24 Nov. 1920, DP; James Weinstein, *The Decline of Socialism in America, 1912–1925* (New York, 1967), 235–236.

33. *NYT,* 25 July 1920; Frank Sheridan to EVD, 14 Oct. 1920, DP. Villard cited in Sinclair, *The Available Man,* 159.

34. *NYT,* 8 Oct. 1920; Robins, *Tomorrow Is Beautiful,* 181.

35. Joseph Tumulty, *Woodrow Wilson as I Know Him* (New York, 1921), 500; Cox cited in Thomas Fleming, *The Illusion of Victory: America in World War I* (New York, 2003), 465.

36. *Christian Science Monitor* (hereafter *CSM*), 3 Nov. 1920; Murray, *The Harding Era,* 80; *NYT,* 2 Nov. 1920.

37. *NYT,* 3 Nov. 1920.

38. *CSM,* 3 Nov. 1920; *Washington Post* (hereafter *WP*), 4 Nov. 1920; *NYT,* 4 Nov. 1920; *CT,* 3 Nov. 1920. Cox allowed the editor of his Ohio newspaper to issue a statement in place of a personal announcement.

39. *CSM,* 3 Nov. 1920; EVD, *Walls and Bars* (Chicago, 2000), 108; *AC,* 3 Nov. 1920.

40. *AC,* 4 Nov. 1920; *NYT,* 3 Nov. 1920.

41. *New York Post* cited in Morello, 94; C. Vann Woodward, *Tom Watson: Agrarian Rebel* (New York, 1938), 473.

42. Joseph Cohen to EVD, 4 Nov., 1920, DP; *NYT,* 31 Oct. 1920; *AC,* 3 Nov. 1920; *New York Call Magazine,* 10 Apr. 1921; DK to EVD, 3 Nov. 1920, DP. James Weinstein argues that the results did not reflect a loss of "popular Socialist consciousness," citing the fact that the party won a number of local races, and radicals split their vote among the Socialist Party, the Farmer-Labor Party, the Non-Partisan League, and the disenfranchised communist

factions. Weinstein does agree with Hillquit's view, however, that the 1920 campaign marked "both the disintegration of the Socialist Party as a truly national organization and the dispersal of the organized radical forces" (*Decline of Socialism*, 237). Debs heard anecdotal evidence that many in the communist factions not only failed to vote for him but tried to turn workers away from the polls, dashing the hope that the campaign might unify the radical forces.

43. *NYT,* 9 Dec. 1920; *WP,* 8 Nov. 1920.
44. On the place of civil liberties in postwar progressivism, see Alan Dawley, *Changing the World: American Progressives in War and Revolution* (Princeton, 2003), 322–323; and Paul L. Murphy, *The Meaning of Freedom of Speech* (Westport, 1972), chap. 7.

14. Lonely Obstinacy

1. Eugene V. Debs (hereafter EVD), *Walls and Bars* (Chicago, 1973), 77, 51.
2. Ibid., 84; *Federal Penal and Correctional Institutions Annual Report* (Leavenworth, 1928); the unpublished account of the prison says that "more prisoners were confined for drug offenses than any other offense . . . 261 men in 1918 imprisoned for narcotics laws" (p. 128). Fellow inmate Joseph Coldwell provides additional details about Debs's role in comforting prisoners sent to die in what the inmates called the "kick-off rooms." Joseph Coldwell Papers, Rhode Island Historical Society.
3. *Milwaukee Leader,* 6 Jan. 1921; Mabel Curry to David Karsner (hereafter DK), 28 Nov 1920, David Karsner Papers, New York Public Library (hereafter DKP).
4. *New York American,* 10 Dec. 1920; Hapgood to Woodrow Wilson (hereafter WW), 9 Nov. 1920, *The Papers of Woodrow Wilson,* ed. Arthur S. Link (Princeton, 1966–1994) (hereafter *WWP*).
5. *San Francisco Journal,* 17 Dec. 1920; telegram from F. W. Galbraith Jr., National Commander American Legion, to WW, 9 Nov. 1920, *WWP; Washington Post* (hereafter *WP*), 10 Nov. 1920; *New York Times* (hereafter *NYT*), 7 and 10 Nov. 1920.
6. Samuel Gompers to WW, 15 Dec. 1920, *WWP.*
7. *WP,* 8 Nov. 1920.
8. Theodore Debs (hereafter TD) to DK, 18 Dec. 1920, DKP; TD to Bertha Mailly, 17 Dec. 1920, Algernon Lee Papers, Tamiment Library.
9. EVD to Branstetter, n.d. (Christmas season, 1920), Eugene V. Debs Papers, Indiana State University (hereafter DP).
10. Samuel Lipman to Harry Weinberger, 20 Nov. 1921, Harry Weinberger Papers, Sterling Library, Yale.
11. EVD, *Walls and Bars,* chap. 8.
12. *WP,* 28 Dec. 1920; Lucy Robins, *War Shadows* (New York, 1922), 264.
13. *NYT,* 25 and 29 Nov. 1920, 28 Dec. 1920.
14. *Amnesty and Pardon for Political Prisoners, Tuesday December 21, 1920, U.S. Senate, Subcommittee of the Committee on the Judiciary,* pp. 6–7.

15. *Amnesty and Pardon*, 25; Lucy Robins, *Tomorrow Is Beautiful* (New York, 1948), 182.

16. "Palmer Under Fire," *Independent*, 5 Feb. 1921. In the summer of 1920 a House committee investigated charges that Justice Department agents had arrested suspects without warrant and illegally detained and deported hundreds of suspected subversives. And in the Senate, the maverick Idaho Republican William Borah, a supporter of the France resolution, introduced a bill against "Palmerism" that threatened fines against any government official found to interfere with the free speech rights of a detainee; Robert K. Murray, *Red Scare: A Study in National Hysteria, 1919–1920* (New York, 1955), 256; *CT*, 20 Jan. 1920.

17. A. Mitchell Palmer to WW, 30 Jan. 1921, *WWP; Christian Science Monitor* (hereafter *CSM*), 1 Feb. 1921.

18. William B. Wilson to WW, 18 Dec. 1920, *WWP;* Joseph Tumulty, *Woodrow Wilson as I Know Him* (Garden City, 1921), 505.

19. Lucy Robins to TD, 31 Jan. 1921, DP; *NYT,* 1 Feb., 1920; Robins, *War Shadows,* 270.

20. Lucy Robins to TD, 31 Jan. 1921, DP.

21. *NYT,* 2 Feb. 1921.

22. *CSM,* 24 Feb. 1921. Evidence suggests this was not issued by the attorney general or directly by the White House, but by the federal superintendent of prisons; *Seattle Union Record,* Mar. 2 1921.

23. Tom Watson, in *Columbia Sentinel,* 7 Mar. 21; "The Republican Victory," *New Republic,* 10 Nov. 1920.

15. Free Speech and Normalcy

1. *Chicago Tribune* (hereafter *CT*), 18 Mar. 1921.

2. Francis Russell, *In the Shadow of Blooming Grove: Warren G. Harding and His Times* (New York, 1968), 443–444, 449; James Giglio, *H. M. Daugherty and the Politics of Expediency* (Kent, OH, 1978), 118–123; *New York Times* (hereafter *NYT*), 26 Mar. 1921.

3. *CT,* 19 Mar. 1921.

4. Lucy Robins, *Tomorrow Is Beautiful* (New York, 1946), 193.

5. Harry M. Daugherty, *The Inside Story of the Harding Tragedy* (New York, 1932), 115–120.

6. *NYT,* 26 Mar. 1921; Robins, *Tomorrow Is Beautiful,* 193.

7. Stephen Reynolds to Theodore Debs (hereafter TD), 23 Mar. 1921, Eugene V. Debs Papers, Indiana Historical Society; *New York Tribune,* 21 Apr. 1921.

8. T. M. Shearman to Harry M. Daugherty, 25 Mar. 1921; Arch Klumph to Warren G. Harding, 26 Mar. 1921, Pardon Attorney Papers, National Archives, College Park, MD (hereafter RG 204).

9. *NYT,* 31 Mar. 1920.

10. Robins, *Tomorrow Is Beautiful,* 194.

11. Robins, *War Shadows* (New York, 1922), 319.

12. *Socialist World,* 15 Mar. 1921; *NYT,* 30 Mar. 1921.

13. *Boston Globe*, 7 Mar. 1921; Ellen Carol DuBois, *Harriet Stanton Blatch and the Winning of Woman Suffrage* (New Haven, 1997), 225–227; Harriet Stanton Blatch, *Challenging Years* (New York, 1940), 317.

14. Upton Sinclair to TD, 13 Nov. 1920, Upton Sinclair Papers, Lilly Library.

15. *Socialist World,* 15 Mar. 1921; Robins to Baldwin, 22 Nov. 1921, quoted in Robins, *War Shadows,* 368.

16. Robins, *War Shadows,* 293, citing Universal Service wire story of 10 Mar. 1921.

17. EVD to Otto Branstetter, 28 Mar. 1921, Eugene V. Debs Papers, Indiana State University (hereafter DP).

18. *Socialist World,* Mar. 1921; *Atlanta Constitution* (hereafter *AC*), 18 Mar. 1921; Otto Branstetter to EVD, 4 Apr. 1921, DP.

19. *Socialist World,* 15 Mar. 1921; *Boston Globe,* 1 Apr. 1921; on the Terre Haute campaign, see *Letters of Eugene V. Debs,* ed. Robert Constantine (Urbana, 1990), 3:200; *Terre Haute Post,* 4 Mar. 1921.

20. Otto Branstetter to EVD, 21 Apr. 1921, Eugene V. Debs Papers, Indiana State Library.

21. *CT,* 13 Apr. 1921; Melvyn Dubofsky, *We Shall Be All* (Urbana, 1988), 262.

22. Otto Branstetter to EVD, 21 Apr. 1921, Eugene V. Debs Papers, Indiana State Library; Robins, *War Shadows,* 325; Otto Branstetter to EVD, 4 Apr. 1921, DP; Samuel Castleton quote in Otto Branstetter to EVD, 3 May 1921, DP.

23. *NYT,* 22 Oct. 1921; Robert K. Murray, *The Harding Era: Warren G. Harding and His Administration* (Minneapolis, 1969), 166.

24. Wells quoted in *Atlanta Georgian,* 7 Dec. 1921; *Christian Science Monitor* (hereafter *CSM*), 3 Oct. 1921; *Terre Haute Post,* 20 Aug. 1921.

25. TD to Stephen Reynolds, 18 Mar. 1921, Eugene V. Debs Papers, Indiana Historical Society; Clyde Miller to Harry M. Daugherty, 24 Mar. 1921, Department of Justice Papers, National Archives, College Park, MD (hereafter RG 60), Central File 77175.

26. *NYT,* 19 Apr. 1921; *CT,* 19 Apr. 1921. See also Dr. Frank Crane, "Debs," *Atlanta Journal,* 11 Mar. 1921.

27. *AC,* 6 July 1921; *NYT,* 27 Oct. 1921; Alvin Owsley to Harry M. Daugherty, 28 July 1921, RG 60, Central File 77175.

28. *NYT,* 13 May 1921.

29. *Washington Post* (hereafter *WP*), 3 July 1921; TD to Joseph Cohen, Joseph Cohen Papers, Tamiment Library; *Socialist World,* June–July 1921; *WP,* 29 July 1921; *CT,* 12 and 27 Aug. 1921.

30. EVD to Mabel Curry (hereafter MC), 12 July 1921, Mabel Curry Letters, Lilly Library; *AC,* 29 July 1921; Giglio, *H. M. Daugherty,* 128. MC to Norman Hapgood, 4 Oct. 1921, Norman Hapgood Papers, Library of Congress.

31. Karsner tried to circumvent this restriction in two ways. First, by publishing a "daily message" in the *Call* from Debs, reprinted from earlier statements, and, second, by working with Hearst papers to infiltrate the prison in the fall of 1921, in hopes of sneaking out an interview. This plan was apparently

abandoned out of fear that it would undermine Debs's chances of a release. TD to David Karsner (hereafter DK), 24 Oct. 1921, David Karsner Papers, New York Public Library (hereafter DKP). On Debs's condition at this time, see David H. Clark to Norman Hapgood, 25 July 1921, Norman Hapgood Papers, Library of Congress.

32. "May First—Behind Prison Bars," 26 Apr. 1935, typescript copy in Joseph Coldwell Papers, Rhode Island Historical Society.

33. Constantine, *Letters of Eugene V. Debs,* ed. 3:216.

34. Broadus Mitchell to EVD, 4 Apr. 1921, DP.

35. EVD to MC, 2 May 1921, Mabel Curry Letters, Lilly Library.

36. James Weinstein, *The Decline of Socialism in America, 1912–1925* (New York, 1967), 239; *Socialist World,* July 1921; Louis Fraina, cited in Nicholas Salvatore, *Eugene V. Debs: Citizen and Socialist* (Urbana, 1984), 329; TD to James Oneal, 1 July 1921, James Oneal Papers, Tamiment Library.

37. *Appeal to Reason* (hereafter *ATR*), 13 Aug. 1921; New York incident cited in *CSM,* 4 Aug. 1921.

38. *Rip-Saw,* Aug. 1921; *NYT,* 3 July 1921; Sally M. Miller, *From Prairie to Prison* (Columbia, MO, 1993), 196–197.

39. *Socialist World,* Aug. 1921; John A. Thompson, *Reformers and War: American Progressive Publicists and the First World War* (New York, 1987), 272–273; Robert K. Murray, *Red Scare: A Study in National Hysteria, 1919–1920* (New York, 1955), 182–186.

40. *Nation,* 6, 13 20, 27 July 1921.

41. William Pencak, *For God and Country: The American Legion, 1919–1941* (Boston, 1989), 155; Samuel Walker, *In Defense of American Liberties: A History of the ACLU* (Carbondale, 1999), 53–54; *Survey,* 1 Feb. 1926.

42. *The Letters of Lincoln Steffens,* ed. Ella Winter and Granville Hicks (New York, 1938), 2:577.

43. *Autobiography of William Allen White* (New York, 1946), 622–623.

44. Norman Hapgood, "Prisoner Number 9653," *Atlanta Georgian,* 12 July 1921; Spurgeon Odell to Oswald Garrison Villard, 14 June 1921, and Villard to Odell, 21 July 1921, Oswald Garrison Villard Papers, Houghton Library.

45. Russell, *In the Shadow,* 460; *Boston Globe,* 30 July 1921; *NYT,* 30 July 1921.

46. Samuel Castleton to TD, 29 July 1921, Castleton Papers, Tamiment Library. The president continued to meet with various amnesty delegations— Gompers, the Socialists, various liberal and church delegations, and even the ACLU, a group widely denounced for its defense of the most unrepentant radicals. Harding was, in fact, the only president willing to meet with the group in its first decade of existence.

47. *ATR,* 10 Sept. 1921, included an excerpt of Daugherty's remarks; *Baltimore Sun,* 27 Dec. 1921. Mencken wrote that Daugherty's claim that America had no political prisoners was "extraordinarily silly." The "imbecility" of this argument, he fumed, "is so obvious that it is hard to imagine even an audience of lawyers listening to its exposition without bombarding its father with dead cats."

48. *WP*, 23 Sept., 7 Oct. 1921.

49. EVD to TD, 15 Nov. 1921, DP; *WP*, 28 Oct. 1921.

50. Robins, *War Shadows*, 337; *WP*, 27 Aug. 1921; *CT*, 28 Aug. 1921; *AC*, 2 Sept. 1921; "A Miserable Subterfuge," *Call*, 28 Aug. 1921, DP; TD to Warren G. Harding, 30 Aug. 1921, DP; *Socialist World*, Sept. 1921; *NYT*, 2 Sept. 1921.

51. DK to EVD, Oct 28 1921, DKP; MC to Witter Bynner, 2 Dec. 1921, Witter Bynner Papers, Houghton Library.

52. *ATR*, 17 Sept. 1921.

53. Biographer Robert K. Murray says Harding used this style often, appearing to support both sides and "relying on time to rescue him." Murray, *Harding*, 125–128; Andrew Sinclair, *The Available Man: The Life behind the Masks of Warren Gamaliel Harding* (New York, 1965), 225–227, suggests Harding used the appearance of weakness in order to attain his goals.

54. Murray, *Harding*, 149.

55. *Atlanta Georgian*, 10 and 15 Nov. 1921; *WP*, 23 Nov. 1921; *Rip-Saw*, Nov. 1921, citing the *Nation. Boston Globe*, 25 Nov. 1921; Winter and Hicks, *Letters of Lincoln Steffens*, 575.

56. *CSM*, 15 Nov. 1921; *Socialist World*, Nov. 1921; Robins, *Tomorrow Is Beautiful*, 202–203; Andrew C. Cooper et. al. to EVD, 15 Nov. 1921, DP; *NYT*, 15 Nov. 1921. For more on this petition, see Robins, *War Shadows*, 370–373; *AC*, 19 Nov. 1921; Otto Branstetter to Bertha Hale White, 15 Nov. 1920, Socialist Party Papers, Duke University Special Collections (hereafter SPP); Oliver Wilson to Bertha Hale White, 16 Nov. 1920, SPP. On picketing, see *NYT*, 19 Nov. 1921; *New York World*, 16 Nov. 1921; *WP*, 23 Nov. 1921.

57. 16 Apr. 1921, clipping in DP; *NYT* cited in Robins, *War Shadows*, 390.

58. *Socialist World*, Dec. 1921; *WP*, 18 Dec. 1921; *Terre Haute Tribune*, 16 Dec. 1921; Bertha Hale White to TD, 20 Dec. 1921, SPP; Otto Branstetter to EVD, 25 Nov. 1921, Eugene V. Debs Papers, Indiana State Library.

59. "Memorandum for the Attorney General: War Time Prisoners," 10 Dec. 1921, Pardon Attorney Papers, National Archives, College Park, MD (hereafter RG 204), Box 1. Robins, *War Shadows*, 367, quotes him as being "inclined to be stony hearted in such matters."

60. "Application for Executive Clemency in behalf of Eugene V. Debs," RG 204, EVD Pardon Case File.

61. *WP*, 23 Nov. 1921; *NYT*, 16 Nov. 1921.

62. Murray, *Harding*, 168. Lincoln Steffens reported in his autobiography that Harding asked him to meet privately with Debs in Atlanta, to ask Debs to agree not to preach "hate" and Bolshevism straight out of the prison gates. Delighted by this chance to move in the corridors of power, Steffens boarded a train for Atlanta and, with special permission from the Justice Department, met with Debs privately for two hours in the warden's office. According to Steffens, Debs agreed not to embarrass the president by turning his release into a propaganda coup for American Bolshevism. Steffens soon found that he did not enjoy the influence over Debs that he had assumed himself to have.

63. Murray, *Harding,* 169.
64. *CT,* 24 Dec. 1921.
65. "Behind Prison Walls," *Century Magazine,* clipping in DP.
66. *New York World,* 26 Dec. 1921.
67. Murray, *Harding,* 168
68. *Boston Globe,* 28 Dec. 1921, clipping in DP; *Washington Herald,* 27 Dec. 1921.
69. *CT,* 28 Dec. 1921.

16. Last Flicker of the Dying Candle

1. *Rip-Saw,* Jan. 1922.
2. *Pittsburgh Post,* 28 Dec. 1921; *CT* and *Boston Transcript,* 27 Dec. 1921.
3. Harry M. Daugherty to Newcombe Carleton, 10 Jan. 1922, Pardon Attorney Papers, National Archives, College Park, MD, RG 204; H. L. Mencken, "Who's Loony Now?" *Baltimore Evening Sun,* 27 Dec. 1921.
4. EVD to Comrade Tuvim, 22 Mar. 1922, Eugene V. Debs Papers, Tamiment Library; EVD to Otto Branstetter, 25 Mar. 1922, Eugene V. Debs Papers, Indiana State Library; Nicholas Salvatore, *Eugene V. Debs: Citizen and Socialist* (Urbana, 1984), 329–330; Theodore Draper, *The Roots of American Communism* (New York, 1966), 324–326.
5. "Stay Away from Terre Haute," *Socialist World,* Jan. 1922; Eugene V. Debs (hereafter EVD) to Theodore Debs (hereafter TD), 5 and 12 Aug. 1922, Eugene V. Debs Papers, Indiana State University (hereafter DP).
6. Ray Ginger, *The Bending Cross: A Biography of Eugene Victor* (New Brunswick, 1949), 421; EVD to TD, 25 July 1922, DP; EVD to David Karsner (hereafter DK), 22 Aug. 1922, David Karsner Papers, New York Public Library (hereafter DKP); Karsner, *Talks with Debs in Terre Haute* (New York, 1922), 202–207.
7. Draper, *Roots of American Communism,* 226; William O'Neill, *The Last Romantic: A Life of Max Eastman* (New York, 1978), 85.
8. James Weinstein, *The Decline of Socialism in America, 1912–1925* (New York, 1967), 253, 331; Karsner, *Talks with Debs,* 66.
9. *New Republic,* 4 Aug. 1921; Karsner, *Talks with Debs,* 68–70.
10. Lucy Robins, *Tomorrow Is Beautiful* (New York, 1948), 176, 214–215.
11. Karsner, *Talks with Debs,* 168–178. Engdahl attacks Debs in the *Worker,* 12 Aug. 1922. Steffens cited in Draper, *Roots of American Communism,* 115; Justin Kaplan, *Lincoln Steffens: A Biography* (New York, 1974), chap. 14; *The Letters of Lincoln Steffens* (New York, 1938), 2:580–581.
12. Stokes in Arthur Zipser and Pearl Zipser, *Fire and Grace: The Life of Rose Pastor Stokes* (Athens, GA, 1989), 233; Robert Minor on free speech cited in David Shannon, *The Socialist Party of America: A History* (Chicago, 1967), 167; *The Liberator,* May 1921.
13. "Call for a National Convention for the Purpose of Organizing a Communist Party in America," *Revolutionary Radicalism* (Lusk Committee Report) (Albany, 1920), 1:742 Scott Nearing, for example, concluded that Americans

lived under an unacknowledged "domestic dictatorship"; John A. Saltmarsh, *Scott Nearing: An Intellectual Biography* (Philadelphia, 1991), 218–219; Max Eastman, "Examples of Americanism," *Liberator,* Feb. 1920; Eastman cited in O'Neill, 92.

14. Debs cited in Edward P. Johanningsmeier, *Forging American Communism: The Life of William Z. Foster* (Princeton, 1994), 177. EVD to Valenburgh, 28 Jan. 1926, DP: "I have heartily favored Soviet Russia from the hour it was born and have supported it with my pen and from the platform to the full extent of my power, but I have been utterly opposed to the cruel Soviet policy which has proscribed the expression of opinion and made a crime of all honest opposition."

15. Lucy Robins, *Tomorrow Is Beautiful* (New York, 1948), 199–201.

16. Not easily discouraged, Robins followed up that spring, asking Debs to consider leading a new organization that she described as a "Labor Red Cross." With support from the AFL, this nonpartisan agency would raise money to support strikers, defend workers in court, and serve as a unifying force for the radical and conservative branches of the labor movement. Debs vaguely promised to consider the suggestion, most likely out of a desire not to hurt his friend's feelings, but soon let the matter drop. Robins, *Tomorrow Is Beautiful,* chap. 21.

17. Samuel Gompers, *Seventy Years of Life and Labor* (New York, 1925).

18. Salvatore, *Eugene V. Debs,* 334–339; Weinstein, *Decline of Socialism,* 240–243.

19. *Socialist World,* May 1923; *Cleveland Plain Dealer,* 12 June 1923; an account of his first speech after prison is in *New York Times* (hereafter *NYT*), 27 Nov. 1922.

20. Department of Justice Papers, National Archives, College Park, MD, RG 60, FBI surveillance file, Cleveland File 1268, 12 June 1923; David Kennedy, *Over Here* (New York, 1980), 224–230; Weinstein, *Decline of Socialism,* 328.

21. David Shannon, *The Socialist Party of America* (New York, 1955), 166; Weinstein, *Decline of Socialism,* 242–243.

22. Saltmarsh, *Scott Nearing,* 208–209; Stephen Whitfield, *Scott Nearing, Apostle of American Radicalism* (New York, 1974), 138–139.

23. DK, "The Passing of the Socialist Party," *Current History Magazine,* June 1924.

24. EVD to DK, 26 Oct. 1925, DKP.

25. Salvatore, *Eugene V. Debs,* 332, 339–340; EVD to Mabel Curry, 5 Nov. 1922, Mabel Curry Papers, Lilly Library.

26. EVD in "Debs Calls the Jury of the People to Try Indiana Governor," *New Day,* 20 May 1922; *Socialist World,* Jan. 1922.

27. *Cincinnati Inquirer,* undated clipping in FBI files, RG 65, National Archives, College Park, MD; "Eugene V. Debs in Cincinnati," *St. Louis Labor,* 19 June 1926; EVD to TD, 13 Sept. 1923, DP. "Anyhow Debs Spoke in Cincinnati," *Nation,* 25 July 1923, 87.

28. Paul L. Murphy, "Communities in Conflict," in *The Pulse of Freedom,* ed.

Alan Reitman (New York, 1975), 34; the reaction against the anti-sedition laws in New York is analyzed in Todd J. Pfannestiel, *Rethinking the Red Scare: The Lusk Committee and New York's Crusade against Radicalism, 1919–1923* (New York, 2003), 127–129; Leon Harris, *Upton Sinclair, American Rebel* (New York, 1975), 197–198.

29. Nearing's experiences speaking on campus are related in Whitfield, *Scott Nearing*, 132–134; for a review of ACLU activities in this period, see *A Year's Fight for Free Speech: The Work of the American Civil Liberties Union from Sept. 1921 to Jan. 1923* (New York, 1923), and Murphy, "Communities in Conflict," 35–42.

30. Robins, *Tomorrow Is Beautiful*. Socialist work for amnesty in this period consisted of work through the General Defense Committee of Chicago, an alliance with liberal groups, and investigative work into the cases of the Oklahoma Socialists jailed during the Green Corn Rebellion. *NYT*, 20 July 1922. The resolution presented to the House Judiciary Committee prompted a hearing that produced a heated exchange between liberals who testified for the bill (Gilbert Roe, Harry Weinberger) and many committee members. *NYT*, 17 Mar. 1922; William Preston Jr., *Aliens and Dissenters* (New York, 1963), 259.

31. *A Year's Fight*, 10; *Nation*, 25 Jan. 1922; Donald Johnson, *The Challenge to American Freedoms* (Lexington, 1963), 185.

32. Unmarked clipping in DKP; *A Year's Fight*, 10–11.

33. Johnson, *Challenge to American Freedoms*, 186–188; O'Hare's own account of the crusade can be found in the relevant issues of her *Rip-Saw*, including Apr.–May 1922.

34. Johnson, *Challenge to American Freedoms*, 186–188; *Rip-Saw*, Apr.–May 1922; *NYT*, 29 Mar., 30 Apr., 3 and 6 May, 10 July 1922.

35. Johnson, *Challenge to American Freedoms*, 191–193; one remained in Atlanta, deemed to be an "insane fanatic."

36. *NYT*, 16 Dec. 1923.

37. *NYT*, 7 Oct. 1925.

38. Geoffrey Stone, *Perilous Times* (New York, 2004), 230–231; James Giglio, *H. M. Daugherty and the Politics of Expediency* (Kent, OH, 1978), 170–175. For Daugherty's version of these events, see his *Inside Story of the Harding Tragedy* (New York, 1932); Preston, *Aliens and Dissenters*, 242–243; Paul L. Murphy, *The Meaning of Freedom of Speech* (Westport, 1972), 188–189.

39. Salvatore, *Eugene V. Debs*, 340–341.

40. Morris Hillquit, *Loose Leaves from a Busy Life* (New York, 1934), 300.

41. Eulogies are in the Debs scrapbooks, DP; *Literary Digest*, 13 Nov. 1926; *Collier's*, 20 Nov. 1926.

Epilogue

1. On government repression of the labor movement, see Andrew Sachs, "Silencing the Union Movement," *Silencing the Opposition: Government Strategies of Suppression*, ed. Craig R. Smith (Albany, 1996).

2. Donald Johnson, *The Challenge to American Freedoms* (Lexington, 1963), 82–83; Paul L. Murphy, *The Meaning of Freedom of Speech* (Westport, 1972), 188–189.

3. Lucy Robins, *War Shadows* (New York, 1922), 91; Oswald Garrison Villard, "New Fight for Old Liberties," *Harper's Magazine*, Sept. 1925.

4. *Lexington Herald*, 11 Jan. 1922, clipping in Bernard J. Brommel Papers, Newberry Library.

5. M. J. Heale, *American Anticommunism: Combating the Enemy Within, 1830–1970* (Baltimore, 1990), chap. 5; Murphy, *Freedom of Speech,* 180; Carl Swidorski, "The Courts, the Labor Movement, and the Struggle for Freedom of Expression and Association, 1919–1940," *Labor History* (Feb. 2004): 61–84; Joseph A. McCartin, *Labor's Great War: The Struggle for Industrial Democracy and the Origins of Modern American Labor Relations, 1912–1921* (Chapel Hill, 1997), chap. 8.

6. Murphy, *Freedom of Speech,* 200–201; Norman Hapgood, ed., *Professional Patriots* (New York, 1927).

7. Heale, *American Anticommunism,* chap. 5; Paul L. Murphy, "Communities in Conflict," in *The Pulse of Freedom,* ed. Alan Reitman (New York, 1975), 62–63.

8. Eric Foner, *The Story of American Freedom* (New York, 1998), 183; Thompson, *Reformers and War* (New York, 1987), 273–274; Edward A. Stettner, *Shaping Modern Liberalism: Herbert Croly and Progressive Thought* (Lawrence, 1993), 144–145; Paul L. Murphy, *Freedom of Speech,* 18–19; David Rabban, *Free Speech in Its Forgotten Years* (New York, 1997), 299–303; Alan Dawley, *Changing the World* (Princeton, 2003), 322–323; on the value of pluralism for some prewar progressives, see Mark A. Graber, *Transforming Free Speech: The Ambiguous Legacy of Civil Libertarianism* (Berkeley, 1991), chap. 3.

9. Murphy, *Freedom of Speech,* 176–177; Harold Lasswell, *Propaganda Technique in the World War* (New York, 1927).

10. J. Michael Sproule, *Propaganda and Democracy: The American Experience of Media and Mass Persuasion* (New York, 1997). Sproule provides a good summary of Miller's role in the Debs case, and his subsequent career as a scholar and activist.

11. Zechariah Chaffee, *Freedom of Speech* (New York, 1941), 3.

12. Fred D. Ragan, "Justice Oliver Wendell Holmes, Jr., Zechariah Chafree Jr., and the Clear and Present Danger Test for Free Speech: The First Year, 1919," *Journal of American History* (June 1971); Rabban, *Free Speech,* chap. 7.

13. Chaffee, *Freedom of Speech,* xiv.

14. Johnson, *Challenge to American Freedoms,* 188–189; *A Year's Fight,* 12–13.

Archives Consulted

American Legion Archives, Indianapolis

Bancroft Library, University of
California, Berkeley
Hiram Johnson Papers

Duke University Special Collections
Socialist Party Papers

Houghton Library, Harvard University
Witter Bynner Papers
John Reed Papers
Oswald Garrison Villard Papers

Indiana Historical Society
Eugene V. Debs Papers
Stephen Reynolds Papers

Indiana State Library
Eugene V. Debs Papers

Indiana State University
Eugene V. Debs Papers

Library of Congress
Newton Baker Papers
William Borah Papers
George Creel Papers
Clarence Darrow Papers
Norman Hapgood Papers
William McAdoo Papers
Gilbert Roe, in La Follette Family
Papers
Woodrow Wilson Papers

Lilly Library, Indiana University
Mabel Curry Papers
Max Eastman Papers

E. Haldeman-Julius Papers
Robert Hunter Papers
Upton Sinclair Papers
Ryan Walker Papers
Fred Warren Papers

National Archives, Chicago
Case File, U.S. v. Debs

National Archives, College Park, MD
Department of Justice, RG 60
Federal Bureau of Investigation,
RG 65
Bureau of Prisons, RG 129
War Department, RG 165
Pardon Attorney, RG 204

National Archives, Washington, D.C.
Supreme Court, RG 267

Newberry Library
Bernard J. Brommel Papers
May Walden Kerr Papers

New York Public Library
David Karsner Papers
Norman Thomas Papers
ACLU Papers

Ohio Historical Society
Warren G. Harding Papers

Princeton University
ACLU Papers
Roger Baldwin Papers

Rhode Island Historical Society
Joseph Coldwell Papers

Sterling Library, Yale University
  Rose Pastor Stokes Papers
  Harry Weinberger Papers

Tamiment Library, New York
  University
  Eugene V. Debs Papers (includes
    papers of August Claessens,
    Samuel Castleton, Seymour
    Stedman, Joseph Cohen,
    Algernon Lee)
  Elizabeth Gurley Flynn Papers
  George Herron Papers
  New York Bureau of Legal Advice
    Papers
  James Oneal Papers

University of Vermont
  John Spargo Papers

Western Reserve Historical Society
  David C. Westenhaver Papers

Acknowledgments

When I began researching this book, students and colleagues often remarked about how timely the story was, raising questions about the impact of war on democracy that seemed to be lifted straight from the day's headlines. That was some years ago, and they were referring to the "wag the dog" accusations against Bill Clinton's administration. The headlines have changed, but the questions raised by the Debs trial and postwar Red Scare have only become more pressing. Over the years since then I have appreciated the chance to talk with students about these matters, most often in a seminar that I have called "War and Truth." Those conversations provided encouragement and inspiration as I wrote this book; it helped to see that these issues are alive for young people today, just as they were for many in Debs's generation.

Research assistance for this project was provided from a variety of sources. The project began while I was teaching at Colby-Sawyer College, with help from a faculty research fellowship, collegial exchanges in the Humanities Department, and library support from Carrie Thomas. I am also grateful for research support from my current academic home, the University of Tennessee, and for encouragement from the History Department's former chair, Todd Diacon. David Leventhal provided energetic research help, and I also received valuable guidance from Anne Bridges at UT's Hodges Library.

Archival visits were funded by a Director's grant from the Indiana Historical Society, an Everett Helm fellowship from Indiana University's Lilly Library, a research grant from the Newberry Library, and a Gilder Lehrman Foundation award for work in the New York Public Library. I am grateful for the assistance from the archivists and research librarians at these institutions, and many more archives cited in the notes. I particularly want to acknowledge David Vancil, curator of the

Debs papers at Indiana State University. In addition to creating a wonderfully accessible collection, he offered friendship, wise counsel, and the occasional Champagne Velvet. Thanks also to Dennis Vetrovec, Dr. Vancil's able assistant.

Much of this manuscript was written during a fellowship year at Emory University's Center for Humanistic Inquiry. The CHI provided a congenial place to write, and allowed me to share this work with scholars from a variety of disciplines. Particular thanks go to CHI director Martine Watson Brownley, Keith Anthony and Amy Erbil on the CHI staff, and my fellow fellow Jonathan Eburne, who was always ready to keep the flame of interdisciplinarity burning late into the night.

Jonathan Prude, Jean Christophe-Agnew, Tom Chaffin, and my late friend Marcia Carlisle provided early encouragement for this project, while Steve Ash, Robert Constantine, David Vancil, and Jeff Norrell offered helpful readings of the manuscript. Patrick Allitt was particularly generous with his time, and much of the book took shape in my mind as we hacked through the roughs of Candler Park. I also want to thank the two anonymous reviewers whose suggestions helped make this a stronger book, manuscript editor Wendy Nelson, and Jennifer Banks, who did much to shepherd the manuscript along. And I am indebted to Joyce Seltzer at Harvard University Press for her encouragement and wise counsel at every stage of this project.

There are days when writing a book feels a bit like being sentenced to a benign version of a prison's dark "hole." And so I am deeply grateful to my family for making sure I never stayed locked away in the library for too long. As ever, my parents offered support and encouragement, while my brother Bruce was a valuable friend and intellectual partner. One of the unexpected pleasures of this project was the chance to visit with the Indiana branch of my family, particularly Barbara and Ryan Toon, who did so much to make me feel at home during my research trips to Indiana. My wife, Lauren, offered encouragement, insight, and companionship, while generously bearing the brunt of my long absences. More than anyone, my children, Charlie and Emma, rescued me from solitary confinement, and for that reason I dedicate this book to them.

Index